GW00482149

The Mirror of the Seas

Frontispiece HRH Prince Philip, KG, KT, the Duke of Edinburgh. By kind permission of the artist, Richard Stone. National Maritime Museum, Greenwich, London.

The Mirror of the Seas

A Centenary History of the Society for Nautical Research

Hugh Murphy and Derek J. Oddy

The Society for Nautical Research
2010

The Mirror of the Seas: A Centenary History of the Society for Nautical Research

First published 2010 by
The Society for Nautical Research
National Maritime Museum, Greenwich,
London SE10 9NF United Kingdom
www.snr.org.uk

© The Society for Nautical Research

The rights of Hugh Murphy and Derek J. Oddy to be identified
as the authors of this work has been asserted by them
in accordance with the Copyright, Designs and Patents Act, 1988.

All rights reserved. No part of this book may be reprinted or reproduced
or utilized in any form or by any electronic, mechanical, or other means, now known
or hereafter invented, including photocopying and recording, or in any information storage
or retrieval system, without permission in writing from the publishers.
The publisher makes no representation, express or implied, with regard to the accuracy
of the information contained in this book

British Library Cataloguing in Publication Data
A catalogue record for this book is available from the British Library

Typeset in Great Britain by Palindrome

Printed and bound in Great Britain by
Bell & Bain Ltd, Thornliebank, Glasgow

ISBN 978-0-902387-01-0

Contents

List of Illustrations and Tables   vii
Preface   ix
Foreword   xiii
Acknowledgements   xv
Abbreviations   xvii

1 Launching the Society for Nautical Research   1
2 Refloating the Society and Saving HMS *Victory* for the Nation   22
3 A Run Ashore: Creating the National Maritime Museum   51
4 The Society Weathers Changing Cirumstances: From Austerity
   to Economy 1946–65   75
5 Doldrums and Squalls: the Society from 1966–85   106
6 Off Course: Deviation from True Bearings   139
7 Crossing the Bar: The Society Enters a New Century   164
8 Making Fast and Paying Off   177

Appendix I: Patrons, Presidents and Officers   191
Appendix II: Honorary Vice-Presidents   193
Appendix III: Lectures and Publications   195
Appendix IV: Consolidated Financial Summary, 1911–2008   199
Appendix V: Selected Obituaries   205

Index   261

List of Illustrations

1 HRH Prince Philip, KG, KT, Duke of Edinburgh, Patron of the Society for
Nautical Research   Frontispiece
2 W. L. Wyllie, RA (about 1890) by R. W. Robinson   10
3 The cover of the first volume of *The Mariner's Mirror*, vol 1: 3   12
4 The contents page of the first issue of *The Mariner's Mirror*, January 1911   14
5 Professor Sir Geoffrey A. R. Callender (1875–1946)   24
6 Admiral Sir F. C. Doveton Sturdee (1859–1925)   26
7 HMS *Victory* in the tideway, 21 October 1921   29
8 The Save the Victory Fund notepaper   31
9 A Save the Victory Receipt   33
10 Sir James Caird (1864–1954)   34
11 Letter from James Caird to Admiral Sturdee   36
12 HMS *Victory* under restoration   39
13 HM King George V visiting HMS *Victory*, 1928   40
14 Sir George P. W. Hope (1869–1959)   41
15 The Victory Museum   45
16 James Richard Stanhope, 7th Earl Stanhope (1880–1967)   54
17 The Queen's House, Greenwich   59
18 *Implacable* in Portsmouth Harbour   66
19 *Implacable* and *Foudroyant* moored in Portsmouth Harbour   67
20 Admiral of the Fleet Earl Mountbatten of Burma (1900–79)   79
21 Frank Carr (1903–91)   81
22 Reginald Lowen (1900–90), with Princess Elizabeth, and Lord Stanhope   85
23 *Cutty Sark*   96
24 George B. P. Naish (1909–77)   108
25 Basil Greenhill (1920–2003)   109
26 Capt. Alan J. Villiers (1903–82)   112

27 HRH the Duke of Edinburgh in naval uniform   129

28 Dr Helen Wallis (1924–95) greeting the Society's Patron   131

29 John Munday and Lt Cdr Lawrence Phillips, two Hon. Secretaries of the
   Society   133

30 HRH The Duke of Edinburgh at the Society's 75th Anniversary   135

31 HRH The Duke of Edinburgh, Roy Clare and Colin White (1951–2008)   169

Colour Plates between pp. 142–3

Plate 1 *Naval Officers of the Great War* (1921) by Sir Arthur Stockdale Cope

Plate 2 *A Panorama of the Battle of Trafalgar* by W. L. Wyllie

Plate 3 *The Battle of the Texel* (1673) by W. van de Velde the Younger

Plate 4 *James Richard Stanhope, 7th Earl Stanhope* (1880–1967) by Sir James Gunn

Plate 5 *Dr Roger C. Anderson* (1883–1976) by Bernard Hailstone

Plate 6 HMS *Victory*'s cutter

Plate 7 HRH Prince Andrew, the Duke of York

Plate 8 The Officers of the Society, 2009

List of Tables

Table 1 SNR income and the costs of producing *The Mariner's Mirror* 1968–1975
      119

Table 2 Subscription income: net cost of *The Mariner's Mirror* and fees charged on
the Society's Restricted Funds 1978–1986   141

Preface

Work on this book started within a few days of the news that the Clyde-built tea clipper *Cutty Sark* had been damaged by fire in her dry-dock at Greenwich. Such a misfortune to the famous ocean-going sailing ship is a reminder to members of the Society for Nautical Research how fragile is the preservation of maritime history. A current example of how not to preserve a ship, the *City of Adelaide*, lies forlorn and unloved at the Scottish Maritime Museum, Irvine. Survivors from the age of sail – many of them British built – lie scattered across the world, having passed out of British registration. Another Clyde-built survivor, the four-masted full-rigged ship, *Falls of Clyde* – formerly a sailing oil-tanker – is afloat in Honolulu but her future remains uncertain as she was unrigged to her lower masts in 2008. The full-rigged ship *Wavertree*, Southampton-built and the last of her kind built in wrought iron, is at New York's South Pier, where she lies alongside the German-built four-masted steel barque *Peking*, while another Clyde-built full-rigged ship, *Balclutha*, is at San Francisco; the Port-Glasgow built, *Glenlee* is at Glasgow Harbour, while two other lower Clyde-built four-masted barques survive, *Pommern* at Mariehamn, Åland, Finland, and *Moshulu* (ex *Kurt*) at Philadelphia.[1]

Given Britain's past pre-eminence in building, sailing, and fighting with ships, it is surprising that there are not more maritime artefacts of former times in the United Kingdom. Yet little physical evidence of this heritage has been preserved. Britain, it seems, has been surprisingly unsentimental in discarding the relics of maritime greatness. Apart from HMS *Victory* in dry-dock in Portsmouth; the teak-built *Foudroyant* (a 38-gun frigate built at Bombay and launched in October 1817) is now on display in Jackson Dock, Hartlepool, under her original name of HMS *Trincomalee*. She is the oldest British frigate afloat, and the second oldest floating ship in the world.[2] Ocean-going ships powered by machinery have fared little better. Archetypal vessels such as HMS *Warrior*, built in 1860, spent much of the twentieth century as *Oil Fuel Hulk C77* in Pembroke Dock before her restoration began in 1987, while HMS *Gannet*, built 1878, has now been restored and lies afloat in Chatham Dockyard. Of similar importance, the ss *Great Britain* launched by Isambard Kingdom Brunel in Bristol in 1843 uniquely combined an iron hull with a steam engine driving a screw propeller.[3] The *Great Britain* continued trading at sea until 1886 but then, after fifty years as a floating warehouse, was abandoned in the Falkland Islands until being salvaged in 1970, and brought home to Bristol to be conserved. Even though two world wars in the twentieth century destroyed much of Britain's marine assets, none of the passenger liners which sailed in the north Atlantic trade before the advent of jet-engined passenger aircraft has survived in Britain, no post-Dreadnought battleship has been preserved nor any aircraft carrier. The largest surviving British warship of the Second World War is the Southampton-class cruiser, HMS *Belfast* moored in the Thames, while the Fleet Air Arm Museum exists as a land-based exhibition at Yeovilton, in Somerset, and is part of the National Museum of the Royal Navy.[4] RMS *Queen Mary*, berthed at Long Beach, California, is showing signs of neglect to her fabric and equipment, despite performing her role as a floating hotel. Also on the West Coast of the USA, but at the other end of the scale, the Tyne-built steam paddle tug *Eppleton Hall* lies at San Francisco, where the ss *Jeremiah O'Brien*, one of only two remaining fully functional Liberty Ships of the 2,710 built during the Second World War, still cruises.

The role of the Society for Nautical Research during the twentieth century has been to preserve maritime artefacts, to support research into maritime subjects and, through its journal, *The Mariner's Mirror*, to write about them. *The Mariner's Mirror* has been much more than a means of recording members' research and thoughts: it has served as an international forum for the interchange of knowledge on maritime matters. It remains the world's pre-eminent scholarly journal in the English language devoted to maritime history in its broadest sense; and is the repository of many of the finest articles yet written on the sea. Founded when commercial sail was dying out, *The Mariner's Mirror* became a repository of all manner of knowledge about the handling and operation of sailing vessels, including the sailing navy, the customs, payment, apparel, signals and technical language used by seamen and the representation of maritime activities by artists. At the local level, the Society's members talked to those handling small craft under sail, as well as inshore fishermen, about the development of their vessels, and devotedly and painstakingly set about taking off the lines of some craft. Although the Society's original members were never able to develop this specialized knowledge into their projected nautical encyclopaedia of the sea – their enthusiasm could not be re-kindled after the Great War and, though it was briefly resuscitated after the Second World War, no work in print ever materialized – they published leaflets, notably on small craft, which attracted much interest.[5] These early, local interests were eclipsed by the Society's interwar achievements which occurred on a scale never envisaged by its founders and only made possible through the generosity of individual benefactors.

The membership of the Society for Nautical Research has included many illustrious figures of the twentieth century and a centenary history must provide space in its appendices to list them, as well as the many members who contributed to the success of the Society as Chairmen and Officers of its Council, as members of the Society's Committees and, above all, as Honorary Editors of *The Mariner's Mirror*. The *Mirror* found little space for the obituaries of many of its distinguished contributors, and while space considerations in this centenary volume militate against a full appreciation of the part they played in the Society's success, Appendix V does provide some acknowledgement for their efforts. In some respects, the Society has been more transient that its successes would suggest. It has never had a base or headquarters of its own, or even a regular office from which to carry on its business; in consequence, there has never been anywhere to house a library or a comprehensive archive of its records.[6] The ephemeral nature of the Society for Nautical Research has given the authors the task of getting to grips with its existence, the driving forces within it, and the relative importance of its leading figures. The Society's records, other than the printed reports of the Council to its annual meetings or reports in *The Mariner's Mirror*, are sparse. The Society held bank accounts and its revenue and expenditure were audited; it purchased securities and applied the proceeds to its purposes. In doing so, the Society for Nautical Research saved Nelson's flagship, HMS *Victory*, for the nation; was the major player in the formation of the National Maritime Museum, Greenwich, and the Royal Naval Museum, Portsmouth, all of which were accomplished in the first four decades of its existence. This alone would justify a centenary account, but the Society's later history also deserves to be told; not only for members new and old, but to the wider audience interested in maritime history and affairs, and conscious both of the importance of seafaring as a basis for Britain's former political and economic strength and the nation's continuing prosperity and importance in international affairs.

Hugh Murphy and Derek J. Oddy
London, October 2009

References

1   A fuller list of vessels preserved in the United Kingdom can be found in The National Register of Historic Vessels, a database listing over 1,200 vessels. Significant vessels not mentioned above include the Leda-class frigate HMS *Unicorn* at Dundee, HMS *Caroline* at Belfast – a survivor of the Battle of Jutland – RRS *Discovery* at Dundee and HMRY *Britannia* at Leith.

See www.nationalhistoricships.org.uk or the larger, but not up-to-date, international register www.worldshiptrust.org/register.html.

2   The uss *Constitution* in Boston harbour, United States of America, is the oldest ship afloat.

3   See infra, Chapter Five.

4   hms *Cavalier* (1944) a Second World War destroyer, survives at Chatham Dockyard. In September 2009, a new National Museum of the Royal Navy was launched, integrating the four existing Service museums: the Royal Naval Museum, Portsmouth, the Royal Marines Museum, Southsea, the Royal Navy Submarine Museum, Gosport, and the Fleet Air Arm Museum, Yeovilton.

5   Members were aware of Admiral W. H. Smyth's *The Sailor's Word-Book* (1857) but their project was for a much more ambitious work.

6   Since becoming a company limited by guarantee, the Society has a Registered Office which is the National Maritime Museum, Greenwich, London SE10 9NF. The SNR's surviving records are held in the NMM's Archives.

Foreword

From HRH *Prince Philip, The Duke of Edinburgh*

 BUCKINGHAM PALACE.

In December 1910, the first Annual General Meeting of the Society for Nautical Research took place at the Royal United Services Institute in Whitehall. It was at that point that my association with the SNR began. It was on that occasion that my maternal grandfather, Admiral of the Fleet, The Marquis of Milford Haven, was elected as the Society's first President. Shortly before he died in 1921, he initiated the project to 'Save the Victory'. Its success ranks as one of the Society's greatest achievements.

In 1952, his son and my uncle, Admiral The Earl Mountbatten of Burma, became Patron of the Society, and held that position until his assassination in 1979. The following year, I was approached by the Society with an invitation to succeed him as Patron. Needless to say, I was honoured and delighted to accept. It so happens that I had already served as a Trustee of the National Maritime Museum, another product of the Society, since 1948.

I have followed the activities of the Society with great interest, and I was delighted to be able to join the members for the Society's 75th anniversary celebrations in 1985. Then in 2005, I opened the Exhibition of HMS *Victory's* foretopsail to mark the bicentenary of the Battle of Trafalgar.

For all these reasons it gives me great pleasure to congratulate the Society on achieving its centenary, and to welcome the publication of this important history.

Acknowledgements

The authors are grateful to the Chairman, Officers and Council of the Society for Nautical Research for their encouragement in the writing of this history.

We have benefited from the support of the Director, Deputy Director and Trustees of the National Maritime Museum, Greenwich, especially Christopher Gray, Secretary to the Board of Trustees, Liza Verity, Dr Pieter van der Merwe and Geraldine Charles, whose guidance in the Archives we have much appreciated. Other members of staff who have been particularly helpful include Eleanor Gawne, Mike Bevan, Andrew Davies, Martin Salmon, Sue McMahon, Janet Norton, Ann Wallis, Jean Patrick, Colin Starkey and Sarah Beighton.

We are very pleased to acknowledge the help of many members of the Society for Nautical Research who responded to our inquiries with their recollections and reminiscences. These include John Munday, Honorary Vice-President, Lt Cdr Lawrence Phillips, Vice-President, Professor Roger Knight, Vice-President, Dr A. P. McGowan, Vice-President, Dr Susan Rose, Vice-President, Alan Aberg, Vice-President, Professor E. J. Grove, Vice-President, Rear-Admiral David M. Pulvertaft, Chairman of the Publications Committee from 2003 to 2009, his successor, Cdr David Hobbs, David Page, Rob Gardiner, David Clement, Arvid Gottlicher, Campbell McMurray, Alex Ritchie, Barbara Jones, Professor Andrew D. Lambert, Patricia K. Crimmin, Professor N. A. M Rodger, Professor R. O. Goss, Mr M. P. J. Garvey and Dr Ann Shirley. Our thanks are due for the comments of the referees who read the typescript in draft and to Dr Paula J. Turner, the Administrative Editor for *The Mariner's Mirror* who has created this book out of our typescripts.

Our thanks are due also to the staffs of the National Archives of England and Wales, Kew, the British Library, Churchill Archives Centre, Churchill College, Cambridge, Diane Clements, Director, The Library and Museum of Freemasonry and to Matthew Sheldon and Stephen Courtney of the National Museum of the Royal Navy

We are very grateful to Richard Stone for permission to reproduce his portrait of

HRH The Duke of Edinburgh which appears as the frontispiece. We are also pleased to acknowledge the Trustees of the National Gallery for permission to reproduce J. M. W. Turner's *The Fighting* Temeraire, and the Trustees of the National Portrait Gallery for permission to reproduce Sir Arthur Stockdale Cope's *Naval Officers of the Great War* and also the portrait of James Arthur Seventh Earl Stanhope. We are also grateful to acknowledge Paul Gunn and Chloe Gunn-Blackburn for permission to use Sir James Gunn's portrait of Earl Stanhope and Donovan Hailstone for permission to use Bernard Hailstone's portrait of Roger Charles Anderson. Other illustrations appear by permission of Churchill Archives Centre, the National Maritime Museum and the National Museum of the Royal Navy. We have attempted to obtain copyright consent for all other illustrations and apologize if any have been used in error without permission.

Finally, we are especially grateful to Mrs Sylvia Caldwell-Smith for the photograph of her grandfather, Sir James Caird. We trust this book truly reflects his remarkable and generous contribution to the maritime history of the United Kingdom and the success of the Society for Nautical Research.

List of Abbreviations

Annual General Meeting	AGM
British Library	BL
British Parliamentary Papers	BPP
Captain	Capt.
Commander	Cdr
Commander-in-Chief	C-in-C
Commanding Officer	CO
Fellow of the Royal Society	FRS
Fellow of the Royal Institute of British Architects	FRIBA
Finance and General Purposes Committee	FGPC
Her Majesty's Royal Yacht	HMRY
His Majesty's Ship	HMS
International Journal of Maritime History	*IJMH*
Lieutenant Colonel	Lt Col
Lieutenant Commander	Lt Cdr
Ministry of Defence (Navy)	MoD (N)
National Maritime Museum, Greenwich	NMM
National Museum of the Royal Navy	NMRN
North Atlantic Treaty Organization	NATO
Navy Records Society	NRS
Official Nelson Commemorations Committee	ONCC
Portsmouth Naval Base Property Trust	PNBPT
Portsmouth Royal Naval Museum Trading Company	PRNMTC
Royal Mail Ship	RMS
Royal Naval Museum, Portsmouth	PRNM
Royal Navy Volunteer Reserve	RNVR
Royal Research Ship	RRS
Royal United Services Institute	RUSI

Save the Victory Fund	STVF
Society for Nautical Research	SNR
Steamship	SS
Training Ship	TS
The Mariner's Mirror	*MM*
The National Archives, Kew	NA
Victory Advisory Technical Committee	VATC
Victory Technical Committee	VTC

1

Launching the Society for Nautical Research

The Maritime World of the Society's Founders

Britain's command of her surrounding seas and oceans was fundamental to the national interest and imperial ambitions of an island nation. It was taken for granted as an established tradition and little thought was given to it in the years following the Napoleonic Wars. Throughout the reign of Queen Victoria, the Royal Navy policed the world's sea lanes against piracy and slave traders and surveyed the oceans' hazards to protect the expanding commerce of Britain's mercantile marine, the world's largest trading fleet. However, confidence that British control of the seas was unchallengeable began to be shaken during the late nineteenth century. Any complacency was dispelled by a series of naval alarms that began in 1884 with an influential newspaper article entitled 'What Is the Truth about the Navy' by 'One Who Knows the Facts'.[1] It was followed in 1888–9 by concerns that the two-power standard of naval superiority, whereby the Royal Navy was expected to have the capability and capacity to defeat the next two strongest naval powers in combination, had been lost. The government's response was to increase naval expenditure by passing the Naval Defence Act 1889, but, before the building programme had taken effect, French aggression in the Far East in 1893 aroused further apprehension that Britain's pre-eminence was under threat.[2] It was also apparent that imperial rivalry between European powers was leading to competitive shipbuilding programmes and that foreign fleets were increasing in size and strength. From the late 1880s onwards, with progress being made applying new technology to the building and propulsion of ships, and the use of electricity to control their operations, it became evident that improved defences were needed against new long-distance weapons, such as the torpedo and the large-calibre gun. This gave rise to the realization that the British naval tradition of closing with the enemy and engaging at short range was unsustainable and much of Britain's fleet was obsolete. The power of the Royal Navy, and its ability to protect the carriage of exports and supply of raw materials and foodstuffs on which the economy depended, meant that naval affairs were major items of news and public interest, and leading newspapers, such as *The Times*, employed a 'Naval Correspondent'.

The Queen's Golden Jubilee in 1887 and her Diamond Jubilee ten years later focused the country's awareness on the extent of the British Empire and the need to maintain Imperial power.[3] To that end the strength of the armed forces was constantly under examination. In an age when trade shows and fairs presenting the progress of commerce and manufactures to the nation were popular, the armed forces felt they too must display their capabilities. The Army Exhibition of 1890 held at the Royal Hospital, Chelsea, was followed in 1891 by a Naval Exhibition on the same site organized by the Royal United Services Institute (RUSI).[4] Popular feeling was harnessed by the formation of the Navy League in 1893 as a pressure group for the support and upkeep of naval expenditure. The League developed a programme of lectures and visits to schools and held a mass meeting in Trafalgar Square in 1896. So began a decade of 'high navalism' culminating in the League seizing a leading role in the commemoration of the centenary of the Battle of Trafalgar in 1905 in the face of Government reluctance to do so. The League emphasized the role of the Royal Navy as the bulwark of the freedom of the seas, and the place of Nelson in the forefront of the national canon of heroes.[5] The novelty of film was also used to popularize the navy. Alfred J. West opened *Our Navy* at The Polytechnic in Regent Street, London, in October 1899. With frequent programme changes, it ran for fourteen years and was seen by more than two million people.[6]

During the years 1896–1905, Britain's maritime position in the world came under close scrutiny, notably following the German Navy Laws of 1898 and 1900. Concern that Britain was exposed by 'splendid isolation' to international criticism during and after the Boer War (1899–1902) brought about an invasion scare in January and February 1900 which envisaged that, with the Royal Navy so widely dispersed, the French Brest fleet might hold the English Channel long enough to land 50,000 or 100,000 men on the south coast of England.[7] The febrile situation surrounding naval affairs led Britain to negotiate the Anglo-Japanese Naval Treaty of 1902 and to seek European alliances initiated by the *entente cordiale* with France in 1904.[8] At home, recognition of the force of growing American and German economic competition found expression in the debate between protagonists of free trade on one hand, and protectionism on the other; but there was also an undercurrent of unease about the physical well-being or, more accurately, the lack of it, of large swathes of Britain's population. The manpower debate, initially concerned with the army but extended by implication to the navy, was based on these presumed inadequacies.[9] Social investigators such as Charles Booth highlighted the blight of poverty, substandard housing and lack of education of London's poorer classes. From another perspective noted authors such as H. G. Wells and George Bernard Shaw were proponents of eugenic population control which focused on unskilled labour and the 'undeserving poor'. These factors were by no means exhaustive but they formed part of a wider context in which the continuing debate on maintaining a two-power standard took place and gave rise to strategic concerns expressed in 1905 by the Royal Commission on the Supply of Food and Raw Materials in time of War.[10]

The public face of Britain's naval power was exemplified by the commissioning in December 1906 of the first all 'big gun' battleship, HMS *Dreadnought*. Her revolutionary technology, including steam turbine engines and a gunnery fire-control system, sparked an escalation in the naval arms race, particularly with Germany. Public awareness of the importance of the sea to Britain's status as a Great Power was consequently high. The popularity of organizations that existed to further British naval expansion could be measured by the growth of the Navy League to 100,000 members by 1914, and the creation of a splinter organization, the Imperial Maritime League, in 1908.[11] The Imperial Maritime League – originating as a faction in the Navy League led by Admiral Lord Charles Beresford – criticized the Navy League as being merely 'an echo' of the Liberal Government and the reform policies of the First Sea Lord, Admiral Sir John Fisher.[12] The Imperial Maritime League lost its main target when Fisher resigned in January 1910 but it served to offset the influence of the National Defence League, an army-inspired pressure group that claimed in 1907–8 that the Royal Navy was unprepared to defeat any sudden invasion of the East Coast of England by a German army of 100,000 men. The imagined German invasion force and its target may well have had its origins in Erksine Childers's 1903 novel, *The Riddle of the Sands*, but though Rosyth had been designated as an east coast naval base in 1903, construction only began in 1909 and was unfinished in 1914.[13] Fisher's strengthening of a Nore Division of the Home Fleet based at Sheerness in 1907 emphasized the Admiralty's recognition of a German threat following from the passing of the German Navy Law of 1906, which provided for the building of six heavy cruisers in addition to the annual budget's provision of two more battleships, and the widening of the Kiel Canal to allow them access to the North Sea. Support for naval expansion from Conservative newspapers pressed the Liberal government of the day towards greater naval expenditure in order to guarantee the Royal Navy's continuing mastery of the seas. Thus the largest item of expenditure in the 'People's Budget' of 1909 was not allocated for social reform measures but for the building of eight new super-dreadnoughts. It could be argued that naval affairs had never had such a high profile. Indeed, the general public in areas such as Clydeside, Tyneside, Barrow, and Merseyside could see for themselves the direct result of the increase in naval construction, in which private shipbuilding firms took the lion's share.[14]

The founders of the Society for Nautical Research (SNR) were therefore members of a society in which there was heated debate about maritime affairs. The modernization of naval bases and the 1893 building programme for the Royal Navy, especially the construction of torpedo-boat destroyers following Fisher's appointment as Third Sea Lord and Controller of the Navy in 1892, had caused controversy which spread beyond rivalries within the navy. Further measures introduced when Fisher was C-in-C, Portsmouth, and as First Sea Lord from 1904, included the speeding-up of shipbuilding in HM dockyards, the design of HMS *Dreadnought*, and the reform of officer training. However, it was the concentration of Britain's fleet in home waters that aroused the public opposition of Admiral Lord Charles Beresford, a dispute which the newspapers reported as though Fisher and Beresford were champion prize-fighters.[15] Moreover, the debate on free trade which divided the Liberals and Conservatives depended upon Britain's supremacy not merely in terms of fighting ships but also upon the dominance of world trade by British shipping and shipbuilders. The British merchant fleet provided food and raw materials for Britain's people and their work and carried British exports to the Empire and other overseas markets. Britain's mercantile marine touched every part of the globe: her docks and wharves teemed with imports of raw materials, semi-finished goods and foodstuffs, and were the conduit for exports of manufactured goods and coal. Her coastwise, short-sea and deep-sea trades were long established through sail and steam, and the emigrant trade was catered for by passenger ships and liners. The sheer variety of vessels regularly seen in Britain's ports and rivers ranged from full-rigged sailing ships and barques to coasting brigs and ketches, while steam-powered vessels ranged from Atlantic passenger liners to cargo liners, colliers, tramps, whalers and fishing vessels. Maritime subjects were ever-present in newspapers and popular discussion, and it was widely recognized that in time of war Britain's food supply would depend upon the capability of the navy to maintain command of the seas.

The extent of change in the second half of the nineteenth century had been dramatic. In Edwardian Britain, a middle-aged person would have lived through the transformation of shipping from sail to steam, and from wood to iron and steel shipbuilding. Moreover, any person interested in technology would also have been aware of the tremendous strides made in marine propulsion and in marine boilers by British engineers such as Charles Randolph and John Elder, Alexander Carnegie Kirk, Walter Brock, Charles Parsons and James Howden.[16] The rapid development of marine technology also encompassed refrigeration of perishable cargoes and mechanical cargo handling.[17]

Edwardian Britain was therefore a society in which maritime affairs were both a source of pride and anxiety: pride in Britain's naval and mercantile power and anxiety that the growth of international competitors might challenge this leadership. It was also a society which was conscious of its maritime heritage and in which marine metaphors – many from the days of sail – permeated all levels of cultural expression. However, by 1910 much of this maritime culture was already in the past. Although many sailing vessels were still to be seen in British ports, there were few British-flagged deep-sea traders under sail.[18] The Board of Trade did not require time in sail as a prerequisite for a Second Mate's Certificate and commercial knowledge of handling vessels under sail was becoming increasingly confined to some coasting and river-trading craft and inshore fishing boats. This meant that one fundamental aspect of Britain's maritime heritage was on the verge of extinction in the years before the First World War.

The Formation of the Society: its aims and objectives

While populist opinion was well catered for by the newspaper reports of political campaigns, such as those by the Navy League, interest in the history of the Royal Navy at a scholarly level was maintained by the Navy Records Society (NRS), formed in 1893. Its early years were prolific: by 1910 the NRS had published its fortieth volume, *The Naval Miscellany*, vol. II, edited by Sir John Knox Laughton, but its output was mainly limited to substantial scholarly edited volumes of original documents.[19] Wider but equally serious maritime interests, including that of nautical archaeology, lacked a dedicated outlet through which to disseminate research findings. There were professional organizations already in existence such as the Institute of Naval Architects, founded in 1860 and incorporated by Royal Charter in 1910; the Institution of Engineers and Shipbuilders in Scotland whose first meeting took place in 1865, and the North East Coast Institution of Engineers and Ship-builders, formed in 1884. These professional bodies published papers pertaining to their disciplines, mostly of a technical nature.[20] In addition, scholarly editions of primary records of voyages, geographical discoveries and other geographical material were covered by the publications of the Hakluyt Society, established in 1846.[21]

The genesis of the SNR took place against this background. The principal creator of the Society was Leonard George Carr Laughton, a naval correspondent for the *Morning Post*, nautical antiquarian, and the son of Sir John Knox Laughton, the founder of the NRS. As Sir Alan Moore recalled, the formation of a Society of Nautical Antiquaries had been discussed as early as January 1907.[22] Carr Laughton and Moore initially considered it might be called the Jal Society after Auguste Jal, the French compiler of the vast *Glossaire nautique*, though Laughton deemed the time was not yet ripe for its formation.[23] There seemed no urgency to form a society, as any research written up could find an outlet in the *United Services Magazine*, for which Moore began to write in 1908.[24] Thereafter, according to Moore, other nautical antiquarians and historians became involved including Harold Hulme Brindley, of St John's College, Cambridge; Roger Charles Anderson, a future editor of *The Mariner's Mirror*, and Chairman and eventually President of the SNR; Robert Morton Nance, later a prolific contributor to *The Mariner's Mirror*, and Gregory Robinson, a marine painter.

By October 1909 active consideration was given to the formation of a society which might be run as an adjunct to the NRS or, if it were to be called the Jal Society, the offices of the NRS could be used to promote it. The proposed society would be subscription-based and would need a large membership. Preparatory to this a list of potential leading members had been drawn up. Carr Laughton spoke to his father who was then secretary of the NRS and to Cdr Charles Napier Robinson who was naval correspondent of *The Times* and also assistant editor of the *Army and Navy Gazette*. In October and November 1909 several informal exchanges over tea and by letter took place on the formation of a Jal Society. Carr Laughton wrote to C. N. Robinson on 12 November 1909 proposing a 'society of marine antiquaries'. He attached an annexe headed 'Proposed Jal Society', listing its objectives as the compilation of a marine encyclopaedia, the production of a magazine and the assemblage of a marine bibliography, including works of art.[25] In replying to Carr Laughton, on 22 November 1909, Robinson suggested that if he could succeed in starting a small society for the production of nautical notes and queries, then this would be, 'the best possible thing for naval archaeology', and that the title should be nautical rather than naval. He suggested something similar in size and shape to the *Navy League Journal*.[26] Thereafter, the preliminary work of starting the society fell upon Carr Laughton. Although Moore had 'no record of what he did till 13 February 1910', Carr Laughton wrote to his father, Sir John Knox Laughton, on 30 November 1909 explaining how far their plans had progressed, and setting out the divisions which had already emerged among the group proposing the new society:

> This Jal Soc. Idea is rather a complicated business. We have approached enough men to get some sort of idea as to the next move, though we have yet to come to a decision.
>
> The young bloods – not necessly young in A.D., but new to the difficulties of such a project – welcome the idea, & would endorse & support any scheme. The old stagers, e.g. C. N. Robinson, Corbett & Leyland, are inclined to be pessimistic. Robinson thinks we can do nothing without money, & doubts whether we can get enough to be of use. The other two seem to think that the scheme is in some way likely to rival the N.R.S. That of course is a misconception, at least as far as intent is concerned.[27]

Julian Corbett apparently thought that any scheme rivalling the NRS would fail, but Carr Laughton summarily dismissed his concern by stating that the difference between the two societies 'would be as wide as the poles asunder'. The next step was to find out how many active nautical antiquarians there actually were; since only if sufficient numbers were interested could the aspiration to form a society be accomplished. At this stage, Carr Laughton envisaged producing 'a sort of glorified Glossaire nautique' or 'Word book' together with a small magazine along the lines of *Notes and Queries*[28] and that in the near future a prospectus for the proposed society should be circulated among members of the NRS.[29]

Meanwhile, Carr Laughton fretted over how to sell the proposed journal to non-subscribers. On 11 December 1909, he wrote to C. N. Robinson:

> Is it not likely that a considerable number of thrifty souls would say to themselves 'Well, all these people do is to publish a magazine. If I can get it as an outsider for 3/- a year, why pay a guinea?' If we're to adopt that course it seems to me that we would have to try to devise some makeweight for the satisfaction of subscribers. If we were Yankees we could give 'em a button, or if Germans a uniform. But, being mere British these useful courses are barred.[30]

The support of Sir John Knox Laughton was certainly welcome, even though he was in his eightieth year. He outlined the proposals for a new society to the NRS Council meeting on 14 December 1909.[31] By February 1910, Carr Laughton and Alan Moore had drafted the contents of a slip of paper, announcing the intention of forming, in Moore's words, 'a Jal society'.[32] This appears as the 'Prospectus' on p. 8. Sir John Knox Laughton ensured notices for it appeared in the next available volume of the NRS, and in the *Proceedings of the United States Naval Institute*.[33] The following month, Carr Laughton wrote to C. N. Robinson asking him to publicize the circular in *The Times* and the *Army and Navy Gazette*.[34]

Carr Laughton then took on the job of Acting Secretary to the proposed society and, with the aid of his father's influential contacts, by 3 April 1910, 43 people had indicated their support, including several admirals, notable among whom was Vice-Admiral His Serene Highness Prince Louis of Battenberg, later to become the new Society's first President. This was certainly enough to form a society but not enough to sustain a journal. In addition, Moore had begun to have doubts about continuing with the name 'Jal Society' as a 'regrettable number of people' had never heard of him. Presciently, Robert Morton Nance, in a letter to Moore, added that a 'Jal Society', 'would seem a little too much as if we were banded together for the study of his works'. This advice was heeded: the proposed society was briefly referred to as the Nautical Antiquary Society and valuable publicity for it was given in articles by Robinson in *The Times* and by Carr Laughton in the *Morning Post*. By 10 April,

Proposal for the Formation of a Society for Nautical Antiquaries

Experience has shown that interest in Nautical Archaeology is active and increasing. At present each individual student whether his motive be historical, artistic or purely antiquarian, must needs rely on his own unaided research: whence it appears that the provision of some means of intercommunication would be helpful. Of various suggestions made, that which seems to find most favour is for the foundation of a periodical wherein subscribers could record the results of their researches into, and bring forward points needing elucidation concerning such matters as the following:–The design, building and equipment of ships; the language and customs of the sea; genealogies; nautical flags, relics, medals, dress and so forth. If after the establishment of a periodical it were thought desirable to proceed to the foundation of a Society, the periodical would still be needed to serve as its official organ.

It is believed that the proposed Society, or periodical, would serve as a useful, if humble, ally to the Navy Records Society, standing to it in the relationship in which a pinnace bears to a great ship, and serving to make discoveries in narrow waters where she herself might not easily come.

In order to know what support might be expected, it is necessary to assume that the annual subscription would probably be fixed at One Guinea: and to ask those who favour this project to communicate, as a preliminary measure, with the Acting Secretary, Mr L. G. Carr Laughton, 5 Ruvigny Mansions, Putney, S.W.

February 1910.

58 names had come forward but not until June were circulars sent out announcing a preliminary meeting of supporters.[35] The delay was occasioned by the death of King Edward VII on 6 May 1910; at the end of May, Carr Laughton wrote to C. N. Robinson, 'Since the King's death things have utterly stagnated.'[36] On 14 June an inaugural meeting took place at the RUSI in London with the marine painter W. L. Wyllie RA in the chair.[37] There were around 40 people present, and the decision to found a society for the study of nautical antiquities was taken. A Provisional Committee of 17 was appointed which held its first meeting on 21 June. Vice-Admiral Sir Reginald Custance took the chair, with Carr Laughton as Acting Secretary. Also present were the Rev. E. W. Matthews, Lieut E. Williams RN, Admiral Sir R. Massie Blomfield, H. H. Brindley, Cdr C. N. Robinson, John Leyland, Douglas Owen, William Gordon Perrin (Admiralty Librarian), and Sir John Knox Laughton of the NRS. It established two sub-committees for rules and finance, and issued the formal Prospectus of the Society for Nautical Research.[38] Although the name Nautical Research Society was used when the Provisional Committee met on 21 June, it offered confusion with the Navy Records Society, and on 19 July the Provisional Committee adopted the name 'The Society for Nautical Research'.

The proposal for a journal with the title *The Mariner's Mirror* was made at the committee meeting on 21 June and though referred to a sub-committee for consideration was never thereafter challenged. According to Moore, it was already common currency.[39] Crucially, at the 19 July meeting, W. G. Perrin informed the committee that the Admiralty would subscribe for around 250 copies of the proposed journal per month to be distributed among the fleet, thereby almost guaranteeing the journal's financial viability. Subsequently, the first general meeting of the SNR took place on 2 December 1910, at the RUSI with Sir Clements Markham FRS in the chair; 125 supporters of the Society were enrolled as members. Thereafter, the Society's aims were clear and intrinsically international in scope. Its objects were:

- To encourage research into Nautical Antiquities, into matters relating to sea-faring, and ship-building in all ages and all nations, into the language and customs of the Sea, and into other subjects of nautical interest.

- For this purpose to publish periodically a Journal, to be called the 'Mariner's Mirror', such journal to contain original articles, notes and queries, pictures and designs, and generally to serve as a medium of inter-communication between members of the Society.

- To collect material with a view to the ultimate publication of a complete and scholarly Nautical Encyclopaedia or Dictionary.[40]

Figure 2 W. L. Wyllie, RA (about 1890) by R. W. Robinson. (Royal Academy of Arts, London)

Aspiring members were asked to apply to the Secretary and Treasurer, Douglas Owen, and would be admitted subject to the approval of Council. Subscription rates of one guinea (£1 1s, or 21 shillings) were payable for the first year of membership and thereafter the rate was set at half a guinea (10s 6d) per annum.[41]

The Membership

The first List of Members of the SNR is dated December 1911. It contains 248 names, including those of clubs and institutions: of these 94 were also listed as members of the NRS in June 1911, and over 80 members were officers of the Royal Navy, including 23 admirals. Only two women braved this stronghold of male interest – Lady Londonderry and Mrs Ethel Pryor.[42] The Society's first President, Vice-Admiral Prince Louis of Battenberg, presided at the Annual General Meeting (AGM) in 1912. The social stature of the Society's President, Vice-Presidents and Councillors was impressive even by the standards of the day. A full list is given in Appendix I. Four of the 18 Councillors were members of the Editorial Committee of *The Mariner's Mirror*, along with the editor, L. G. Carr Laughton, and Douglas Owen, the Hon. Secretary and Treasurer.[43] That a number of members and Councillors considered themselves to be 'Nautical Antiquarians' should not, however, be taken as meaning they were primarily concerned with aspects of antiquity: they were antiquarians in the best sense of the word, who saw the past as part of the present and who did not regard, as Moore remarked of Harold Hulme Brindley, that something that had gone out of use was necessarily done with.[44] Indeed, in Nietzsche's sense, antiquarianism is a form of history aimed at creating a feeling of connexion to one's own history – a sense of perspective still present in *The Mariner's Mirror* today.[45]

The Mariner's Mirror

From the outset, the Society's existence was indelibly linked to, and determined by, the future and viability of its journal. At the first full meeting of the members of the Society on 2 December 1910, L. G. Carr Laughton was appointed Editor of what was planned as a monthly periodical with an Editorial Committee, including the Hon. Editor, responsible for it. The inaugural issue of *The Mariner's Mirror* took place on 11 January 1911. Its name was taken from a sixteenth-century precursor, the English translation by Anthony Ashley of Lucas Janszon Waghenaer's *Speculum Nauticum*, published in 1588. The pale grey-green cover bore beneath the gothic script of 'The Society for Nautical Research' a reproduction of the title page of Waghenaer's *Mariner's Mirror*, showing a representation of a great ship, of seamen's costumes, and of navigational instruments in the year in which the Great Armada was overthrown. This, in amended form, still adorns the cover of the journal today. Nonetheless, the initial design came in for some trenchant criticism from Gregory Robinson, who drew the cover from 1912 to 1923.[46] The central space (figure 3), was only partly occupied by the title in Roman capitals and four lines of ordinary print, as a reproduction of volume 1:3 shows.
   Robinson dropped the gothic heading, and changed the central inscription with

Figure 3 The cover of the first volume of *The Mariner's Mirror*, vol 1: 3. (Society for Nautical Research)

the addition of 'The Journal of the Society for Nautical Research' on a white rather than on a pale green cover. The first issue ran to 32 pages, and its list of contents is reproduced in figure 4. The edition also included two high-quality illustrations; a very rare mezzotint after an original painting of William van de Velde the Younger, by Godfrey Kneller, 1680, engraved by J. Smith, 1707, in the possession of T. H. Parker of London, and another scarce mezzotint 'A Fresh Gale' after the original by van de Velde, engraved by Richard Houston.[47]

There were teething troubles in the production of *The Mariner's Mirror*. The February 1911 issue, costing one shilling, was delayed by a printers' strike and, as the year progressed, further delays in publication occurred, despite a notice in the August issue that 'A plan has now been adopted which the Committee believe will ensure the clearing off of arrears before the close of the year'. However, the Report of the Council for 1912 noted that 'owing to various causes, but chiefly to the serious demands involved on the time of the Hon. Editor, the publication of the journal fell in the latter part of the year into arrears'.[48] Even so, the fact that the Society's journal had come to fruition in such a remarkably short period was testament to the determination of the founders of the SNR. The initial success of *The Mariner's Mirror* brought an increase in the Society's membership, which almost doubled to 248 by December 1911. Although *The Mariner's Mirror*'s success or failure ultimately depended upon the measure of literary support obtained from members, whether in the form of a repository for their discoveries or brief research notes, or as a medium from which they could pursue their enquiries, there were organizational problems to be overcome. Carr Laughton was, in the eyes of other members of the Editorial Committee, given to procrastination. Organizational difficulties remained unresolved and ran on from 1911 into 1912. Tensions between the Editorial Committee members mounted. In November 1912 Douglas Owen, the Hon. Secretary and Treasurer, wrote in exasperation to C. N. Robinson that Carr Laughton's promises and explanations were alike worthless:

> He is a Rotter. Personally I sh[oul]d disregard them all & view the facts as they stand . . . Unless we can devise some other means of issuing the journal, we had better face the situation and wind up. Personally I will have nothing more to do with it officially, if *he* has. I was a fool to accept his promises and to withdraw my resignation. I ought to have had enough sense to know that sooner or later we should have the whole thing to go through again.

By the next post Robinson received further but more measured indications of disquiet from Alan Moore:

> I cannot think that the Admiralty will go on with their support if we continue

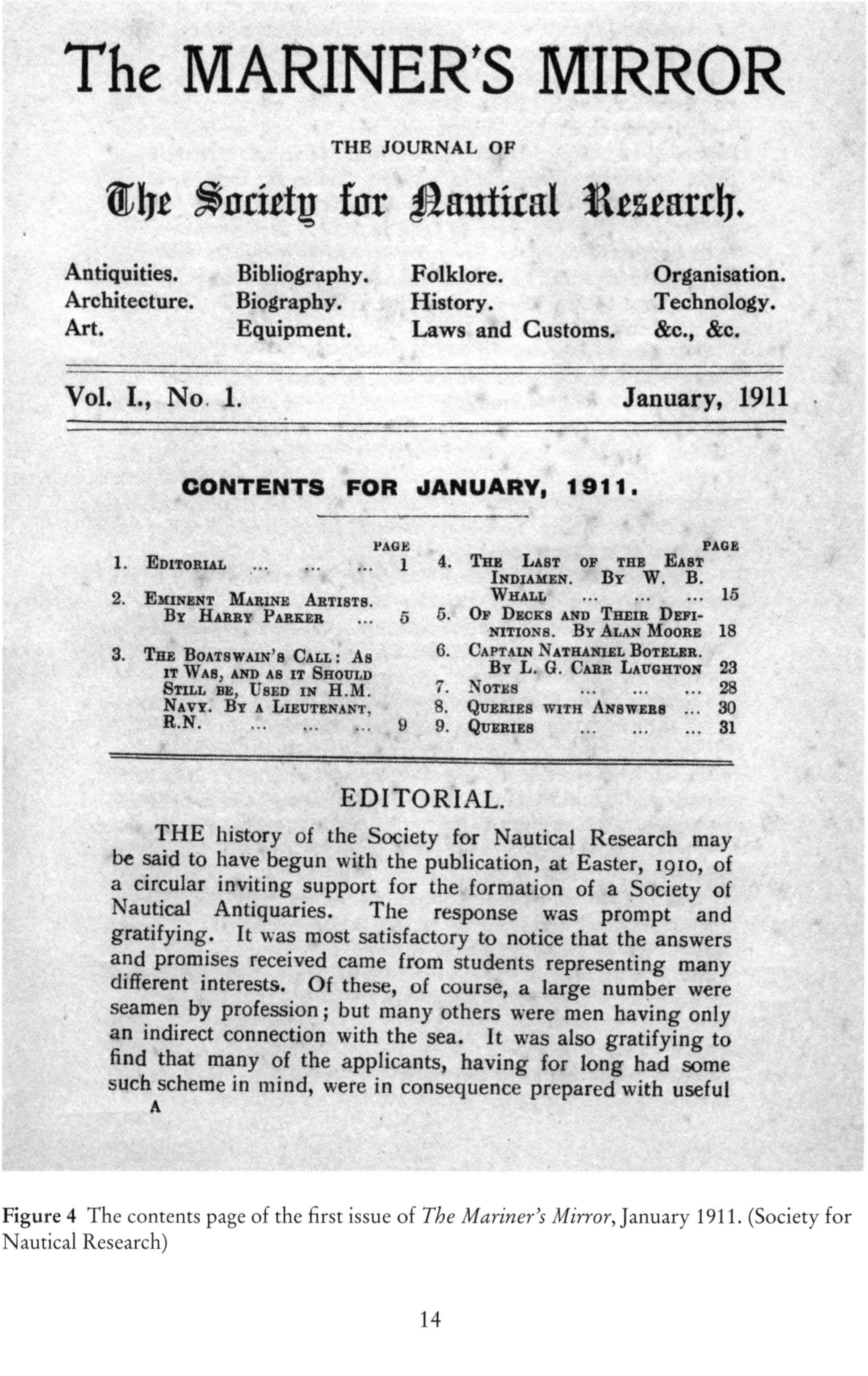

The MARINER'S MIRROR

THE JOURNAL OF

The Society for Nautical Research.

Antiquities.	Bibliography.	Folklore.	Organisation.
Architecture.	Biography.	History.	Technology.
Art.	Equipment.	Laws and Customs.	&c., &c.

Vol. I., No. 1.   January, 1911

CONTENTS FOR JANUARY, 1911.

	PAGE
1. EDITORIAL	1
2. EMINENT MARINE ARTISTS. By HARRY PARKER ...	5
3. THE BOATSWAIN'S CALL: AS IT WAS, AND AS IT SHOULD STILL BE, USED IN H.M. NAVY. BY A LIEUTENANT, R.N.	9
4. THE LAST OF THE EAST INDIAMEN. BY W. B. WHALL	15
5. OF DECKS AND THEIR DEFINITIONS. BY ALAN MOORE	18
6. CAPTAIN NATHANIEL BOTELER. BY L. G. CARR LAUGHTON	23
7. NOTES	28
8. QUERIES WITH ANSWERS ...	30
9. QUERIES	31

EDITORIAL.

THE history of the Society for Nautical Research may be said to have begun with the publication, at Easter, 1910, of a circular inviting support for the formation of a Society of Nautical Antiquaries. The response was prompt and gratifying. It was most satisfactory to notice that the answers and promises received came from students representing many different interests. Of these, of course, a large number were seamen by profession; but many others were men having only an indirect connection with the sea. It was also gratifying to find that many of the applicants, having for long had some such scheme in mind, were in consequence prepared with useful

A

Figure 4 The contents page of the first issue of *The Mariner's Mirror*, January 1911. (Society for Nautical Research)

in our unpunctuality and since those members who at the beginning had most matter to unburden themselves of are now beginning to dry up as far as ready copy is concerned, it seems to me that the remedy lies in making the MM quarterly, but would the Admiralty continue to co-operate?[49]

Such was the overall dissatisfaction with Carr Laughton's performance that the members of the Editorial Committee called a Special Meeting of Council on 11 November 1912 in accordance with Rule IX to:

Decide upon the steps necessary to secure the resumption of the publication of the Journal, of which no issue has been made since the June number.[50]

This had the desired effect. The Report of the Council for 1912 explained that a sub-committee had been appointed to deal with the matter and the arrears had been made good. For the coming year, 1913, an 'Editorial Committee of six joint Hon. Editors was appointed, each to be responsible in turn for one issue of *The Mariner's Mirror*, with L.G. Carr Laughton as Advisory Editor'.[51] Tension continued as this 'solution' proved in practice to be exceptionally cumbersome and 'led more than once to a good deal of confusion and of unnecessary correspondence'. By the end of the year 1913, the Council gladly accepted the offer of R. C. Anderson to act alone as editor, though Carr Laughton did not give up the editorial chair gracefully. On 10 January 1914 Anderson wrote to C. N. Robinson 'Considering that he showed himself *utterly* incompetent as an Editor it sh[oul]d be better for him to let other people try without his interference'.[52] By way of compensation, Carr Laughton was made a Vice-President of the SNR in 1914.

Looking back at the first issues of *The Mariner's Mirror*, one is immediately struck by the quality of the writing and analysis, and the sheer output of the founders of the journal, particularly R. C. Anderson, Carr Laughton, Alan Moore and R. Morton Nance. To begin with, their articles and other contributions from the Society's Council formed the bulk of the journal's content. Moreover, to widen the range of contributors, two of the founders adopted a *nom de plume* as when S. Goodwin and Olaf Hartelie (say it aloud!) began to supply articles.[53] In accordance with one aim of the Society, the compilation of a 'Nautical Encyclopaedia or Dictionary' was announced in an editorial of September 1911 and in the November issue a methodology on referencing was explained.[54] Clearly, this was a huge task and no timescale was put upon it. However, although there were many other expressions of good intentions to complete the project, and despite the fact that many members worked assiduously towards its completion, no publication ensued.

During this formative period, the SNR's relationship with its sister organization, the NRS, was close and dual membership between the societies was a feature – a situation that still pertains today. Moreover, this relationship gave the SNR a natural constituency of membership, which helped to underpin its survival. It is a moot point whether the Society would have come about were it not for the existence of the NRS. However, both for the present and for the future, historians are fortunate that Britain has two such learned societies – one devoted to the history of the Royal Navy and its personnel, and the other to maritime history in its widest sense. Indeed, *The Mariner's Mirror* can also lay claim to have been the pioneering journal of nautical archaeology.

Barely Afloat Before Being Laid Up

From its formation the Society began to generate income from entry fees and the half-guinea (10s 6d or 55p) annual subscription. Its first-year income from 250 members came to £262 10s, while a few paid subscriptions up to two years ahead.[55] A few shillings were even received as donations from sympathizers who declined to become members. Thus, at the end of its first year in existence the Society's success was measured by a substantial cash balance of £138 10s 1d. However, in financial terms, the SNR's existence was linked to, and determined by, the health of *The Mariner's Mirror*, and its finances were dominated by the printing and postage of it to members. Fortunately, *The Mariner's Mirror* also generated income through its sales to non-members, especially when the Admiralty bought significant numbers for distribution to ships and shore establishments until publication ceased temporarily in 1914.

The Society records contain no information as to whether or not having a headquarters building for the SNR was ever discussed at the time of the Society's formation. A London headquarters would have given the SNR a focal point at the heart of the Empire in which members could congregate, hold meetings and from which it could attempt to influence debate on nautical matters. Despite its influential membership, however, no wealthy benefactor had appeared at this stage, and it is likely that the founders of the Society decided to walk before they could run.

The initial growth in membership stalled by 1912 when there were 276 members; in the following year 23 new members joined. Vice-Admiral Prince Louis of Battenberg presided at the 1912 AGM 'at which a Code of Laws for the proper government' of the Society was instituted.[56] In the following year he again presided at the summer meeting and, in an address, formulated what he conceived to be the Society's principal function – vigilance over the safeguarding of objects of naval and national importance. In this regard, successful representations regarding the preservation of Lord Nelson's last will and testament were made and it was withdrawn from the ruck of documents at Somerset House and placed under special protection by the side of William Shakespeare's.[57] The SNR also attempted to increase the scope of its activities by organizing, through R. C. Anderson, 'a small, but quite effective, historical display at the Amsterdam Shipping Exhibition' of 1913.[58] That initiative brought the Society to the attention of a wider circle of businessmen and scholars, and was the first attempt to internationalize its role.

Presiding over the summer meeting of 1914, Prince Louis again returned to his theme of the previous year, the duty of the SNR to guard with patriotic vigilance the nation's treasures where these were of a maritime or nautical character. He also referred to the timbers of an old ship which had recently been unearthed during excavations at Woolwich. The Board of Admiralty had appointed three members of the SNR to investigate the remains and to determine, if possible, its age and origin. This was inherently difficult as ships' timbers differed but little between the sixteenth and eighteenth centuries, and nothing but the backbone of the vessel and a few broken ribs remained. The examination concluded that the ship in question was a ship of the line of 1650 or thereabouts. She had sunk, they thought, in what had been known at the time as 'Woolwich Creek'.[59] That the Admiralty had consulted the SNR on this matter was testament to the professional expertise within its ranks and also put down a marker for future collaboration. Nevertheless the impact of the report on the 'Woolwich Ship' was somewhat submerged in the critical days of August 1914.

Within hours of the outbreak of the Great War, every member of the executive of the SNR had put his services at the disposal of the state. The SNR duly suspended its activities, and after the appearance of the September 1914 issue of volume 4 of *The Mariner's Mirror*, further publication was held in abeyance for the duration of the war.

References

1 *Pall Mall Gazette*, 15 September 1884. This was the first in a series of articles, followed by 'The Truth about Our Coaling Stations', 16 October 1884 which created the first 'naval panic'. R. Hough, *First Sea Lord: An Authorized Biography of Admiral Lord Fisher* (London, 1969), 79–81, suggests that it was written by the editor of the *Pall Mall Gazette*, W. T. Stead, himself, but instigated by H. O. Arnold-Foster (1855–1909) with the collaboration of the then Capt. J. A. Fisher, commanding the gunnery school at Portsmouth, HMS *Excellent*. A. D. Lambert, *Admirals: The Naval Commanders That Made Britain Great* (London, 2008), 281, notes that Fisher was 'discreetly backed' by Admiral Sir Geoffrey Hornby, the outstanding modernizer of the Victorian navy. See also D. M. Schurman, *Imperial Defence 1868–1887*, edited by J. F. Beeler (London, 2000).

2 For background, see R. Hough, *First Sea Lord*, ch. 5 or A. J. Marder, *British Naval Policy, 1880–1905* (London, 1961).The 'two-power standard' may have become a popular measure later but did not hold good in the ironclad era of the 1880s. See R. F. Mackay, *Fisher of Kilverstone* (Oxford, 1973), 181, for the assessment that following Stead's articles 'Britain

was only a little ahead of France in numbers of ships, that both France and Italy were superior in armament (the "Admirals" class having been delayed by painful slowness in the production of their breech-loaders) that Chili [sic] and Brazil had acquired ironclads superior to British cruisers in the Pacific and South Atlantic; that the Royal Navy was short of personnel'.

3   Marder, *Naval Policy*, 45, 'The jubilee naval review at Spithead in 1887 exhibited to the people the weakness as well as the strength of the navy'.

4   See K. Littlewood and B. Butler, *Of Ships and Stars: Maritime Heritage and the Founding of the National Maritime Museum, Greenwich* (London, 1998), 17–18. The exhibition was attended by more than two million visitors.

5   'The term "navalist" as used in this volume refers to those people, civilians and officers, who actively support a big-navy policy. "Navalism" is the big-navy movement', Marder, *Naval Policy*, ix, Explanatory Note. See also Lambert, *Admirals*, 282–3 for the origins of the 'big navy' campaign by W. H. Smith and Admiral Sir Geoffrey Hornby during 1887–8.

The centenary of Trafalgar in 1905 was to a large extent played down by the British Government, which had signed the *Entente Cordiale* with France in 1904. The royal family appeared to have been persuaded to leave London on the weekend of celebrations and only one official service was sanctioned at St Paul's Cathedral, at which the King was represented by a naval officer. Despite this, events were organized throughout the Empire. See D. Shannon, *Nelson Remembered: The Nelson Centenary 1905* (Karawara, W. A., 2007). However, J. Rüger, *The Great Naval Game Britain and Germany in the Age of Empire* (Cambridge, 2007), 228, emphasizes the artificiality of Franco-British 'friendship' and the 1905 centenary celebrations.

By the bicentenary of the Battle of Trafalgar in 2005 a number of biographical and historical treatments of Nelson appeared in print in addition to a veritable flood of re-issued books. On the latter point, Robert Southey's *Life of Nelson* (London, 1813), had gone through more than 50 editions by 1914 and a further 50 by 2000. Some of the better recent treatments are: T. Coleman, *Nelson: The Man and the Legend* (London, 2002), J. Sugden, *Nelson: A Dream of Victory, 1758–1797* (New York, 2004), R. J. B. Knight, *Nelson: The Pursuit of Victory: The Life and Achievements of Horatio Nelson* (London, 2005), A. D. Lambert, *Nelson, Britannia's God of War* (London, 2005), and C. White, *Nelson: The New Letters* (Woodbridge, 2005).

6   See Rüger, *Great Naval Game*, 65.

7   Marder, *Naval Policy*, 374–7.

8   The Anglo-Japanese Naval Treaty, 1902, was renewed in 1905 and 1911. It permitted the withdrawal of Britain's weak naval squadrons from the Far East.

9   This debate was characterized by articles in the *Contemporary Review*, e.g. 'Miles' (pseudonym of Sir Frederick Maurice) 'Where to Get Men', LXXXI (1902), 78–86; Sir F. Maurice, 'National Health: A soldier's study', LXXXIII (1903), 41–56. The theme was taken up by the director-general of the Army Medical Service in a memorandum on physical unfitness of men offering to enlist, British Parliamentary Papers (hereafter BPP) 1903 (Cd.1501) XXVIII, 919 and was a precursor to the *Report of the Royal Commission on the Supply of Food and Raw Materials in time of War*, BPP 1905 (Cd. 2643) XXXIX. The navy encouraged its association with 'amateur sea enthusiasts, coastwise sailors, and yachtsmen' by forming the Royal Naval Volunteer Reserve in 1903. See A. J. Marder, *From the Dreadnought to Scapa Flow. Vol. 1: The Road to War, 1904–1914*, (London, 1961) 33.

10 See *Report of the Inter-Departmental Committee on Physical Deterioration*, BPP, 1904 (Cd. 2175) XXXII, and the equivalent investigation in Scotland, *Report of the Royal Commission*

on Physical Training in Scotland, BPP, 1903 (Cd. 1507) XXX. For the general background, see G. R. Searle, *The Quest for National Efficiency, 1899–1914* (Oxford, 1971), and G. R. Searle, *Eugenics and Politics in Britain, 1900–1914*, (Dordrecht, 1976).

11   See Hough, *First Sea Lord*, 232, for the Imperial Maritime League's creation and support for Lord Charles Beresford's opposition to Fisher's reforms. Beresford's allies in forming the Imperial Maritime League were Rudyard Kipling, Fred T. Jane and A. Conan Doyle.

12   See W. M. Hamilton, *The Nation and the Navy*, (New York and London, 1986), 154–6.

13   E. Childers, *The Riddle of the Sands: A Record of Secret Service* (London, 1903). It was followed by a number of other books both German and English of an even more alarmist nature; see Hough, *First Sea Lord*, 202, and also Marder, *Naval Policy*, 466–7, on the clamour for an east coast naval base and August Niemann, *The Coming Conquest of England* (London, 1904), 476.

14   Of the 45 dreadnoughts (both battleships and battle-cruisers) completed or building for the Royal Navy at the end of 1914 (including vessels commandeered from export customers) 17 came from two Royal Dockyards – nine from Portsmouth and eight from Devonport – and 28 from private firms; 12 from the Clyde, nine from Tyneside, five from Barrow, and one each from the Thames and the Mersey. For a breakdown of the private yards involved, see M. Lindberg and D. Todd, *Anglo-American Shipbuilding in World War II: A Geographical Perspective* (Westport, CT, 2004), 42. A fine analysis of the impact of naval orders on a particular region, which covers this period, is H. B. Peebles, *Warship Building on the Clyde: Naval Orders and the Prosperity of the Clyde Shipbuilding Industry, 1889–1939* (Edinburgh, 1987), 1–87. For an overall analysis of naval history in this period, see A. J. Marder, *From the Dreadnought to Scapa Flow: The Royal Navy in the Fisher era, 1904–1919* (London, 5 vols, 1961–70).

15   Concentrating the fleet in home waters was made possible by the Anglo-Japanese Naval Treaty, 1902.

16   Inventors, respectively, of the compound marine steam engine, the triple-expansion marine steam engine, the quadruple-expansion marine steam engine, the marine steam turbine, and the forced draught system applicable to marine boilers.

17   For an analysis of the rise of refrigeration and cargo handling in Britain's meat trade, see D. J. Oddy, 'The growth of Britain's refrigerated meat trade, 1880–1939', *The Mariner's Mirror*, 93:3 (2007), 269–80.

18   R. & H. Green of Blackwall, noted for their 'Blackwall frigates', had sold their last vessel, *Carlisle Castle*, by 1890, National Maritime Museum, Greenwich (hereafter NMM), Green Blackwall Collection. Devitt & Moore continued to trade under sail to Australia until the end of the First World War. They carried cadets, which amounted to the last ocean-going training in sail under the Red Ensign. See NMM, MSS DEM; see also A. G. Course, *Painted Ports: The Story of the Ships of Messrs Devitt and Moore* (London, 1961).

19   For Knox Laughton, see A. D. Lambert, *The Foundations of Naval History: John Knox Laughton, the Royal Navy and the Historical Profession* (Chatham, 1998). For a centenary history of the NRS, see A. B. Sainsbury's pamphlet, *The Centenary of the Navy Records Society, 1893–1993* (London, 1993).

20   The *Transactions of the Institute of Naval Architects*, later the Royal Institute of Naval Architects, have been published since 1860. For the Institute of Engineers and Shipbuilders in Scotland, see *Mirror of History: A Millennium Commemorative Volume* (Glasgow, 2000). See also J. F. Clarke, *A Century of Service to Engineering and Shipbuilding: A Centenary History of the North East Coast Institution of Engineers and Shipbuilders, 1884–1984* (Newcastle, 1984) and A. Jarvis, 'British Provincial Engineering Institutions and the

Maritime Industries', in D. J. Starkey and H. Murphy, eds, *Beyond Shipping and Shipbuilding: Britain's Ancillary Maritime Interests in the Twentieth Century* (Hull, Maritime Historical Studies Centre, 2007).

21 To date the Hakluyt Society has published six series of books together with some online publishing. For the complete bibliography, see www.hakluyt.com.

22 *Mariner's Mirror* 44:4 (1955), 267–80, Sir Alan Moore, 'The beginning of the SNR'. At the time, Moore was Carr Laughton's sailing companion: he later became a naval medical officer and inherited a baronetcy.

23 *Ibid.*, The *Glossaire nautique* was published in Paris in 1848; see Moore, 'Beginning of the SNR', 268.

24 *Ibid.*, 268–9. Moore agreed to write a series 'on the Evolution of the Ship'.

25 Letter from L. G. Carr Laughton to C. N. Robinson, 12 November 1909. Letter inserted in Cdr C. N. Robinson's bound copy of *The Mariner's Mirror*, (1911), NMM archives.

26 *Mariner's Mirror* 44:4 (1955), 274.

27 NMM SNR/1 L. G. Carr Laughton to Sir John Knox Laughton, 30 November 1909.

28 First published in 1849 by Oxford University Press and still extant.

29 NMM SNR/1 L. G. Carr Laughton to Sir John Knox Laughton, 30 November 1909.

30 Letter from L. G. Carr Laughton to C. N. Robinson, 11 December 1909. Letter inserted in C. N. Robinson's bound copy of *The Mariner's Mirror*, (1911), NMM archives.

31 *Ibid.* NMM SNR/1 Minute Book.

32 Moore, 'Beginning of the SNR', 269–74.

33 See Lambert, *The Foundations of Naval History*: 204–5.

34 Letter from L. G. Carr Laughton to C. N. Robinson, 11 March 1910. Letter inserted in C. N. Robinson's bound copy of *The Mariner's Mirror*, (1911), NMM archives.

35 Moore, 'Beginning of the SNR', 276.

36 Letter from L.G. Carr Laughton to C. N. Robinson, 30 May 1910. Letter inserted in C. N. Robinson's bound copy of *The Mariner's Mirror*, (1911), NMM archives.

37 See reports in *The Times* and *Morning Post* on 15 June 1910 and *Lloyd's List* on 18 June 1910.

38 Moore, 'Beginning of the SNR', 276–7. See also SNR 1/1.

39 *Ibid.*, 277.

40 These objects contained within the Rules of the SNR, formed part of its Prospectus and are alluded to by L. Carr Laughton in an editorial in *The Mariner's Mirror*, 1, January 1911. They were quoted by Moore, 'Beginning of the SNR', 278; see also SNR 1/1.

41 *Ibid.*

42 NMM SNR/1 SNR List of Members, December 1911.

43 The four were John Leyland, Alan H. Moore, W. G. Perrin and Cdr C. N. Robinson.

44 Moore, 'Beginning of the SNR', 269.

45 F. Nietzsche, *Untimely Meditations*, D. Brezeale, ed., R. J. Hollingsdale, trans., (Cambridge, 1997), 57–125.

46 Moore, 'Beginning of the SNR', 279.

47 *Ibid.*

48 SNR 3/1 Minute Book No. 1. Report of the Council of SNR for 1912.

49 Owen to Robinson, 3 November 1912 and Moore to Robinson, 4 November 1912. Letters inserted in Cdr C. N. Robinson's bound copies of *The Mariner's Mirror*, NMM archives.

50 SNR 3/1 Minute Book No. 1. Report of the Council for 1912.

51 Report of the Council for 1912; the six Joint Editors were R. C. Anderson, John Leyland, C. N. Robinson, A. H. Moore, W. G. Perrin and W. Senior. For an additional viewpoint, see

Lambert, *The Foundations of Naval History*, 171. It appears that Leonard Carr Laughton was under considerable stress, amounting almost to a mental breakdown. He was also Secretary of the NRS, but resigned from the post in 1913, having neglected its day-to-day business. His father, Sir John, 'doubted his sanity'.

52 Anderson to Robinson, 10 January 1914. Letter inserted in Cdr C. N. Robinson's bound copies of *The Mariner's Mirror*, NMM archives.

53 S. Goodwin (or R. C. Anderson) contributed four articles in 1911 and 1912 while Olaf Hartelie (C. N. Robinson) wrote six articles from 1911 to 1922.

54 *Mariner's Mirror* 1:9 and 1:11 (1911), 245–6, 289–92.

55 NMM SNR/3/1 Statement of Accounts for 1911.

56 NMM SNR 2/28 Annual Report of 1938, 'A Brief Chronicle of the first 27 Years', 70.

57 *Ibid*.

58 R. C. Anderson, 'The First Fifty Years', *Mariner's Mirror*, 47:1, (1961), 4.

59 *Ibid*., 71.

2

Refloating the Society and saving
HMS Victory *for the Nation*

With so many members contributing to the war effort during the Great War, the
Society was dormant from 1914 to 1919. The pre-war Editor of *The Mariner's
Mirror*, R. C. Anderson, who had been a member of the Royal Naval Volunteer
Reserve since 1903, served in Gibraltar during the war. In 1916 he found time to get
married and, as a wedding present, gave his new wife, Romola, a lifetime
membership of the SNR.[1] Evidently Anderson intended that the SNR would not be
a short-term phenomenon and, nearly five years after its suspension, *The Mariner's
Mirror* reappeared under his editorship in July 1919. In his editorial of January 1914,
Anderson had expressed a wish to see the circle of contributors widened and the list
of subjects covered become more varied. He returned to this theme in his first post-
war editorial stating that 'the remedy for any suspicion of "a one-man show" lies in
the hands of the members themselves'. Noting that the late F. T. Jane (1865–1916)
had got into trouble for saying there was 'too much Nelson about the Navy League',
Anderson expressed the view that there was 'too much shipbuilding about *The
Mariner's Mirror*, and that he knew that many members felt the same'. He admitted
that he was not in the position of making rash promises, but thought that he would
have the support of the Editorial Committee and the Society in general in
interpreting the scope of the journal very widely, 'so that any work connected with
our subject would be sure of a welcome'.[2] Editors, of course, are in the hands of their
contributors; but perhaps it will surprise modern readers to note that *The Mariner's
Mirror* resumed as a monthly journal where it had left off, without any
acknowledgement of the war, or its impact on the Society's membership. Those
series in progress in 1914 continued as though no interruption to publication had
occurred: thus volume 5:9, appearing in September 1919, offered readers 'Naval
Museums III' as a continuation of the series abandoned in volume 4:9, of September
1914. It followed that the contents of volume 5 largely consisted of the contributions
of founder members, with Morton Nance contributing three articles and Anderson

two. This was understandable; as much of the research published had been under-taken at periods during the war, and the journal had to be filled to maintain membership. There was nothing to foretell the major themes that came to dominate the Society's activities in the interwar years.

The immediate post-war problem was to revive the membership of the Society after the interregnum. This depended largely upon the efforts of the SNR's Hon. Secretary and Treasurer, Sir Douglas Owen. Given the exigencies of war, Owen had great difficulty in contacting the widely dispersed membership of 1914, but he persevered. During *The Mariner's Mirror*'s suspension, the hope had been expressed that members whose subscriptions were paid by bankers' orders would not think it necessary to countermand these orders; and the question of subscriptions paid without value received would be addressed on the resumption of publication. Many members did keep up their annual subscriptions of 10s 6d throughout the war, despite the non-production of the journal, and this left the Society in a far healthier financial position than would otherwise have been the case. Although subscription income had fallen from £104 in 1915, it still totalled £70 in 1918. Thus the total amount of subscriptions received from 1915 to 1918 was £337 1s 0d. Total income from 1915 to 1918 came to £460, including bank interest, against which costs amounted to only £59 so that after the First World War ended, the SNR had £137 cash in hand in December 1918.[3] During 1917 and 1918, the Hon. Treasurer requested the Society's bankers, Coutts and Co., to invest surplus funds in War Loan stock; by the end of 1918, the SNR held £500 5% War Loan (redeemable 1929–47) purchased at a cost of £520 9s 1d.[4] Finally, in 1919, members who had continued to pay their subscriptions were informed how the Society's financial prospects stood and were given the choice of a refund or to treat their contributions as a donation.[5]

During the course of the war death thinned the Society's ranks, including five Vice-Presidents and three Councillors.[6] Accordingly, in the immediate post-war period it was decided that the Society's Council should be reconstructed, and members of the Editorial Committee of *The Mariner's Mirror* met in tandem with the Council to consider re-publishing the journal. Estimates of the cost of printing and publishing were obtained; the result mirrored inflation elsewhere in the economy, and showed a marked advance on pre-war costs. Crucially, had it not been for the Admiralty's renewal of its patronage and their order for 300 copies of *The Mariner's Mirror*, the Society, as it stood, would not have been financially viable. Sir Douglas Owen resigned as Hon. Secretary and Treasurer in October 1919 due to ill health and died shortly afterwards. His successor, Colonel W. G. Simpson, also resigned in 1920 but during his tenure it was resolved that the annual subscription as of 1 January 1920 should be one guinea (£1 1s 0d) instead of 10s 6d: also that the first year's subscription for new members should be £1 11s 6d instead of one guinea. This increase reflected the

Figure 5 Professor Sir Geoffrey A. R. Callender (1875–1946), Hon. Secretary and Treasurer of the Society, 1921–46. (© National Maritime Museum, Greenwich, London)

fact that production costs of *The Mariner's Mirror* had more than doubled since early 1914. Nevertheless, the SNR continued to run a surplus until 1922.

Colonel Simpson's successor was Geoffrey Arthur Romaine Callender, who volunteered for the post of Hon. Secretary and Treasurer. He was a member of the teaching staff at the Royal Naval College, Osborne, when the Council appointed him on 22 October 1920.[7] When Osborne closed in 1921, Callender moved to the Royal Naval College, Dartmouth, but in the same year – 1921 – he was appointed professor of history at the Royal Naval College, Greenwich, from which post he was more centrally placed to run the SNR's affairs. In his first Treasurer's Statement to the Council, Callender explained that there were difficulties in meeting the printer's bills which he attributed to the limited range of the SNR's activities; namely, that the

Society had 'focussed themselves so exclusively on *M.M.* that many members regard the Journal as the sole end of our existence'. In fact, Callender suggested that some of the recent loss of membership could be attributed to a lack of interest in *The Mariner's Mirror*. He reminded the Council that there were 'other spheres demanding our attention': the Nautical Encyclopaedia 'to which we stand committed' by the Society's original aims. Somewhat creatively, he went on to include a Naval and Nautical Bibliography, the establishment of a national naval museum – in Callender's view the Society's 'first duty' – and the rescue of HMS *Victory*, none of which had been in the SNR's original objectives.[8] The problems facing *The Mariner's Mirror* led Callender to put two alternatives before the Council: changing the *Mirror* to a quarterly journal, or a rapid expansion in membership, which would require other activities such as a museum to attract them. Accordingly, at the Annual Meeting, the Council urged every member to recruit for the Society.[9]

One operational change which might have helped regenerate the Society was the question of establishing a permanent London address, Unlike the older learned societies, the SNR had never given any consideration before the war to having premises where members could hold meetings and socialize. Indeed, there is only one recorded instance, at the 1922 AGM, of a member urging the need for a London headquarters upon the SNR.[10] While a London headquarters would have provided a meeting point for members in and around the capital, it would also have been a centre of contact for visiting members from other regions and countries. Perhaps, on reflection, the matter was never fully considered; perhaps the founders were so used to meeting each other in the venues of other organizations which pre-dated the SNR that having their own meeting place had never seemed necessary. Establishing a journal was the overwhelming aim of the founding members, many of whom were already associated with other clubs and societies that provided the SNR with facilities when requested. Among other locations for its meetings, the Society had originally used the premises of the RUSI in Whitehall and, later, the Royal Naval College, Greenwich.[11] However, once Professor Callender was established in Greenwich as Hon. Secretary and Treasurer, he had no inclination for any of the SNR's affairs to be transferred to central London beyond his immediate control, so that members' wishes would have fallen upon stony ground.

By this juncture it had become apparent that, given the rising costs of sustaining a monthly publication and the strain on the editor, the production of *The Mariner's Mirror* must be subject to radical re-thinking, and it was decided at the Annual Meeting in 1921 that in the first instance a report on its prospects should be undertaken.[12] Before it was completed, the Society's President, Prince Louis of Battenberg, now first Marquis of Milford Haven, died on 11 September 1921. He had been a resourceful and inspiring leader, and his work on behalf of the SNR had

Figure 6 Admiral Sir F. C. Doveton Sturdee (1859–1925), President of the Society, 1922–5. This oil sketch in 1920 was a study for Plate 1. (© National Maritime Museum, Greenwich, London)

constituted his principal interest during the last few years of his life. He was succeeded as President in the spring of 1922 by Admiral of the Fleet Sir Frederick Charles Doveton Sturdee, the victor of the Battle of the Falklands. Admiral Sturdee achieved his greatest prominence in the SNR after some fifteen years of disappointments in his career brought about by internal politics in the Royal Navy. As a pre-war supporter of Admiral Lord Charles Beresford he was not trusted by Admiral Sir John Fisher or even Sir John Jellicoe who, during the Great War, 'would not like Sturdee in the van or rear' of the Grand Fleet. Being passed over in favour of more junior admirals left Sturdee feeling very bitter at 'the weight of Their Lordships' displeasure', and his final appointment was as C-in-C at the Nore from 1918 to 1921. Neither during the war nor afterwards did his exposition of naval strategy and tactics find universal approval. After the war only his public fame as the victor of the Falklands and his lectures on 'Seapower and the Empire', as well as on moral questions, such as 'Citizenship and the Empire' or 'Astronomy and Religion', remained to sustain him. For Sturdee, the British Empire stood 'between Freedom and Bolshevism, its downfall is the aim of all Communists'.[13] His reiteration of the importance of naval history found its place in the post-war SNR and for him HMS *Victory* became almost a sacred symbol. Her preservation would emphasize the navy's importance as the interwar rivalry between the navy and the air force began. Indeed, under the combined leadership of Sturdee and Callender, the SNR's agenda for the interwar years was firmly set in line with what before the war had been termed 'navalist' policy. The Royal Navy was threatened by the restrictions of the Washington Treaty of 1921, and by the new claims of air power on defence expenditure. The SNR's interwar work to develop *The Mariner's Mirror*, to preserve and restore HMS *Victory*, and to create a major maritime museum was important to focus patriotic feelings on seapower as indispensable for the maintenance and defence of the British Empire.

Admiral Sturdee's first task was to oversee the report upon the state of *The Mariner's Mirror*. In March 1922, Cdr H. S. Lecky RN and G. E. Manwaring, the report's authors, produced an uncompromising assessment of the journal's potential. In their opinion it was essential to put *The Mariner's Mirror* on a sounder basis than hitherto to ensure the Society's independent existence. They found that the editor, R. C. Anderson, had never refused articles, and suggested that an Editorial Board be charged to aid him in his endeavours.[14] The Council appointed a Board in June consisting of Sir Julian Corbett, Cdr C. N. Robinson, H. H. Brindley and W. G. Perrin. One omission from the Board was Callender but, as his position in the SNR strengthened, Callender never allowed this exclusion to occur again. However, R. C. Anderson relinquished his office as Editor soon afterwards, and was succeeded by W. G. Perrin. Thereafter, the position, simply put, was either to persist in a monthly publication or change to a quarterly. It was decided to test opinion at the Annual Meeting, and to give members who could not attend the opportunity to participate in a postal ballot on retaining a 32-page monthly issue, or changing to a quarterly publication of 96 pages. Subsequently, at the Society's AGM of 1923, it was agreed to defer the results of the postal ballot until the arguments for and against were summarized. On this, the President invited W. G. Perrin to sum up. Perrin admitted that it was on his own recommendation that this matter had arisen for debate. He had no doubt that the majority of members would wish to retain a monthly publication – it was something to look forward to and served as a means to keep members constantly in touch with the Society. However, he thought that the balance of advantage lay in a quarterly. His reasoning was that if the Society was to keep its head above water it was essential to offer a product that members of the general public would buy. Moreover, the present membership was not enough to keep the journal alive and, but for the support of the Admiralty, the Society would long since have had to close it down. Perrin did not mince his words: experience had shown that in its present format the public did not support the journal; it was 'too much like a parish magazine'. Indeed, as a monthly publication no article which developed a subject in any serious length could be included – it had to be published over several monthly issues. A quarterly publication would solve this, and indeed attract contributors because of it. Perrin was supported in his views by Vice-Admiral Ballard. Significantly, two founder members, R. C. Anderson and Gregory Robinson, opposed the change. Nevertheless, the motion was put to the meeting to convert the *Mirror* from a monthly to a quarterly journal as from 1 January 1924, and this was carried by 25 votes to four. Admiral Sturdee then announced the results of the postal ballot of members. He had received 95 proxies of which 31 were cast to retain the monthly publication and 64 for the substitution of a quarterly. This, he thought, supplemented and endorsed the decision of the meeting. John Leyland then moved that W. G. Perrin should be invited to accept office as Honorary Editor of the Society's journal which was duly seconded. However, Perrin intimated that there were certain stipulations he felt compelled to make, which the meeting accepted on the proviso that they would need Council approval.[15] Under Perrin's editorship it was decided to transfer the printing of the new quarterly journal to the University of Cambridge Press.

The Society suffered a heavy blow with Perrin's sudden death in 1931. Much of his life had been devoted to subjects naval and maritime, and he was also the author of a definitive volume on British flags.[16] For nearly twenty years Perrin had served as Secretary of the NRS, and he edited *The Mariner's Mirror* for eight years. R. C. Anderson once again stepped into the breach until relieved in the summer of 1932 by the Admiralty Librarian, David Bonner Smith. Bonner Smith continued as editor until 1939, when once again R. C. Anderson took over.

Saving HMS Victory

Floated out at Chatham Dockyard on 7 May 1765 and commissioned in 1778, HMS *Victory* – the sixth ship to bear this name – remained on active service until 1812. By 1815, the Admiralty, displaying its customary lack of sentiment, had consigned her to the ship-breaker's yard. Primarily due to the efforts of a private individual, John Poole, the national conscience was stirred and, Nelson's flagship was saved and even modernized in 1820. Thereafter, the Admiralty was charged to maintain the iconic *Victory* in reasonable condition at Portsmouth. Visitors were allowed on board from time-to-time, and *Victory* served as a tender to HMS *Wellington*, and in other roles as a guard ship or stationary flagship at various times. During these years, while *Victory's* maintenance was begrudged, her condition deteriorated.[17] Indeed, as Alan

H.M.S. "VICTORY" in harbour October 1921, flying signal.

Stephen Cribb, Photo, Southsea

Figure 7 HMS *Victory* in the tideway, 21 October 1921. (Sturdee Papers, Churchill Archives Centre, Churchill College, Cambridge)

Aberg has noted, quoting Sir Geoffrey Seymour in 1886: '. . . a more rotten ship . . . never probably flew the pennant. I could literally run my walking stick through her sides in many places.'[18] This observation was prescient as *Victory* began to leak heavily in the following year and underwent emergency repairs. On 23 October 1903 she was rammed by HMS *Neptune*, which was being towed to the breakers. Badly holed, *Victory* had to be docked to avoid sinking.[19] Nevertheless, she was restored to her berth in the harbour after each of these incidents, and Sir Philip Watts, in a paper to the Institution of Naval Architects on the centenary of Trafalgar, reported that she was in a good state of repair.[20] However, her condition continued to give cause for concern. The SNR had noted *Victory*'s deterioration before 1914, but when war was declared Council did not feel it appropriate to raise the matter formally with the Admiralty.

By the end of the Great War, Nelson's flagship at Trafalgar was in a deplorable condition. In the spring of 1921 the President of the SNR, Prince Louis, called attention to her serious state of disrepair and, with the committed support of the Society, urged the Board of Admiralty to take appropriate steps to ensure her integrity and seaworthiness.[21] With Prince Louis's death in September 1921, the Society lost his powerful influence and contacts when making the case for *Victory*'s restoration. However the Admiralty offered considerable assistance by arranging for a survey to be carried out, and were happy to view the project as a form of partnership with the SNR. Crucially, the Admiralty agreed to meet the initial costs of dry-docking and the cost of a steel cradle to support the hull. Dockyard Officers at Portsmouth added their support and offered No. 2 Dock as a berth. Accordingly, *Victory* was moved from the tideway to No. 2 Basin on 16 December 1921 for the removal of ballast and in a three-day process was berthed in No. 2 Dock on 14 January 1922. Although supported by the steel cradle, she sat low in the dock with much of her hull hidden from view and the droop of her bow evident.[22] Indeed, when King George V visited Portsmouth Dockyard on 3 July 1922, it was reported that 'he did not like the low position of HMS *Victory* and he gently but expressively motioned with his hands and said, "Get her up." '[23]

In April 1922, with Admiralty acquiescence, the Council of the SNR decided to make a public appeal for financial support to save *Victory*. Given the state of its own finances, the SNR had little choice but to raise funds by public subscription. In the aftermath of the Washington Treaty, the Admiralty's major pre-occupation was in maintaining the operational fleet and ensuring its future size and tonnage. No funds were available for *Victory*'s restoration, as distinct from repairs, but a communiqué from the Admiralty dated 7 April 1922 set out the terms of its participation. The Board was not prepared to replace *Victory* in the water ever again, so a seaworthy restoration was out of the question, but when the Society had raised sufficient money, the Dockyard would restore *Victory* 'on lines recommended by the SNR' to as near as possible her Trafalgar state. In doing so it was incumbent upon the Society to remove many of the later anachronisms which had been inflicted on *Victory*. This not only included the unsightly museum on board, but also such matters as whether to replace the current wire rigging. Visitors would also be allowed on board as soon as possible to restore income to the former harbour boatmen who might wish to act as guides.[24] To this end the Society launched the Save the Victory Fund, (STVF) on Trafalgar Day 1922. The SNR's President, Admiral Sturdee (who suggested the term 'Save the Victory'), eagerly undertook the chairmanship of the Fund.[25] There was much enthusiasm for the ship's preservation among the senior ranks of the Society. Callender was shocked by the 'irreverence of the crowds' who came on board after the ship was dry-docked: he felt men should remove their hats on boarding while C. N. Robinson similarly saw *Victory* as a 'sea cathedral'. Callender's distaste for unseemly behaviour and the flippancy of the guides reflected the greater accessibility which dry-docking had introduced, and reinvigoration of popular interest which delighted the First Lord on his visit to Portsmouth.[26]

At the same time as the STVF was announced, a distinguished Victory Appeal Committee was set up to promote and run the appeal. This was also chaired by

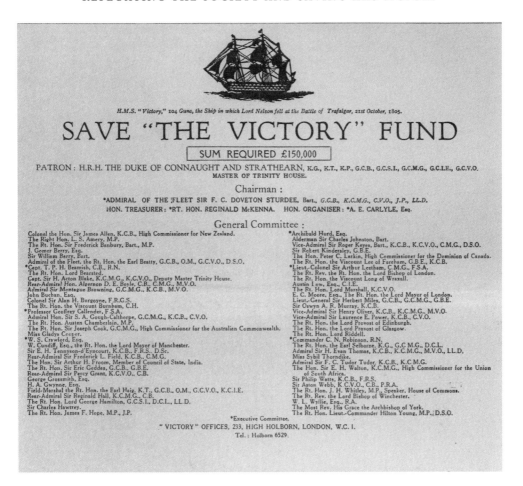

Figure 8 The Save the Victory Fund notepaper showing the widespread support for the appeal. (Sturdee Papers, Churchill Archives Centre, Churchill College, Cambridge)

Sturdee under the patronage of HRH The Duke of Connaught, and consisted of over 50 members. They included the Fund's Treasurer, Reginald McKenna, three Bishops; two Lord Mayors and two Lord Provosts, the Speaker of the House of Commons, the First Lord of the Admiralty and five of his predecessors, and all four High Commissioners for the Dominions.[27] Sturdee, and no doubt most of the committee, considered *Victory* 'an imperial asset', as shown by his lecture given at the Royal Colonial Institute in December 1922, entitled 'The *Victory* and what it means to the Empire'.[28]

By undertaking to raise funds for *Victory*'s restoration the SNR implicitly called into question why the Admiralty had allowed the ship to deteriorate so markedly in the first place. Once she had been surveyed, however, the cost of the project was put at just over £100,000: alarmingly, this was double the previous estimate.[29] Indeed, the initial report on her condition pointed to major damage to her hull, which was badly 'hogged'.[30]

As soon as the intention to restore *Victory* to her Trafalgar condition was announced, the Society received a range of suggestions. These included a proposal to replace all rotten timbers taken out by a 'modern' material – ferroconcrete – while another suggested raising the ship up on to a multi-tiered platform on the north shore of the Thames opposite Greenwich to create a '*Victory* Cenotaph'.[31] The views of SNR members also varied as to the best outcome. Mr Wheatley Cobb regarded any plan that did not return the *Victory* to a sound condition afloat as a failure, but Sir Alan Moore thought it impossible to re-rig the ship beyond keeping her lower masts and rigging in place, while H. H. Brindley felt it would be 'too expensive to reconstruct as at Trafalgar'.[32] For those who wished *Victory* restored to that state, there was no evidence that she could support her full rig while in dry-dock. Before restoration work could be contemplated, however, accurate information as to *Victory's* original Trafalgar state was essential, so L. G. Carr Laughton and others embarked upon research into her rigging and original plans. Additionally, much information on her condition at Trafalgar was given by the marine painter, W. L. Wyllie, and his son, Lieutenant-Colonel H. Wyllie OBE. Underpinning these researches, the SNR happily took up the role of technical advisers to the Admiralty on the ship's restoration. At the Admiralty's request, a Victory Technical Committee (VTC) was set up. This was chaired by seventy-six-year old Sir Philip Watts, a Vice-President of the Society since 1910, and a former Director of Naval Construction responsible for the technical aspects of the *Dreadnought* programme.[33] Initially, discussions centred on hull and rigging, but the VTC soon moved to secure missing ordnance.

The early response to the Appeal was slow, which to a large extent reflected the state of the economy. It coincided with widespread unemployment, a depression in trade, and general financial stringency and belt-tightening, coupled with the un-certainties engendered by two general elections between October 1922 and October 1924. Initially, as in the matter of taxes, it appears that the poor contributed disproportionately more than the better-off: on one occasion it was said that Sturdee raised £65 in pennies.[34] In July 1922, C. N. Robinson asked the advice of Mr Lints Smith, the Manager of *The Times*, on how best to raise the money the Appeal required. Smith advised Robinson to get a professional publicity agent and suggested that he should approach W. S. Crawford. The firm agreed to provide office accom-modation for the Victory Appeal Committee at 233 High Holborn, WC1, where A. E. Carlyle and A. T. Spens acted as Appeal Secretaries.[35]

It is hard to over-estimate Carlyle's importance to the success of the Appeal. He was on personal terms with L. S. Amery, the First Lord of the Admiralty, and

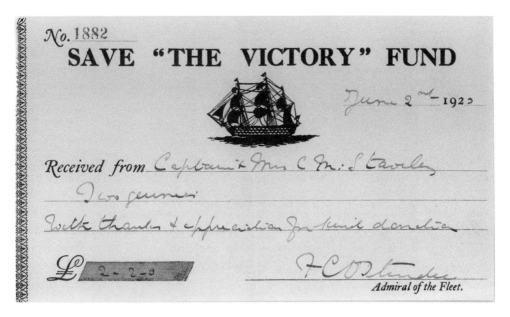

Figure 9 A Save the Victory Receipt. Capt. and Mrs C. M. Staveley were Admiral Sturdee's son-in-law and daughter. (Sturdee Papers, Churchill Archives Centre, Churchill College, Cambridge)

persuaded him to write to Sturdee to explain why the Navy Estimates could not cover restoration work: 'If paid for out of Navy Estimates, the cost would have to be deducted out of a provision that is barely sufficient to meet all the needs of the Navy today'. Amery continued:

> Would this be in accordance with the spirit of Nelson? There can only be one answer to such a question. And that there is enough patriotism and liberality amongst our British race to contribute individually the amount required for such a splendid object I cannot for the moment doubt.36

Sturdee's own letter to *The Times* concluded:

> I am gratified with the wide spread nature of the response to my appeal, but the total sum received to date is utterly inadequate to even commence the work. I would that a few of our well known patriotic and public benefactors would come forward and provide a sum sufficient to start the work without delay, and thus assure the success of the undertaking. By so doing they would earn the undying gratitude of the whole British Empire.

'This is the paragraph that did it,' wrote Carlyle triumphantly to Callender, '. . . & I am so glad I thought of getting Amery to write to Sir Doveton.'[36] The situation

Figure 10 Sir James Caird (1864–1954). Sir James Caird's generosity was fundamental to the Society's achievements in the interwar years. (Portrait supplied by kind permission of Mrs Sylvia Caldwell-Smith)

changed dramatically when Amery received a letter dated 27 February 1923, from James Caird, a partner in Turnbull Martin & Co., the managers of the Scottish Shire Line, who wished to be known only as 'A Well Wisher of the Navy'. Caird's letter offered £50,000 towards the *Victory*'s restoration.[38] This was the first of many benefactions to the SNR by the Scottish shipowner. Amery forwarded Caird's letter to Sturdee the following day. Although Sturdee had embarked upon a nationwide lecture tour to drum up funds, enlisting stars of the stage, and the display of 'Save the Victory' posters free of charge by many railway companies, the Appeal had raised only £3,000 at the beginning of 1923.[39] From March 1923 onwards, James Caird effectively underwrote the *Victory* project. Writing to Sturdee on 2 March, he requested the name of the bank for a further contribution and wrote again the next day stipulating that he should be known as 'A well wisher'. Caird invited Sturdee to lunch with him at the Caledonian Club in London on 9 March and the following day expressed concern that, 'when you open the old ship up', more work might be necessary. His letter continued 'You can ask any time' for an additional £25,000, but requested no publication of this offer. Caird repeated this in a further letter to Sturdee, dated 16 May 1923, which gave the SNR what amounted to a blank cheque:

> On my way to the City this morning I read with much interest your speech & Mr Amery's appealing for Funds and I trust your appeal will meet with the success it so well deserves.
>
> Work, I note, is to begin on the "Victory" the 1st of June and I hope will not cease until the good old ship is completely restored. As you Know I am with you to that End in event of you meeting with any difficulty.[40]

A special gift of £600 enabled a cinematic film entitled *The Romance of HMS Victory* to be produced, directed by the navy's former official film-maker, Frederick Engholm, with captions based on Professor Callender's book *The Story of HMS Victory*.[41] It was shown to the King and Queen at Balmoral on 19 September 1923 with Admiral Sturdee in attendance. Sturdee chaired a Save the Victory lunch at the Criterion Restaurant, Piccadilly, on 9 October 1923, which followed a trade showing of the film to the press at the Alhambra Cinema in Leicester Square. The film went on general release in Trafalgar Week 1923. Crucially for *Victory*'s future preservation, Sturdee, in reply to a letter from Callender in April 1924, agreed that the STVF might become a permanent endowment for the ship, provided that a surplus remained after repairs and restoration were completed.[42]

As early as June 1921, Sir Julian Corbett, mindful that an appeal should not go on too long, had urged that when the figure of £50,000 had been collected, restoration should begin immediately.[43] Thus Sturdee, on receipt of Caird's initial munificent donation, asked the Admiralty to proceed with *Victory*'s restoration. Following the dry-docking in January 1922, it was estimated that from one-third to one-half of *Victory*'s fabric needed replacement, with rot evident in her external planking and gun-ports. Due to numerous alterations, she bore only a superficial resemblance to her fighting appearance at Trafalgar. Even though *Victory* had been much altered by her 1798 refit prior to Trafalgar, she was largely transformed as a fighting ship by Sir Robert Seppings's modernization in 1820, sixty-one years after her keel was laid at Chatham. In consequence, her bow had been rebuilt to conform to more modern standards. Over the years, her original steering gear had been removed and she had been stripped of many fixtures and fittings. Restoration work began in 1923 on 1 June – 'a suitable naval day' – selected by Sturdee. He arranged a ceremony at 2.30 p.m. at

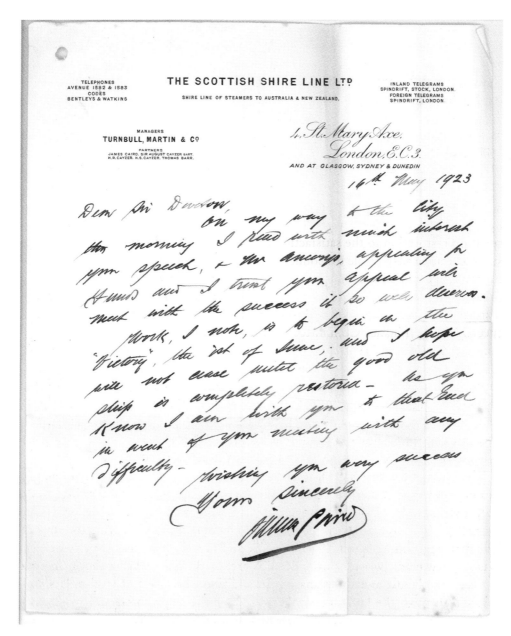

Figure 11 Letter from James Caird to Admiral Sturdee. (Sturdee Papers, Churchill Archives Centre, Churchill College, Cambridge)

which Earl Howe, as the descendant of an Admiral who had flown his flag in *Victory* at sea in wartime, lowered the figurehead to symbolize the start of the restoration.[44] It took ten years to complete but Sturdee, who died on 7 May 1925, did not live to see it.

By the end of 1923 the Appeal, augmented by Caird's donations and the accumulated interest thereon, stood at nearly £80,000 and the bulk of this sum had been deposited at interest in the Midland Bank.[45] Additionally, sales of a commemorative medal struck out of 6 cwt of copper sheathing removed from *Victory* had raised over £600, and an improved design struck by the Royal Mint was set to replace it.[46] Members of the public contributing to collection boxes placed at Portsmouth Dockyard also boosted the fund. For some time it had been the intention of the Society to close the Victory Appeal on Trafalgar Day 1924, its second anniversary, by which stage it had reached £81,000. At the end of 1924, over £20,000 had been spent on restoration to the satisfaction of the VTC. The adoption of the VTC as a sub-committee answerable to Council was formally announced by Admiral T. P. H. Beamish, when chairing the Society's 1925 AGM. The work on *Victory* had by necessity to continue apace, and for this reason the all-encompassing STVF, as distinct from the Victory Appeal, remained open. The SNR Council appointed a special Victory Finance Committee for the administration of the funds with Vice-Admiral Sir George Price Webley Hope, Admiral President of the Royal Naval College, Greenwich, as its chairman and with eight other members.[47] By 9 March 1926, receipts to the STVF, including interest on cash on deposit amounting to £5,350 17s 10d, totalled £98,885 18s 4d, and by 1927 the figure expended on restoration of *Victory* approached £90,000. Payments from the fund directly allocated to restoration work amounted to £48,808 8s 4d. With sundry other expenses the balance left in the STVF stood at £46,387 18s 4d.[48]

The initial work in restoring *Victory* and subsequent progress concentrated on dealing with the permanent support of the ship in dry-dock and alterations to the hull. Between March and April 1925, a three-stage lift paid for by the STVF was carried out by flooding No. 2 Dock and re-blocking the keel to bring the ship up. The first stage, on 12 March 1925, was witnessed by the members of the VTC. The existing steel cradle was then extended upwards to the hull and teak chocks inserted between the cradle and the planking. In addition, three sets of steel pillars were inserted through the hull to take the weight of the ship's masts and spars; these pillars were stepped on external steel plates located on the concrete plinth under *Victory's* keel.[49] As the restoration programme progressed, members of the Society were given the privilege, by courtesy of the Admiral Superintendent, of being allowed to proceed straight from the dockyard gate to *Victory* without restrictions or formalities.[50] By 1928 restoration of the rigging had moved on apace: a decision of 1925 to re-rig with wire had been rescinded and hemp specified instead.[51] The fore topmast was hoisted on 12 January and the main topmast on 2 February. A week later all three topmasts were in position. The fore yard was then crossed, followed by the main yard in April, and the fore-topsail yard in May. On 20 June the swaying up of the spanker gaff confirmed that the restoration was many weeks ahead of schedule.[52]

Accordingly, by July 1928, the project had been completed as far as the restoration of the rigging, topsides, and the permanent support of *Victory* in dock was concerned, and the project was given the royal seal of approval when King George V visited the ship on 17 July.[53] The Royal Standard was broken out at the main top-gallant masthead (203 feet high and then the loftiest structure in Portsmouth) and the King was piped aboard. After a tour of the ship he unveiled a commemorative tablet, designed by H. S. Rogers FRIBA, and executed in oak and synthetic ivory inlay, which read as follows:[54]

HMS VICTORY

LAID DOWN 1759 LAUNCHED 1765

WAS AFTER 157 YEARS OF SERVICE

PLACED 1922 IN HER PRESENT BERTH

THE OLDEST DOCK IN THE WORLD

AND RESTORED TO HER CONDITION

AS AT TRAFALGAR

UNDER THE SUPERINTENDENCE OF THE

SOCIETY FOR NAUTICAL RESEARCH

TO COMMEMORATE THE COMPLETION OF

THIS WORK THIS TABLET WAS UNVEILED

ON 17TH JULY 1928 BY

H.M. KING GEORGE V

Restoration work continued until January 1929 when a payment of £2,285 for work done in 1928 practically exhausted the STVF.[55] In consequence, lacking further financial resources to complete the restoration, the SNR approached the Admiralty and in April their Lordships formally agreed to carry out maintenance 'as part of the ordinary naval repair and maintenance programme'. What remained to be done by this stage in terms of restoration was of relatively minor importance. This led the SNR to discharge two of its committees, the Victory Finance Committee and the VTC. However, the Admiralty remained keen to retain a committee to assist them in supervising *Victory*'s maintenance. Accordingly, the VTC was replaced with the Victory Advisory Technical Committee (VATC) which, after the death of Sir Philip Watts, was chaired by Admiral Sir George Hope.[56]

Figure 12 HMS Victory under restoration. This picture shows the ship in No. 2 dock after being refloated and raised in 1925. (Society for Nautical Research)

The Society in the later 1920s

Following Admiral Sturdee's death, the Society took several months to find a new President. At the AGM on 14 May 1925, the Council was charged with finding a successor. They were 'practically unanimous' that the First Sea Lord, Admiral of the Fleet, David, The Earl Beatty (1871–1936) should be approached. Beatty pointed out that his duties as First Sea Lord would prevent him taking an active role in the Society's affairs, and suggested that the executive duties be passed to a newly created office of Chairman of Council.[57] On the Society's behalf, Beatty approached Vice-Admiral Sir George Hope. Beatty and Hope were both formally elected at a Extraordinary General Meeting on 8 July 1925. Vice-Admiral Hope's distinguished naval career had led him to become Deputy First Sea Lord in January 1918 during the Great War, and a naval representative at the signing of the Armistice. He had been appointed Admiral President of the Royal Naval College, Greenwich, until February 1926 and was supported enthusiastically by Professor Callender, initially even for the post of SNR President. With Hope as Chairman and Callender as Hon. Secretary and Treasurer, the SNR entered a remarkably stable period of leadership which lasted into the post-war era and was terminated only by Callender's death. From 1925 until 1946 Callender achieved a remarkable degree of control over the

Figure 13 HM King George V visiting HMS *Victory*, 1928. The King was introduced to leading members of the Society. At the far end (behind the King) are James Caird and Geoffrey Callender. Visible in front of the King are (l. to r.) Cdr C. N. Robinson, L. G. Carr Laughton, the tall figure of Sir Alan Moore and W. L. Wyllie. On the extreme right is Wing Cmdr H. Wyllie. (© Society for Nautical Research)

SNR's policies and activities, presaged by his Treasurer's statement in 1921, and by his vigilant membership of all its committees.

The publicity achieved by the restoration of HMS *Victory* reversed the SNR's decline in membership and the Society returned to solvency as a result. In 1924 the initial membership fee was abolished in the hope that by so doing more new members would accrue. The Society was now large, with a prominent public image; it had secured a role in the preservation of the nation's maritime history, and was the custodian of a fund for the preservation of *Victory's* fabric. At the AGM in 1926, Sir George Hope announced that, with the consent and approval of King George V, HRH The Duke of Kent had agreed to become the first Patron of the Society. In 1936, Hope succeeded Earl Beatty as President but also remained Chairman until 1951.[58]

At the AGM in 1928 the Society agreed to extend the privilege of Life Membership to individual members, allowing them to compound subscriptions in all

Figure 14 Sir George P. W. Hope (1869–1959). He is wearing the uniform of a rear-admiral but was promoted to vice-admiral in 1920 and admiral in 1925. He was Chairman of the Society, 1925–51 and President, 1936–51. (© National Maritime Museum, Greenwich, London)

future years by a single payment based on a fixed scale determined by age. Provision was also made for the appointment of not more than six Honorary Vice-Presidents of the Society, who, 'by distinguished service should have advanced the Society's interests and aims'. The meeting elected the first two Honorary Vice-Presidents: one was Sir James Caird, knighted in 1928 for his philanthropic generosity and enthusiasm for all things naval and maritime; the other was Henry S. Wellcome who, at his own expense, restored the Surgeon's Cabin and Dispensary of HMS *Victory*.[59]

Art, Monuments and Memorabilia

Once the principle of applying donations to specific causes had become established, the Society applied it rigorously. At the 1926 AGM it was decided to erect a memorial plaque to commemorate the work of the great seventeenth century Dutch marine artists the van de Veldes, father and son. An account opened in 1926 recorded the receipt of £29 1s 6d from members of the Society, and £8 1s 6d from non-members. By 1928, the van de Velde Memorial Fund had attracted only another £6, totalling £44 4s 0d. Since the estimated cost of the memorial was no more than £80 and the growth of the fund so slow, it seems surprising that the memorial was not subsumed under the Society's general account. An anonymous donation in 1927 allowed the design and sculptural work to proceed and the completed memorial was installed in the Baptistry of St James Church, Piccadilly, where both artists were buried. It was ceremonially unveiled on 1 May 1929 by His Excellency Jonkheer R. de Marees van Swinderen, Envoy Extraordinary and Minister Plenipotentiary from the Netherlands.[60]

Other specific accounts were begun in the 1920s, some of which were temporary or minor. The most important was the Macpherson Collection Endowment Fund, established in 1927 to purchase marine paintings and drawings. Its first-year income came to over £10,000 and from 1929 to 1946, it held over £11,500 in government securities as Appendix IV, Parts 1and 2A show.[61] Two temporary sets of accounts were the Victory Museum Fund and the Chelengk Fund (later known as the Nelson Relics Fund) which was to provide funds for the acquisition of the diamond plume of triumph given to Nelson in 1798 after the Battle of the Nile by the Sultan of Turkey. Both these accounts were transferred to the STVF in 1933, when the Victory Museum Fund had a balance of only £184 4s 8d, and the Nelson Relics Fund, after the purchase of Nelson's Chelengk, totalled £38 12s 0d. Two other small accounts in the 1930s were the Victory Panorama Annexe Fund and the Coastal Craft Fund. The former, begun in 1933, had reached nearly £4,900 by 1938, though some £2,000 seems to have been transferred to it from the STVF that year. The closure of Portsmouth Dockyard to the public during the war years cut off the Fund's principal source of income. The war similarly affected the Coastal Craft Fund as there was no activity after 1939 when its balance was down to £12 15s 6d.

The final account of this minor series was the *Implacable* Fund which did not appear formally as an SNR account until 1940.

Towards a Victory Museum

Once *Victory*'s restoration was assured, the SNR moved to ensure the preservation and safety of the Nelson memorabilia held on board. During the ship's restoration, discussions had taken place with the Admiralty on the future of the small onboard collection of Nelson relics and other naval memorabilia. Clearly these could not remain while work took place, and demolition of the 'ungainly edifice' which comprised the onboard museum was one the first priorities in the restoration.[62] Accordingly, in March 1924 the Admiralty and the SNR discussed the creation of a permanent home for the collection. The discussion was then widened to include the amalgamation of the Nelson souvenirs with the existing Dockyard Museum. The latter had been established in 1911, but the discussions centred on its development in a new building or buildings. Admiral Sturdee, who had initially suggested housing the Nelson relics formerly on *Victory* separately from the Dockyard Museum's contents, opposed the Admiralty's proposal that the cost of the new museum should be met by the STVF. He was also opposed to the Admiralty's suggestion that a new Victory Museum should form a wing or annexe to a much larger building which was to replace the existing Dockyard Museum. Sturdee attended a meeting of the VTC at the Admiralty and laid his objections before it. Although he soon found that the VTC did not share his objections, he nevertheless remained convinced that the new Victory Museum should be entirely separate from the Dockyard Museum.[63] The VTC, by contrast, preferred the Admiralty proposal of a combined museum, and saw no good purpose would be served by the erection of two separate museums in the same dockyard. This was not resolved before Sturdee's death, by which time the main obstacle to reconciling differences was financial. Sturdee initially had to find £6,500, and it seemed to him unsound to sink such a sum, privately raised, into a scheme, the general effect of which would be to improve state-owned Dockyard buildings.

The matter was resurrected at the Society's AGM of 1926 with Admiral Sir George Hope in the chair. Hope recalled that the idea of a Victory Museum was very dear to the late President's heart, and its erection, 'if such a thing be possible, was a pious duty of the Society for Nautical Research'. Hope then offered a pragmatic solution that there should be one, not two museums in Portsmouth Dockyard and that the SNR would only fund accommodation for its own exhibits. In doing so it would not contribute to improved accommodation for the Dockyard Museum. However, the Society noted with regret that owing to financial stringency the Admiralty was unable to move the project along. Moreover, in view of this, the Society would shelve its existing proposals, whilst expressing its conviction that 'the only businesslike procedure would be for the two building schemes to run concurrently'. Before a general discussion ensued, it was pointed out that the Admiral Superintendent had kindly consented to house the Society's exhibits temporarily in the Dockyard Museum; that Nelson's Funeral Barge[64] had been given special accommodation in one of the Dockyard buildings; and that the joint museum under contemplation was cruciform in ground plan, one transept being apportioned to the *Victory* exhibits. It was eventually agreed that:

The Victory Museum, if and when erected, should form a wing or annexe of a larger building which should accommodate also the exhibits in the Dockyard Museum; and that further action should be postponed until the final estimates for the restoration of HMS *Victory* showed whether there would be a surplus adequate for the erection of such a building as that which the Admiralty approved.[65]

In the interim, pending the resumption of the project, the SNR continued to accept and store objects for the new museum, and these acquisitions and donations were detailed in Annual Reports. They included what was then considered to be Nelson's death mask from Her Majesty Queen Mary, which she purchased in 1924.

By 1929 the Society had identified a site between the starboard side of *Victory* and the harbour with two existing buildings on it, as ideal for the new museum. Of these, the Old Rigging House was built around the same period as the ship; the other was more modern. It was also decided to construct an annexe alongside one of the buildings to house a panorama of Trafalgar painted by a founder member of the SNR, W. L. Wyllie RA. The foundation stone was laid by Wyllie himself on 24 May 1929, and the annexe was formally opened by King George V on 29 July 1930. The SNR had raised £726 to meet the building costs.[66] A small fee of 2d was charged for admission, and the proceeds of this levy in a few short years defrayed the entire cost of building. The panorama depicted the Battle of Trafalgar at 14.00 hrs, when *Victory* was interlocked with the French *Redoubtable* and the English *Temeraire*. A spectator, pushing open the door, found himself seemingly in the wardroom of the French ship *Neptune* and, looking through the stern windows, beheld the battle.

As to the proposed Victory Museum, the Old Rigging House, which had more aesthetic value than the other, had been constructed on unsuitable ground. The rickety and insecure state of its foundations, which required considerable reinforcement to sustain an edifice of greater weight, led to it being demolished. Thereafter, the difficulties of adapting the site and preserving the façade of brickwork ultimately meant that earlier estimates in the region of £7,000 to £8,000 for the building were unrealistic, and a figure of £11,500 was mooted. These problems, allied with the Society's dogged pursuit of the creation of a new NMM at Greenwich, meant that it was diverted from its aim of having a museum to hold Nelsonian and dockyard relics at Portsmouth until 1935. Nevertheless, the Society's and, specifically, the late Admiral Sturdee's reservations about the Victory Museum had been addressed. On the appointment of the VATC in 1929, the Admiralty agreed to place the arrangement and direction of the proposed museum under that Committee, which consisted entirely of SNR members. Their Lordships were also willing to entrust the VATC to remove from the existing Dockyard Museum any objects it deemed worthy of display in a Victory Museum and to dispense with the rest. Thus, there

Figure 15 The Victory Museum. The Museum was designed by H. S. Rogers FRIBA. (By courtesy of the National Museum of the Royal Navy)

would not be dual buildings or management. Moreover, *Victory* herself would be kept free of the encroachment of exhibits which spoiled her appearance in previous years. Accordingly, at the 1929 AGM the Society agreed to institute a public appeal to raise the then estimated cost of the new museum.

It had already been decided in 1929 that the proceeds from the sale of *Victory* souvenirs should, in the first instance, go to a naval orphanage. A maximum sum of £200 was set, beyond which any surplus should go to the STVF. It was further decided that the selection of articles for sale as souvenirs should rest with the Society. Subsequently, the gain to the STVF in the first year of operation of a souvenir stall in the temporary Victory Museum amounted to £400.[67]

In 1935, Professor Callender appointed his friend, the architect H. S. Rogers, to draw up plans that would retain the existing façade of the building. These were completed with some difficulty as the Panorama Annexe was constructed to Wyllie's requirements without reference to the size, position or proportions of the proposed museum. After a succession of delays postponed the placing of the contract, con-struction work on the museum began in the autumn of 1937, but not before the SNR had secured the co-operation of the Admiralty and Treasury to raise the balance of the £11,000 costs. Finally, in July 1938, the Victory Museum and Gallery opened to the public,[68] the accumulated proceeds from admission to the Trafalgar Panorama having helped to the tune of £1,800. Appropriately, the Victory Museum's first curator was the CO of HMS *Victory*, Lieutenant English. At its official opening on Monday 25 July 1938, the C-in-C, Admiral of the Fleet, the Earl of Cork and Orrery noted:

> The Museum deals primarily with Nelson: and this surely is most fitting. For it was from Portsmouth that Nelson sailed for Trafalgar and to Portsmouth that his flagship returned. It is not intended to make this museum representative of naval history in general nor of Portsmouth history in particular, but a museum to illustrate the chronicles of the period covered by the active career of HMS *Victory*, which flew the flag in turn of Keppel, Howe, Kempenfelt, St. Vincent, Hood and Nelson – an epoch of sixty years. The museum will thus form an annexe, as it were, to HMS *Victory*; and all visitors to the flagship, it is hoped, will proceed to the Museum and inspect, among much else of interest the remarkable panorama of Trafalgar which should help the least imaginative to visualise the most famous sea battle of all time.[69]

The opening of the Victory Museum brought a surprising announcement from Sir George Hope at the AGM. He had already proposed to Council that the VATC be discharged and its function passed to the Trustees of the NMM. This was based, in Alan McGowan's view, on 'the well meant but injudicious advice' of Sir Geoffrey Callender. The Trustees, most of whom were SNR members – would serve not only as Trustees of the Victory Museum in perpetuity but of Nelson's flagship also.[70] The Council accepted this proposal, despite the Admiralty's wishes expressed in 1929 that the SNR should retain the VATC in existence after the restoration work was completed. This major change in the SNR's responsibilities was not put to the membership: once the Admiralty had approved it on 16 June 1938, members were informed of the change at the AGM on 19 July. The STVF, however, still remained under control of the SNR.[71]

The restoration of *Victory* proved highly popular with members of the public. Indeed, since the visit of King George V in July 1928, some 1,867,241 people had visited Nelson's flagship.[72] Moreover, the restoration and subsequent preservation of HMS *Victory* came to serve as a model for all future projects of this type.

References

1   *Mariner's Mirror* 76:3 (1990), 203, obituary for Romola Anderson.

2   *Mariner's Mirror*: 5:1 (1919), editorial.

3   SNR/3/1 Council Minute Book, handwritten loose sheet, being a wartime financial summary.

4   NMM SNR 1/2 SNR Statement of Accounts for 1914–1918 prepared for 1919 AGM.

5   NMM SNR 1/2 Report of the Council to the AGM, November 1919.

6   *Ibid.*, respectively Vice-Presidents: Lord Brassey – the Lord Warden of the Cinque Ports; Lord Inverclyde – shipping magnate, Sir John Knox Laughton, Sir Clements Markham – formerly President of the Royal Geographical Society and Cdr Sir George Vyvyan; Councillors – Cdr E. Cunninghame Graham, Mr W. Boulthee Whall and Lieutenant E.E. Williams.

7   NMM SNR 6/1 Council Meeting in the Admiralty Library, 22 Oct. 1920. Geoffrey Arthur Romaine Callender (1875–1946) had joined the Royal Naval College, Osborne, in 1905, shortly after its foundation, and was promoted to be head of English and history in January 1913. He moved to be head of the history department at the Royal Naval College, Dartmouth, in 1921, but was appointed as the first Professor of History at the Royal Naval College, Greenwich when it became a staff college and war college for the Royal Navy.

8   NMM SNR 3/1 Minute Book No. 1.

9   NMM SNR 3/1 SNR Council Minute Book 1920, Treasurer's Statement; Minute Book No. 1, Report of the Council to the AGM, June 1921.

10 *Mariner's Mirror,* 8:3 (1922), 215.

11 Once the NMM had opened, with Geoffrey Callender installed as its first Director, the museum became the preferred location for the SNR's meetings.

12 Report of the Annual Meeting, 15 June 1921 published in *Mariner's Mirror* 7:3 (1921).

13 Sir Frederick Charles Doveton Sturdee's surviving papers are held at the Churchill Archives Centre, Churchill College, Cambridge. See SDEE 5/14. See also A. Temple Patterson ed., *The Jellicoe Papers*, vols I and II (NRS vols 108 and 111, 1966, 1968), especially vol. II, 126–7 for Beatty's comment to Jellicoe that Sturdee was 'very bitter' over the uncertainty of his retaining command of the 4th Battle Squadron.

14 NMM SNR Minute Book No.1, Report from Lecky and Manwaring on the Future Conduct of the Society's Journal to President and Council of SNR, 7 March 1922.

15 *Mariner's Mirror* 9:3 (1923), 209–11, Report of AGM. No record of Perrin's 'stipulations' survives.

16 W. G. Perrin, *British Flags* (Cambridge, 1922).

17 Admiral Sir Richard Saunders Dundas to Sir Charles Wood, First Lord of the Admiralty, 3 September 1857: 'I am sorry that you are not disposed to find the *Victory* defective, & if she is once repaired you will not get rid of her of another term of years, & I look upon her & the *Impregnable* as occupying the places of effective Guard ships and costing money without any countervailing advantages'. Papers of Sir Charles Wood, Halifax MSS (A4/128, f6.): Borthwick Institute, York University. The authors are grateful to Professor Andrew Lambert for this reference.

18 A. Aberg, 'Saving the *Victory*', *Mariner's Mirror*, 91:2 (2005), 358. See also, J. McKay, *The 100-Gun Ship* Victory (London, 1987), which provides a chronology of repairs, re-building and refits after her decommissioning.

19 See NMM SNR 6/1 for an account of HMS *Neptune*'s disastrous last voyage.

20 See A. Bugler, HMS Victory *Building, restoration and repair* (London, 1966), 36. Also, Aberg, 'Saving the *Victory*', 362.

21 For the life of HSH Prince Louis of Battenberg, later, First Marquis of Milford Haven, see Admiral Mark Kerr, *Prince Louis of Battenberg* (London, 1934). See also P. Ziegler, *Mountbatten* (London, 1979).

22 Bugler, *HMS* Victory, 37–9. Divers were used to measure the distortion of *Victory's* keel, so that blocks could be prepared, but the height of the tide made the docking difficult. The droop of the bow was attributed to the pull generated by many years swinging at anchor.

23 *Ibid.*, 40.

24 AGM of the SNR, 1922, *Mariner's Mirror* 8:3 (1922), 211–12.

25 Churchill Archives Centre, Cambridge, SDEE 1/19/2.

26 NMM SNR 7/2 Callender to Sturdee, 10 September 1922; NMM SNR 7/3 L. S. Amery to Sturdee, 18 February 1923.

27 NMM SNR 3/1 Minute Book No. 1, Report of the Council for 1922.

28 Aberg, 'Saving the *Victory*', 361; Churchill Archives Centre, Cambridge, SDEE 1/19/1, Report in *The Times*, 8 December 1922; handwritten lecture.

29 Aberg, 'Saving the *Victory*', 361.

30 Sir Philip Watts' interim report, dated 12 February 1923, showed that from foremast to stem the bow drooped about 18 inches and from the mizen aft to the rudder post there was a further droop of about 8 inches. *Victory's* deck lines were affected. NMM SNR 7/3.

31 See NMM SNR 7/1 and 7/4.

32 For these comments see NMM SNR 7/4.

33 The Committee was variously called the Technical Restoration Committee, the Advisory Technical Committee as well as the Victory Technical Committee. The members were Sir William Smith CB, R. C. Anderson, L. G. Carr Laughton, W. L. Wyllie, RA, Lt Colonel Harold Wyllie, and Professor Geoffrey Callender.

34 Littlewood and Butler, *Of Ships and Stars*, 40.

35 Given the slow rate of accumulation of moneys, it was found necessary to establish a guarantee fund to provide liquidity to continue the appeal. The guarantee fund was on deposit at the London Joint City and Midland Bank, over which the fund's Treasurer, Reginald McKenna, presided, and was entirely underwritten by Society members. See NMM SNR 7/2, Callender to Sturdee for the balance on 22 September 1922, which was £850. 15s., also NMM SNR 3/1 Minute Book No.1, Report of the Council for the year 1923.

36 NMM SNR 7/3 L. S. Amery to F. C. Doveton Sturdee, 12 February 1923.

37 NMM SNR 7/3. Carlyle to Callender, 1 March 1923.

38 Churchill Archives Centre, Cambridge, SDEE 1/19/2.

39 Littlewood and Butler, *Of Ships and Stars*, 40.

40 *Ibid.* Sturdee's personal charm was put to good effect: by 18 March Caird's letter listed weights of fish he had caught.

41 AGM of the SNR, 1924, *Mariner's Mirror* 10:3 (1924), 318.

42 Aberg, 'Saving the *Victory*', 362.

43 *Mariner's Mirror* 8:3 (1922), Report of the Annual Meeting, 14 June 1922.

44 NA ADM 1/8655/20.

45 NMM SNR 3/1 SNR Minute Book No.1, Report of the Council for the year 1923.

46 *Ibid.*

47 NMM SNR 2/28 Annual Report 1938: The SNR. A Brief Chronicle of the first 27 Years. A Committee to review the Rules of the Society as instituted in 1912 had been appointed in 1925 on the death of Sir Doveton Sturdee. The Committee's recommendations were accepted by members at an Extraordinary General Meeting on 17 March 1926; the principal change was the creation of a new executive post, for which any member of the Council

would be eligible. The first occupant of the post of Chairman of the Council, in the first instance, appointed by Council in July 1925, was Vice-Admiral Sir George Hope who was by virtue of his office an *ex officio* member of all SNR committees, and thus could bring together the different strands of opinion within the Society, and give it direction.

48 *Mariner's Mirror* 12:3 (1926), 330. See AGM of the SNR, 1926. These figures differ from those in the Treasurer's Annual Accounts shown in Appendix IV due to a variation in the audit date.

49 Bugler, *HMS* Victory, 41–4.

50 AGM of the SNR 1926, *Mariner's Mirror* 12:3 (1926), 324–34. Members could apply to the Hon. Secretary for a ticket valid for six months.

51 See NMM SNR 7/1 Minutes of the Victory Technical Committee, 18 November 1926.

52 NMM SNR 2/18 Report of the Council for the Year 1928.

53 When *Victory* was first berthed in No. 2 Dock, with her keel resting on ordinary docking blocks, she was supported in a longitudinal sense by a cradle made of strong steel frames. The decision to correct the trim of the ship and raise her level rendered the original cradle useless, and presented anew the problem of longitudinal support. The problem was solved by the reconstruction of the cradle; the original steel frames were utilized, and were reshaped to conform to the shape of the ship's body on the one side, and to the declivity of the dock-wall on the other. As to permanent support, a concrete wall was built on the floor of dock, five feet wide at the base, and three feet six inches wide at the top, upon which *Victory* was supported, her keel reposing upon capping blocks of oak. The wall varied in height from 9 feet forward to 5 feet aft.

54 NMM SNR 2/18 Report of the Council for the Year 1928. These materials proved to be unsuitable and a new Tablet was provided in 1946 made of bronze and enamel set in an oak frame. See NMM Trustees' Minutes, 8 April 1946.

55 *Mariner's Mirror* 15:3 (1929), AGM of the SNR, 1929, 289.

56 *Ibid.*, 289–290.

57 See *Mariner's Mirror* 11:2 and 11:3 (1925), AGM of the SNR, 1925, 230–2; EGM, 8 July 1925, 335–6. Beatty retired as First Sea Lord in 1927. For his life, see, W. S. Chalmers, *Rear Admiral RN: The Life of Beatty* (London, 1951).

58 *Mariner's Mirror* 22:3 (1936), AGM of the SNR, 1936.

59 James Caird was granted a baronetcy in the New Year's Honours list in 1928. For Henry Wellcome, who was later knighted in 1932, see R. Church and E. M. Tansey, *Burroughs Wellcome & Co.: Knowledge, Trust, Profit, and the Transformation of the British Pharmaceutical Industry, 1880–1940* (Lancaster, 2007).

60 *Mariner's Mirror* 15:3 (1929), 302–12.

61 See Chapter 3, 55–7, for the origins of the Macpherson Collection of marine paintings and drawings and its purchase by the Society.

62 Statement of Admiral Sir George Hope to the AGM of the SNR, 1926; '. . . pre-restoration, the Victory Museum was one of the outstanding features of the ship. The building extended over most part of the Main or Upper Gun Deck and its roof presented a most unprepossessing appearance and filled the entire space between the Quarter Deck and Forecastle'.

63 NMM SNR 7/1. A meeting of the Victory Sub-Committee on 9 July 1924 resolved: 'That the Museum to be constructed be called the <u>Victory Museum</u> and be large enough to house the Exhibits at present in the Dockyard Museum and in a separate wing at its end, the Victory relics, and that Sir Philip [Watts] should convey the terms of this Resolution to Sir Doveton Sturdee'.

64 It had been the State Barge of King Charles II. On 8 January 1806, it was employed in the

funeral procession to convey the body of Lord Nelson from Greenwich to Whitehall Stairs, en route to St Paul's Cathedral.

65 *Mariner's Mirror* 12:3 (1926), AGM of SNR, 1926.
66 Aberg, 'Saving the *Victory*', 362–3.
67 NMM SNR 2/28 Annual Report 1938. The SNR. A Brief Chronicle of the first 27 Years.
68 *Ibid.*, 364.
69 NMM SNR 1/6 Report of the Council for the year 1938.
70 A. McGowan, HMS Victory: *Her Construction, Career and Restoration* (London, 1999), 122.
71 AGM of the SNR, 1938; *Mariner's Mirror* 24:4 (1938), 375.
72 NMM SNR 1/6 Report of the Council for the year 1938.

3
A Run Ashore:
Creating a National Maritime Museum

The Society's interest in museums began formally in 1913 when it was asked to assist in the reorganization and rationalization of the collections of the Royal Naval Museum at the Royal Naval College, Greenwich. A catalogue of the museum's contents was duly completed in 1914, although doubts were expressed that the museum would remain in Greenwich if war broke out. During the Great War, owing to the fear of air raids, the museum's contents were dispersed. The larger paintings were removed to Bodmin in Cornwall. Other items were stored in the basements and cellars of the Royal Naval College and elsewhere. The war put into abeyance any further developments, and while periodic discussions on the creation of a national naval museum were undertaken in SNR circles immediately after the war, little or no progress ensued.[1]

When Geoffrey Callender moved to the Royal Naval College, Greenwich, in 1921, he set himself the task of harnessing the SNR's resources towards the creation of a national and unified collection of maritime artefacts. Initially, he became involved in the separate but ultimately related project of reviving the Royal Naval Museum at Greenwich.[2] He found it in chaos – a large number of ship models had gone to the newly created Imperial War Museum, some 300 or more objects had been dispersed to the Science Museum, and the remaining College collections were confused with those of the Royal Navy's oldest charity, Greenwich Hospital.[3] Nonetheless, by 1924, the fundamental reform instituted by Callender was the setting up of a Royal Naval Museum Committee including R. C. Anderson, which became accountable for keeping the displays contemporary, judging new acquisitions, and was responsible for all questions relating to the administration of the museum.[4] In 1925 Callender informed the SNR Council that during the past year the Admiralty had commissioned the Society, through the aegis of its Publications Committee, to prepare a new Catalogue of the Royal Naval Museum 'on scientific lines'. Accordingly, all exhibits had been re-numbered, an inventory made, and an investigation into their provenance and history was proceeding rapidly.[5]

At this point events began to turn in Callender's favour. Having reorganized the Royal Naval Museum, he then learnt that the Royal Hospital School was planning to leave its premises south of Romney Road which centred on the Queen's House. A sizable estate had been bequeathed to the Admiralty at Holbrook, near Ipswich – and Arthur Smallwood, the Director of the School, was keen to re-locate it there; however financial questions relating to the move remained unanswered. Callender became aware that if such a move occurred, the Queen's House might be taken over by the Office of Works for restoration with a view to opening it as a historic building. He also learnt that the contents of the Royal Naval Museum were to be transferred to the old School buildings (possibly to make more space available in the College) and in consequence formed the idea that the Queen's House would be a suitable home for a maritime museum. Callender described these developments at Greenwich to the SNR Council in 1925.[6] He gave the Council the historical background and noted that if it was necessary 'to begin at the very beginning; to find a suitable site, to erect a suitable building and so on, then the task might be abandoned as impracticable due to its magnitude'. Nonetheless, the Admiralty collection of ship models could form the nucleus around which 'any collection of really national proportions should be gathered together'. Indeed:

> No scheme should be more instant in its appeal to members of the Society for Nautical Research than the establishment of a National Maritime Museum such as those which already exist in countries less renowned than Britain in connection with the sea.

This is the first recorded use in the SNR Records of the title 'National Maritime Museum'.[7] At a Council meeting in February 1925, Callender stated that the impending changes to the Greenwich site 'offered a golden opportunity for establishing a Naval and Nautical Museum of a National character, which has from the outset been one of the chief aims of the Society for Nautical Research'.[8] In this assumption, Callender was imposing his own agenda on the Society: it had patently not been one of chief aims of the SNR, or it would have formed one of its original objects. However, the idea of creating a national maritime (or nautical and naval) museum might well have been implicit within the SNR's range of activities in its formative years. While Callender was certainly manipulative in pressing the SNR to accept a national museum as one of its aims, the title was a delicate issue, for the Admiralty was concerned to prevent its historical collections being dissipated or placed in any institution not under their Lordships' control.

Callender's view that the Queen's House might be a suitable venue for a national museum was not as limiting as it seems but in view of the lukewarm response of the Office of Works to the idea, Admiralty support for the SNR's idea was crucial. What was particularly important was that the Admiralty should be willing to allocate at least some of the other buildings of the Royal Hospital School for a new museum. Nevertheless, as late as May 1927, 'the project to establish a new museum at Greenwich was still in jeopardy'.[9] However, by that stage the greater force in Whitehall – the Admiralty – was with the Society and by June 1927 the Treasury had also accepted the proposal. In his Chairman's Report to Council for 1927, Admiral Sir George Hope repeated Callender's assertion that 'the establishment of a Naval and Nautical Museum on a national scale has been constantly advocated by all those interested in Nautical Research and it may be said to have been one of the prime causes for the Society's foundation'; moreover, 'in the past year a great move forward has been made'. Chairing the Society's AGM in June, Admiral Hope read an official pronouncement resonant with historical detail that proclaimed it to be the product of Callender's pen. Noting that the Royal Hospital School was to vacate its premises at Greenwich, he announced that in the interim the appropriate depart-ments of state concerned had agreed that 'at the earliest possible moment the Queen's House should be converted into the National Naval and Nautical Museum which had been awaited for so long'.[10]

At this stage, Hope was unable to be specific about administrative questions. However, on 22 November 1927, the Admiralty made an official announcement:

> It having become necessary for a body of trustees to be appointed to take charge of the interests and property of the National Naval and Nautical Museum which is eventually to be accommodated in the Queen's House at Greenwich, The First Lord of the Admiralty has obtained consent of the following, Earl Stanhope, DSO, MC, Civil Lord of the Admiralty, Admiral Sir George P. W. Hope, Chairman of the Council of the Society for Nautical Research, Sir Lionel Earle KCB, KCVO, Secretary of the Office of Works, Mr Roger C. Anderson, FSA, Member of the Council of the Society for Nautical Research, Professor Geoffrey Callender, FSA, Royal Naval College Greenwich.[11]

Thus three of the five Trustees – Hope, Callender and Anderson – were the most influential members of the Society. At their first meeting, held concurrently with the Admiralty's announcement, the Trustees appointed the Admiralty Librarian and Hon. Editor of *The Mariner's Mirror*, W. G. Perrin, as Secretary. However, it was the Chairman of the Trust, James Richard Stanhope, 7th Earl Stanhope, and 13th Earl Chesterfield, KG, PC, DSO, MC (1880–1967) who became the driving force in bringing the museum into existence. At the time the Trust was established, Stanhope held office in Stanley Baldwin's Conservative government and had previous minor government experience in 1918 as Parliamentary Secretary to the War Office. Although formerly an army officer between 1901 and 1908, and again from 1914 to

Figure 16 James Richard Stanhope, 7th Earl Stanhope (1880–1967), photographed by H. Walter Barnett. This portrait shows Lord Stanhope as an interwar politician. (© National Portrait Gallery, London)

1918, Stanhope was an enthusiastic supporter of the proposal to establish a national maritime museum and from 1930 onwards his experience as a Trustee of the National Portrait Gallery guided the National Maritime Museum Trust towards museum policies that were acceptable in Whitehall. Like many of his contemporaries, Stanhope was averse to the ongoing loss of British art and other historical collections to the USA and eager to consolidate nautical pictures and memorabilia in the proposed museum at Greenwich, even at the risk of offending either the Science Museum or the Imperial War Museum. In the autumn of 1931, he was briefly Parliamentary and Financial Secretary to the Admiralty but was moved to be Under-Secretary of State for War between 1931 and 1934 and to become First Commissioner of Works (with a seat in the Cabinet) during 1936–7. Thus what became the National Maritime Museum Trust was chaired by a political insider able to identify correctly the lack of progress by the early 1930s as paralysis in the Treasury. Stanhope also had experience of holding office in the Board of Admiralty and later the Office of Works, the two departments with responsibility for converting the School buildings into a museum.

The establishment of the National Maritime Museum Trust meant there was a recognized body in which the property of the new museum could legally be vested. Up to this point those who advocated a national maritime museum had been placed in a dilemma – not until a physical home of sufficient stature could be found for potential exhibits were donations of national importance likely to be forthcoming. This was particularly the case with private, rather than state-owned property. Indeed, the naval aspect of the new museum was soon established as the Lords Commissioners of the Admiralty promised to give practically the entire contents of the Royal Naval Museum, Greenwich, to the new museum, and to transfer to it on 'permanent loan, the paintings of the pre-existing 'National Gallery of Naval Art' (a Naval Gallery in the Painted Hall).[12] These included the oldest surviving Chatham Chest, (the early seventeenth-century coffer of the eponymous charity that dated back to the Armada), Drake's so-called astrolabe, a compass and dipping needle of Captain James Cook, the entire West Collection of Nelson relics, and an array of Admiralty scale models of the Royal Navy's men-of-war from 1670 to 1870. In addition, the Admiralty were also prepared to donate other Nelson relics, and the sheer draughts, plans and profiles of the ships built for the Royal Navy from the middle of the seventeenth century, and a substantial collection of half-models illustrating the progress of naval construction from the days of the *Devastation* to those of the *Dreadnought*.[13] By the end of the 1920s, Greenwich was the accepted locus of a national maritime museum and Sir George Hope, no doubt prompted by Callender, saw its future as 'a People's Palace of British Sea-Power'.[14]

The Macpherson Collection

In the interwar years many notable private collections were in danger of being sold abroad. Among them was one numbering many thousands of maritime prints and dozens of paintings, and other items assembled by the noted collector and yachtsman, A. G. H. Macpherson (1873–1942).[15] Plainly, a collection of such national importance was unlikely to be formed again, and Admiral Hope urged that it was of such value that a national effort was needed to retain it in the country.[16] The sentiment accorded with a general public feeling that too many cultural assets were being lost – mainly to the USA – which led to the subject being debated by the Royal Commission on National Museums and Galleries between 1927 and 1930. Shortly after Hope's announcement in June 1927, Macpherson intimated his willingness to co-operate with the Society's desire for his collection of over 11,000 items to be retained for the nation. In the interim, a Society member, Captain Harry Parker, an authority and dealer in naval prints, valued the collection.[17] Macpherson not only accepted Parker's valuation, which amounted to £120,000, but generously agreed to accept three-quarters of this amount to give the British people an opportunity to purchase his collection. On 8 August 1927 the SNR launched a public appeal to raise the money over the signatures of Prince George, the Duke of Kent, its Patron, and others who included the novelist Thomas Hardy. With the appeal up and running, the publicity brought to the Society's attention:

> an experienced man of business [who] was able to arrange with Mr Macpherson that on immediate payment of £25,000 for the purchase of part of the Collection, the whole Collection, with the additions Mr Macpherson was still making, should remain under option to us for six months.[18]

The anonymous 'man of business' was none other than James Caird who again came to the Society's rescue. He paid Macpherson the initial sum of £25,000 and the agreement was signed. This was just as well, as the option expired on 30 April 1928, by which stage the Society, with the administrative aid of two practising solicitors as the appeal's Honorary Secretaries, had raised only £30,000, including Caird's deposit. Although there were myriad donations from home and abroad, most had been small. Originally it had been decided that to ensure the appeal's success, leaders of shipping and allied interests should be approached, but before doing so, the opinions of several prominent businessmen were sought. The results were disappointing; shipping was experiencing a depression and, in consequence the idea for a business appeal was dropped. On the expiry of the original option the Society faced a series of questions, given added focus by the fact that Macpherson had substantially added to his collection, including an important set of marine paintings of the Dutch and English schools. By the terms of the option agreement, the value of the collection had risen to £108,000 and it seemed impossible to separate these later additions – which included paintings by Brueghel, Storck, van de Velde, Backhuysen and Monamy – from those which had originally been included. Clearly, with less than £5,000 raised (excluding Caird's donation), the Society was in danger of being publicly embarrassed. Caird again intervened anonymously, promising to donate £10 for every additional £100 raised. This offer received widespread press attention and increased the level of small subscriptions without relieving the Society's embarrassment. With the total unlikely to be realized in time, Caird decided to complete the purchase himself, including the later additions. Not only would the Trustees of the appeal then have the entire collection in hand, but also a sum equal to all the subscriptions from other sources. Caird also promised to pay the administrative expenses and upkeep of the collection until it was transferred for display in the Queen's House. In addition, Caird also donated a further £6,000 to the Trustees of the National Naval and Nautical Museum as the nucleus of an endowment which would enable the Trustees to make the collection more accessible for use by students and the public at large. Another anonymous gentleman had also donated £1,000 for the same object, and given the desirability of expanding this nucleus of money it did not seem appropriate to close the Macpherson Collection Appeal at that stage. Indeed, it was envisaged that those who were ready to add to it by gifts of paintings, prints and models, or to give money for the endowment fund, would facilitate the appointment of a curator to oversee the collection and from time to time add to it.[19] Thus, almost entirely due to James Caird's generosity, the Society escaped being crushed by the financial burdens generated by Callender's ambitious plans for the preservation of Britain's maritime heritage. With the preservation of HMS *Victory* and the Macpherson Collection assured for the nation however, establishing the National Naval and Maritime Museum still remained to be achieved.

The Trust at Work, 1928–1933

Once the National Maritime Museum Trust was established, a possible venue identified and a substantial amount of potential exhibits already pledged, the momentum for the creation of the national maritime museum had gathered sufficient pace to ensure a reasonably quick resolution. This proved not to be the case, as ten years elapsed before it opened to the public. The delay was partly explicable in that a new school had to be built at Holbrook in Suffolk before the Royal Hospital School could vacate its existing premises; moreover, its buildings at Greenwich required substantial refurbishment and conversion. Although the Duke of York, later King George VI, had laid the foundation stone at Holbrook in 1928, the school took five and a half years to complete, and it was not until the summer term of 1933 that the Royal Hospital School was able to leave Greenwich. As Hope later noted in relation to the Greenwich site, in 1933 'there seemed no immediate prospect that the site would be conveyed to us, or the buildings converted to the use we had in mind'.[20]

Between 1928 and 1934, the progress made by the Trust depended upon three men: Lord Stanhope as chairman, Professor Callender as his adviser, and Sir James Caird as provider of the necessary funds, in addition to his own forays, also with

Callender's guidance, into the marine art market on behalf of the future museum. Originally, Caird had no part in the Trust's deliberations but in 1928, largely on the urging of Lord Stanhope, he was invited to participate in its meetings. He could not be a Trustee – only original members could be replaced according to the Deed of Trust. The solution to this was the creation of the Macpherson Collection Trust – to which the original NMM Trustees appointed themselves and James Caird as well and thereafter convened joint meetings of both bodies.[21]

For the first two years (1928–9) little progress was made. Even though Stanhope was the Civil Lord of the Admiralty in Baldwin's government, he found his own party, the Conservatives, 'distinctly sticky'. Surprisingly, when he was out of office from 1929 to 1931, Stanhope thought it easier to work with James Ramsay MacDonald's Labour government since 'the Labour people were keen on novel forms of education and in museums generally'.[22] Nevertheless, the Trust's main problem was to convert the First Lord of the Admiralty, A. V. Alexander, to their point of view. By October 1930, the lack of progress made the Trustees feel it would be desirable that a further commitment to the museum should be forthcoming from government, but the developing economic crisis prevented any announcement being made. However, at the Tenth Meeting of the Trustees in 1931, official approval of the Board of Admiralty was reported for the substitution of the name 'National Maritime Museum' in place of the 'National Naval and Nautical Museum' and for the addition of Sir James Caird to the museum Trustees as distinct from his membership of the Macpherson Collection Trust.[23] When the National Government was expanded in November 1931 by the coalition between MacDonald's National Labour and the Conservatives, Stanhope returned to office as Under-Secretary of State for War, a post he held until 1934. The post of First Lord of the Admiralty went briefly to Sir Austen Chamberlain, who retired after the Invergordon Mutiny.

The new First Lord of the Admiralty, Sir Bolton Eyres-Monsell made a visit to Greenwich on 18 November 1932, when Callender showed him the Queen's House 'and a good many of our acquisitions'. Although the First Lord was interested in the Queen's House and its history, he commented: 'It is all very well speaking of making this into a museum; but I object very strongly to the idea of this splendid place being taken out of naval control'.[24] Callender's worries about the outcome of the meeting were heightened by the sudden intervention of the Admiral President of the Royal Naval College, Sir Barry Domvile. Replying the following day, Stanhope advised Callender that they should do nothing until matters calmed down as he suspected that 'Domvile, or rather more likely, Mrs Domvile is at the back of all this business, as he wishes the whole of the N.M.M. to come under his personal control, so that he may be president of the College and of the Queen's House and Museum'.

Stanhope went on to propose that Hope, Caird and Callender should meet him at

Figure 17 The Queen's House, Greenwich, was the original focus for the National Maritime Museum. Its limited size meant that the adjacent Royal Hospital School buildings were essential to accommodate the Museum. (© National Maritime Museum, Greenwich, London)

his London home in Eaton Square in order to impress upon Caird that he must not let himself be persuaded by anyone that the museum should be under Admiralty control, nor was the Trust able, by the nature of its Deed, to hand over its treasures to any other body.[25] Callender, however, thought that such a meeting would be too unsettling for Caird. The difficulty for the Trustees was that they held a considerable amount of art and historical artefacts, which was being regularly augmented by Caird's purchases. From 1928 to 1934, Caird, advised by Callender, spent over £300,000 on art and artefacts for the new museum.[26] This material would form the nucleus of the NMM collections but was kept in the Painted Hall and the Royal Naval Museum at Greenwich which the Trustees did not own.[27] During the winter of 1932–3, Stanhope was involved in a game of bluff with the Admiralty, the Treasury and the Office of Works, and from January 1933 onwards began to hold meetings of the Trustees in his room at the War Office rather than in the Admiralty Library.[28] By the spring of 1933 Stanhope wrote to Callender: 'I don't care a d—n for the Admiralty once we have been taken over by the Govt. & established under the

Office of Works vote, but I don't want to have a row till then'. While meetings with senior Whitehall officials such as Sir Vincent Baddeley of the Admiralty stressed Callender, Stanhope reassured him that no one 'should have to put up with the criticisms & silly superiorities of the Baddeleys – least of all the Director & I intend to try to persuade you to be the first'.[29] To some extent the Trustees' meetings were formal occasions upon which the 'inner circle' of Stanhope, Callender and Caird informed the other Trustees what they had been buying in the London art market.[30] Sir Lionel Earle, one of the original Trustees, retired in 1933, his place being taken by his successor at the Office of Works, Sir Patrick Duff. The lengthy construction period at Holbrook, to which the Royal Hospital School would move, enforced further delays until Easter 1933.[31]

By this stage, Caird had formed a close friendship with Geoffrey Callender; several times a month they would lunch together at the Reform Club, and thereafter Callender would accompany Caird as the latter looked to add to his already substantial private collection of art and antiques to be donated to the NMM. In the interim, all came under Callender's care at the Royal Naval College. Contemporaneously, the SNR launched a number of public campaigns to save various collections and items of historical importance for the new museum. There were, of course, tensions with existing museums and libraries regarding the collecting policies of the Trust but Callender poured sufficient oil on troubled waters to overcome most objections. Arrangements were made with the National Portrait Gallery (aided by Lord Stanhope's presence on its Board) and the British Museum and these generally held up well. From time to time spats occurred with the Science Museum, the Imperial War Museum and, intermittently, with the Admiralty regarding overlapping collecting policies but no major disputes arose.

In the interim, the Society promoted an exhibition of prints at the Guildhall in London, in October 1928, chosen by Caird and Macpherson from the Macpherson Collection. The exhibition was moved to the Whitehall Gallery in the following year, and went on tour to Plymouth, Birkenhead and lastly Hull in March 1930. Unfortunately it was not very well attended anywhere and the Trust lost money, which in part was due to damage to exhibits in transit. Thereafter no other loan exhibitions were contemplated other than those already booked.[32] In July 1930 an exhibition of the ship models in Caird's collection opened in the Painted Hall at Greenwich. It now comprised the whole of the famous TS *Mercury* collection of ship models and other artefacts, once owned by the cricketer C. B. Fry and his wife Beatrice but later purchased by Caird to prevent its dispersal abroad. The occasion was augmented by the presentation to the new museum of a chelengk, or diamond plume of triumph usually worn in a turban. This notable relic of Nelson's victory at the Battle of the Nile, like the Mercury models, had been in danger of being sold abroad until the Society brought it to the attention of the public in 1928 by instituting the Chelengk Fund. In 1929, Lady Barclay stepped in and offered the chelengk to the nation through the National Art Collections Fund.[33]

Despite the inherent difficulties in establishing the new museum, welcome news was received in April 1933 that Sir Warren Fisher, Permanent Secretary at the Treasury, had agreed in principle that it should be established on the same basis as the other national museums and galleries. He also suggested that a small inter-departmental committee comprising Treasury, Admiralty and Office of Works officials should discuss the project and make recommendations. This *ad hoc* National Maritime Museum Committee consisted of Sir John H. McCutcheon Craig of the Treasury, Sir Oswyn Murray for the Admiralty in the chair, and Sir Patrick Duff of the Office of Works. Crucially, at its first meeting the Committee noted that the Admiralty would not be responsible for the museum and that the proposed museum should come under the Civil Service Vote, with the Office of Works being responsible for the buildings, fixtures and fittings and related charges. Moreover, the Committee agreed with Stanhope's suggestion that Geoffrey Callender would be eminently suitable to be the museum's first Director.[34] While this was positive news from the Society's point of view, the second meeting of the NMM Committee, to which both Stanhope and Callender were invited, did not go well. Duff and Murray suggested that Greenwich was too far from central London, but Stanhope defended the proposed location. This turn of events seems to have brought Callender to the edge of a mental breakdown. His mood was not aided by the Committee's suggestion that the Civil Lord of the Admiralty should visit Greenwich and assess the situation. Towards the end of May 1933, the interdepartmental Committee came to view the Greenwich site. Amidst this continuing uncertainty, Lord Stanhope, as Chairman of the NMM Trustees, took a unilateral decision to approach Sir James Caird and ask him to finance the renovation and adaptation of the West Wing of the former school buildings for use by the new museum.[35] Stanhope realized that the Trustees had to satisfy the other parties involved, particularly the Treasury, that a private contribution of sufficient merit could be made to the overall project. A related concern was that the Director of Greenwich Hospital was determined to obtain some monetary recompense for use of the Royal Hospital School's vacated buildings by charging a market rent for them, on the same principle that the Admiralty already paid rent to the Hospital for use of its former residential buildings by the Royal Naval College. Caird quickly agreed to defray the costs of converting the West Wing.[36]

Given the uncertainty over the direction of the project one thing was certain: there was no likelihood of the new museum being able to afford such rent. As in the past, with the project in danger of becoming embroiled in a morass of competing interests, Sir James Caird brought much needed clarity to the situation. In a letter to the Prime Minister, Ramsay MacDonald, in December 1933 he offered not only to make a formal deed of gift of his purchases of art and artefacts to the museum but also to cover the full cost of equipping it at approximately the sum estimated. Caird laid down conditions for this largesse: the project should commence in the financial year 1934–5 and the museum should be controlled by Trustees appointed by the Prime Minister of the day, who would be directly responsible to the Treasury. In addition, the site, comprising the Queen's House and School buildings in their grounds amounting to some ten acres, should be incorporated into Greenwich Park with the Government providing the necessary funds to lay out and maintain the grounds as part of the Park. MacDonald took Caird's letter with him to his home in Lossiemouth to consider it over the Christmas holiday.[37]

Momentum by this stage was clearly with the NMM Trust. Subsequently it was agreed that the School buildings were to be transferred free of charge, and without payment of rent; however, if at some future point the buildings ceased to be used as a museum they would revert back to the Greenwich Hospital charity. Noting the role of the SNR in calling attention 'to the fact that many of our unique naval relics had passed by sale to public or private collections in foreign countries' and that others were in 'imminent danger', MacDonald put the proposal before the Cabinet on 19 February 1934 with the agreement of the Chancellor of the Exchequer, the First Lord of the Admiralty and the First Commissioner of Works.[38] In March 1934 he announced in the House of Commons that a Bill for the establishment of a National Maritime Museum would be introduced shortly. Cabinet discussion on the form of a bill resumed on 30 May 1934:

> The President of the Board of Trade welcomed the proposal very warmly. It was a deplorable fact that this country, which ought to take the lead in all maritime matters, possessed no Maritime Museum on a National scale. The thanks to Sir John [sic] Caird could not be too cordial.
>   The Prime Minister said that, generally speaking, he was disinclined to send letters of thanks on behalf of the Cabinet. On this occasion he proposed to write himself to Sir John [sic] Caird, and he would go so far as to tell him how cordially the Cabinet had accepted his offer.[39]

At MacDonald's request Stanhope, an Honorary Vice-President of the Society, accepted the chairmanship of the new and permanent NMM Board of Trustees. Ultimately twelve men, (excluding Geoffrey Callender as the museum's first Director) were chosen by the Prime Minister to make up the Board. Only Duff of the existing NMM Trust refused appointment.[40]

On 8 July 1934, some seven years after Hope's initial announcement, Stanhope proposed the second reading of the National Maritime Museum Bill in the House of

Lords and on 25 July the resultant Act received the Royal Assent – coincidentally on the very day that the Society held its twentieth AGM. The school buildings at Greenwich were made over to the Office of Works and demolition of some parts began while the reconstruction of others proceeded. In 1935, in recognition of the munificent generosity of Sir James Caird, the Society commissioned Sir William Reid Dick to make a bust (originally in bronze, but subsequently in marble) of him for the Caird Rotunda outside the new Caird Library. The Rotunda, designed by Sir Edwin Lutyens, was completed the following year. Finally, on 27 April 1936, it was possible to put the first exhibits in place.

Fittingly, the Society's AGM in 1937 was held in the newly opened National Maritime Museum. A decade before, Hope had described it as 'a People's Palace of British Sea Power' – words put into his mouth by Callender – and concluded by calling it the 'Maritime Museum'. The doors of the new museum were opened to the public on Thursday, 29 April 1937.[41] Over the first weekend 10,000 people were admitted. The figures for May and June combined were 75,000. Membership of the Society stood at over 900, and the cherished goal of 1,000 members was in sight.[42]

Nautical Archaeology – Henry V's Grace Dieu

In the field of pure nautical research the year 1933 was also important. Some leading members of the Society and their friends, especially R. C. Anderson, and F. C. P. Naish and his two sons, aided by the technical knowledge of Mr Prynne, an officer of the Royal Engineers, and by the researches of L. G. Carr Laughton and G. S. Laird Clowes investigated the remains of a wreck in the Hamble river above Bursledon. They succeeded in determining with a degree of confidence, practically amounting to certainty, that the Hamble wreck was that of Henry V's largest ship, the *Grace Dieu*, built at Southampton in 1418. She had been laid up there in 1434, and burned in her mud berth in 1439. This *Grace Dieu*, unlike the *Henry Grace à Dieu* of Henry VIII, was not a carvel-built vessel but one built in the earlier clinker fashion of Northern Europe, though in her case the planking was of three thicknesses. In short the discovery of these remains revealed for the first time the details of construction of a large clinker-built ship.[43]

Other Matters

At the 1936 AGM of the Society, Admiral Hope reminded members that during the introduction of the National Maritime Museum Bill in Parliament, Lord Stanhope had demonstrated the claims of the SNR to be considered the originators of the proposal. Hope desired through the establishment of a new association to be called the Friends of the National Maritime Museum, 'to perpetuate the close connection of this Society with the foundation of the Museum'. A sub-committee had worked out the proposed details and Callender put their draft report before the meeting. Only Society members would be eligible to become Friends and their election would be subject to Council approval. Each 'Friend' would receive a badge denoting that status, but could only become a Friend on the recommendations of three existing ones. The draft report was approved but it remained for the NMM Board of Trustees to sanction the proposed association. Anyone disposed to be considered a 'Friend' had to join the Society and pay the annual subscription of one guinea. The Friends' silver and blue enamel membership badge displayed three anchors emblematic of the old Navy Board and entitled its owner to free entry to the museum on paying days, as well as tickets to the Print Room and Reading Room.[44] With the approval of the NMM's Trustees all Society members who had served on its Council or as officers or auditors were appointed Friends without submitting themselves for election. Moreover, the establishment of the Friends also opened up the possibility of further donations to the museum's burgeoning collections. In the following year, Society members were the first to pass through the doors of the museum's new Nelson-Ward Gallery, which held many new items presented by this descendant of Nelson's daughter, Horatia. The Reverend Nelson-Ward was a member of the Society and a Friend of the museum. As Admiral Hope commented, he had 'dowered England with a donation worthy of our national hero, and in a spirit of princely generosity which proves him the lineal descendant of the most recklessly generous soul that ever lived – Nelson himself'.[45]

In 1937, G. S. Laird Clowes died. He had been the instrumental force in establishing the Society's Coastal and River Craft Sub-Committee in 1934 with the object of awakening public interest in old types of such vessels, and in the work of the Society in identifying and securing records of them.

Implacable *and* Foudroyant

The *Implacable* Fund related to the 74-gun Third Rate, formerly the *Duguay-Trouin*, under which name she had fought in the combined French-Spanish fleet at Trafalgar. The *Duguay-Trouin* was in Rear-Admiral Dumanoir de Pelley's van and barely engaged in the main battle, but fell into British hands at the later action against Sir Richard Strachan's squadron off Ferrol on 4 November 1805.[46] She was taken into the Royal Navy and renamed *Implacable*.

The saving of *Implacable* from the ship-breakers was always associated with the name of Geoffrey Wheatley Cobb (1851–1931), and the support given to him by Sir Owen Seaman (1861–1936), the editor of *Punch* from 1906 to 1932.[47] In 1909, Cobb made a personal appeal to King Edward VII to save *Implacable*, which was to be sold off by the Admiralty. Cobb was successful in cancelling the sale and the ship was handed over to him 'for preservation' in 1911.[48] It only became apparent later that *Implacable* 'still remained, and remains, the property of the Admiralty but there are no funds out of which she can be maintained'.[49]

Cobb had the vessel moved to Falmouth and maintained her alongside the 46-gun frigate, *Trincomalee*, which he had bought in 1897 and renamed *Foudroyant*.[50] Thereafter Cobb used both ships as naval training establishments for young boys. *Implacable* lay at Falmouth until repairs could be carried out at Plymouth in the 1920s. By then Cobb was short of funds to restore her. At first, it appeared that the SNR would rescue Cobb from his financial plight. Letters surviving after Admiral Sturdee's death in 1925 reveal his intention that the SNR should restore *Implacable* in the same way as HMS *Victory*. In June 1924, Sturdee opened an account at the National Provincial Bank, Southsea, entitled 'The Sea Fund', of which he was the sole Trustee.[51] The fund was based on another anonymous donation made by James Caird 'for a new purpose to refit the "Implacable" at Falmouth'. After Sturdee's death, the funds in the deposit and current accounts totalled £19,266 14s 7d. Sturdee left instructions that in the event of his death the donor's identity would be revealed to the bank so that the donor could continue to draw cheques to maintain *Implacable*. He wrote: 'I expect some £10,000 will be left on deposit for some years for future maintenance of the ship after the outfit is complete.'[52] However the bank did not accept this arrangement that a trustee-less account could exist and on 20 September 1925 James Caird wrote to Lady Sturdee acknowledging that the Sea Fund balances had been transferred back to him and that he would 'duly honour the promises we made during your late husband's control of the Banking a/c'.

With *Implacable* in dry-dock at Devonport, a Dockyard survey led the Admiralty to estimate that repairs would cost £12,500 – a figure well within the Sea Fund's balance which had been returned to James Caird – but *The Mariner's Mirror* for October 1925 carried in its Editorial Notes the following re-direction of Admiral Sturdee's plan:

> It is only too evident that, with H.M.S. *Victory* to look after, the Society for Nautical Research cannot shoulder so heavy a responsibility as the restoration of the *Implacable* would entail.[53]

In other words, Professor Callender wanted to channel all Caird's gifts towards the restoration of the *Victory*. Behind this expression of intent, it seems that Callender had persuaded Caird not to pursue Sturdee's plans for *Implacable* but to transfer the majority of the Sea Fund to the STVF, which received a donation of £15,000 in November 1925.[54]

Figure 18 *Implacable* in Portsmouth Harbour. From *The Story of the* Implacable, this race between sailing craft illustrates her youth training activities in the late 1930s. (Original picture supplied by the British Library)

After Sturdee's death, two SNR members, Sir Owen Seaman, and Sir Vincent Baddeley, First Principal Assistant Secretary at the Admiralty, approached Callender on Cobb's behalf requesting access to the Society's anonymous benefactor. Callender was less than enthusiastic, and did his best to demolish Cobb's case, but did pass on the request to James Caird who initially agreed to support the venture by an endowment of £250 per annum to cover the cost of training four boys.[55] Some SNR members formed an *Implacable* Committee chaired by Seaman to raise sufficient funds to save the ship. Despite the fact that the ship's restoration was not official SNR policy, Callender ensured that he was Deputy Chairman of the *Implacable* Committee, since its work cut across the Society's ongoing commitment to HMS *Victory*.

Fortunately for *Implacable*'s survival, with the Admiralty's approval, Admiral of the Fleet Earl Beatty, then President of the SNR, made an appeal in 1925 for funds to restore the ship.[56] Beatty's appeal raised almost £25,000 and supplementary appeals increased that total to £33,000 by 1937. By 1927 the Fund had raised £25,000 and repairs were underway. At this point Cobb took *Foudroyant* back to Milford Haven, leaving *Implacable* 'under the direction of her Committee'. After Cobb died in 1931, his widow consulted Lt Col Harold Wyllie, the son of W. L. Wyllie RA and 'made over

Figure 19 *Implacable* and *Foudroyant* moored in Portsmouth Harbour. In 1940 a bomb struck *Foudroyant*'s port gunwhale forward and passed through the heads to explode in the mud between both ships. (Original picture supplied by the British Library)

ownership of the *Foudroyant* to the *Implacable* Committee. The two ships were now the sole responsibility of the Committee'.[57] A temporary respite followed an appeal by the Duke of York in 1931, when 'nearly ten thousand pounds were subscribed'.

Implacable was towed to Portsmouth in 1932 to provide holiday training afloat for youth groups and was berthed in Portsmouth Harbour from June 1932 onwards. The *Implacable* Fund was spent in reconditioning the ship's hull and restoring her original between-decks appearance. *Foudroyant* was also towed from Milford Haven to Portsmouth in the same year, the cost of her transport being paid by Sir James Caird.

When Sir Owen Seaman died in 1936, the SNR finally gave recognition to the volunteer *Implacable* committee. Chaired by Admiral Humphrey Hugh Smith, with Callender as his deputy, it continued to finance the use of both *Implacable* and *Foudroyant* for children's holidays. The onboard administration was led by Harold Wyllie. By 1936 he was superintendent of *Implacable* and *Foudroyant* with a small number of riggers and shipwrights carrying out ongoing repairs. At the Society's AGM, it was noted that a minimum sum of £3,000 per annum was needed for the upkeep of *Implacable* and *Foudroyant* including the wages of shipwrights and the cost of moorings. As the chairman of the *Implacable* Committee, Admiral Smith explained that the finances were in a very parlous state, and money was coming in but very slowly. In April 1938, Christopher Stone, an SNR member, broadcast a radio appeal for funds which brought in £559 2s 7d, though the ships' running costs that year totalled £2,700.[58] An 'Admirals' Appeal' in 1939 brought a gift of £1,000 from the Pilgrim Trust. Despite the public goodwill the ships engendered, the SNR took no formal responsibility for either of them but gladly accepted public credit for the *Implacable* appeal and repair work.[59]

The SNR in the Second World War

During the Second World War the Society continued its activities on a reduced scale. No Reports of Council appeared until 1944–5, but Callender continued to write short reports in his capacity as Secretary and Treasurer. At the outset he noted that much of the overseas membership of the Society had been lost owing to German tyranny and oppression. Moreover, owing to civilian upheavals in Britain many members also changed addresses without notice. Given these factors it seemed pointless to update the list of members.[60] Nevertheless, the Society's subscription income held up well compared with the average of £900 per annum in the late 1930s, and remained at around £750 for the war years. By 1945 it had recovered to £900 per annum. Unlike the years 1914 to 1918, the Society continued to publish *The Mariner's Mirror* throughout the conflict, which meant that revenue and expenditure retained some semblance of peacetime operations. Crucially for the financial health of the Society, the Admiralty continued to take *The Mariner's Mirror*. From the beginning of the war it bought sufficient copies to circulate among ships in commission. That demand steadily increased and by 1945 the Admiralty was purchasing, on average, 900 copies of each issue.[61]

R. C. Anderson took over editorial duties for the third and last time in 1939, succeeding D. Bonner Smith who had previously followed him in 1932. On the outbreak of war, Anderson had warned members that *The Mariner's Mirror* would be reduced in size. Despite this warning he could scarcely have foreseen that by 1942 it would be half its pre-war length, though he was able to claim that it still contained three-quarters of its pre-war contents.[62] The rationing of paper, like many other wartime products, was under government control; in this instance under the 'Paper Controller' which meant that in addition to the scarcity of paper, photographic prints were costly. Anderson, however, felt that it was necessary to keep them in the journal when they were required as evidence.[63] By 1945 the wartime introduction of lighter paper permitted the number of pages to increase again.[64]

Sales of Society publications were erratic with almost no revenue accruing from sales of occasional publications to non-members or souvenirs from the Victory Stall in 1941 and 1943, but revenue in 1942 and 1944 reached about £500 per annum and peaked at £1,400 in 1945. Despite inflationary pressures, printing costs were below £600 per annum throughout the war. Accordingly the Society ran some substantial surpluses, with cash balances reaching £2,200 in 1942. From then on the surplus cash was invested in war savings. At the outbreak of war the Society held £970 in 3.5 per cent War Loan. In 1943 it invested £2,000 in 3 per cent Savings Bonds (redemption date 1960–70), and a further £2,000 in 1944–5 in 3 per cent Savings Bonds (1965–75). From 1944 onwards the Society's holdings were valued at over £4,900. Three smaller specific funds were mostly held in abeyance for the duration of the war.

Visits by the public to HMS *Victory*, previously a good source of revenue, ceased with the closure of Portsmouth Dockyard for the duration of the war. The ship herself was under the care of the NMM's Trustees rather than the SNR. They met only irregularly until 1942 and the ship was barely mentioned, though in October 1944, the Trustees discussed whether they might enter a claim against the Admiralty relating to the deterioration in *Victory*'s condition while she was on 'war work'![65] Of serious concern to the SNR was the air-raid damage to *Victory*: the ship was shaken by a near miss on 10 January 1941 and the museum had some windows and fittings broken by the blast. Temporary repairs were effected, since with the shortage of office accommodation, the C-in-C had ordered the Expense Account Department to use the Victory Museum.[66] More seriously, a high-explosive bomb landed in No. 2 Dock two months later on 10 March 1941.[67] Some 10 feet of the dock wall and dock side was destroyed as well as four sections of the steel cradle upon which the ship rested. In the forepart of the ship 'the false keel, keel, floor timbers and keelsons immediately under the riding bitts' were completely destroyed for about 20 feet and a hole 15 ft by 8 ft was made in the hull.[68] Nevertheless, the symbolic value of HMS *Victory* remained intact: the King and Queen visited the ship on 4 December 1941 and were given lunch on board by the C-in-C Portsmouth, Admiral Sir William James; later in the month the King and Crown Prince of Greece paid a visit while numerous service personnel, especially Canadians, were allowed on board.[69] A visit by the Archbishop of Canterbury in May 1943 led Capt. Grant, the CO, to report:

> The visit was quite a success. The weather was fine, the Commander-in-Chief and the Archbishop addressed the audience from the Starboard Cat-Head. The crowd that assembled by the dockside to hear the addresses, was not too large for the accommodation. I should say it numbered from 5,000–6,000. The addresses were relayed to other parts of the dockyard and that may account for the fact that the figures were not higher.
>
> I thought the C.-in-C. gave a very inspiring address, more especially in what he said about H.M.S. *Victory*. His Grace the Archbishop never mentioned the ship.[70]

Further shortage of barrack space in Portsmouth meant that during 1943–4, the ship was used as overflow accommodation – which hindered the death-watch beetle 'census' that Capt. Grant was carrying out: 'Now that there are so many ratings berthed on board, the decks are kept so scrupulously clean at all times' so that his men found it hard to make an accurate count of the beetle carcasses!

When preparations began for re-rigging the ship in 1945, Harold Wyllie expressed fears that re-rigging the foremast and bowsprit would inflict further damage as it was recognized that the forepart of *Victory*'s hull had been already strained from riding at her mooring in the tideway until 1922.[71] Repairs had not begun in June 1945 when Capt. Grant, *Victory*'s CO, wondered whether there was a case for leaving the bomb damage unrepaired: 'As it is now of great interest to the visitors, and I am still of the opinion that there is a fine source of revenue by charging visitors to leave the ship through the bomb hole'.[72] However HMS *Victory* was fully re-rigged by 21 October 1945 and able to fly Nelson's Trafalgar signal. There were no payments advanced from the STVF between 1941 and 1946 for work on the ship, but donations continued to be made and the Fund's income in 1946 totalled just over £1,140. Cash at the bank, which had been erratic during the 1930s, rose steadily reaching over £1,000 in 1942 to over £4,305 in 1946.

The Macpherson Collection Endowment Fund also saw its cash holding at the bank rise from over £410 in 1939 to £1,543 in 1946. The Fund continued to hold nearly £11,527 in securities which had been credited to the account since 1928.

The *Implacable* Fund remained more active than the small funds under the Society's control. Work on *Implacable* stopped in 1940, and wages paid were wound down. Between 1941 and 1946, the only expenditure was for the storage of boats. The *Implacable* Committee's Chairman, Vice-Admiral Humphrey Hugh Smith, despite being in his sixties, volunteered for active service. He was lost on convoy duties on 27 September 1940. Thereafter, the Committee continued under its Deputy Chairman, Professor Callender, for the duration of the war. The Superintendent of *Implacable* and *Foudroyant*, Lt Col Harold Wyllie, served as a wing commander in the Royal Air Force (as he did in 1918) until 1943, when, at the request of the Admiralty, he was specially released to return to the ships with the rank of Lt Cdr RNVR.

With Portsmouth subject to enemy action, the *Implacable* Committee had offered *Implacable* and *Foudroyant* to the Admiralty for wartime service. Their Lord Commissioners accepted the offer, despite the fact that in August 1940 a bomb had struck *Foudroyant* forward on the port gunwale and, smashing through the heads, had exploded in the harbour mud between both ships.[73] After a survey they were both transferred to Admiralty control on 1 March 1941, and used as storeships. As an *Implacable* Committee Report put it:

In what other countries can ships be found built in the lifetime of Napoleon and still afloat in the Hitlerite epoch to fling their defiance at the oppression of liberty.[74]

Auspiciously, in 1942, when Mrs Wyllie began serving on the *Implacable* Committee, she became the first woman to join a Society committee.[75] Mrs Wheatley Cobb, who had sold the *Foudroyant* to the *Implacable* Committee in return for a mere token payment, died the following year. Both *Implacable* and *Foudroyant* ceased to be storeships in 1943 and became a fully commissioned Training Establishment with Harold Wyllie conducting training duties.[76] Both ships survived the war but their physical conditions deteriorated badly.

In 1942 the Society lost its patron, HRH The Duke of Kent on active service.[77] Other notable deaths were those of Admiral Sir Cyril Fuller, who had conducted the operations of the Cameroons Expedition in 1914–15; J. Holland Rose, Vere Harmsworth Professor of Naval History at Cambridge, A. G. H. Macpherson, and Cecil King the marine painter who had designed the monument to the van de Veldes erected in St James's Church, Piccadilly on 1 May 1929.[78]

From 1 January 1940 to 31 December 1945 the Society lost 285 members, though the resulting decline in aggregate was only 18, and on 1 January 1946 total membership numbered 896. R. C. Anderson shouldered the burden of editing *The Mariner's Mirror* throughout the entire period of a long and trying war, and kept the journal punctual to the end.[79] The Society had risen from small beginnings to become a learned society of note and the coming peace offered it new challenges and opportunities.

References

1   The antecedents to the museum's long and involved gestation are admirably set out in the context of the growth of museums generally and, from the 1860s onwards, in an increasing historical awareness of naval history, by Littlewood and Butler, *Of Ships and Stars*, 1–44. The narrative in this chapter is indebted to those authors for their detailed work on the foundation of the NMM and the role of the SNR in its establishment.

2   Throughout this chapter 'Royal Naval Museum' refers to the Admiralty Museum in the Royal Naval College, Greenwich, and not the Royal Naval Museum in Portsmouth Dockyard discussed in Chapter 2.

3   Greenwich Hospital is an ancient Crown charity providing charitable support including annuities, sheltered housing and education to serving and retired personnel of the Royal Navy and Royal Marines and their families. Its main beneficiary today is the Royal Hospital School, which was founded at Greenwich in 1712 and moved to Holbrook near Ipswich on 22 March 1933. By the 1920s, most of the former Hospital buildings were occupied by the Royal Naval College. The Seamen's Dreadnought Hospital for merchant seamen remained next to Romney Road until after World War II when the National Health Act came into operation.

4 Littlewood and Butler, *Of Ships and Stars*, 44.

5 NMM SNR 3/1 SNR Minute Book No.1. Report of the Council for the Year 1925.

6 *Ibid.*

7 *Ibid.* cf Littlewood and Butler, *Of Ships and Stars*, 52, who cite Callender in the 1930s attributing the title 'National Maritime Museum' to Rudyard Kipling. See NMM 5/17 Callender to Mrs Cope Cornford, 9 November 1937, claimed to remember Kipling suggesting it at a meeting with Lord Stanhope. However, see Minutes of the Third Trustees Meeting, 14 June 1928, for their discomfort with the name 'National Naval and Nautical Museum' and the decision taken at the Fifth Meeting, 28 October 1929, to 'adhere to the name "National Maritime Museum"'.

8 NMM SNR 3/1 SNR Minute Book No.1, Council Meeting 19 February 1925.

9 Littlewood and Butler, *Of Ships and Stars*, 48.

10 *Mariner's Mirror*, 13:3 (1927), AGM of the SNR 1927, 200–12.

11 AGM of the SNR, 1928. See also A. Newman, *The Stanhopes of Chevening: a Family Biography*, (London, 1969), 344, for James Richard Stanhope, 7th Earl, as Civil Lord of the Admiralty with responsibility for Buildings.

12 The Royal Naval Museum's artefacts at Greenwich were confused with relics formerly held by the Greenwich Hospital School. AGM of the SNR, 1927. Thanks are due to Dr Pieter van der Merwe for pointing out the existence of the 'National Gallery of Naval Art'.

13 AGM of the SNR, 1927.

14 *Mariner's Mirror*, 13:3 (1927), 200–12: AGM of the SNR, 1927.

15 For an appreciation of Macpherson's qualities as a sailor, see J. S. Hughes ed., *Macpherson's Voyages* (London, 1944).

16 AGM of the SNR, 1927.

17 Capt. Parker was a director of T. H. Parker, Dealer in Prints, Drawings and Paintings, 12A Berkeley Street, Piccadilly, W1.

18 *Mariner's Mirror*, 14:3 (1928), AGM of the SNR, 1928, 261–4.

19 *Ibid.*, 263–4.

20 Sir George Hope's address to the AGM of the SNR, 1937.

21 Littlewood and Butler, *Of Ships and Stars*, 53.

22 NMM 5/48, Callender to Hope, 26 April 1930.

23 NMM Trustees' Minutes, Tenth Meeting, 6 July 1931.

24 NMM 5/50, Callender to Stanhope, 18 November 1932.

25 NMM 5/50, Stanhope to Callender, 19 November 1932.

26 Littlewood and Butler, *Of Ships and Stars*, 55.

27 NMM 5/50, Stanhope to Callender, 6 March 1933.

28 NMM 5/50, Stanhope to Callender, 23 December 1932.

29 NMM 5/50, Stanhope to Callender, 6 March 1933.

30 NMM 5/50, Stanhope to Callender, 4 March 1933.

31 Negotiations took place between the NMM Trust and the representatives of the Royal Hospital School on the allocation of premises. The NMM Trust desired the use of all the buildings of the Royal Hospital School south of Romney Road in Greenwich. Eventually, the intervention of Sir Eric de Normann (1882–1982) of the Office of Works was crucial: Normann ordered an inspection of the premises; which resulted in all the buildings, with the exception of the gymnasium and the large swimming pool, being allocated in principle to the nascent NMM.

32 Littlewood and Butler, *Of Ships and Stars*, 57.

33 AGM of the SNR, 1930. The Chelengk was later stolen in a smash-and-grab raid on the museum in 1951 and never recovered.

34 NMM 5/50, Stanhope to Callender, 6 March 1933.

35 NMM 5/50, Stanhope to Callender, 24 June 1933.

36 Littlewood and Butler, *Of Ships and Star*, 66.

37 *Ibid*, 68.

38 NA CAB 24/247, C.P. 50(34), NMM. Sir James Caird's offer. Note by the Prime Minister.

39 NA CAB 23/79. Discussion on NMM Bill in Cabinet.

40 The new Trustees appointed by Ramsay MacDonald on 7 August 1934 were Admiral of the Fleet the Earl Beatty (1871–1936); Sir William Berry (1865–1937), Vice-President of the Institute of Naval Architects; Sir Percy Mackinnon (1872–1956) former Chairman of Lloyd's of London; Captain H. F. David, retired Master of RMS *Olympic*, and a member of the Society of Master Mariners; the Earl of Ilchester (1874–1959), a trustee of the National Portrait Gallery and the British Museum; Sir Frederick Kenyon (1863–1952), President of the Society of Antiquaries; Admiral Sir Herbert William Richmond (1871–1946) Professor of Naval and Imperial History at Cambridge University; and Walter Runciman (1870–1949) formerly President of the Board of Trade.

41 Littlewood and Butler, *Of Ships and Stars*, 92, the opening was delayed by the death of King George V on 20 January 1936, a period of national mourning and the subsequent abdication of Edward VIII.

42 AGM of the SNR, July 1937.

43 NMM SNR 2/28 Annual Report for the Year 1938: A Brief Chronicle of the first 27 years, 92.

44 AGM of the SNR, 1938.

45 AGM of the SNR, 1939.

46 For this action see M. Robson, *The Battle of Trafalgar* (2005), 150–3.

47 G. W. Cobb was a South Wales coal-owner of Caldicott Castle, Monmouthshire, which had been bought in 1885 by his father Joseph Cobb, a railway promoter, who began restoring it.

48 Littlewood and Butler, *Of Ships and Stars*, 38. *Foudroyant* had been Nelson's flagship from 1789 to 1790. Cobb, after a lengthy press campaign, had put up his own money to rescue *Foudroyant* from German ship-breakers and she was brought back to the Thames in 1882 and moored at Greenhithe. Subsequently repaired, although the limited company formed for the purpose was declared bankrupt and was wound up in September 1895, Cobb came into possession of *Foudroyant*, then lying on the mud at Erith. The following year commanded by Cobb and with a uniformed crew of 27 men and boys, *Foudroyant* was exhibited at Woolwich and later undertook a tour of home ports. Unfortunately when anchored off Blackpool on the night of 15–16 June 1897 she dragged her anchors and ran aground. Successive attempts to salvage her ended disastrously; and by August 1898 all that remained of *Foudroyant* was her keel embedded in the sand.

49 *Implacable* Committee, *The Story of the* Implacable (1939). See appeal.

50 For *Trincomalee*, now berthed at Hartlepool, see A. D. Lambert, *Trincomalee: The Last of Nelson's Frigates* (Rochester, 2002).

51 Churchill Archives Centre, Cambridge, SDEE 6/8. Copies of letters from Sturdee to the National Provincial Bank dated 6 June and 14 June 1924, sent to Sturdee's solicitors, Minet May & Co., after his death.

52 Churchill Archives Centre, Cambridge, SDEE 6/8. Sturdee to National Provincial Bank 14 June 1924.

53 *Mariner's Mirror* 11:4 (1925), 339.

54 See Littlewood and Butler, *Of Ships and Stars*, 41–2 for this payment. The accounts of the STVF compiled by Callender concealed this payment by providing only combined totals for the years 1922–6.

55 Littlewood and Butler, *Of Ships and Stars*, 41–2.

56 See NMM SNR/2/27, Annual Report for 1937, 16.

57 Lambert, *Trincomalee*, 112.

58 See *The Story of the Implacable* (1939), The 'Implacable' Fund accounts for 1938. The greatest injustice was that the Admiralty, which owned *Implacable*, charged the Committee for mooring her.

59 See *The Times*, 17 June 1939, leading article 'A Veteran in Distress' which accompanied the 'Admirals' Appeal', a letter signed by every Admiral of the Fleet, the Master and Deputy Master of the Honourable Company of Master Mariners and the Deputy Master of Trinity House.

60 NMM SNR 2/30 Hon. Secretary's and Treasurer's Report for the Year 1940.

61 NMM SNR 3/3 Council Meeting held in NMM Boardroom, 5 June 1946.

62 *Mariner's Mirror*, 28:1 (1942), 91.

63 *Mariner's Mirror*, 29:4 (1943), 186.

64 *Mariner's Mirror*, 31:2 (1945), 50.

65 NMM Trustees' Minutes, 9 October 1944.

66 NMM SNR 7/26 Victory Correspondence. Report by Cdr A. Grant CO, to Callender, 29 January 1941.

67 NMM SNR 7/26 Report by Cdr A. Grant CO, to Callender, 12 March 1941.

68 NMM SNR 7/27 Lt Cdr H. Wyllie to CO, HMS *Victory*, 11 September 1945. See also Bugler, HMS *Victory*, ch. 9.

69 NMM SNR 7/26 Capt. Grant's reports.

70 *Ibid.*, July Report, 1943.

71 Harold Wyllie was transferred from the RAF to the navy in 1943.

72 *Ibid.*, Captain A. Grant to Trustees, 20 June 1945.

73 Lambert, *Trincomalee*, 117.

74 NMM SNR 2/30 Hon. Secretary and Treasurer's Report for the Year 1940, *Implacable* Report.

75 *Mariner's Mirror*, 10:3 (1924), 319. AGM of the SNR, 1924. Miss Isabel G. Powell was elected to the Council.

76 NMM SNR 2/31 Hon. Secretary and Treasurer's Report for the Years 1942–3.

77 See AGM of the SNR, 1926, also *The Times*, 27 May 1926, 'Prince George as Patron'.

78 NMM SNR 2/31 Hon.Secretary and Treasurer's Report for the Year 1941. NMM SNR 2/28 A Brief Chronicle of the first 27 Years, 84.

79 NMM SNR 2/34 Report of the Council for the Years 1944 and 1945.

4

The Society Weathers Changing Circumstances: From Austerity to Economy, 1946 to 1965

Prior to the Second World War, the Society had achieved a great deal: HMS *Victory* had been saved for the nation and the Victory Museum at Portsmouth had been established; the NMM had been founded at Greenwich and its collections augmented; the Society's membership had increased; and *The Mariner's Mirror* continued to reflect a wide range of interests in maritime history. On one front only, the Society had not achieved its early intentions: the originally promised nautical encyclopaedia or dictionary had not been forthcoming.

The founding members of the SNR considered it essential to establish a journal in which to publish their research, so that in the early years of the Society's existence *The Mariner's Mirror* took priority over all other activities which might have formalized the conduct of the Society on a face-to-face basis other than at annual general meetings. Once the NMM had opened, with Sir Geoffrey Callender installed as its first Director, the museum became the preferred location for SNR's meetings. It is nevertheless puzzling that, given the Society's crucial role in establishing the museum, and with the museum's Trustees almost entirely composed of SNR members, no provision for a representative Trustee for the Society was ever made. Initially, Callender's pervasive role in the SNR seemed to be a sufficient link, and the establishment of the Friends of the National Maritime Museum a means of perpetuating the Society's close connexion with the museum. However, the SNR was soon disabused of any early assumptions that its role in establishing the NMM would forever secure some influence in the museum's decision-making.

It was evident in the immediate post-war period, and indeed afterwards, that the museum Trustees had independent ideas. An early example concerned a SNR proposal which Sir George Hope passed on to the Trustees. The Admiralty had given permission for the museum to use as a badge the three anchors – the emblem of the old Navy Board. The SNR proposed that a three-anchor flag should be made to fly over the museum's buildings. The idea, at that juncture, did not impress the

Trustees, whose number included Sir George Hope and Roger Anderson – in their view that as a national institution the museum was entitled to fly the Union Flag and 'that no improvement upon this privilege could be appropriately considered'.[1]

National Marine Photograph Collection

Undaunted, the SNR continued to try to develop the NMM's resources. At the Society's AGM in July 1947, Basil Greenhill proposed the inauguration of a Photographic Records Sub-committee, the rationale being that in the United Kingdom and all over the world there were very many small private collections of marine photographs, but there was no place where a student could study a photographic collection of all types of ships over the last century. His proposal entailed the investigation of methods by which the Society could acquire a National Marine Photographic Collection to be based at the museum. Subsequently, the Sub-committee was chaired by the author and seafarer, Alan Villiers.[2] By 1950 the Photographic Records Sub-committee had amassed a collection of 70,000 prints for the museum's collection, retaining around half the negatives (some of which were copy negatives from prints), and three exhibitions were mounted in Bristol, Cardiff and Edinburgh, and later on in the year at Crosby, Liverpool. Meanwhile a cine camera had been purchased for the Photographic Records Sub-committee and a team led by Engineer-Cdr H. Oliver Hill travelled to Restronguet Creek, near Falmouth, in Cornwall, to film the last English fishing fleet under sail. The Coastal Craft Sub-committee continued to collect the lines of many types of small craft for the historical record, and the Society reached out to the ship-modelling community through a meeting held at the NMM on 20 May 1950.[3]

Implacable and Foudroyant

The question of taking responsibility for HMS *Implacable* and the *Foudroyant* remained unresolved. The one survivor of the Battle of Trafalgar still afloat, *Implacable*, had not fared well. After the war, the Admiralty handed her back in a deplorable state, but *Foudroyant*, (which had been in the care of the Ministry of War Transport) less so.[4] Accordingly, the Report received by the SNR Council found the state of both ships to be 'shocking':

> Everywhere was evidence of lack of proper care having been taken: locked storerooms had been broken into, boats were damaged or missing and bollards and bulwarks had been smashed and torn away. Heavy lighters and other craft had been made fast alongside without fenders, loosening and breaking the

strakes through chafing; and the crowning offence had been, in order to keep the decks tight, instead of caulking, to lay cement on the waterways and round the hatch coamings of the *Implacable*. This cracked and allowed rainwater to lodge beneath it, rotting the beam ends, lodging knees and timbers in the wake of the main and lower decks. At the time and repeatedly afterwards Lt-Colonel Harold Wyllie had warned them of this danger, but no attempt was made to prevent or stop the rot. The *Foudroyant* also showed signs of having been grossly neglected; but she had been spared the laying of concrete, and so, though she is at present unfit for use, her condition is not so bad.[5]

By 1948 the possibility of saving *Implacable* from the ship-breakers hung in the balance. Frank Carr had proposed at the 1947 AGM of the Society that *Implacable* be restored and brought to Greenwich and put in a dock alongside the Royal Naval College. He communicated this to the museum Trustees in October. Crucially, at this stage, Sir James Caird, feeling 'cautiously optimistic', offered to pay for the cost of a survey.[6] However, in the winter of 1947, surveyors estimated the cost of restoration as £150,000, with another £50,000 required for re-rigging.[7] There might be additional costs later. At this, the SNR rapidly distanced themselves from *Implacable*: Capt. Bosanquet, speaking at the 1947 AGM, referred to the *Implacable* as 'a totally independent activity'.[8] The museum Trustees, meeting on 12 January 1948, likewise doubted such a sum could be raised by public appeal.[9] In April 1948 Carr urged the revived *Implacable* Committee chaired by Admiral Sir Percy Noble to attempt to interest other bodies in the restoration of the ship, and promised support but in a personal capacity only.[10] Prince Philip, HRH The Duke of Edinburgh, visiting the NMM in April, shortly before he became a Trustee, gave his support to Carr and promised to raise the matter with the Prime Minister, Clement Attlee.[11] When the museum's Trustees met in October, Sir James Caird:

> Was strongly of the opinion that the Trustees should have nothing to do with any scheme in view of all the circumstances; the reports of the experts on her bad condition, the lack of docking facilities, the amount of money required immediately, (and which might ultimately run into the sum of £500,000), the need of an Endowment Fund, and the cost of upkeep, rigging, repairs, staffing etc.[12]

The Technical Committee of the London County Council reported in 1949 that the hull was in such poor condition there was no way of preserving *Implacable* in order to place her in a dry-dock at Greenwich and that as such the ship should be broken up.[13] Realistically, in the continuing conditions of post-war austerity and without the backing of the LCC and other public bodies, it would be well nigh impossible to raise the necessary funds to restore *Implacable* and as such her fate was effectively sealed. *Implacable* was stripped of her figurehead and stern carvings and mouldings, towed from Portsmouth on 2 December 1949 and scuttled over the Owers Deep.[14] Thus the last survivor of Trafalgar other than *Victory* sank to her watery grave, loved by some, but not loved enough to be saved. However, the teak-built frigate, *Foudroyant* continued to be berthed at Portsmouth and to be used as a training ship for boys and girls during the summer holidays.

Recommissioning the Society: an era of change

After the war, membership numbers were known to have declined but the total did not make allowance for those members in enemy territory during the war, who could not be contacted after hostilities ceased. Strenuous efforts to make contact resulted in some re-joining the Society. This success prompted the Council to comment somewhat optimistically that membership numbers indicated 'a vigorous and healthy constitution on which good hopes for the future may be based'.[15] In fact, losses in the Second World War meant that on 1 January 1947 the total of 894 members was still below the 1938 figure.[16] Not until 1949 was the 1938 membership total passed. Increasing the membership remained an absolute priority for the continued health of the Society. Subscription income post-war began to exceed £1,000 per year and though the post-war inflation in costs was absorbed, a small loss was recorded in 1950. Nevertheless, capital had grown during the war to almost £6,000 invested in government securities, which produced a modest level of investment income. Although the Society continued to keep sizable cash balances there was no great margin to enable the SNR to weather unexpected financial storms. In 1949 SNR membership reached over 1,000 for the first time and sub-scription rates remained unchanged at one guinea (£1 1s).[17]

Change at the top

The most significant loss during the war had been the Society's Patron, the Duke of Kent, and to replace him required the exercise of some tact. In June 1946, Callender suggested approaching the Duchess of Kent to invite her to take the place of her late husband.[18] Palace officials, however, thought 'that the Office of Patron should really be held [by] a man' and suggested approaching Admiral Lord Louis Mountbatten.[19] This suggestion commended itself to Callender 'because his father had been our President (and a very keen one) when the Society was first formed' but Lord Mountbatten was then Viceroy of India and later became the new independent state's first Governor-General.[20] The subject of the Society's Patron was then in abeyance until the summer of 1947. By late July, Admiral Sir Aubrey Smith suggested to Reginald Lowen, the

Figure 20 Admiral of the Fleet Earl Mountbatten of Burma (1900–79), Patron of the Society 1950–79. (© National Maritime Museum, Greenwich, London)

Acting Hon. Secretary, that Lieutenant Philip Mountbatten might be approached to become Patron 'if he was considered suitable' as 'there are so few Royalties, and they are so much in request, that there is something to be said for being first in the field'.[21] This did not command the immediate support of the Council. As Roger Anderson pointed out 'it would be as well to wait until Mountbatten becomes Duke of something or other, and this probably won't happen till just before the wedding in November'.[22] It was not until September 1951 that Admiral of the Fleet the Earl Mountbatten of Burma became the next Patron. In his acceptance letter, he wrote, 'I know what a great interest my Father took in the Society, and it was through him that I first became a reader of *The Mariner's Mirror*.'[23]

The sudden death of Sir Geoffrey Callender from a heart attack in his office at the NMM on 6 November 1946 was the end of an era for the SNR. Callender had combined the posts of Hon. Secretary and Hon. Treasurer since 1921; and from 1925 had run the Society in conjunction with Admiral Sir George Hope, who occupied the position first of Chairman of the Council from 1925, and later, from 1936, of President. After Callender's death, the offices of Hon. Secretary and Hon. Treasurer were never held jointly again. Callender – certainly since the death of Admiral Sturdee in 1925 – had exercised a pervasive personal influence on the development of the Society. Callender's championing of a NMM on personal and patriotic grounds had centred on securing the Queen's House, and related buildings, and his friendship with Sir James Caird and the support of Earl Stanhope ensured the fulfilment of his ambition to be the museum's first Director.[24] According to Sir George Hope, Callender had turned down other appointments including a professorial chair at Oxford.[25] Two days before his death at the age of 71, Callender had his last lunch with Sir James Caird. He was, by this stage, well past the standard Civil Service retirement age. Only the exigencies of war and his intimate knowledge of the museum's collections, coupled with the support of Caird and Earl Stanhope, as Chairman of the museum's Trustees, had kept Callender in post. Callender's style was nothing if not autocratic – to a large extent, he *was* the museum. As Stanhope wrote to Caird in September 1945, 'Anderson, and to some extent Cork [the Earl of Cork and Orrery], have their knives into Callender. They say, (quite rightly) that we must prepare for a new Director'.[26] Callender's funeral service took place on 11 November 1946 in the Chapel of the Royal Naval College, after which he was buried in Blackheath. Sir James Caird paid for the entire funeral, and purchased such of his books which were useful to the museum library.[27]

Upon Callender's death, his assistant Reginald Lowen, who had borne much of the administration during the war while Callender was domiciled in Oxford, became Acting Director of the NMM. The SNR's Council immediately asked him to be the SNR's Hon. Secretary while Capt. Bosanquet became Treasurer.[28] It seems that Callender's successor as professor of history at the Royal Naval College Greenwich, Michael Lewis, was approached by Lord Stanhope to become the museum's second Director but turned down the opportunity.[29] Instead, Frank George Griffith Carr was appointed on 1 May 1947. Formerly an Assistant Librarian in the House of Lords, he was a long-standing SNR member and since 1934 had been Secretary of the Society's Coastal Craft Sub-committee. The Council offered its congratulations to Carr on his appointment, noting that the Society would always regard the museum as its offspring.[30] Nevertheless, this marked a further break between the NMM and the SNR for Carr never held any SNR office after his appointment to the Director's post. It was noted at the Annual General Meeting of 1948 that Reginald Lowen had relieved Capt. Bosanquet as Hon. Treasurer in October 1947. Bosanquet had been Hon. Auditor until 1946, a post he had held since the Society's formation in 1910.[31] Lowen held the post of Hon. Treasurer until 1963 when it passed to Mr E. C. D. Custance. Lowen was replaced as Hon. Secretary in 1947 by George Naish.[32]

Figure 21 Frank Carr (1903–91), Director of the NMM. (© National Maritime Museum, Greenwich, London)

Both Lowen and Naish were employees of the NMM, but did not get on well at a personal level. Lowen was a steady and reliable administrator, while Naish, enthusiastic and knowledgeable, was unpredictable and at times, mercurial.[33]

To compound matters further, Naish was at the centre of increasing dissension among the museum staff. He was disappointed by not succeeding Callender as Director, and barely mollified by being appointed Assistant Director from October 1947 on the recommendation of Frank Carr. Indeed, the staff seem to have divided into two hostile camps; those who supported Naish and those supporting Lowen. By October 1950, following a critical review of the NMM by the Treasury's Organization and Methods Division, Lord Stanhope abolished Naish's post as Assistant Director.[34] As a result, Naish's relationships with both Carr and Lowen deteriorated markedly and, with the appointment by the Trustees of a new Deputy Director, Cdr William Edward May RN (retd), in 1951, Naish was further marginalized. The fact that two of the Society's principal officials barely tolerated each other, together with Naish's enmity towards Carr, did not augur well for the conduct of Society or museum business or the relationship between the Society and the NMM. Evidence of continuing friction occurred in 1956, when Carr complained to the NMM Trustees that the SNR was booking meetings in the museum's board room and lecture room without reference to him or his deputy, Cdr May. Matters had come to a head on 12 September – the previous day – when such a meeting clashed with an international conference of 250 persons booked to use the same facilities on the same day. No member of the museum staff was mentioned in the minutes, though responsibility for the clash was obvious, and R. C. Anderson, as SNR President and a senior member of the Board of Trustees, was left to apologize on behalf of the Society.[35]

Before the AGM of 1951, the Society's President and Chairman, Sir George Hope decided that he could no longer hold office. Hope had been Deputy First Sea Lord at the end of the First World War and was present alongside Admiral Sir Roslyn Wemyss, the First Sea Lord, at the negotiations for and signing of the Armistice at Compiegne at 11a.m. on 11 November 1918. He had succeeded Sturdee as Chairman in 1925, and Earl Beatty as President in 1936. His resignation was accepted by the Society with the greatest reluctance and marked by the presentation of a clock.[36] Roger Anderson, owing to his outstanding services to the Society, duly succeeded Hope as President, and Professor Michael Lewis was elected Chairman. The following year, in his first presidential address to the Society's AGM, Anderson informed members that a full-time curator of the Victory Museum, Instructor-Captain T. E. Jackson RN (retd), had been appointed from 1 May 1952, and that his salary would be paid by the Society.[37] Moreover, the Society also agreed to fund the enlargement of the museum when labour and materials could be spared from more urgent work in the Dockyard.

An interesting *vignette* came to light when Mr G. R. G. Worcester, a member of Council, proposed the election of the Society Officers for the year 1952. Worcester recalled that when he was sent to a Japanese prisoner-of-war camp, the Japanese allowed three books per person to be kept. He took with him Roger Anderson's *Sailing Ships*, Sir Alan Moore's *Last Days of Sail* and the Bible. These three books provided the basis of his knowledge of nautical research.[38]

In 1953, L. G. Carr Laughton, who had been the leading light in the foundation of the Society and Hon. Editor of *The Mariner's Mirror* for almost four years from 1910, was made an Honorary Vice-President. Such recognition of his contribution would seem to have been long overdue; but Carr Laughton had aroused Callender's dislike, particularly in view of disputes on the VATC over the restoration of *Victory*'s bows. Callender summarized it tartly:

> I do not think that it is an unfair summary to say that the Committee divided on this subject. The majority were convinced that the ship at Trafalgar wore the appearance that she now has to-day. There was, however, a minority of one,

namely Mr L. G. Carr Laughton, whose knowledge of such matters is certainly very considerable. He maintained that we were making the wrong decision and he, in due course, entered a protest.[39]

Perhaps Carr Laughton's greatest legacy, as Gregory Robinson pointed out, 'was that *The Mariner's Mirror* was for free discussion so that we might reach true conclusions'.[40]

In the following year, 1954, the Society's greatest benefactor, Sir James Caird, died at his home in Wimbledon, after a long illness, aged 90. Without his generosity, *Victory* would not have been saved; neither would the purchase of the Macpherson Collection and the Mercury ship models have been possible nor the foundation of the NMM. When so many in the Society and beyond cavilled at the costs; Sir James, contrary to the popular myth about the tightfistedness of Scotsmen, put his hand in his pocket and came up with the money. The Society was never able to undertake any grandiose schemes of preservation or restoration again.

The Mariner's Mirror

During the war, the production of *The Mariner's Mirror* had substantially increased owing to extra Admiralty orders. While this was entirely welcome both for the reputation of the journal and the augmentation of the Society's coffers, continuing Admiralty support could not be taken for granted in peacetime. So it proved shortly after the war ended when, without consultation, the Admiralty withdrew its support for the distribution of *The Mariner's Mirror* to ships in commission in the Royal Navy. The loss of Admiralty support, which by December 1945 averaged 900 copies of each issue, nevertheless came as something of a shock to the Society. With the January 1946 issue ready for despatch, the Office of the Director of Victualling informed the Society's printers, Cambridge University Press, that no further copies of *The Mariner's Mirror* would be required. Subsequently a letter to the Director of Victualling remained unanswered; and the Society deemed it necessary to take the matter to a higher authority. In February 1946, Callender, as the Society's Treasurer, wrote to a Principal Assistant Secretary at the Admiralty. Although it was acknowledged, four months elapsed without reply before Admiral Sir Aubrey Smith, a Vice-President of the SNR, offered to approach the Secretary of the Admiralty on the Society's behalf.[41] Smith's approach was ultimately to no avail.[42]

Plainly, with the loss of Admiralty support and increases in printing costs, receipts from sales of *The Mariner's Mirror* suffered such a serious reduction – as can be seen in Appendix IV, Part 2A – that membership, and therefore the Society's main income, had to be increased. Income was primarily derived from members' subscriptions, sales of *The Mariner's Mirror* to non-members, occasional publications, and a small amount of interest from investments. One suggestion adopted after the Society's AGM of 1946 was the use of covenants allowing the Society to reclaim income tax. Initial uptake of this means of increasing the Society's revenue was disappointing: only 31 members signed Deed of Covenant forms in the first year.[43] The Covenant forms entailed nothing more than members agreeing to subscribe one guinea per annum for seven years but it was hoped that an increase in the uptake would defray increasing printing costs and also allow an increased number of pages in the journal. As production costs of *The Mariner's Mirror* had increased, the question of increasing subscriptions also arose at the 1948 AGM. A Compounded Subscription (Life Membership) of £25 in one lump sum was proposed by Admiral Hall and subsequently adopted, though one alternative proposal suggested £15 as sufficient, and another opposed life membership as uneconomic for the Society.

In June 1946, Roger Anderson, the Hon. Editor of *The Mariner's Mirror*, expressed a wish to resign in order to pursue his own research. Anderson had acted in an editorial capacity for nearly twenty years and had shouldered the editorial burden of producing the journal during the war years. He was succeeded by Cdr Hilary P. Mead, RN, who held office for seven years before stepping down at the end of 1953, when Mr G. R. G. Worcester replaced him. Mead had a difficult job through the period of post-war austerity, paper restrictions, controls and rising prices. As his successor pointed out, the cost of printing had risen since 1939 by nearly 150 per cent and that of paper even more. *The Mariner's Mirror* had been reduced from 112 to 80 pages per issue, and the number of plate illustrations from about ten to four. There was at that time no prospect of reducing costs while maintaining quality, and the austerity limit on the journal's size of 80 pages per issue had to be continued unless income was increased by a substantial rise in circulation or other means.[44] This was a final blow to the long-delayed publication of a 'Maritime Miscellany' celebrating the coming-of-age of the Society in 1931. Callender had been unsupportive of the proposal and by December 1937 had only four chapters in draft while a fifth was being re-written.[45] Post war, rising costs made any such separate issue unsustainable. In 1950, over twenty years later, it was decided to publish the already-completed contributions in various issues of *The Mariner's Mirror*.[46] Another disappointment was that the *Mirror* remained bereft of a general index. Over many years three individual members had undertaken to produce one but the last, C. J. Britton, had died while working on it in 1947. A similar situation pertained with the continued non-production of a nautical encyclopaedia or dictionary, which had always been sidelined by Callender's obsession with the creation of the NMM.

Figure 22 Reginald Lowen (1900–90), right, with Princess Elizabeth, and Lord Stanhope.
HM The Queen, when Princess Elizabeth, was being shown the pre-war Visitors' Book of the
National Maritime Museum. (© National Maritime Museum, Greenwich, London)

The Post-war Finances of the SNR 1946–1960s

When Reginald Lowen took over as Treasurer, his first year's accounts summarized
the Society's expenditure to date on its principal objectives. By the end of 1947, he
calculated that since 1922 the Society had expended £100,275 on the restoration and
maintenance of HMS *Victory*, an enormous sum which dwarfed all other SNR
transactions. By comparison, the Victory Museum had cost only £8,467.[47] This
expenditure aside, the post-war financial position of the Society was one of steady if
unspectacular growth. Indeed, the Society entered 1946 in a reasonably strong
financial position even though its subscription had remained unchanged since 1920.
On the balance sheet, invested funds totalled £4,937 at cost with around £1,000 on
both deposit and current accounts with the Society's bank.[48] This later allowed the
purchase of £1,000 2.5 per cent Defence Bonds which brought total investments up
to nearly £6,000, and produced an annual income of about £178.[49] The Society's

income and expenditure account showed an excess of income over expenditure of £160 which, though satisfactory, marked a large decrease of £1,550 when compared with the surplus of the previous year of £1,712.[50] This financial deterioration was almost entirely due to the loss of Admiralty support for the Society's journal. However, due to increased receipts from the souvenir stall and dockside collecting boxes at Portsmouth and other donations, the Society was able to repay all of its outstanding debts in relation to the Victory Museum and Panorama Annexe accounts.[51] Indeed, during 1946 *Victory* attracted a record total of 193,443 visitors and the Society later obtained approval for re-rigging the ship but, with the scarcity of Italian hemp, sisal cordage was used.[52]

Subscription income rose steadily, passing £1,000 in 1948 and £2,000 in 1964, though post-war inflation meant that annual expenditure rose faster over the same period from around £1,200 in 1948 to more than £2,900 in 1964. The foresighted wartime policy of placing spare cash in government savings bonds produced a steady income flow rising from around £160 per year in the late 1940s to over £800 per year in the late 1960s. However, this source of income was more than matched from various items sold such as journals, including back numbers, occasional publications, plans and indexes, advertising in *The Mariner's Mirror* and minor items, such as sales of the Society's tie. Together, these commercial activities showed an income which rose from under £300 per year in the late 1940s to around £1,500 in the late 1960s. It followed that the Society began to hold increasing amounts of cash, since current and deposit bank accounts together rose from around £300 per year in the early 1950s to some £1,500 per year in the mid-1960s. Evidently the Society's finances were increasingly stable, since its main income and expenditure accounts showed losses occurring in only three years, each of which was attributable to changes in the pattern of its investment holdings. Investments at cost amounted to £5,937 in 1947 and had risen to £11,900 in 1969, though the accounts began to show current market values from 1954 onwards.[53] Careful appraisal of the market led the Society to sell low-interest wartime savings bonds and Treasury stock and to re-invest the proceeds in higher-yielding post-war issues, as well as some companies quoted on the stock exchange. By 1969 the market value of the SNR's investments was put at £15,600.[54] Given the position in 1946, this marked a steady if unspectacular performance in the period of the long post-war boom in international trade and investment opportunities. Despite the SNR's financial stability, declining surpluses in the early 1950s, culminating in a loss of £79 in 1955, triggered the first rise in subscription rates since 1920 from £1 1s to £1 10s.[55]

Besides the accounts for running the Society, the SNR still kept a number of special-purpose accounts, three of which had originated in the interwar years. Appendix IV sets out in more detail a summary of the funds administered by the

Society. The first of these, the STVF, had acquired responsibilities extending beyond HMS *Victory* to include the Victory Museum, while the Macpherson Collection Endowment Fund concentrated on the purchase of maritime artworks for the NMM.[56] Besides these two sizable holdings, the Coastal Craft Fund amounted to little more than the petty cash utilized by Basil Greenhill and its last accounts were filed in 1950.[57]

Fortunately, the STVF remained buoyant throughout this period through donations, admission tickets and sales. Its revenue rose to over £3,000 in 1953 and £5,000 per year from 1957 onwards. During the 1960s, annual revenue rose from over £6,000 in 1961 to over £16,000 in 1969. The Fund's assets, which were under £10,000 in the late 1940s, reached £20,000 in the mid-1950s. The continual demands on the STVF from the Victory Museum and the ship limited the growth of assets, but during the 1960s annual asset values exceeded £20,000 substantially in every year bar one. The Macpherson Collection Endowment Fund also came to have a substantial balance. The year 1952 saw the largest expenditure yet from the Macpherson Fund, £300, for its contribution towards the purchase from Lord Halifax, of a large painting of the Battle of the Texel by van de Velde which was eventually hung in the Hall of the Queen's House.[58] Throughout the 1940s and 1950s the annual values recorded in the accounts amounted to some £13,000–£14,000 and exceeded £15,000 in almost every year in the 1960s.

One new substantial fund managed by the Society was the Walker Bequest. Bequeathed by Mrs Dorothy M. Walker from the residue of her estate for the purposes of 'The Museum of Naval Trophies and other articles of historical interest in Portsmouth Dockyard', it was valued at £6,825 when received in 1953.[59] Through judicious investments the Walker Bequest came to exceed £10,000 by 1961, and £20,000 by 1969. The bequest was of substantial importance in offsetting the need for the STVF to contribute to the Victory Museum. Taken together, the accounts show that the Society was administering substantial sums of money in the post-war years. This was not unnoticed by the membership and at the 1954 AGM, Mr R. A. Skelton, Map Librarian at the British Library, pointed out that the Society was holding funds amounting to £43,000. He therefore proposed the appointment of Trustees to be responsible for securing a continuous financial policy. The meeting accepted his proposal for a new Rule appointing three Trustees elected by the members.[60]

HMS Victory, *the Society and the Admiralty*

In 1948, a decade had passed since the Society had relinquished the responsibility for looking after HMS *Victory* and the Victory Museum to the NMM Trustees. When the

Trustees met in May 1948, Roger Anderson suggested that it was illogical that they should have the responsibility for HMS *Victory* formerly exercised by the VATC, yet did not control the STVF.[61] Using the pretext that the STVF had become an onerous burden for the Treasurer and Auditors to administer, the SNR's Officers, led by Sir George Hope, meekly proposed to transfer control of the STVF to the NMM Trustees at the July 1948 AGM. At a stroke, another of the main pillars of the Society's existence was abandoned. The rationale for the change, as Anderson, a Vice-President of the SNR and an NMM Trustee seconding the motion pointed out, was that 'it is not unreasonable that the people who are looking after the ship should have the handling of the money to do with it'. Whilst this may have seemed reasonable to the assembled members who accepted the proposal unanimously, few, if any, saw its true import. Indeed, Anderson's statement and the silence of his fellow Officers on the real reasons for this *volte face* was indicative of a culture that Council knew best and would not deem to consult the members on such important but ultimately controversial matters.

Repairs and maintenance

The Victory Museum had suffered damage in the blitz and was not able to re-open until June 1946 when the war damage had been repaired.[62] All capital expenditure in the immediate post-war years was strictly controlled by Board of Trade licences for building materials and imports, and the STVF could make no major outlay until 1953, when nearly £2,300 was provided for showcases and fittings. From 1955 to 1958 electrical work in the museum, together with an extension and stairs, required over £2,500; while further restoration work in 1958, including repairs to the roof of the entrance hall, took a further £2,250. Between 1962 and 1964 the extension work consumed £12,630; yet in 1967 a further £3,565 needed to be spent on weatherproofing, decorations, treating the floor and restoring the *Panorama*, as well as over £500 on more showcases. Finally, in 1969, air-conditioning was provided for the *Panorama*, together with further repairs, for roughly £320.[63] Meanwhile HMS *Victory* herself required several substantial payments towards her upkeep: in total the SNR paid out £30,000 in three equal amounts in 1960, 1965 and 1966. More specifically work on *Victory*'s rigging required payments of over £440 in 1965 and almost £5,100 in 1967, while several small amounts were allocated to ship's furniture in 1948, 1964 and 1969.[64]

HMS *Victory: warship or heritage site?*

HMS *Victory* had fared far better than the Victory Museum, despite her wartime bomb damage. Her commanding officer also looked after the museum but by 1949 it was felt better to separate the two roles. An advertisement for a full-time curator of HMS *Victory* was placed in the national press. A sub-committee interviewed several candidates but no appointment was made – a situation which was unchanged a year later. The STVF totalled about £9,000 invested or held by the Society and was added to day-by-day by means of collecting boxes at Portsmouth, entrance fees to the Victory Museum and Wyllie *Panorama* and sales at the souvenir stall. Although the Society had offered the handling of the STVF to the NMM Trustees following the AGM of June 1948, the Trustees later explained they were unable to accept it since, under the terms of the National Maritime Museum Act, all appointments had to be approved by the Treasury, thus the administration of the STVF had to remain with the Society.[65] When the NMM Trustees had at first accepted the Society's offer they had not realized the NMM could not pay a curator for the Victory Museum from the STVF. A curator appointed by the Trustees would have to be a civil servant and his salary would have to be included in the NMM's Estimates.[66] One has to question why Sir George Hope and Roger Anderson let this matter go to the NMM Trustees in the first place. Both had been members of the Board of Trustees since 1927 and should have understood its operations and its Civil Service constraints.

In July 1948, Frank Carr visited HMS *Victory* to consult with the C-in-C Portsmouth, Lord Fraser of North Cape (June 1947 to October 1948) over the appointment of a curator for the Victory Museum. However, the outcome was unacceptable to the NMM Trustees, who had been responsible for the Victory Museum and its contents since 1938, even though the SNR paid for its upkeep. The C-in-C sought ultimate control over the curator and the Victory Museum. By this stage the Society had interviewed a number of candidates for the position of curator, but their choice, Cdr Higham, was not approved by Fraser's successor as C-in-C Portsmouth, Admiral Sir Algernon Usborne Willis (October 1948 to September 1950). Admiral Willis wished the position to be a filled by an ex-member of the lower deck who had reached the rank of lieutenant rather than a cadet-entry officer, who had not attained the rank of commander on the Active List.[67] This was precisely the opposite of the Society's original intention to appoint a cadet-entry officer rather than an ex-member of the lower deck as curator.[68]

Underpinning these events was the fact that in the immediate post-war years, relations between the Society and the Royal Navy's C-in-Cs Portsmouth became strained over the status of HMS *Victory* as a commissioned ship, and particularly as the flagship of the C-in-C Portsmouth. Pre-war the C-in-C, Admiral of the Fleet the Earl of Cork and Orrery – an SNR member – had made little use of *Victory* for official purposes, and visitors' access to the ship had been almost unrestricted.[69] During the war the Royal Navy's demands for additional facilities meant *Victory* was used as an accommodation ship and *Victory*'s wardroom was used for courts martial, a practice which continued until 1957.[70] With the Dockyard closed to the public, the Victory Museum was also commandeered for offices. Problems arose, not only after *Victory* was damaged by bombing, but because Admiralty House, the official residence of the C-in-C, also suffered bomb damage and its remaining usable parts became offices. From early in 1941, HMS *Victory* was a symbolic attraction for official visitors. By the time the Dockyard re-opened to the public after the war, the potential conflict between access to *Victory* for visitors and her role as a commissioned ship had not been resolved. Concerns put forward by members of the public that access to *Victory* had become considerably restricted reached the SNR and the Trustees of the NMM.[71] In response to their approaches, the C-in-C Portsmouth, Admiral Sir Geoffrey Layton (September 1945 to June 1947), explained that until war damage to Admiralty House was repaired he had no option but to use the Great Cabin of *Victory* for entertainment purposes and access to it and the wardroom would continue to be limited. In October 1946, Layton met four Society representatives and pointed out to them that the day-to-day use of *Victory* as a live flagship with the C-in-C coming and going, periodic parading of guards and bands and so on, had considerably enhanced interest in the ship and increased visitor numbers.[72] At this meeting, it was apparently agreed that Nelson's furniture, which had been removed and sent for restoration, should not be returned to the ship but instead put on view in the Victory Museum.[73]

The restrictions on public access to Nelson's cabin continued throughout the summer of 1948, during Lord Fraser's time as C-in-C, because no finance was available for repairs and redecorations to Admiralty House until October of that year.[74] By then, Lord Fraser had become First Sea Lord and Chief of Naval Staff and the appointment of C-in-C Portsmouth had passed to Admiral Sir Algernon Willis. Representatives of the SNR and the Trustees of the NMM met Admiral Willis, on board HMS *Victory* on 15 October 1948.[75] The attitudes of both sides had hardened during the delay, as additional events of the previous twelve months remained unresolved. Surprisingly, the strongest complaints from among the Trustees were made by Admiral Sir Charles Little, himself formerly C-in-C Portsmouth from 1942 to 1945. His position was portrayed by the Secretary of the Admiralty in a memorandum to the First Lord:

> Incidentally, I believe that what gave rise originally to the attack by the Society for Nautical Research was Admiral Sir Charles Little's disgust at a very large cocktail party held on board the VICTORY in the late Commander-in-Chief's time when the condition of the decks towards the end of the party left a great deal to be desired.[76]

The restrictions on access to Nelson's cabin on *Victory* for visiting members of the public were exacerbated by the installation of a galley in Nelson's quarters and a pantry nearby, which successive C-in-Cs required for entertainment purposes. The Society's position throughout was that there were far too many official occasions; moreover, the Society had raised the money to save the ship in the first place and the restoration and furnishing of the vessel had been subsequently carried out on the basis that it would be open for inspection by members of the public. Relationships between the parties continued to deteriorate, and by 30 June 1949, Admiral Willis unilaterally suspended any transfer of entrance fees to the Victory Museum to the STVF. This had been a valuable addition to the Fund for many years.[77]

In June 1950 the Council of the SNR and the Trustees of the NMM issued a joint memorandum to the Admiralty. While the signatories, Lord Stanhope, for the NMM, and Sir George Hope, for the SNR, welcomed the maintenance of HMS *Victory* as a live flagship, it was a cause of regret that she was used for official entertainment purposes 'on not infrequent occasions' although it was recognized that special occasions justified it. They regretted that as a consequence of such official entertainment (which they also noted that the First Lord of the Admiralty, Viscount Hall, approved of or at least found unavoidable) that:

A pantry and kitchen equipment should be continued to be installed in Lord Nelson's night cabin and in the Admiral's lobby, these therefore being no longer maintained as they were in 1805.

The memorandum further considered that:

it would not be possible to restore the Trafalgar appearance of the cabins if modern furniture, a wireless set, etc., not in keeping with the period, were also to be retained.

In addition it was also noted that, with the First Lord's approval, it would still be necessary for the C-in-C Portsmouth to make *ad hoc* arrangements with regard to Nelson's furniture when official entertainment was taking place on board. Thus Lord Stanhope and Admiral Hope expressed the wish that a different policy regarding *Victory* 'in the eyes of the Public the Valhalla of British naval history – may some day prevail'. Then, with a little more steel, the memorandum concluded that the Trustees would recommend that the *Victory* furniture should be displayed in the Victory Museum and should not be removed without the approval of the Council of the SNR.[78]

In reply, Viscount Hall reiterated that he regarded the galley in the lobby as necessary for official entertainment but that he thought it was inconspicuous and 'does not seriously detract from the 1805 condition of the ship'. However, he noted that Admiral Willis had stated that he would be willing to remove the pantry from the Admiral's night cabin, and that he, as First Lord, endorsed this proposal, so that this part of the Admiral's quarters would in future be open to the general public. Moreover, Hall also noted that the Nelson furniture would be adequately cared for on board and that *Victory* was the right place for it. Nevertheless, if the NMM Trustees and the SNR still insisted that the Victory Museum was the proper place then he would raise no further objection.[79]

This presaged a thaw in the rather icy relationship between the parties, and by January 1951, discussions between the Society and the Admiralty had resulted in the removal of the pantry from Lord Nelson's sleeping cabin.[80] Their Lordships were also reinstating the transfer of entrance fees to the Victory Museum back to the STVF, 'subject to the deduction of all expenses incurred by Navy Votes on account of the Museum or arising from its presence in the Dockyard'. Accordingly, instructions were issued to the new C-in-C Portsmouth, Admiral Sir John Arthur Power (September 1950–September 1952), with retrospective effect to 30 June 1949, when previous payments to the STVF were suspended.[81]

Ultimately, the question of a new curator for the Victory Museum was not resolved until Capt. Jackson was appointed in May 1952. Following his appointment, takings in fees tripled compared with the previous year, as over 235,000 visitors had visited HMS *Victory* up to June 1953, the best year since 1947. The problem of death-watch beetle infestation persisted and a committee of experts visited the ship in April 1953 and as a first measure recommended fumigation.[82]

In 1948, the NMM Trustees had appointed a new VATC but it had only met once, on 14 July 1949, since when it lay dormant.[83] By 1953, legal opinion evinced that the arrangement of 1938 whereby the Trustees of the NMM took over the functions of the former VATC, after its discharge by the Admiralty, was *ultra vires*. Following that decision, Admiral Sir Charles Little, a Trustee and former C-in-C, suggested in 1953 that the museum's Trustees should have nothing more to do with *Victory* or the Victory Museum.[84] This drastic proposal did not meet with the approval of his fellow Trustees, but differences of opinion between all parties remained unresolved. The touch-paper was again lit in January 1954 when Professor Michael Lewis noted:

> that he had been concerned to learn, almost by chance that the Admiralty proposed to deck over the open waist of the Victory, thus altering her Trafalgar state without consulting the Trustees of the National Maritime Museum or the Council of the Society.

This proposal to lay a deck over the boat skids was intended to prevent water lying on deck and seeping into the hull. The alternative – setting awnings – was in keeping with the period but required more hands than the CO could muster.[85] Lewis approached the Admiral-Superintendent of the Dockyard who agreed to hold up the work for the time being. At the same time the NMM Director, Frank Carr, informed Sir John Lang, the Secretary of the Admiralty, that the NMM Trustees and the Council of the SNR wished for a round table conference to consider questions affecting *Victory*.[86] According to Sir Victor Shepheard, the Director of Naval Construction, this was urgent in view of a report identifying, 'advancing rot in the ship's hull and forecasts of the necessity of extensive repairs costing hundreds of thousands of pounds in a period of thirty to fifty years'.[87] Sir John Lang, however, was slow to move. This reflected the uncertainty which had existed in the Admiralty since 1939 over who was responsible for historical advice on *Victory*'s preservation,. He consulted the new C-in-C Portsmouth, Admiral Sir George Creasy. A powerful man who had served as Fifth Sea Lord and Vice-Chief of Naval Staff, he was currently NATO C-in-C Channel Command. As Admiral Creasy saw it, the SNR 'took a false step in transferring their advisory functions to the Trustees of the National Maritime Museum' under the influence of Sir Geoffrey Callender. Although both Sir John Lang and Admiral Creasy questioned the validity of the NMM's Trustees to advise on *Victory*'s preservation while the expertise and the money was held by the SNR, the only post-war meeting of the VATC in 1949 had been accepted by the Admiralty. Admiral Creasy recommended Lang should hold a meeting including the SNR as they 'did all the work to bring about the restoration of VICTORY and the ship is morally theirs'.[88]

The conference finally took place on 11 February 1955 in the Permanent Secretary's room at the Admiralty with Sir John Lang in the chair. Taking a lead from Admiral Creasy; the Admiralty representatives 'stressed that whatever solution was reached, the Admiralty would wish to deal with a single body'. Finally, it was agreed that the VATC should be formally reconstituted. The Admiralty would be responsible for the circulation of information to members of the VATC and for summoning it to meet and would provide facilities either on *Victory* or in London. The VATC would select its own chairman, but this would not be an Admiralty representative. Subsequently the Board of Admiralty approved these arrangements and the first meeting of the new VATC was held on 30 June 1955 on board *Victory*. As a result of some 6,000 test borings all over the hull it was reported that 'nearly the whole of the bottom of the ship below the orlop deck is so rotten or defective that complete renewal will be required'. It was also pointed out that:

> when the ship was restored to her Trafalgar condition in the late 1920s, it was already appreciated that major constructional repair would be necessary to the lower part of the fabric of the hull. The money then available from the Save the VICTORY Fund was principally devoted to the repair of the upper works and

the restoration of the ship to the appearance which she bore at Trafalgar. The major problems of structural decay were not then dealt with; they were perhaps too alarming to be considered at that time.[89]

Restoration would begin when the survey had been completed. The VATC was to meet formally twice a year in the spring and autumn.[90] It had been agreed on 11 February 1955 that:

> All questions involving naval archaeology and the preservation of the *Victory* as an historical monument would be referred to the committee, and it was the intention that the committee should be used as a really effective instrument.[91]

This implied that the old VATC had been a less than effective instrument in the preservation of *Victory* after 1929 and that both the Admiralty and the NMM Trustees had been to a degree complicit in this. If the VATC was once more to be effective in the preservation of *Victory* it also put into perspective the Society's lack of supervision of the ship following the completion of the 1920s restoration. It is unclear whether the VATC ever met afterwards and certainly no further work of significance had taken place when the VATC was disbanded in 1938 on Callender's advice. Only the barest maintenance took place throughout and beyond the Second World War.

After the round table conference of February 1955, the Admiralty asked the SNR Council to submit the names of four Society representatives. The new Committee began meeting on 30 June 1955 and elected Professor A. E. Richardson, President of the Royal Academy, to be its chairman.[92] Since entry fees to the Victory Museum had been restored as from 1949, the STVF had built up a balance of over £20,000. The SNR therefore committed £10,000 from the STVF, which the Admiralty used to purchase teak for *Victory* in 1956.[93]

Cutty Sark

In the interim, efforts had been made to save the Clyde-built 921-ton composite clipper, *Cutty Sark*, the last of her kind.[94] She had been purchased at Falmouth by Captain Wilfred Dowman in 1922 from Portuguese owners with the aim of restoring her to her former glory. Captain Dowman died in 1936 and his widow, Catharine, was no longer able to afford the ship's upkeep.[95] In 1938 *Cutty Sark* sailed from Falmouth – her last voyage at sea – to the care of the Incorporated Thames Nautical College at Greenhithe, Kent, for use as a training ship. She remained there throughout the war years. Subsequently, in January 1949, Sir William Currie had asked his fellow NMM Trustees if they would be interested in taking over the vessel.

However, the museum's Trustees deferred discussions on the subject pending a resolution on the future of the *Implacable*, all of which was, in reality, a charade. The Trustees had to justify their existence, but as the museum was publicly funded there was no chance of extensive funding for matters outside its immediate sphere of influence, that is, its collections. The exception to this rule was, of course, the personal philanthropy of one Trustee, Sir James Caird. *Cutty Sark* was later surveyed by the kindness of Lloyd's Register of Shipping, first as she lay afloat, and second when she was berthed at the expense of the London County Council. It was found that her condition, as befitted Clyde workmanship, was tolerably good. Her iron frames were generally in fair condition, but her iron floors had deteriorated badly. On the other hand, her hull planking was in first-class condition as was her keel and her keelsons. Her poop deck would have to be renewed but by and large she was in much better condition than originally hoped for and therefore the cost of repairing her was less than expected. Prince Philip – a committed and hugely influential supporter of the project – was crucial to saving *Cutty Sark* for the nation, together with Frank Carr, who expounded the view that *Cutty Sark* should represent to the Merchant Navy what *Victory* represented to the Royal Navy. Preferably, she should be berthed at Greenwich in a dock alongside the pier there. Carr foresaw that an appeal would have to be mounted across the world to restore her and hoped that the Society would offer both its support and technical expertise to the project.[96]

By 1953 the appeal for *Cutty Sark*, to which the SNR, as usual, gave moral support, had been very successful. Although undertaken thirty years later than the Save the Victory Appeal, the amount raised for it was over double than that of its predecessor. Indeed, when around £200,000 had been subscribed or promised, the ship's papers were handed over in May 1953 to Prince Philip, who accepted them on behalf of the *Cutty Sark* Preservation Society.[97] The project to that date had overcome considerable difficulties. The London County Council, though unwilling to underwrite the estimated £250,000 cost of the project, promised to provide a site at Greenwich. Eventually, plans were formulated for berthing of the ship in a purpose-built dry-dock. In the interim, the vessel remained at Greenhithe and was later towed to Dead Man's Buoys about half a mile above Greenwich Pier for the Festival of Britain in 1951. During the year surveyors reported that it would cost an estimated £70,000 to restore and re-rig the ship and a further £175,000 to construct a dry-dock at Greenwich.[98] *Cutty Sark* was eventually towed into her purpose-built dry-dock on 10 December 1954. Thereafter, she was painstakingly restored and officially opened to the public by Queen Elizabeth II accompanied by Prince Philip on 25 June 1957, as a national monument to Britain's merchant seamen and ships of the days of sail.

Figure 23 *Cutty Sark* moored at Dead Man's Buoys, Greenwich, with her topgallant-masts lowered. (© National Maritime Museum, Greenwich, London)

An Index and a Nautical Dictionary

At the 1953 AGM, the Society's Chairman, Roger Anderson, noted with typical insouciance that the only part of the original programme of the Society that it had not yet accomplished was a Nautical Dictionary. He stated that the founder-members who had drafted the Rules of the Society had left a 'comfortable loophole' in this respect 'as Rule 2 speaks of collecting material for ultimate publication, and "ultimate" can be as far off as we like. Even if the Society dies before the Dictionary appears, there will still be no real grounds for complaint' – so much, then, for treating the objects of the Society as a duty. Neither the saving of *Victory* nor the establishment of a national maritime museum were original objects of the Society, but Anderson had not demurred.

During the 1950s, the end of the saga of non-production of a general index for the first 35 volumes of *The Mariner's Mirror*, which had been bedevilled by misfortune and disappointment, also seemed to be in sight; Anderson noted that it was a year away from fruition.[99] Before its appearance, Cambridge University Press warned that there would be considerable increases in printing costs during 1955, with the result that the annual subscription was raised to 30 shillings from 1 January 1956.[100] The general index to volumes 1–35 of *The Mariner's Mirror*, compiled by Roger Anderson, was published by Cambridge University Press in 1956 and sold steadily. At the 1956 AGM, Anderson, in a *volte face* to his previous comments, now pledged the Society to produce a nautical dictionary primarily based on the vast amount of index cards and slips of paper which Leonard Carr Laughton had accrued before his death. Anderson saw it as a challenge to try to produce the nautical dictionary before the Society's 50th anniversary in 1960.[101] By the 1958 AGM, the information on the slips had been typed to the letter 'S' and a start made on listing the sources used by Laughton and his helpers in compiling them.

In the interim, the Society had set up an appeal fund to complete the work of pre-servation of an historically valuable collection of ships' figureheads and other relics of shipwrecks preserved in a small outdoor museum run by Lt Cdr Thomas Dorrien Smith RN, called 'Valhalla' in the garden of Tresco Abbey in the Isles of Scilly. Elsewhere, money from the STVF had been allocated to repair the roof of the Victory Museum and to insure exhibits, and a new catalogue stand was offered for *Victory*, whose CO, Lt Cdr Langley, in a departure from past practice, was now invited to meetings of Council.[102] In 1959, the Treasurer, Reginald Lowen reported that the covenant system of membership, in abeyance since 1957, was about to be reinstated, as the Inland Revenue had, in principle, recognized the Society as a 'Charitable Body'. Capt. Jackson, curator of the Victory Museum, confirmed that the building and its contents had been insured for £30,000 and £15,000 respectively.[103]

Fifty Years of Nautical Research: 1910–60

On the occasion of the Society's fiftieth anniversary, Roger Anderson mused on how best to celebrate it, and suggested that the Society should elect a new President to replace him. His successor was the Society's then Chairman, Professor Michael Lewis who, on behalf of the Society, presented Anderson with a framed portrait in oils by the artist Bernard Hailstone. It had been originally commissioned by Anderson's wife, Romola, but was subsequently paid for by the Society as a token of its esteem.[104] Anderson recalled that it had been seventy years since he last sat for a portrait with his mother and a dog, and that the dog had been the best sitter! Such was the muted extent of the Society's 50th anniversary celebrations. Predictably, given past failures, hopes that a nautical dictionary would be published by this stage were again dashed; little progress had been made apart from experimental work defining and illustrating terms under the letter 'A'. The Society, through the STVF, had given another £10,000 for the purchase of teak for *Victory* (aided by the sale of over £5000 Conversion Stock), and the total number of visitors to the ship in 1960 was 255,000. Membership of the SNR had reached 1,022, and the Tresco Valhalla Appeal had raised just over £400. It was closed in 1963, as no donations had been received since 1961.[105] Earlier, the Society had been represented on a committee to endow an annual lecture in the name of the historical geographer Professor Eva Taylor. The inaugural E. G. R. Taylor lecture took place on 17 October 1960 and in the same year the eighty-year-old Professor Taylor was elected as the Society's first female Honorary Vice-President.[106]

From January 1962, Capt. T. Davys Manning OBE, RNVR, became Editor of *The Mariner's Mirror* in succession to George Worcester who, after seven years in office, wished to retire. The Publications Committee which had been set up to advise Worcester, was abolished in favour of a 'panel of experts' drawn up by the President of the Society. This panel could be approached individually by the Editor at his discretion when in need of expert advice.[107] By this stage the seemingly inexorable rise in production costs of *The Mariner's Mirror* gave real cause for concern. Annual subscriptions in 1961 amounted to £1,400 but expenditure on the production of the journal cost some £200 more. Moreover, Cambridge University Press had warned that they would increase their charges by 50 per cent with effect from January 1963. In response, the Society appointed a small sub-committee to examine its financial policy, future expenditure and possible new sources of income. Before it could report however, Michael Lewis stated at the 1962 AGM that the Society would have to reduce expenditure and increase income. In the former case he wondered whether *The Mariner's Mirror* might be shortened and the number of expensive illustrations reduced. Secondly, it might be necessary 'to employ a not-so-good publisher who charged less'. Lewis nevertheless accepted that 'it would be plain suicide to risk ruining the *Mirror* itself in the process. A much worse *Mirror* would certainly be an income-loser, because it would inevitably reduce membership through large-scale resignations'. On the income side, raising subscription levels was an option, however unpalatable this would be to sections of the membership: the Society had experienced the resignations of over 100 members as a result of the rise of 9s in 1956. Another option was the obvious one of increasing membership to around 2,000, and lastly an increase in covenanted subscriptions was also desirable.[108]

When the sub-committee eventually reported it was evident that it had concentrated on increasing the Society's income: no substantial changes were recommended to the nature, size or format of *The Mariner's Mirror*. Neither, after canvassing a number of alternative printers were Cambridge University Press abandoned. Of five main recommendations – all accepted by Council – a continued drive for new members had priority. Over the two years since Lewis had exhorted the membership to be more proactive in introducing friends and colleagues to the Society some 239 new members had been enrolled – in arithmetical terms almost one member in four had done his or her bit for recruitment. However deaths and resignations over the period numbered 120. The result was that the Society had gained 113 new members, and membership in June 1963 numbered 1,130, the highest-ever total. Second, an increase in covenants was sought. Third, increased dividends from existing investments were envisaged: in fact, some £2,000 from accrued savings had been invested giving the Society an increased yearly income of nearly £100. The last two recommendations concerned the Society's institutional members – first, the institutional subscription was doubled to 60s per annum; second, was a greatly enhanced contribution from the Cambridge University Press. CUP already made an invaluable contribution to the Society's coffers through its non-member 'sales subscribers' of nearly £500 per annum. However, as the institutional subscription was previously the same as the individual one, CUP had not put its full marketing weight into attracting institutions from all over the world. With the new institutional subscription, however, CUP was confident that it could increase income by at least £200–£300 per annum. Of the twelve kindred journals published by CUP, all except the SNR had been charging its institutional members at least double the individual subscription. In reality, the Society could no longer afford to ignore such a universal trend, but still put its individual members – some 88 per cent of the Society membership – first by keeping the existing subscription at 30s.[109]

In August 1962, through the STVF, the second extension to the Victory Museum was begun. The post-war rigging of sisal on *Victory* had stretched badly, necessitating re-rigging in hemp on the advice of the VATC. The Society, through the STVF, offered up to £12,000 for the purpose and more if spread over a number of years. The restoration of *Victory's* hull was well under way; re-furnishing and re-decoration of the Great Cabin had been completed, and re-rigging in hemp began. Visitors to *Victory* numbered 274,000 in 1963, and a record number of 181,500 visited the Victory Museum. Profits from the sale of some 40,000 brochures at the Victory catalogue stall; plus the revenue from collection boxes and museum admission fees, had risen to £6,846, an increase of £1,682 10s 11d over the previous year. Investment income increased to £1,683 – a creditable performance, and the extension to the museum was completed in March 1963 which, including new show cases and fittings, cost £5,645. In addition, to foster a sense of Society identity, John Munday had designed a Society tie sporting a spouting sea monster taken from Waghenaer's *Speculum Nauticum*, which is still in use today. By 1963, 250 ties had been sold at £1 each.

In 1962, a new but constitutionally separate Southern Branch of the Society, SNR South, was started by Professor J. S. Bromley, in consultation with Council. Its inaugural lecture, given by Frank Carr, was heard at Southampton University. That SNR South had needed to be formed at all was an indictment on the limited ambitions of the Society and its lack of regular face-to-face meetings.[110] During 1963, Reginald Lowen, the Society's Treasurer since 1948, resigned to spend the rest of his life with his family in Australia. As a mark of esteem the Society presented him with a cheque for £100 and a silver desk calendar. He was succeeded by Mr E. C. D. Custance DSC, at the 1963 AGM.[111]

The bicentenary of the launching of *Victory* at Chatham was marked in 1965.[112] Unfortunately, just prior to the programme of celebrations, *Victory's* CO, Lt Cdr V. H. Bracher, was struck down by illness and later died in hospital. He was succeeded by Lt Cdr Whittingham. In the same year Capt. Jackson retired after thirteen years as curator of the Victory Museum. The Society marked the occasion with the presentation to him of a gold watch. His successor was Capt. A. J. Pack RN (retd). To celebrate the bicentenary nine different functions were arranged, seven of which were in Portsmouth and two at Chatham, with the Society's Hon. Secretary, George Naish, attending all of them.

On 1 January 1965, the Society's membership stood at a record level of 1,306 and, as a result of the steady increase in subscription income, the size of *The Mariner's Mirror* had been increased from the 80 pages of the austerity years to 96 pages, and more illustrations were included. The marked increase in membership reflected the increasingly effective use of administrative resources in attracting new members, including the provision of an assistant secretary, Mrs Pamela Gueritz, who was in turn succeeded by Mrs A. B. Sainsbury.[113]

In stark contrast to the heyday of the Society's influence in the interwar period, the two post-war decades witnessed a decline in the prominence of the Society. Without real responsibility for the *Victory*, less so for the Victory Museum; without formal connexions to the NMM and with two of its principal officers at odds, economy generally held sway and vision was lacking, even though the Society was now on a far better financial footing than previously due to the increase in membership and a more pro-active approach to its investments. Relations with various C-in-Cs Portsmouth over *Victory* deteriorated seriously in the post-war period, but had stabilized by the mid-1950s. Indeed, increases in investment income had allowed the Society greater scope in preserving and restoring *Victory* and in updating and modernizing the Victory Museum. *Implacable* had gone, but *Cutty Sark* had been saved, though not by the Society. The Society's relations with the NMM, now firmly controlled by its Trustees, had been under strain. However, with the aid of Cambridge University Press, *The Mariner's Mirror* had gained and maintained a growing international reputation.

References

1   NMM SNR 3/3 Council Meeting, NMM, 5 June, 1946.
2   Including Greenhill and Villiers, the other members were Engineer Cdr H. Oliver Hill, with a member of the museum staff, Michael Robinson being co-opted.
3   *Mariner's Mirror*, 36:1 (1950), AGM of the SNR, 1950.
4   NMM SNR 2/36 Report of the Council for the Year 1946, *Implacable* Report.
5   *Ibid.*
6   NMM Trustees' Minutes, 6 October 1947.
7   NMM Trustees' Minutes, 12 January 1948.
8   See SNR 2/27 Annual Report for 1937, 32. Capt. Bosanquet had conveniently forgotten that in 1937 it had been stated that: 'The *Implacable* Committee is a Committee of the Society for Nautical Research'.
9   NMM Trustees' Minutes, 12 January 1948.
10   *Mariner's Mirror,* 33:4 (1947), AGM of the SNR, 1947, 213. The *Implacable* Committee's Hon. Sec. and Treasurer was Capt. Clement Brown. See 217, for Capt. Bosanquet's comment.
11   Littlewood and Butler, *Of Ships and Stars*, 130–1.
12   NMM Trustees' Minutes, 11 October 1948.
13   See NMM Trustees' Minutes, 11 July 1949, for extracts from the LCC Report.
14   NMM Trustees' Minutes, 3 October 1949.
15   NMM SNR 1/7 Report of the Council for the Years 1945 and 1946.
16   NMM SNR 1/8 Report of the Council for the Year 1947.
17   NMM SNR 1/8 SNR Membership at 1 January 1949 was 1,010.
18   NMM SNR 6/19, Callender to Admiral Sir Aubrey Smith, 21 June 1946.
19   *Ibid.*, Lord Herbert from York House, St James's Palace, to Admiral Sir Aubrey Smith, 3 October 1946.
20   *Ibid.*, Callender to Admiral Sir Aubrey Smith, 19 October 1946. Callender claimed that he had suggested to the SNR's Chairman, Admiral Hope, after the Duke of Kent's death that

Lord Louis Mountbatten be approached but 'Hope jumped on the proposal pretty heavily'.

21 *Ibid.*, Admiral Sir Aubrey Smith to Lowen, 29 July 1947.

22 *Ibid.*, R. C. Anderson to Admiral Sir George Hope, 14 August 1947.

23 *Ibid.*, Earl Mountbatten of Burma to R. C. Anderson, 18 September 1951.

24 See above, Chapter 3 and NMM 5/50, Stanhope to Callender, 6 March 1933.

25 *Mariner's Mirror,* 33:4 (1947), 212. See Sir George Hope's address to the AGM of SNR, 1947.

26 Littlewood and Butler, *Of Ships and Stars,* 119.

27 Littlewood and Butler, *Of Ships and Stars,* 123. The cost was £28. 3s. 0d.

28 *Mariner's Mirror,* 33:4 (1947), 212; *Mariner's Mirror,* 34:4 (1948), AGM of SNR, 1948, 228. Lowen had acted as an unofficial assistant secretary for the SNR since 1936, handling membership matters on Callender's behalf. See NMM SNR 6/8, 6/12 and 6/17.

29 *Mariner's Mirror,* 56:3 (1970), Obituary of Professor Michael Arthur Lewis CBE.

30 NMM SNR 1/8 Report of the Council for the Year 1947.

31 *Mariner's Mirror,* 34:4 (1948), AGM of SNR, 1948.

32 NMM SNR 1/8 Report of the Council for the Year 1947, both Lowen and Naish were elected at the Council Meeting held at the NMM on 8 October 1947.

33 Littlewood and Butler, *Of Ships and Stars,* 125, 137-140. Personal correspondence from former members of NMM staff.

34 *Ibid.* Cdr W. E. May formerly worked at the Admiralty Compass Observatory, Slough.

35 NMM Trustees' Minutes, 13 September 1956.

36 See NMM Trustees' Minutes, 16 January 1952 for an appreciation of Sir George Hope's services to the NMM.

37 Capt Jackson was formerly Education Officer, Portsmouth Command.

38 *Mariner's Mirror* 38:4 (1952), AGM of SNR, 1952.

39 NMM SNR 7/26 *Victory* Report July 1943.

40 *Mariner's Mirror,* 39:4 (1953), AGM of SNR, 1953.

41 NMM SNR 3/3 Council Meeting, NMM Boardroom 5 June 1946.

42 NMM SNR 6/23, even as late as November 1962, the Society's Patron, Earl Mountbatten resurrected the case for the supply of *The Mariner's Mirror* to the fleet but without success.

43 NMM SNR 1/7 Report of the Council for the Year 1946.

44 *Mariner's Mirror,* 40:1 (1954), Editorial by G. R. G. Worcester.

45 The coming-of-age volume had originally been proposed at the Society's AGM in 1932. In July 1933, Prof. Callender reported to the AGM that 'of the thirty-two chapters promised in what I may style our prospectus, over twenty are now ready to go to press'. At the 1935 AGM, Callender admitted that further delay had been occasioned by 'the very onerous editorial duties' he faced. The following year he told the AGM that 'the book is already far advanced' and suggested its publication might coincide with the opening of the NMM. For the limited progress he made, see NMM SNR 6/10, Secretary's Papers (1937), following which Sir George Hope admitted to the 1938 AGM that fifteen chapters had been returned to their authors for revision.

46 *Mariner's Mirror,* 36:4 (1950), AGM of SNR, 1950, 356.

47 NMM SNR 2/37 Annual Report of the SNR (1947).

48 Investments were £950 War Loan 3.5% Registered Stock 1952 or after, at Cost £937 4s 0d, £2,000 3% Savings Bonds 1960/70, and £2,000 Savings Bonds 1965/75.

49 NMM SNR 2/36 Hon. Treasurer's Report to the Council for the Year 1946.

50 For these and other figures quoted from the SNR accounts, see Appendix IV.

51 NMM Trustees' Minutes, 10 February 1947. Lowen's recommendation to use the STVF to

pay off the debt on the Victory Museum took account of the outstanding costs of the *Victory* furniture restoration and the proposed extension to the Victory Museum to house the Royal Barge.

52   NMM SNR 1/7 Report of the Council for the Year 1946, 8. *Victory's* masts and spars had been sent up and re-rigged in time for Nelson's signal to be flown on 21 October 1945.The initial re-rigging in 1945 was in sisal but it was showing signs of deterioration as early as January 1946. See NMM Trustees' Minutes, 4 February 1946. In 1948, Admiral Sir Henry Kitson pointed out at the Society's AGM, that hemp for RN vessels was usually impregnated with Stockholm Tar as it was being laid up, and the amount of stretch per fathom which could be got in the Rigging House was known. This was not the case with the sisal being used for the post-war re-rigging of *Victory*, which, though treated with a preservative, was issued white and this not only affected the stretch and spring back of the rope but also added to the difficulty of providing suitable blacking which would penetrate but not injure the rope. The nature of the rope used greatly increased the difficulty of turning in the deadeyes and hearts. The throat and round seizings had to be constantly re-passed in order to get the hearts and deadeyes turned in really snug after a pull had been got upon the lanyards. There were over 450 of these seizings on the standing rigging alone, all of which had to be clapped on in a seamanlike way. For the Final Report on re-rigging *Victory*, see NMM Trustees' Minutes, 10 January 1949.

53   In 1954 the SNR's investments were valued at £6,080.

54   NMM SNR 2/59 Annual Report for 1969, Balance Sheet.

55   NMM SNR 4/26, statistical summary, 1911-1983.

56   NMM SNR 2/37 Annual Report for 1947, 17. The Victory Museum and Panorama Annexe Fund merged with the STVF in 1947.

57   NMM SNR 2/40 Annual Report for 1950.

58   *Mariner's Mirror,* 38:4 (1952), AGM of SNR, 1952.

59   *Mariner's Mi*rror, 39:4 (1953), AGM of SNR, 1953.

60   AGM of SNR, 1954, 8.

61   NMM Trustees' Minutes, 6 May 1948.

62   NMM Trustees' Minutes, 8 April 1946. A check of exhibits by *Victory's* CO revealed that three exhibition cases had been forced and a collection of coins and medals stolen. After a police investigation only three medals were recovered.

63   See STVF accounts for relevant years in NMM SNR 2/43–2/59.

64   See STVF accounts in NMM SNR 2/50–2/59.

65   NMM Trustees' Minutes, 11 October 1948; see also *Mariner's Mirror,* 35:4 (1949), AGM of SNR, 1949.

66   NMM SNR 2/56 Report of the Council for the Year 1956.

67   NMM SNR 7/29 Letter from Capt. Blamey, Office of C-in-C Portsmouth to George Naish, SNR Secretary, 16 July 1949.

68   NMM SNR 7/29 Letter from George Naish to Capt. Blamey, 22 July 1949.

69   NA ADM 1/22710. See memorandum from Sir John Lang to Viscount Hall, First Lord, 12 August 1949, para. 3. Pre-war entertainments appear to have been supplied with food from delivery vans in insulated containers.

70   NMM Trustees' Minutes, 8 April 1946; Trustees' Minutes 9 May 1957. The Ward Room would no longer be used and Capt. Hardy's quarters would also be restored and open to the public.

71   NMM, Trustees' Minutes, 8 April 1946. A naval officer visiting HMS *Victory* complained to Callender that he had been refused entry to Nelson's cabin. His indignation was aroused by

his knowledge that the public had subscribed for the ship's restoration, not the Navy Vote.

72   NMM SNR 7/29 Letter from Admiral Sir Algernon U. Willis to Admiral Sir Charles Little, 13 September 1948. The four Society representatives who visited Admiral Layton were, Sir George Hope, Sir Osmond Brock, Lord Catto and Sir Geoffrey Callender. See also, NMM, Trustees' Minutes, 28 October 1946. Delays in the reconstruction of Admiralty House meant that restricted access to HMS *Victory* would continue until 1950 or 1951.

73   NMM Trustees' Minutes, 24 June 1946. Damage had resulted from wartime storage in the Forts and careless treatment in transporting it back to the ship. Repairs might cost £200 or more. This would be charged to the STVF.

74   NA ADM 1/22710. See cover note by the Civil Engineer-in-Chief dated 8 June 1949.

75   *Ibid.* See Minutes of the Meeting. Lord Fraser of North Cape, who had been appointed C-in-C Portsmouth on 30 June 1947, became First Sea Lord and Chief of Naval Staff in 1948.

76   *Ibid.*, Lang to Viscount Hall, 12 August 1949. The 'late Commander-in-Chief's time' was during Lord Fraser's appointment as C-in-C Portsmouth from June 1947 to September 1948.

77   NA ADM 1/22710. Sir Algernon Willis's letters are noted for intemperate or 'politically incorrect' language. See also NMM SNR 7/31 Letter dated 5 January 1951 from L. Pughe to George Naish, Hon. Secretary of the SNR.

78   NMM SNR 7/31 Memorandum on HMS "Victory", 20 June 1950. For a detailed discussion on the furnishing of *Victory*'s cabins, see also the NMM Trustees' Minutes, 17 April 1950.

79   NMM SNR 7/31 Letter from Viscount Hall to Earl Stanhope dated 28 July 1950.

80   NMM Trustees' Minutes, 9 January 1951.

81   NMM SNR 7/31 Letter from L. Pughe to George Naish, Hon. Secretary of the SNR, 5 January 1951.

82   *Mariner's Mirror*, 39:4 (1953), AGM of SNR, 1953. The Committee of Experts comprised Frank Carr, Dr R. C. Fisher and Mr E. C. Harris of the Forest Products Research Laboratory, Dr H. J. Plenderleith of the Research Laboratory of the British Museum, and Dr H. Hay and Mr D. A. Mattinson of the Ministry of Works.

83   NMM SNR 2/56 Report of Council for the Year 1956, and AGM of SNR, 1956.

84   Littlewood and Butler, *Of Ships and Stars*, 141.

85   NMM Trustees' Minutes, 14 January 1954.

86   NMM SNR 3/4 Minutes of Council Meeting, 6 January 1954. See NA ADM 1/27660 Letter from Frank Carr to Sir John Lang, 5 March 1954.

87   See NMM Trustees' Minutes, 13 May 1954. Sir Victor Shepheard, Director of Naval Construction, sent a report from Mr W. J. Holt to the Trustees.

88   NA ADM 1/27660. Admiral Sir George Creasy to Sir John Lang, 10 January 1955. Creasy joined the navy in 1908 and had undoubtedly been in contact with Callender at Osborne.

89   NMM Trustees' Minutes, 20 July 1955, summarizing the VATC meeting on 30 June 1955.

90   McGowan, HMS Victory, *Her Construction, Career and Restoration*, 122–3.

91   NMM Trustees' Minutes, 10 March 1955.

92   NMM SNR 2/45 Report of the Council for the Year 1955. The composition of the VATC from 19 May 1955, was:
      Admiralty – the Director of Naval Construction, the Admiral-Superintendent Portsmouth, the Manager, Constructive Department, Portsmouth, and Dr R. C. Fisher of the Forest Products Research Laboratory;
      NMM – A. J. Villiers, Professor A.E. Richardson (Chair of VATC), J. N. Robertson of Lloyd's Register and Frank Carr;
      SNR – R. C. Anderson, Professor Michael Lewis, E. H. B. Boulton (a timber consultant), and George Naish.

Despite the Admiralty's preference for the SNR, Professor Sir Albert Richardson was a nominee of the NMM. After his death in 1964, the Admiralty ignored the SNR and approached Viscount Runciman as Chairman of the NMM Trustees to find a successor. Runciman nominated Sir Colin Anderson as Richardson's successor. See NMM Trustees' Minutes, 13 May 1964.

The VATC's current chairman is Jonathan Coad, who succeeded Dr Alan McGowan.

93 NA ADM 1/27660. Despite the Admiralty's generous press release, Sir John Lang was concerned that the VATC should be the sole provider of technical advice and wary lest the SNR should tell them how to spend the money!

94 Although originally designed (Hercules Linton) and built by the Dumbarton firm of Scott and Linton, the firm went bankrupt after building the hull, thus *Cutty Sark* 961 tons gross was completed by Denny Brothers' River Leven Shipyard at Dumbarton. Launched in 1869, the year the Suez Canal opened, to compete in the tea trade, *Cutty Sark* was already an anachronism. She was subsequently engaged in the wool trade from Australia until the 1890s when she was purchased by Portuguese interests and renamed *Ferreira*.

95 For this period, see, A. Platt, S. Waite and R. T. Sexton, 'The *Cutty Sark's* Second Keel and History as the *Ferreira*', *Mariner's Mirror* 95:1 (2009), 8–32.

96 *Mariner's Mirror*, 37:4 (1951), AGM of SNR,1951.

97 The ceremony took place on 28 May 1953.

98 Littlewood and Butler, *Of Ships and Stars*, 155.

99 NMM SNR 2/44 Report of the Council for the Year 1954.

100 NMM SNR 2/45 EGM of SNR, 12 October 1955.

101 NMM SNR 2/47 Report of the Council for the Year 1957 and AGM of SNR, 1957.

102 NMM SNR 2/48 Report of the Council for the Year 1958 and AGM of SNR, 1958.

103 NMM SNR 2/49 Report of the Council for the Year 1959 and AGM of SNR, 1959.

104 Michael Lewis, in turn, was replaced as Chairman by Alan Villiers.

105 NMM SNR 2/48 Report of the Council 1960, AGM of SNR, 1960. The total sum paid to Cdr Dorrien Smith from the Tresco Valhalla account was £792 13s 11d, of which £350 was received from the Carnegie Trust; £100 from the Dulverton Trust; £100 from the Drapers Company and £242 13s 11d, contributed by members of the Society and other interested parties.

106 The inaugural Eva G. R. Taylor Lecture was delivered at the Royal Geographical Society on 17 October 1960 by Dr Eric Axelson. The title was 'Henry the Navigator and the Sea Route to India'. The Royal Geographical Society accepted the trusteeship of the fund which amounted to around £600.

107 NMM SNR 2/51 Report of Council for the year 1961.

108 NMM SNR 2/52 Report of Council for the year 1962 and AGM of SNR, 1962.

109 NMM SNR 2/53 Report of Council for the year 1963 and AGM of SNR, 1963.

110 *Ibid.*

111 *Mariner's Mirror*, 50:3 (1964), AGM of SNR, 1964. Eric Custance was the manager of Lloyd's Bank in Blackheath Village, south-east London.

112 NMM Trustees' Minutes, 27 November 1964. The NMM decided to make no celebrations in the museum but some items were loaned to Chatham for display.

113 *Mariner's Mirror*, 51:4 (1965), AGM of SNR, 1965. On 1 January 1966, membership reached another record total of 1,434.

5
Doldrums and Squalls:
the Society from 1966 to 1985

The latter part of the 1960s was primarily a period of consolidation for the Society. Both investment income and membership numbers held up well and the Charity Commission granted a formal Certificate of Charitable Status for all the funds the Society administered.[1] However, the Society was facing the future without either the benefit of major financial backing, such as that provided by the late Sir James Caird, or the former political influence of Earl Stanhope, now in his mid-eighties. As the post-war boom in the economy waned, the lack of significant general funds not committed to specific purposes, restricted the Society's horizons. Thus, limited opportunities meant that the annual visit to HMS *Victory* in Portsmouth Dockyard was the only regular occasion that the Society moved its business from the London metropolitan area. As regards membership in the British Isles, Professor Michael Lewis noted in an editorial to *The Mariner's Mirror* in January 1966 that Northern England 'figures but indifferently, apart from 60 members in Lancashire and Cheshire'. Wales had only 16 private members and Scotland 30, with only one institutional member.[2] The reality was that, for the international membership in particular, *The Mariner's Mirror* was the Society; it served, as it had done since its inception, to inform and promote dialogue among members across the world and to sustain their loyalty. Throughout its history, despite a continuing increase in overseas subscriptions, which accounted for some 40 per cent of the membership in the 1960s, the Society remained essentially Anglocentric. Too often, Council and AGM rhetoric was couched in distinctly English terms. Moreover, despite the attempt to cloak the Royal Navy in British terms, HMS *Victory* remained essentially an English icon. All through its post-1918 history, the Society could be accused of being *Victory*-obsessed, not that the preservation of *Victory* and the aim of restoring her to her 1805 condition was not a worthy cause in itself, but simply because the Society's interwar successes allowed it to rest on its laurels in the post-war years.

Two of the Society's principal officers, Reginald Lowen and George Naish were distracted from SNR affairs by change at the NMM. Frank Carr, the NMM Director since 1947, had never been really in full control and was constantly undermined by Lowen and Naish, despite the steadying hand of Cdr May as Deputy Director. Moreover, by 1966, Carr's relationship with Lord Runciman, Stanhope's replacement as Chairman of Trustees, had deteriorated to the point that he was forced to retire a year earlier than he intended. Carr did not take the decision of the Trustees gladly as he suffered considerable financial loss in his pension arrangements. Carr's replacement as Director by Runciman's favoured candidate, Basil Greenhill, formerly British Deputy High Commissioner in East Pakistan, was officially announced on 5 August 1966. Before Carr retired on 22 December 1966, his final report to the Trustees expressed bitter regret that he had devoted the best years of his life to the museum. There had also been a rather unedifying and increasingly acrimonious correspondence in the national press between Carr and Greenhill. Thereafter, Carr refused to enter the museum until Greenhill retired in 1983. The Trustees then discussed the future of George Naish: in 1967 he was already sixty years of age but, in recognition of his service to the museum, he was promoted to the position of keeper, and in effect, second-in-command to Greenhill, depending on when May retired as Deputy Director.[3]

Exhibiting the SNR's achievements

W. L. Wyllie's *A Panorama of the Battle of Trafalgar* was returned from restoration in Manchester in March 1967, though the problem of temperature and humidity control continued to be investigated with a view to improving the conditions under which it was displayed in Portsmouth. An unusual application of the STVF, prompted by the Ministry of Defence (Navy), was the purchase of a portrait of Lord Nelson by the eighteenth-century English artist, Sir William Beechey, 'for the Nation' which would be hung in HMS *Victory*. The Government, because of 'the austere economic climate', felt unable to authorize its purchase from public funds.[4] The picture was obtained at a specially reduced price of £3,000 despite the interest of two American collectors of Nelson relics who were separately prepared to pay £10,000.

The Nelson exhibition in Japan

In the middle of 1967, the Society, the NMM and other bodies including Lloyd's Register received an unusual request from the Board of Trade and the Central Office of Information to lend exhibits for a Nelson Exhibition to take place in Japan. Two large department stores in Tokyo and Nagoya were prepared to make available a

Figure 24 George B. P. Naish (1909–77), the Society's Hon. Secretary, 1947–77. (© National Maritime Museum, Greenwich, London)

whole floor of their respective premises to house the exhibition. George Naish's immediate reaction, as Hon. Secretary, was one of horror that 'priceless items should be lent for what seemed to be undiluted commercialism'. The idea was backed by the British Embassy in Tokyo as a way of encouraging trade, but, according to Naish there was a 'deeper and more aesthetic reason which persuaded one that co-operation was justified'. This was due to:

The fact that Japan having been closed to the outside world for most of her history, the Japanese people had been starved of culture other than that of their

Figure 25 Basil Greenhill (1920–2003), Director of the National Maritime Museum, 1967–83 and a Vice-President of the Society. (© National Maritime Museum, Greenwich, London)

own indigenous variety. Thus, while she has an abundance of temples and shrines, and her own classic art there are few museums in the country covering other fields. Add to this the fact that the Japanese as a race thirst for more and more education in all spheres, the justification for loaning these items seems real enough.[5]

As expense did not seem to be a criterion, those items deemed necessary for the exhibition but which because of the potential hazards of a long sea journey could not be lent, were faithfully reproduced. For example, replicas were made of Nelson's

Great Cabin in *Victory*, Wyllie's *A Panorama of the Battle of Trafalgar* on a canvas 44 feet by 12 feet, and the display of 73 models of ships engaged at the Battle of Trafalgar made for the Prince Consort, were all reproduced down to the minutest detail. In the first week of the exhibition in Nagoya over 250,000 people attended. As Naish, who attended the exhibition for ten days at the invitation of the promoters, later noted, the Japanese:

> seemed to have a special place in their hearts for all things British, and for the Royal Navy in particular. Understandable perhaps, against the background that their own national hero, Admiral Togo (1848–1934), the victor of the Battle of Tsushima against the Russians at the beginning of the century, received his early training in Britain (1871–1878) and his flagship at the battle, the Mikasa, was built at Barrow-in-Furness. What it meant however was that there was an unlooked for bonus in permitting the exhibition in promoting Anglo-Japanese friendship.[6]

The Society Becalmed – 1968

During 1968, Lt Col A. J. L. Hughes, who had indexed *Mariner's Mirror* for the past fourteen years and who had kept all index cards since volume 40, retired from his voluntary annual labour. Mr W. O. B. Majer, a stalwart member of SNR South, stepped into the breach by volunteering to do the index work. It was also reported at the AGM that the Americans had their eye on the ss *Great Britain*, a unique record of Victorian engineering and shipbuilding skill, lying beached in the Falkland Islands. 'Certain persons', including Dr E. C. B. Corlett, a naval architect and salvage expert, wished to see her towed back to her home port of Bristol and replaced in the dock where she was built, to be exhibited as the very first ocean-going iron screw steamship of just under 3,000 tons. Richard Goold-Adams, a member of Council, spoke in favour of her return to Bristol and this received the general support of the meeting.[7]

The year 1969 saw the establishment of a small Symposium Account to handle funds for the various symposia the Society sponsored. At the AGM, the President, Michael Lewis, declared that he would serve only one more year in office. Unfortunately he did not see the year out and died at the age of 80. Elected as Chairman in 1951, and President since 1960, membership under Lewis's presidency had increased by more than 50 per cent: in June 1970, membership stood at over 1,600. The following year, the AGM faced a proposal to increase subscriptions from 1 January 1972. The Treasurer, Eric Custance noted that: 'Deeds of Covenant had more than doubled in the past six years, membership had increased by about 400 and Cambridge University Press have sold £300 of the Society's publications, but costs have overtaken us'. He asked that the individual subscription of 30s (£1.50p), be doubled to £3 and institutional subscriptions to £6. Professor Lewis was succeeded as President by Alan Villiers, who retired in 1974 and he, in turn, was succeeded by Rear-Admiral E. F. Gueritz.

The ss Great Britain *Project*

In the meantime, the Society had become more involved in the ss *Great Britain* Project. ss *Great Britain*, the first large ship to be built of iron; the first to possess watertight bulkheads and a double bottom, had been scuttled in Sparrow Cove near Port Stanley in the Falkland Islands since 1937.[8] The aim of the project was 'to bring back from the other side of the world, recondition and put on display the most historic modern ship in the world'. The Society's connexion (similar to its earlier association with *Implacable* and *Foudroyant*) was as fund stakeholder until the Project Committee launched its first appeal: it was not committed financially to the project.[9] The cost of salvage and towing *Great Britain* to the British Isles was put at £75,000 and the contract to return her to Bristol was given to Messrs. Risdon Beazley Ltd.[10] Richard Goold-Adams informed the 1970 AGM that he had spent 'one of the most exciting 48 hours of his life'. He was at Avonmouth when *Great Britain* 'magnificent in her rust' was towed in on her 300-foot pontoon, a scheme financed by Jack Hayward at a cost in the region of £150,000. SS *Great Britain* was taken off the pontoon and allowed to float on her own bottom before being towed upriver to dry-dock on 4 July 1970.[11] In January 1971 the Society handed over its custodianship of the Fund to ss *Great Britain* Trading Co. Ltd. and ss *Great Britain* Project Ltd, and the Society was indemnified against any liability.

The Portsmouth Block Mills

On New Year's Day 1969 the Society's President, Alan Villiers, had received a letter from the Admiral Superintendent, Portsmouth, Rear-Admiral A. M. Power MBE, suggesting that the Marc Brunel-designed Block Mills within the Dockyard be converted to a museum. Admiral Power understood from private conversations that the Society might be interested. On 8 January the SNR Council met to consider Power's suggestion and agreed with it.[12] The Block Mills were erected in 1800 to house machinery designed by Henry Maudsley to manufacture wooden blocks for the Royal Navy. The machines worked continuously from 1806 to 1968 when the Mills were closed down and the machines partially dispersed. The building had been designated as an ancient monument and it now became the Society's aim to restore the Mills to their original condition and replace the machinery which could be

Figure 26 Capt. Alan J. Villiers (1903–82), Chairman of Council, 1960–70 and President of the Society, 1970–74. This picture was taken on a sailing craft in the Indian Ocean in the late 1930s. (© National Maritime Museum, Greenwich, London)

recovered. A committee was subsequently formed representing the Society, the Director of the Science Museum, which had acquired eight pieces of machinery, the Director of the NMM, the City of Portsmouth and the Inspectorate of Ancient Monuments. The Admiral Superintendent would negotiate between the Society and MoD (N) to formalize the foundation of a separate museum in the Dockyard recording advances in dockyard technology as promoted by the Royal Navy.[13] By April 1969 the Society had accepted in principle taking over the Block Mills, the ultimate objective being to reconstruct them. As Admiral Power was anxious to hand over the mills as soon as possible; the Society decided to utilize the Victory Museum Walker Bequest to meet certain expenses. The aim was to retain the block-making machinery not yet removed together with its overhead power-transmission mechanism, including the shafts, gears and counterweights, but the Society was not in a hurry to open a museum.[14] The background to this state of affairs was that in February 1968 the Ministry of Public Works and Buildings had reported to the Admiral Superintendent that there were practical difficulties which would prevent the redevelopment of the Block Mills. The walls were structurally unfit to take new internal floors and loading for modern workshop use. The structural problems were further complicated by the fact that the buildings were erected over the original 1691 ship basin on two-tier brick vaults, the lower of which formed a reservoir for draining nearby docks. This eventually led to the closure of the Block Mills and dispersal of the machinery. However, as the Ministry of Public Works were unlikely to agree to demolition, the suggestion of an industrial museum was made.[15] By the middle of 1969, uncertainty remained over the structural integrity of the Block Mills. The decision on the Block Mills remained in abeyance into the 1970s as the Department of the Environment could not find the £25,000 needed for the fabric of the building.[16] In the end the problems surrounding the project proved insurmountable and it was abandoned.

The Macpherson Collection Endowment Fund

In March 1971, an important change in the provision of the Macpherson Fund was agreed. Before the Second World War, Mr A. G. H. Macpherson had amassed a collection of marine art, which he wished to sell and the Society launched a public appeal for it to be saved for the Nation. This appeal was in danger of sinking without trace in the late 1920s, until Sir James Caird stepped in and purchased the entire collection for the future NMM. No Deed of Gift, or Trust Deed or other governing instrument underpinned the Macpherson Fund. Sir James Caird disregarded the money collected from the public towards the purchase of the collection and it was left on deposit and administered by the SNR. However, it was long established that income from the residue of the fund should be used to augment the existing Macpherson Collection.

That was the theory, but in practice, Sir Geoffrey Callender, Reginald Lowen, Frank Carr and later Basil Greenhill – who did not want the NMM to become an art gallery – used the Fund as they liked. Callender, for example, used it to pay for the planting of shrubs in the museum grounds – the Society's auditor, Capt. Bosanquet, objected to this but Callender ignored him, and it was just after a meeting with Bosanquet and Lowen to discuss such a matter that Callender died. Greenhill used the Macpherson Fund to meet the cost of various symposia drawing on it to pay for the travel and other expenses of overseas contributors to NMM conferences. In so doing he ignored the SNR Symposium Committee he had set up and chaired. George Naish, the Society's Hon. Secretary who was employed at the NMM, had told Greenhill that the Council could use the Macpherson Fund pretty much as it liked for 'nautical research'. By 1971 the situation was that the Macpherson Fund income was spent at the NMM Director's discretion after funds had been passed from the SNR.[17]

A change in apportioning the Macpherson Fund was introduced in 1971 because of the Society's lack of general funds. The nautical archaeology membership within the SNR's Council wanted to aid projects such as the surveying of the Tudor warship *Mary Rose* in the Solent and the investigation of the Marsala Punic ship in Sicily. To this end it was suggested in Council that some of the income of the Macpherson Fund be used for nautical research purposes other than those of the NMM. It was agreed that the Society's President would talk to the Director and Trustees of the NMM at their next meeting. After some discussion, it was decided that the *Mary Rose* Project would materially benefit from assistance and £250 was allocated to it from the Macpherson Fund.[18]

Clearly, by their past misuse of the Macpherson Fund, the NMM was hardly in a position to object to the wider interpretation of its objects. By February 1972, Alan Villiers, the President, explained that the NMM Trustees had agreed to accept half the income from the Macpherson Fund on a yearly basis and that the other half could be used by the SNR, including the provision of a Cumulative Index for *The Mariner's Mirror* after volume 35.[19] This extended use of the Macpherson Fund for purposes other than its original objects was indicative of the Society's desire to fund research initiatives but that it lacked the money to do so otherwise.

The Marsala Punic Ship

In March 1972, Honor Frost requested assistance from the Macpherson Fund towards the expenses of her 1972 season expedition to excavate the wreck of a Punic ship off the northern shore of Isola Lunga on the west coast of Sicily. This ship subsequently became known as the Marsala Punic ship. Indeed, this was the first time such a ship had been discovered, and in view of the fact that Punic ships had been considered to have been the models for Roman ships the discovery was, in terms of nautical archaeology and history generally, of the greatest importance. Dated by its pottery to the third century BC, the ship was in a remarkable state of preservation, the wood having retained not only its original colour but also the signs and guide lines incised or painted upon it initially by the Punic shipwrights. The Council agreed to use the Macpherson Fund to give Ms Frost £250 and a further £250 was allocated to the *Mary Rose* Project in the Solent, which was still at the investigation stage.[20]

Later, Honor Frost reminded Council that the reconstructed ship had been abandoned in a dilapidated building since 1978 and there had followed 'three years of expostulation'. She had recently tackled the Mayor of Marsala pointing out a deadline, after the New Year, after which she would have to disband her team, and saying that if the ship perished 'it would be a lasting disgrace to the town'. The Mayor had subsequently given an interview to the Sicilian press and Frost was told that she could 'tranquilly proceed' as repairs were starting. On checking the situation Ms Frost found that there were no workmen in the building and 'evidently no intention of putting them there'. However, an architect from Milan had been commissioned to deal with the matter. By March 1981 the unstable situation regarding the housing of the Marsala Punic Ship had apparently been resolved. Ms Frost intimated that she would travel to Marsala in April to ascertain the current situation regarding the ship.[21] This episode left the SNR in no doubt that it would be unwise to support any projects outside British waters.

A Royal Naval Museum, Portsmouth

On 11 January 1972, the C-in-C Portsmouth, Admiral Sir Horace Law, sent a memorandum to the Society on the future administration of the Victory Museum, having discussed it in very broad terms with the President, Alan Villiers:

> 1. An American lady, Mrs J. G. McCarthy, OBE, the daughter of Paul Mellon, the noted American art collector, had a rare and expensive collection of Nelsonia, and has offered it on permanent loan to the Royal Navy. The Admiralty Board had agreed to make available part of No. 11 Store, abutting the Victory Arena, to exhibit this collection. Work was already in hand to convert this space for a Museum and it was intended to hold the opening ceremony on 4 May 1972.
> 2. The Submarine Museum was in poor accommodation in HMS *Dolphin*, which was not easily accessible to the general public. The museum had to be re-sited when some new building took place in HMS *Dolphin*. The Trustees believed that it should be moved to Portsmouth where it could be seen by more people.
> 3. With nearly half a million visitors to HMS *Victory* each year, there should be a 'Modern Navy' exhibition for them to see as well as the best of the past.

Admiral Law went on to note, 'I believe that such a Royal Naval Museum complex would be incoherent and incomplete were the Victory Museum not to form a part of it. Furthermore, I believe that the Society would have much to gain by their Museum being "recognized" officially'. In expectation of the Society's support for such a scheme, Law further informed the SNR Council that in anticipation of Council's agreement, he had approached the Admiralty Board proposing that the three new elements mentioned above should, with the Victory Museum, be formed into a Royal Naval Museum complex. The Admiralty Board had welcomed the concept in principle and awaited the outcome of discussions thereon between Admiral Law and the Society. Quite unreasonably, Law requested the Society's decision within a matter of days by 1 February 1972.[22]

In an annex to his memorandum, Law anticipated some of the questions that may have concerned the Society. The location of the new museum would be on the ground floor of Nos 9, 10 and 11 Stores, which led up to the Victory Arena, plus the present Victory Museum. Official 'recognition' meant that MoD (N) would be responsible for staffing and maintaining the new museum and providing services, for example, electricity, and telephones. To ensure that interest in the project would not lapse, as had happened with other museums in the past, there would be a Board of Trustees, representing the Secretary of State MoD (N), the C-in-C Naval Home Command, the Port Admiral, Portsmouth, the SNR, the NMM, Mrs McCarthy (during her lifetime), and the Trustees of the Submarine Museum. Drawn from the Trustees would be an Executive Committee to deal with routine matters. On the question of who would 'own' the items presently exhibited in the Victory Museum, over 40 per cent of which were naval trophies on loan, with the remainder being straightforward acquisitions, mostly through the STVF, or gifts by donors, Law proposed that both should be combined and vested as the property of the new Board of Trustees. On staffing, Admiral Law suggested that a civilian complement should be engaged but the 'Modern Navy' part of the exhibition should be staffed by active service personnel, as part of HMS Victory's Ship's Company. Law also suggested that if the proposals were accepted, the curator of the Victory Museum, Captain Pack, should be put in overall charge of the museum complex, with special responsibility for planning its future development. Moreover, he would be able to ensure that the present Victory Museum's interests and development were continued. Capt. Pack would report to the Board of Trustees. On the question of admission charges, Law would resist any suggestion that the public should be charged to look over his flagship, however it would be more economic in terms of staff and more acceptable to visitors to make one charge to cover the entire museum, with moneys being used by the Trustees for acquisitions and to aid the development of the museum. As to the STVF, the fund would no longer be used to defray the cost of salaries and services. Voluntary contributions from the bookstall should continue to be used for the benefit of HMS Victory, and the Walker Bequest should be transferred to the new Trustees for a similar purpose. Law noted that if the Society did not wish to enter this arrangement then it would be invidious to have two separate museums, staffed to different standards. Furthermore, a Navy Department Complement Review Team had frowned on the present practice whereby ratings from HMS Victory were loaned to the Victory Museum. Admiral Law believed that the formation of a Board of Trustees with a suitable Trust Deed would preserve the independence of the museum, and that it was important to strike while the whole idea of a Portsmouth Royal Naval Museum was to the fore.[23]

The SNR Council considered Admiral Law's memorandum at a meeting in February 1972 and decided that it must agree with the C-in-C's wishes. However, the Society's Trustees would have to take legal advice before handing over the Walker Bequest to any other body.[24] Subsequently, by July 1972, the Society had agreed with

Law's initial proposals and the new C-in-C Portsmouth from 15 May 1972, Admiral Andrew Lewis, informed the Society that the Admiralty Board had agreed that the Victory Museum and McCarthy Collection should be combined. This cleared the way to create the nucleus of the combined museum to be called the 'The Portsmouth Royal Naval Museum' (PRNM). Accordingly, the Treasury Solicitor had been asked to put in hand the preparation of a Trust Deed for the establishment of the museum, and the appointment of a Board of Trustees to manage it, including three representatives from the Society. As the transfer of Mrs McCarthy's collection still had to undergo various legal formalities, Admiral Lewis proposed that it and the Victory Museum should be run in conjunction without waiting for the establishment of the Trust Deed. From 25 August 1972 the employment of the curator of the Victory Museum should be taken over by MoD (N) and paid for by public funds as part of the revised complement of the proposed combined museum. With effect from the same date, an admission fee should be charged for the combined museum at a level of 10p (2s) for adults and 5p (1s) for children.[25]

It remained for the Society to agree to the Trust Deed establishing the new Naval Museum and to transfer the Walker Bequest to it. By October 1973 the Society's Trustees had signed away the Victory Museum, but remained in control of the Walker Bequest, until it was handed over. On 6 December 1973 the Society's Chairman, Helen Wallis, the Hon. Secretary, George Naish and the Hon. Treasurer Eric Custance attended the first meeting of the Trustees of the PRNM in the Signal Tower, Portsmouth.[26] In the Chair was the Under Secretary of State for the Royal Navy, Mr Anthony Buck, MP. At this meeting an Executive Committee to handle the day-to-day running of the museum was appointed and was chaired by the Port Admiral, Rear-Admiral S. L. McArdle. Other members included Capt. Pack as the new Director of the museum.[27]

It was agreed that trading activities and therefore the profit at present wholly accruing to the STVF should in effect be diverted to the PRNM Trustees, who would apportion the profit:

1. to the SNR for STVF, broadly in line with its recent contributions for work on the ship;
2. for development of the PRNM;
3. to provide an Accession Fund for the PRNM;
4. to the Trafalgar Day Orphans' Fund as at present.

Thus the STVF remained under the Society's control, but it was agreed by the SNR representatives that the Society should offer, say, £20,000 to £30,000 per annum, for repairs to *Victory*, being the excellent profits made recently by the Society's Business Manager, Lt Cdr Pearce. This would enable the MoD (N), to hand over a similar sum to the PRNM. It was pointed out that were the MoD (N) to receive these funds they would have to go via the Treasury who well might not and – if history was any guide – would not release them in the required manner. Given this, it was then considered that since the Society had now three Trustees on the new PRNM Board, could they not transfer moneys direct? The SNR representatives did not commit the Society; instead they said that they would consult the SNR Trustees and Council on 16 January 1974. However, at the PRNM Meeting, the Society's representatives became irritated by the Director, Capt. Pack. He had written that, in relation to the Victory Museum, conservation had been a much neglected field in the past and that the new PRNM was severely handicapped by not yet having any funds. Helen Wallis took umbrage at the first charge and Eric Custance pointed out that the Society had offered the Walker Bequest months ago. In any event, the SNR had agreed that it would provide an Acquisitions Fund from the annual income of the Bequest amounting to some £1,490. Capt. Pack, nevertheless, had a point. He could have also mentioned the historically low level of staffing under SNR auspices at the Victory Museum, but declined to do so.[28]

At the January 1974 Council Meeting, it was agreed to transfer £20,000 immediately from the STVF to the PRNM, so that work could commence on building a shop for the new museum, and that the sum might rise to £30,000 if necessary. Eric Custance pointed out that this gift would not upset investments, as the Society had £36,000 in a deposit account. It was also proposed and accepted to raise the salary of the Business Manager, Lt Cdr Pearce, to £150 per annum.[29] Subsequently, the PRMN Trustees agreed to build a museum shop, to pay the fees of an architect and to engage a solicitor to undertake the incorporation of the new trading company; all to be paid for by the grant of £20,000 from the SNR. The Admiralty Board, however, wishing to avoid any hint of a subsidy from public funds to the proposed trading company, whose activities were the responsibility of the SNR, gave their approval on the understanding that the Trustees would meet the entire capital cost of converting No. 9 Storehouse to accommodate the new shop, and that the proposed trading scheme would be largely self-supporting.[30] By April 1974, the Walker Bequest had finally been handed over by the Society to the PRNM Trustees, with the Hon. Treasurer, Eric Custance, remaining a Trustee of the Bequest.[31]

The Mariner's Mirror

During the 1960s, all advertisements in *The Mariner's Mirror* became the responsibility of Cambridge University Press at more realistic commercial rates; and as of 1 January 1967 all subscriptions of members in the USA and Canada were raised from $4.30 to $5.[32] That year an agreement was signed with Messrs Kraus of

Liechtenstein to reprint volumes of *The Mariner's Mirror* from 1 to 35. Volume 57:4 (1971) under the editorship of Capt. T. Davys Manning was the last issue of *The Mariner's Mirror* to be printed and published by Cambridge University Press. Capt. Manning had increasingly been beset by illness and by March 1971 was in a Nursing Home. By the next issue, volume 58:1 (1972), which was printed by Staples and Co., of St Albans, Capt. Manning had died. He was succeeded as Hon. Editor by Professor Christopher Lloyd, who stepped down as Chairman to be replaced temporarily by Helen Wallis, with Brian Dolley becoming Assistant Editor.[33]

At the June 1973 AGM of the Society, the Hon. Editor, Professor Lloyd, complained that over half the contributions for *The Mariner's Mirror* came from the United States. Musing that perhaps the Society might take this as a compliment, he noted that home members could usefully look to their laurels. The last three issues of the journal each had 128 pages but the May issue had 136; however rising prices would probably result in a reduction in the number of pages. The Society's Business Manager at Portsmouth Dockyard, Lt Cdr Pearce, reminded members that he held 'a vast and heavy stock of old *Mariner's Mirrors*. As it was they went all over the world, but he had had to move 10,000 back numbers of the journal seven times and would like to ease the weight off the floors of his present office in the Dockyard'.[34]

Printing costs for *The Mariner's Mirror* continued to give cause for concern. Table 1 shows that the journal had cost just over £4,000 to produce in 1968 but more than double that amount in 1973.[35] This, of course, mirrored the general inflationary conditions prevalent in the national economy but it meant that from 1968 to 1973 the Society's subscription income had fallen well below the publication and distribution costs of its journal, even though the subscription rate had doubled in 1972. By 1974, economies in the production of the journal, including a significant reduction in the number of pages, brought production costs down to just over £5,000, well below subscription income of over £7,600. Unfortunately, the additional cost of printing the

Table 1: SNR income and the costs of producing *The Mariner's Mirror* 1968–75

Year	Annual subscription rate (£)	Subscription income (£)	Total income (£)	Printing and distribution expenditure (£)	Surplus or loss on publications (£)	Journal size in pages/ year (pages)
1968	1.50	2,541	4,947	4,023	924	394
1969	1.50	2,735	5,486	4,674	812	432
1970	1.50	2,891	5,999	5,602	397	474
1971	1.50	2,915	6,343	6,200	143	471
1972	3.00	6,762	8,578	7,050	1,528	486
1973	3.00	7,432	10,423	8,700	1,732	474
1974	3.00	7,639	10,993	5,068	2,571	454

Cumulative Index for *The Mariner's Mirror*, as well as the reprinting of occasional booklets, meant that the true publication outlay for 1974 was £3,613 more than subscription income. According to the Hon. Treasurer, Eric Custance, the Society would just about scrape through 1975 financially, but membership numbers needed to increase and subscriptions would soon have to be raised again.[36]

The Portsmouth Royal Naval Museum Trading Company

During the mid-1970s, the success of the shop on board HMS *Victory* and the new shop ashore raised problems for the Society. The Society had appointed Lt Cdr Pearce as Business Manager for both shops and the return on their investment was regularly producing £5,000 a year which went to the STVF. In April 1975, the SNR Council sought the opinion of the Charity Commissioners on the probity of these activities given the SNR Trustees' responsibility to administer the STVF and keep it in a healthy state, but bearing in mind the Charity Commission's requirement that charities should not trade.[37]

The SNR Council therefore proposed to transfer the sale of souvenirs to the Trustees of the PRNM. They, in turn, would form the Portsmouth Royal Naval Museum Trading Company Ltd (PRNMTC) to handle sales. All its profits would be covenanted to the Trustees of the PRNM, which would distribute them to:

1. The STVF – in about the same proportions as had over the last 10 to 15 years been put into the ship (i.e. £5,000 p.a.) but adjusted to 1975 prices by use of Government statistics OR 10 per cent of those profits, whichever was the greater;
2. PRNM for an acquisitions fund;
3. Trafalgar Day Orphans Fund (about £3,000 p.a.);
4. Development of PRNM.

A degree of conflict arose between the expectations of the Trustees of the PRNM and the desire of the SNR to protect its income for the STVF. By September 1975, the PRNM Trustees, although nominally including the SNR's Chairman, Hon. Treasurer and Hon. Secretary, came to expect the free transfer from the STVF of the shops' stock and working capital in return for the annual share of the profits for the foreseeable future. The Society's Hon. Treasurer, Eric Custance, who was the only SNR representative at this meeting, resisted this proposal strongly, insisting that the transfer of a business involved payment for the assets transferred.

When this became known, one member of the SNR Council, Major-General Michael Prynne CB, CBE, wrote to the Hon. Secretary, George Naish, noting that:

Our first task – which has nothing to do with the PRNM – is to ensure that the source of funds which souvenir sales have provided to the STVF is not jeopardized.

General Prynne had little confidence that future MoD (N) policy would provide adequately for HMS *Victory*'s maintenance without substantial contributions from the STVF. Furthermore, Prynne had long thought that more could be done about *Victory* (which would mean more money) 'especially if one day she ceased to be a fancy-dress office and can truly be restored to being a Trafalgar fighting ship'. Prynne strongly shared Eric Custance's fears that should the Souvenir Stall's sales fall under Civil Service administration, 'it would go the way of all "nationalized industries" – and become both inefficient and loss-making'. Prynne was thus fundamentally opposed to any transfer but, if such transpired, the STVF 'must be thoroughly and adequately safeguarded'. Prynne thought that the free transfer of assets 'seemed a remarkably impudent suggestion'. To him the physical assets (shop and stall) had been 'bought with money subscribed to, and which would otherwise have gone to, the STVF', so that, 'it would therefore be entirely wrong to transfer the capital in exchange for an undertaking with regard to the distribution of part of the profit of its sale'. Prynne did not think that the PRNM Trustees would 'part with a car on this basis. They must think that we are mad'. He then expressed the opinion that 'phased deferred repayment, provided that it could be ensured, might be more satisfactory . . . and should not be departed from' as it seemed to be in line with the advice of the Charity Commissioners.

Underpinning General Prynne's opposition to the assets and goodwill of the Souvenir Sales being transferred to another organization was the legal doctrine of *cy près*. He noted that:

> The STVF is used to restore an old ship (the first restoration on this scale in the world). If the needs of Victory fall short of the means available, the nearest aim would be the restoration of other old ships, not the financing of an organiz-ation with different aims. The Society for Nautical Research would be highly culpable if, under considerable but eminently resistible pressure, it disposes of one of its greatest assets, its ability to maintain a fund (the STVF) which fulfils its own stated object.[38]

At the SNR Council Meeting on 29 October 1975, the matter of the PRNMTC's relationship with the STVF was discussed. A resolution was put to the meeting that:

> The Trustees of the Society, as custodians of the STVF, be requested to transfer to the Trustees of the PRNM the stock of the STVF shop, on board and ashore, in toto or in a series of blocks as may be agreed, and conditional on the following terms:
> 1. Trustees of the PRNM to be responsible for deferred payments to the STVF of the value of the stocks transferred as assessed on 31 December 1975, by

instalments calculated to effect payment in full in the shortest possible time over a maximum of ten years and at a minimum rate of £7,000 per annum, such payments to be a charge against the gross profits, Value Added Tax at current rates if assessed being payable as a separate item by the Trustees of the PRNM on the transfer date.

2. That the Trustees of the PRNM will pay to the Society for the STVF an annual sum hereinafter defined as £5,000 or such a sum as shall be equivalent in purchasing value of £5,000 on 31 December 1975 calculated in accordance with Government statistics, or a third of the net disposable trading profits, whichever is the lesser.

3. That the [present] Business Manager be engaged by the new Trading Company on terms not less advantageous than those currently conferred upon him by his engagement by the STVF and so that no redundancy liability lies against that Fund or the SNR.

When the resolution was put to Council and discussed at length, only General Prynne thought that the proposal should be dropped, but Eric Custance reminded him that MoD (N) could terminate the agreement that the Society could trade on the ship at three months' notice. After discussion, the Society's President, Chairman, and three Trustees signified that they were in favour of the resolution. It was then put to the vote with only Prynne voting against the motion.[39] Subsequently, on 2 June 1976, the PRNMTC was at last incorporated as a private limited company by guarantee with no share capital.[40]

Continuing Work on HMS Victory

HMS *Victory* faced the constant problem of infestation by death-watch beetle. However, this did not cause undue alarm, with the situation being monitored closely by Mr Baker of the Forest Research Laboratory. Moreover, one man was now employed on full-time beetle watch.[41] The Wellcome Foundation donated a new insecticide to overcome the death-watch beetle problem and this was used in an experimental way. Counting death-watch beetles during the mating season continued with numbers rising from 276 in 1975 to 1,301 in 1976 and 1,771 in 1977. An instance had occurred of beetles even scoring healthy *lignum vitae*.

In 1966, for the third time in a decade, the STVF donated funds to purchase another batch of teak worth £10,000 for HMS *Victory*'s preservation.[42] The restoration work on *Victory* was more visible in the 1970s than in the previous decade in view of the near disastrous fire on board in 1973. From the moment the fire started in the cavity between the ship's double hull, the shipwrights and firemen raced against time to stop the smouldering fire spreading along the whole length of the hull. Smoke was so dense firemen had to wear breathing apparatus. After one hour's fire-fighting, a crucial stage was reached when the fire appeared to worsen and a call went out for the city's turntable ladder. From this the shipwrights could reach the outside of the hull to cut away part of the oak planking, enabling firemen to direct water into the cavity. This was the turning point and the fire was soon controlled, leading to the headline in Portsmouth's *The News*: 'After two-hour fire battle: Victory is ours'.[43] In the course of 1974 the Great Cabin on *Victory* was stripped and the Captain's cabin turned into a copy of the Great Cabin. The ward-room was also stripped and extensive repairs carried out. The Admiral's Great Cabin was moved down a deck into the wardroom before it could be returned to its proper place. The Society hoped that in due course the wardroom would be restored to its Trafalgar condition and offered to pay for it through the STVF.[44] During 1977, the refit of the main mast was completed but the mizen had since been undressed, with the topgallant and top masts struck, so as to fit in with the current major recon-struction work on the stern which was concentrated on the Admiral's Great Cabin and the Captain's Cabin under the poop.[45] By January 1978, Lt Cdr Whitlock reported that the restoration of the Great Cabin on *Victory* would probably be completed by the autumn. With hemp no longer available, the VATC agreed to the mizen being dressed in grade one manilla. However, certain ropes would be made of black polypropylene to assess the effect of air pollution: this material had already been used successfully on the USS *Constitution*, which remained afloat berthed in Boston, USA. By 1979 the VATC had approved the use of staple polypropylene for all future rigging on *Victory*. This material had a higher initial cost than manilla but had a considerably longer lifespan.

The major works on HMS *Victory*, facilitated by a grant of £10,000 from the STVF for the work in the Great Cabin were completed by October 1978 in time for the Trafalgar Night Dinner, and a new bus for *Victory's* crew was purchased for £4,250.[46] However, the portrait of Lord Nelson bought in 1967 to hang in *Victory* proved to be a copy and the insurance premium was reduced accordingly.[47]

The CO of HMS *Victory* reported that during the year 1976 475,300 visitors had visited the ship, an increase of over 52,000 on the previous year; and that an experiment with a guide operating a tape recorder with the commentary in French had proved so successful that a commentary in German would shortly be ready.

Carrying the Society Forward into the 1980s

On 12 March 1974, Alan Villiers wrote to the new Chairman of Trustees of the NMM, Admiral Sir Charles Madden, expressing disquiet that the Society's office in the museum was to be taken over for other purposes due to the museum's lack of office space. The occasion for this letter was the retirement of George Naish from the staff of the NMM. The Director, Basil Greenhill, later to become a Vice-President of the SNR, had refused to reconsider the Society's request to retain its presence in the museum. Villiers pointed out that, since its foundation, the museum had been the effective centre of the Society, from which many of the museum's senior officers were drawn. Indeed, for practical purposes, it had been the Society's headquarters. The Society would find it difficult to rent an office in or around London because of the cost implications.[48] No discussion of these matters can be found in Council minutes though Naish remained Hon. Secretary until 1977, but it is evident that the relationship between the Society and the museum was under strain.[49]

In October 1974, Rear-Admiral Gueritz was elected to the presidency of the Society and he recorded the Council's appreciation of Alan Villiers' services to the Society first as Chairman and later President from 1970 to 1974.[50] Much of 1975 was taken up with discussions regarding the Society's relationship to the new PRNM and its associated trading company. The Society also lost a number of distinguished members including, in 1976, the last founder member, the author and historian, thrice Hon. Editor of *The Mariner's Mirror* and Chairman of the Trustees of the NMM, R. C. Anderson. Cost increases again preoccupied Council deliberations, and the fact that the Post Office's postal charges took nearly 20 per cent of the annual subscription income in the United Kingdom, led to the Society arranging for all overseas copies of *The Mariner's Mirror* to be posted in Limerick, Eire. At the beginning of the year the decision was also taken to raise subscription levels for individuals from £3 to £5 and for institutions from £5 to £7.50.[51]

At the AGM in August 1977, the continuing saga of the non-production of a nautical encyclopedia or dictionary took another turn when yet a further sub-committee, this time under the chairmanship of General Prynne, was asked to examine and report on the matter. Again, subscriptions were not enough to meet the costs of production of *The Mariner's Mirror*, with the shortfall met by other sources of income. However, there had been a welcome increase in those members covenanting their subscriptions and the number now stood at 550. Moreover, the Society's investment income had risen to £1,532. Crucially, with the Royal Naval Museum Trading Company commencing business on 2 June 1976, the Trading Company had covenanted £5,000 per annum out of its profit to the STVF.

Captain R. S. Clement Brown, reporting on the training activities of the Foudroyant Trust, noted that 1976 had been a very successful year despite a sand dredger colliding with the ship – the entire cost of which was met by the dredger's insurers. Richard Goold-Adams reporting on the ss *Great Britain* project noted that the number of visitors to the ship was increasing steadily and in June 1977 stood at

130,000 per annum.[52] He added that as soon as funds were raised work would begin on the decking. It emerged that despite handing over the ss *Great Britain* accounts in 1971, the SNR had unofficially retained an interest in the project. The Hon. Treasurer, Eric Custance, had continued to be 'heavily involved in ss Great Britain'. Recalling events later, Helen Wallis wrote:

> In late 1977 Council became aware that, without their authority, SNR was paying all ss GB's postal charges (and possibly other ss GB expenses). In the subsequent, but deliberately unpublicized furore all connection with ss GB was cut, and Eric Custance resigned as Hon Treasurer. There was not, as far as we knew, any formal ss GB fund run by the SNR.[53]

On 30 July 1977, the Society's Hon. Secretary since 1947, George Naish, died. A memorial service was held on 22 September in the Chapel of the Royal Naval College, Greenwich. Naish was succeeded by another NMM employee, Philip Annis, FSA.

During 1976, the Society established a sub-committee of the Council to serve as an Executive Committee. It began meeting in 1977. Its membership comprised the Officers and Trustees of the Society, together with any co-opted members, and considered, *inter alia*, applications for grants in order to make appropriate recommendations to the quarterly Council Meetings. The Council noted with relief that the rise in subscriptions in the previous year had not caused many resignations and that income had just matched the printing costs of *The Mariner's Mirror*. The death of George Naish occasioned several changes in the representation of the Society on the Board of Trustees of the PRNM and on the Executive Committee of the Portsmouth Royal Naval Museum. The new Hon. Secretary, Philip Annis, joined the Chairman and Hon. Treasurer as Trustees, and Mr Basil Bathe, a Vice-President, did likewise on the Executive Committee. Lt Cdr Pearce, the Business Manager of the Royal Naval Museum Trading Company Ltd., reported a record year for profits from the two souvenir shops and the Victory Buffet.[54]

Importantly, at the Society's AGM in June 1978, Admiral Gueritz asked the membership to endorse three lines of action recommended by Council as being of the greatest relevance and importance to its aims. These were:

> 1. The Society should give its moral support and, whenever possible, its financial backing to enterprises intended to explore, to preserve or to present elements of our maritime history;
> 2. To play a full part in the development of co-ordinated action for the creation of adequate resources in skills as well as money to preserve ships and craft and to develop maritime history centres;

3. To join actively in the co-ordination of advice and encouragement to legislators, nationally and internationally, on matters which affect the preservation of our maritime heritage.[55]

No one cavilled at these worthy aims: but the likelihood of the Society advancing cash to other groups in significant amounts – something it had always avoided in the past given its limited financial resources – did not come under any serious scrutiny; neither did the continued Anglocentric parochialism implicit in its limited aims. Later in the year Philip Annis resigned as Hon. Secretary to take up the post of Deputy Director of the NMM. He was succeeded by yet another museum employee, John Munday, its Head of the Department of Weapons and Antiquities. The Society's Treasurer, Eric Custance, retired with his wife to Ludlow in Shropshire, and was replaced by the former CO of *Victory*, Lt Cdr Peter Whitlock. By the Society's AGM of 1979, Professor Christopher Lloyd had retired as Hon. Editor and was made a Vice-President of the Society; he was replaced by Brian Dolley who was also Company Secretary of the PRNMTC. Such was the pressure on the Society's financial position that new subscription rates for *The Mariner's Mirror* had been agreed for 1980 with ordinary membership doubling from £5 to £10 and institutional membership likewise to £15. This reflected a large rise in production costs: *The Mariner's Mirror* had cost over £16,000 in 1978, which was an increase of £2,000 on the previous year and in 1979, the cost was expected to be approximately £20,000.[56] The year 1979 also witnessed the bicentenary of the commissioning of *Victory*. To mark it, a party of seamen and Royal Marines in modern and in period dress walked from the site of the old single dock at Chatham to Portsmouth via the Pilgrim's Way and the Downs. A birthday cake with 200 candles was ceremonially cut with a cutlass by the C-in-C Portsmouth.[57]

On forwarding yet another sizable (£10,000) cheque in 1979 for re-rigging HMS *Victory* in polypropylene, Gueritz had written to the MoD (N) stating that:

> There had never been a time when it was more important for the maritime interests of the country to be properly served by the education of the young and the development of amenities and facilities which support not only the young, but also the more mature members of the population as well.[58]

Not surprisingly, given the notoriously short attention span of ministers, Gueritz received no response to this plea but, undeterred, proposed to pursue it with the new Conservative government on two fronts. One was on maritime history centres of which Greenwich and Portsmouth were examples; and the other was in the matter of cadet organizations. The rationale for the latter was that there should be some movement towards attracting younger members.[59] Little did Gueritz realize that the

Conservative Governments from 1979 onwards led by Margaret Thatcher, and her successor John Major, would preside over the almost complete destruction of Britain's maritime industries under withering international competition, management ineptitude, trade union intransigence and government short-sightedness on a colossal scale.[60]

It would be fair to state that, however belatedly it had moved, by 1979, the Society had at least attempted to widen its appeal and influence. Undermining any real success in this regard, however, was its lack of financial resources, barring its closed funds, and the need to keep a reserve. This meant that it could only really make token awards to worthy projects. Gueritz had been effectively hamstrung in this regard by his predecessors' inability to look beyond balancing subscription income with expenditure on *The Mariner's Mirror*. True, there had been a move towards investment in securities in the post-1945 period to boost the Society's range of funds but there had never really been an adequate response beyond raising the subscription level largely to cover increased production costs. Moreover, the small sums given as a result of the re-interpretation of the objects of the Macpherson Fund could no longer be counted on: in March 1979 a further change in the Society's attitude to the use of money from the Fund had taken place. On the advice of its Executive Committee a motion was put forward to the Council requesting that the Society's Trustees should use the Fund exclusively for the purchase of specific objects by the NMM. In the absence of any Trust Deed this meant the reversion to the original purpose of the Macpherson Fund. The museum would be asked to acknowledge publicly items acquired with the aid of the Fund and to inform the Society accordingly.[61]

The Society's 1979 AGM was notable, in contradistinction to previous AGMs, as it was not the usual supine affair where Council was given an easy ride. Members commented on various matters such as a possible re-design of the cover of *The Mariner's Mirror* to present a more modern image, the holding of the AGM outside normal office hours so that working members rather than the leisured rich, retired and senior museum staff, could attend, and the introduction of postal voting for the election of Officers and Council for the same reason. Gueritz noted these points and promised that they would be debated in Council.[62] Here, finally, was an opportunity to reform the Society for a more modern age but the opportunity was lost. Once again, the long-running saga of the nautical dictionary rumbled on to no definite conclusion. Revived by Roger Anderson, the project had been taken over by General Michael Prynne, until he and his wife were tragically killed in an automobile accident in September 1977. Thereafter, a Dictionary Sub-committee had been formed under the chairmanship of Dr N. A. M. Rodger to examine the feasibility of the project which had formed one of the Society's original objects. Dr Rodger approached Oxford

University Press to seek their collaboration but his proposal was turned down.[63]

On 27 August 1979, the Society suffered a grievous loss when its Patron, Admiral of the Fleet the Earl Mountbatten of Burma, was murdered at Mullaghmore, County Sligo, Eire, by the explosion of a bomb planted on his yacht by elements within the Irish Republican Army. The Society was represented at Earl Mountbatten's state funeral by its chairman, Helen Wallis, and its secretary, John Munday. The Society's President, Rear-Admiral Gueritz, also attended the funeral in his capacity as Chief Honorary Steward of Westminster Abbey.[64]

Modernizing the Mirror

The May 1978 issue of *The Mariner's Mirror* was the first produced in photoset lithography instead of letterpress. Not only did this result in a small cost saving, it also permitted a more flexible choice of illustrative material. In June 1979 the Hon. Editor, Brian Dolley, indicated that he wished to canvass ideas to improve *The Mariner's Mirror* and that he would in due course seek the Council's approval to build a small team of assistants. Since the SNR's earliest days it had been the Council's approach to *The Mariner's Mirror* to offer advice on submitted articles. Regarding this, Admiral Gueritz stated that 'he felt no shame in consulting about articles'. His and the Council's advice would provide support for the Editor without inhibiting his freedom or 'imposing an undue degree of orthodoxy. The journal should be academically free'. Gueritz later invited comment, and one member not unreasonably proposed the formation of an editorial board. Gueritz, somewhat bizarrely, replied that:

> Council was anxious that there should be no disquiet on this score. They were not prepared to allow any Hon. Editor to be brought under fire without his having adequate support, and if such would prove necessary the Council would not hesitate.[65]

This implied that Council knew best – a debatable point in matters of editorial content at the best of times – and also ignored any occasion when individual editors might deserve to be brought under fire owing to their acts or omissions. Gueritz's response showed a lack of knowledge of the Society's history. The SNR had had an Editorial Committee from 1911 to 1922, when it was replaced by a Publications Committee from 1922 onwards.

Admiral Gueritz reiterated that it was understood that members of Council were at the disposal of the Hon. Editor. Honor Frost remarked that there was inadequate protection at present for the Editor in the absence of an Editorial Board. Professor Lloyd thought that the Council was the protector, but that it was essential for the

Figure 27 HRH the Duke of Edinburgh in naval uniform. He became Patron in 1980 after Earl Mountbatten's death. (© National Museum of the Royal Navy)

Editor to be given latitude. Roger Knight stated that it was important for it to be seen that a form of Editorial Board was operating, which was not the case at present, though Brian Dolley thought that a Board should not appear to be 'a form of censorship. In sixty years the *Mirror* had not had one'.[66] N. A. M Rodger observed that although editorial consultation already took place, window dressing was necessary. After further discussion the President asked if Council was in favour of a Board: to him, Council itself was the responsible body, and he wondered whether an intermediate body was necessary. This effectively curtailed debate and the matter was left in abeyance.[67] In recognition of her services, Mrs Celia Dolley was appointed Hon. Assistant Editor of *The Mariner's Mirror*.[68] The Council decided in 1980 to discontinue the publication of annual indexes in order to preserve resources for periodic indexes at possibly five-year intervals. This decision was taken in the expectation that this would increase the value and utility of *The Mariner's Mirror*. In 1981 a ten-year index for volumes 56 to 65 was published. Compiled, as was the index to volumes 36 to 55, by Mrs Elizabeth Rolfe, it was issued free of charge to members owing to a generous grant from the Lily Lambert McCarthy Foundation.

During the years 1979–80 the Society discussed appointing Overseas Corresponding Members, an idea canvassed eagerly by Brian Dolley, who travelled extensively in southern Europe each summer and helped out in the field on the Marsala Punic ship project. Unhappily, the first such honour, intended for Barone G. B. Rubin de Cervin, of Venice, proved to be a posthumous one, so that the first actual Overseas Corresponding Member appointed was Monsieur Lucien Basch, of Brussels. Dr John de Courcey Ireland, a SNR member for over thirty years and founder of the Maritime Institute of Ireland in Dublin, also accepted Council's nomination as an Overseas Corresponding Member.[69]

In March 1980, the Chairman, Helen Wallis clarified the position of the Society's Executive Committee as she was anxious that its function should be generally understood. She explained that it did not make decisions for Council, but worked to prepare business and clarify issues for full Council meetings. This was all well and good but, since the Executive Committee consisted of the Society's senior officers, chairmen of committees and Trustees, their control of agenda gave them a distinct advantage, both in prior knowledge and tactics.

The first copies of the late Admiral Ballard's *The Black Battlefleet*, edited by G. A. Osbon and Dr N. A. M. Rodger and published in conjunction with the Nautical Publishing Company of Lymington, were on their way from Italy. Wallis also reported on a meeting she had with a Mr Abraham of DS16 MoD (N) which had explained the part that the Society played in the maintenance of HMS *Victory*. As a result there would be regular annual meetings with MoD (N) around October or November each year to discuss the form of subvention which in the past had been on an *ad hoc* basis, and which 'had given rise to much uncertainty in Whitehall about the Society's activities'.[70]

By December 1981, Helen Wallis had noted a proposal on the agenda of a forthcoming meeting of the PRNM trustees to drop 'Portsmouth' from its title. Wallis deemed this undesirable in view of the role of Greenwich as the national museum for the history of the Royal Navy and the limitations of staff and facilities at Portsmouth. She also noted that the name of the Victory Museum had been changed by the PRNM to the Victory Gallery without reference to Council, and that PRNM

Figure 28 Dr Helen Wallis (1924–95) greeting the Society's Patron. Dr Helen Wallis was Chairman of the Society, 1972–89. (© Society for Nautical Research)

had apologized as a result.[71] However, by March 1983, Council agreed to the museum's title being changed to Royal Naval Museum, Portsmouth.

On 3 March 1982, Captain Alan Villiers DSC, the Society's former chairman (1960–70) and President (1970–4), died. Lord Runciman, then Chairman of the Trustees of the NMM gave an address at the Memorial Service in Oxford on 22 May. Arrangements were in hand to publish an annual maritime bibliography as a grant of £4,500 over three years had been awarded by the British Library to help with the expenses of the publication. During the annual visit to *Victory*, members witnessed the return of HMS *Glasgow* from the Falklands conflict from the vantage point of *Victory's* poop deck.[72] The Council asked its President, Admiral Gueritz, to write to the Admiral of the Fleet Sir Terence Lewin with the Society's greetings and warmest congratulations on the Forces' achievements in the South Atlantic during the Falklands Conflict. He did so and received a pleasant reply. He then suggested that the SNR should write on Sir Terence's elevation to the Peerage, as also to C-in-C Fleet and others who had been recently been honoured, which was agreed.[73]

The November 1982 issue of *The Mariner's Mirror* was considerably larger than its predecessor solely due to the fact that three of the articles had been subject to generous grants (two anonymous, the other from Bermuda Maritime Museum Trust). In 1982, four grants provided 117 pages out of the total of 470 for volume 68 – a size that had only been exceeded nine times before.[74] In December 1982 a member of Council, Roger Morriss, reported the suggestion of Ms Patricia Crimmin of Royal Holloway College, that a reduced student subscription should be introduced. Brian Dolley thought this undesirable owing to administrative difficulties and added work-load in dealing with different rates. However, he was willing to arrange the supply of the journal to approved centres at reduced rates, with Royal Holloway as a pilot centre.[75] Membership during 1982 had remained constant with new members replacing those lost, but no mention of the possibility of student members becoming full members, as their careers progressed in later years, was raised

At a Council meeting on 9 March 1983, it was agreed to present a motion to the AGM to alter the Constitution of the Society to increase the number of Vice-Presidents from six to ten. By November 1983, Basil Greenhill had retired as Director of the NMM and been replaced by Dr Neil Cossons. Council noted that in due course the latter would be invited to become a Vice-President of the Society. The Hon. Editor, Brian Dolley, had obtained Council's approval to purchase a Sirius 16-bit computer to aid the compilation of membership lists and details at a cost of £5,000 plus VAT. He also urged the purchase of an Adler word processor at a cost of £2,300. This produced type of a high standard with some typesetting capacity and the production of a Cumulative Index was possible on such a machine. Council approved the purchase. Meanwhile the possibility of a contractual relationship with an American publisher, Gales of Detroit, Michigan, and a lexicographer, Mr Laurence Urdang, to compile and produce the long-awaited nautical dictionary was discussed at a special meeting of Council on 9 November 1983. In Dr Rodger's opinion the contract with Gales was the only offer the Society was likely to get. On the second draft of the proposed contract Council had insisted on a clause therein limiting the project to five years. Rodger pointed out, correctly, that the Society had neither a completed manuscript of a dictionary nor the means to complete it. A Trustee, Dr Susan Rose, thought that some areas of the contract could prove fertile ground for litigation. Neither Dr Rose nor her fellow Trustee, Lt Cdr Andrew David, was happy with the contract and Dr Rose thought it was onerous and that the Trustees should not agree to its signing. Dr Roger Morriss went as far as to state that a nautical dictionary should no longer be an aim of the Society. What was missing in the proposed contract was a specific limitation of liability in favour of the Society. It was agreed that a three-part contract would be preferable and that letters of intent should be exchanged between parties.[76] At a later meeting, Admiral Gueritz made it clear to Council that although considerable anxiety had been expressed at the meeting on 9 November on the contract for a nautical dictionary, the decision to pursue its production in principle had been taken and a more informal arrangement with Mr Urdang should be made in the form of a letter of intent in the following (abridged) terms:

> Council has agreed to make available to Laurence Urdang Inc, for the sole purpose of the proposed Gale/Urdang Nautical Dictionary project the material of the Carr Laughton bequest held in the NMM, and material from the Society's journal, with explicit copyright licence free of charge specifically licensed to the Nautical Dictionary Project – the Society to make available the services of an research assistant to process contributions from UK sources and to act as a point of contact for the project in the UK.

Further discussions made the points that no contract would be entered into with Gales, that there was no prospect of an alternative project with a UK-based publisher and that a research assistant would be prepared to work on an expenses only basis to a limit of no more than £500 per annum.[77]

During 1984, on his retirement from the staff of the NMM, the Hon. Secretary, John Munday, announced his resignation and was succeeded by Lt Cdr Lawrence Phillips RNR who at that stage was the Command Public Relations Officer to the C-in-C Home Command, Portsmouth. At the September Council meeting, the first attended by Lt Cdr Phillips as Hon. Secretary, John Munday was invited to become a Hon. Vice-President of the Society and at the December meeting Lt Cdr Phillips's wife, Jennifer, was appointed Hon. Deputy Secretary. In 1984 the work of the Hon. Editor and the Hon. Assistant Editor was considerably increased by the transfer of the membership distribution records to the computer, which had become fully operational in June,[78] and the production of the long-delayed first Annual Bibliography. The bibliography appeared in November, compiled by Mrs Mary Patrick (NMM), Dr Michael S. Partridge and Dr Simon Ville.[79]

The Society's 75th Anniversary

In 1985 the Society celebrated its 75th anniversary of its founding by holding a Council meeting on 14 June at the RUSI, the venue of the Society's first meeting, with its Patron, Prince Philip, HRH The Duke of Edinburgh, in attendance. Later, in the evening at a reception for members in the Banqueting Hall of the Old Royal Palace at Whitehall, the Duke recalled that at the first AGM held in December 1910 his maternal grandfather, The Marquis of Milford Haven was elected as the Society's first President. His son, and Prince Philip's uncle, Lord Mountbatten eventually

Figure 29 John Munday and Lt Cdr Lawrence Phillips, two Hon. Secretaries of the Society. (© Society for Nautical Research)

succeeded the Duke of Kent as the Society's Patron and held that position until he was killed in 1979. When approached by the Society to become its Patron, Prince Philip was 'delighted and honoured to accept'. He then presented on behalf of the Society a replica of the ship's belfry in HMS *Victory* made from her oak and copper to the Director of RUSI. Among the official guests was the Minister of State for the Armed Forces, Lord Trefgarne, and the Presidents of the Hakluyt Society, the Society of Antiquaries, the Navy Records Society, the Royal Naval College, Greenwich, the Chairman of the British Library and the directors of various national maritime museums at home and abroad.[80]

On the following day, at the Society's AGM in Portsmouth, subscription rates, which had been held for six years, were raised from £10 to £15 for individual members and from £15 to £20 for institutions. During 1984, 393,000 people had visited *Victory*, the lowest total in a decade and around 62,000 below average – a

Figure 30 HRH The Duke of Edinburgh at the Society's 75th Anniversary. From left to right: Rear-Admiral E. F. Gueritz (the longest-serving President); the Duke of Edinburgh is shaking hands with Lt Cdr Phillips. On Cdr Phillips' right is Brian Dolley (light-coloured suit) and Capt. Bill Lapper (Senior Trustee). To Cdr Phillips' left are Capt. Peter Whitlock, Annette Gould and Mrs Jennifer Phillips. (© Society for Nautical Research)

decrease in part attributable to the close proximity of the *Mary Rose* and interest in her.[81] Of equal importance to the Society's long-term prospects was the formation on Trafalgar Day 1985 of the Portsmouth Naval Heritage Trust, with its registered office at the museum, comprising the *Mary Rose*, *Warrior* and the museum, with *Victory* in close association. A separate body, the Portsmouth Naval Base Property Trust (PNBPT), had been formed to take over responsibility for the buildings within the Heritage Area, with an endowment of £6m to maintain them.[82] The museum itself had a grant-in-aid but it was essential to receive an income from the commercial development of the area. In his first report, *Victory's* new commanding officer, Cdr Lawrence Jay, who took over from Lt Cdr C. P. Addis MBE, RN, reassured members that notwithstanding the new and far reaching changes imminent at Portsmouth, *Victory* would remain the flagship of the C-in-C, and be commanded by a serving officer. Potentially, and of equal import to the financial health of the

Society, was the retirement from an Honorary Vice-Presidency of Mrs Lily McCarthy, through whose foundation various gifts had been made to the Society during the years since the death of her husband, John McCarthy.[83]

References

1 Certificates of Charitable Status were granted to the SNR, STVF, Macpherson Fund and the Walker Bequest.

2 *Mariner's Mirror*, 52:1 (1966), Editorial. In 2008, Wales had 13 individual members and four institutional members, and Scotland had 18 individual members and 8 institutions

3 The events surrounding Frank Carr's departure and Greenhill's succession are discussed in greater detail by Littlewood and Butler, *Of Ships and Stars*, 186–93. Carr had originally suggested Greenhill, but when offered the job after interview Greenhill told the NMM Trustees he could only come at the start of 1967, but not later, for career break reasons – since he was due for another foreign posting after a spell in London,

4 NMM SNR 7/3 Portrait of Nelson for HMS *Victory*, 27 June 1967.

5 NMM SNR 7/40 Naish personal memo, undated.

6 *Ibid*.

7 *Mariner's Mirror* 54:4 (1968), AGM of SNR, 1968.

8 See Preface; designed by Isambard Kingdom Brunel, she was laid down in 1838 and launched at Bristol in 1843. Her maiden voyage across the Atlantic was in 1845. See also E Corlett, *The Iron Ship* (Bradford-on-Avon, 1975, London, 1990), 218.

9 The SS *Great Britain* Fund was established at the Society's AGM of 1968.

10 NMM SNR 2/59 Report of the Council for the Year 1969 and AGM of SNR, 1969.

11 *Mariner's Mirror*, 56:4 (1970), AGM of SNR, 1970.

12 NMM SNR 7/41 Letter from G. P. B. Naish to Admiral Power, 9 January 1969.

13 NMM SNR 2/59 Report of Council for the year 1969 and AGM of SNR, 1969.

14 NMM SNR 7/41 Letter from George Naish to Admiral Power, 10 April 1969.

15 NMM SNR 7/41 Letter from MoD (N) to Admiral Power, 28 February 1968.

16 NMM SNR 3/8 Minutes of SNR Council Meeting, 20 January 1971.

17 NMM SNR 6/33 Letter from George Naish to Alan Villiers, 23 September 1971.

18 NMM SNR 3/8 Minutes of SNR Council Meeting, 30 June 1971, and NMM SNR 6/33 letter from George Naish to Alan Villiers, 23 September 1971.

19 NMM SNR 3/8 Minutes of SNR Council Meeting, 18 February 1972.

20 NMM SNR 3/8 Minutes of SNR Council Meeting, 29 March 1972.

21 NMM SNR 3/13 (3), Minutes of SNR Council Meeting, 11 March 1981.

22 NMM SNR 7/43 Memorandum from Admiral Sir Horace Law to the President, Officers and Council of the SNR, 11 January 1972.

23 *Ibid*.

24 NMM SNR 3/8 Minutes of SNR Council Meeting, 18 February 1972.

25 NMM SNR 7/43 Letter from Admiral Andrew Lewis to the President of the SNR on provisional administration of Victory and McCarthy Museums, 27 July 1972.

26 Helen Wallis was a map librarian at the British Library.

27 NMM SNR 3/10 Private Memorandum to President, Officers and Council of SNR, December 1973.

28 *Ibid*.

29 NMM SNR 3/10 Minutes of SNR Council Meeting, 16 January 1974.

30 NMM SNR 3/10 Memorandum from the Office of Naval Home Command, Portsmouth, to Helen Wallis, Chairman, SNR, 28 March 1974.
31 NMM SNR 3/10 Minutes of SNR Council Meeting, 3 April 1974.
32 *Ibid.*
33 Brian Dolley had an interest in Staples Press.
34 *Mariner's Mirror*, 59:3 (1973), AGM of SNR, 1973.
35 NMM SNR 3/10 Minutes of SNR Council Meeting, Treasurer's Report, 16 January 1974.
36 NMM SNR 3/11 Minutes of SNR Council Meeting, 18 June 1975.
37 NMM SNR 3/11 Minutes of SNR Council Meeting, 9 April 1975.
38 NMM SNR 3/11 Letter from Major General Michael Prynne to George Naish, 23 September 1975.
39 NMM SNR 3/11 Minutes of SNR Council Meeting, 29 October 1975.
40 Companies House, Company No. 01261270.
41 NMM SNR 2/57 Report of Council for the year 1967; AGM of SNR,1967.
42 NMM SNR 2/56 Report of the Council for the Year 1966; AGM of SNR, 1966.
43 NMM SNR 7/43: excerpt from Portsmouth's *The News*, 27 February 1973.
44 *Mariner's Mirror*, 61:2 (1975), Report of the Council for the Year 1974.
45 *Mariner's Mirror*, 63:2 (1977), Report of the Council for the Year 1977.
46 *Mariner's Mirror*, 65:2 (1979), Report of the Council for the Year 1978. How the purchase of a crew bus was thought to be appropriate expenditure from the STVF seems beyond belief at the present day.
47 NMM SNR 3/13 Minutes of Council Meeting, 5 April 1978.
48 NMM SNR 3/36 Letter from Alan Villiers to Admiral Sir Charles Madden, 12 March 1974.
49 The position was in fact less clear-cut than Alan Villiers' letter suggests. On George Naish's retirement from the museum staff, he lost his office in the East Building but conducted SNR affairs from a room in the museum's annex in Feathers Place until his death in 1977.
50 NMM SNR 3/10 Minutes of Council Meeting, 9 October 1974.
51 This was agreed at an Extraordinary General Meeting on 10 March 1976. The effective date of increase was 1 January 1977.
52 *Mariner's Mirror*, 63:3 (1977), AGM of SNR, 1977.
53 NMM SNR 17/6, 1 June 1993: Letter from Chris Swinson (Hon.Treasurer) to Rear-Admiral Roger Morris seeking information about the ss *Great Britain* Project. The Treasurer's records showed a subsidiary fund in that name. Quotations from Helen Morris to Swinson, 4 June 1993.
54 *Mariner's Mirror*, 64:2 (1978), Annual Report for the Year 1978.
55 *Mariner's Mirror*, 64:3 (1978), AGM of SNR, 1978.
56 *Mariner's Mirror*, 65:3 (1979), AGM of SNR, 1979.
57 *Mariner's Mirror*, 65:2 (1979), Report to Council for the Year 1978.
58 *Ibid.*
59 *Ibid.*
60 For this period, see L. Johnman and H. Murphy, *British Shipbuilding and the State since 1918: a political economy of decline* (Exeter, 2002). See also, A. Jamieson, *Ebb Tide in Britain's Maritime Industries* (Exeter 2003), L. Johnman and H. Murphy, 'The rationalisation of slow speed marine diesel engine building in the UK, 1912–1990', and 'The development of the British ship repair industry, 1945-1985: an overview', in D. J. Starkey and H. Murphy, eds, *Beyond Shipping and Shipbuilding: Britain's Ancillary Maritime Interests in the Twentieth Century* (Hull, 2007).
61 NMM SNR 3/13 (3) Minutes of Council Meeting, 7 March 1979. Reasonable provisions for

expenses and management were to be allowed.

62 *Mariner's Mirror*, 65:3 (1979), AGM of SNR, 1979.
63 NMM SNR 3/13 (3) Minutes of SNR Council Meeting, 7 March 1979.
64 *Mariner's Mirror*, 66:3 (1980), AGM of SNR, 1980.
65 *Mariner's Mirror*, 65:3 (1979), AGM of SNR, 1979.
66 See Chapter 1 for the formation of an Editorial Committee in 1912.
67 NMM SNR 3/13 (3) Minutes of SNR Council Meeting, 6 June 1979.
68 NMM SNR 3/13 (3) Minutes of SNR Council Meeting, 15 October 1981.
69 *Mariner's Mirror*, 68:2 (1982), Report of the Council for the Year 1981. NMM SNR 3/13 (3) Minutes of SNR Council Meeting 11 June 1981.
70 NMM SNR 3/13 (3) Minutes of SNR Council Meeting, 13 March 1980.
71 NMM SNR 3/13 (3) Minutes of SNR Council Meeting, 2 December 1981.
72 *Mariner's Mirror*, 69:2 (1983), Report of the Council for the Year 1982.
73 NMM SNR 3/13 (3) Minutes of SNR Council Meeting, 13 October 1982. Also AGM of SNR, 1982.
74 *Mariner's Mirror* 68:4 (1982), Editorial.
75 NMM SNR 3/13 (3) Minutes of SNR Council Meeting, 2 December 1982.
76 NMM SNR 3/13 Minutes of a Special Meeting of Council, 9 November 1983.
77 NMM SNR 3/13 Minutes of SNR Council Meeting, 1 December 1983.
78 A generous contribution from the Lily Lambert McCarthy Foundation paid for the computer.
79 *Mariner's Mirror*, 71:2 (1985), Report of the Council for the Year 1985.
80 *Mariner's Mirror*, 71:3 (1985), AGM of SNR, 1985.
81 *Ibid*.
82 Under the provisions of the National Heritage Act, 1985.
83 *Mariner's Mirror*, 72:3 (1986), AGM of SNR, 1986.

6

Off Course: Deviation from True Bearings

Any society with maritime interests whose Chairman adopts the metaphor of 'tilling fields' at its AGM, as Rear-Admiral Morris did in 1989, must be in shoal waters, if not aground.[1] Four years earlier, the SNR had ended its 75th anniversary year with a small deficit. The cost of the royal reception, the printing of colour plates in two issues of *The Mariner's Mirror* in 1985, the Cumulative Index and the 1984 Annual Bibliography had been major expenses. The February 1986 issue of *The Mariner's Mirror* alone had cost over £9,000. Had it not been for a major grant from the British Library towards the cost of the 1984 Annual Bibliography and contributions from other benefactors, membership subscription rates would have had to be increased. During 1985 the STVF disbursed some £23,000 on HMS *Victory*. However, as Lt Cdr Peter Whitlock, the Hon. Treasurer, noted, the establishment of Portsmouth Historic Dockyard meant that 'the forthcoming change of status of the ship and the introduction of admission charges would have a serious effect on voluntary contributions'.[2]

During the later 1980s, the SNR continued its efforts to expand its numbers and to develop new initiative. The introduction of an Associate Membership scheme at reduced subscription to encourage young persons and students to join the Society was considered in 1986 but there was insufficient support for this to proceed. A series of meetings for maritime history students was planned and a committee under Dr Susan Rose was asked to develop this idea. Also in 1986, the Council approved a project for Evan Davies, Deputy Head of Strategic Studies at the Royal Naval College, Dartmouth, to produce a history of the Royal Naval College, Osborne. On the wider academic front the Society continued its sponsorship – in association with the British Commission for Maritime History – of a series of International Commission for Maritime History Seminars at King's College, London. One outcome of the Society's 75th anniversary was the launch of the Anderson Research Fund to provide a biennial essay prize of £250 for the encouragement of maritime research, while the development of a more active role for the Society outside London and the Home Counties remained an objective.[3]

Throughout the 1970s and 1980s the SNR faced a decline in the purchasing power of its funds for the furtherance of maritime history. Despite the fact that preservation work on HMS *Victory* was now on a minor scale, there were steep rises in the cost of hardwoods. The Society's public reputation suffered as contributions from the STVF were no longer as obvious as they had been. Other learned societies, particularly those linked to professions, had expanded, as had the museum sector in general. In short, the Society's influence had been waning since the Second World War and the consensus of opinion from certain sections within its ranks was that it had failed to adapt to the modern age. Academically, the reputation of *The Mariner's Mirror* was undistinguished, as the Editor, Brian Dolley, was in sole and unsupervised control of the journal's content. Other journals of comparable longevity and stature had editorial boards comprised mainly of distinguished academics but editors of *The Mariner's Mirror* had always had too much responsibility thrust upon them. No Chairman or President had either the inclination or vision to make changes, so that the Council had failed to put in place the necessary academic supervision required.

Management Fees and Honoraria

Since 1978, the Society's finances had benefited from the practice of charging management fees to administer the STVF and the Macpherson Collection Endowment Fund. This practice followed a suggestion by Brian Dolley to Blease Lloyd, the SNR's auditors.[4] Between 1978 and the end of 1986, the total fees derived by the Society from this practice amounted to £38,610, of which £32,661 had been charged to the STVF and £5,949 to the Macpherson Fund.[5]

Management fees were levied on the restricted funds as a percentage of the value of each fund at the end of each financial year, rising from approximately 0.5 per cent of the fund's values, to approximately 1.5 per cent by the mid 1980s. This helped to keep the Society in modest profit. Had not subscription rates doubled in 1980 and had not management fees been charged in increasing amounts, the Society would have posted losses for these years. Management fees prevented substantial increases in subscriptions at frequent intervals, with the probable result that a substantial number of members would be lost.

According to its own rules, however, the Society was clearly not in the business of providing management services, since it already paid stockbrokers' fees for the management of the funds. There was growing disquiet at the increasing level of management fees among some of the Society's Trustees, Council members and the Hon. Secretary, Lt Cdr Lawrence Phillips. The Council had let this develop without

Table 2 Subscription income, net cost of *The Mariner's Mirror* and fees charged on the Society's Restricted Funds 1978–86

Year	Subscription income	Net cost of Mariner's Mirror	Current value of restricted funds		Management fees charged		Fee Income from restricted funds
			STVF	MCEF	STVF	MCEF	
	(£)	(£)	(£)	(£)	(£)	(£)	(£)
1978	15,036	16,061	150,994	34,090	515	245	760
1979	14,255	16,751	184,231	38,624	740	205	945
1980	23,843	22,522	211,171	38,749	2,148	650	2,798
1981	27,298	22,246	264,425	45,768	2,634	680	3,314
1982	27,007	27,158	298,164	45,955	3,278	700	3,978
1983	25,393	30,497	336,216	49,510	3,523	700	4,223
1984	27,364	34,498	403,930	50,038	5,860	952	6,812
1985	29,204	39,213	434,635	54,834	6,585	996	7,581
1986	31,891	41,083	488,844	56,295	7,380	821	8,201

Key: STVF = Save the Victory Fund; MCEF = Macpherson Collection Endowment Fund.
Note: Subscription rates were doubled on 1 January 1980.

question for over a decade. The practice of paying honoraria from these fees to Officers – but not to Trustees – gave serious cause for concern from 1987 onwards, lest it be declared *ultra vires* by the Charity Commissioners. Lt Cdr Phillips felt that, as a public servant, he could no longer afford to be associated with the way the Society's affairs were being run, and contemplated resigning as Hon. Secretary.

At a Council meeting in September 1987 several options were canvassed by the President, Rear-Admiral Gueritz, who stated that on the basis of figures provided up to 5 April 1987 there was an apparent profit of £2,664. However, to be realistic, no account should be taken of management fees charged against the two funds, which indicated a deficit of £5,000. There was therefore a need to create a contingency reserve so that the Society's investment of £40,000 could be retained intact, and the Executive Committee proposed that this reserve should be set at £15,000. The first opportunity for subscriptions to rise would be in January 1989, assuming approval at the 1988 AGM. Noting that *The Mariner's Mirror* consumed the greater part of the Society's expenditure, Admiral Gueritz explained that if no action was taken on finances 'it would become necessary to cease publication'. The stark alternatives, which he put to the meeting, were:

1. To have three issues per year without change in editorial policy;
2. To have four issues per year of reduced size.

It transpired that the Hon. Treasurer, Peter Whitlock, and the Hon. Editor, Brian

Dolley, had already taken 'remedial action in anticipation of Council's wishes'. The cost of the November 1986 issue of *The Mariner's Mirror* had been £10,500 but for February 1987 it would be reduced to £9,000: the cost of the May issue was similar. The August issue had also been reduced by 25 pages, which in a full year would reduce a volume from 500 to 400 pages. In the ensuing discussion a number of points were forcefully made. Antony Preston was of the opinion that three issues per year would be disastrous: he believed the Society 'had to be seen to be in business, the loss of credibility would be fatal and readers would feel cheated'. Preston suggested that a Publications Committee be established to help the Editor 'as it was unfair to put the responsibility on one man'. Without decisive change, the President felt that an increase in subscriptions in 1989 'was imperative'.[6]

Captain William Lapper RN (retd), the senior Trustee – who believed that charging management fees was justified – emphasized that the 'Council had to bear in mind that the SNR was a commercial operation'. This was an extraordinary statement for a trustee of a society which had charitable status. In support, Brian Dolley agreed that 'the Society had been selling itself cheap for 75 years'. However, members of Council – who were supposed to monitor the Officers' conduct of Society business – finally expressed grave concerns at the amounts levied from the two Trustee-supervised Funds. For example, in 1986, £8,937 had been spent on the restoration of HMS *Victory* and £7,380 had been charged in management fees! Capt. Lapper requested that the principle of charging management fees should be verified by Counsel. Nevertheless, the Trustees 'felt that regardless of this, the amounts which had been taken in recent years had been excessive and that it might be necessary to repay the amounts which had been taken'.[7] Indeed, if the Charity Commission took the latter course, then the Society would have to repay a total of £38,612 which would almost bankrupt it.

It was eventually agreed that *The Mariner's Mirror* should be reduced in size to a degree that would save £7,000 per annum in printing and associated costs, to offset the loss of income from management fees. Total costs over the next two years should not exceed £36,000 per annum. The creation of the contingency reserve of £15,000 was endorsed, and a substantial rise in annual subscriptions was to be put before the 1988 AGM. The Council also agreed that up to £800 should be spent taking legal advice on the charging of management fees to the STVF and the Macpherson Collection Endowment Fund.[8] The disquiet on Council was evident and it is pertinent to ask just how well informed its members were (or indeed the general membership at large) about the activities of the Society's Officers and Trustees? Ominously, it seems likely that honoraria paid to the Society's Officers came out of 'management fees'. The likelihood was that the Charity Commissioners would regard both practices unfavourably, and the Officers and Trustees should have been

Plate 1 *Naval Officers of the Great War* (1921), by Sir Arthur Stockdale Cope. This picture shows the first three Presidents of the Society: Admirals Battenberg, Sturdee and Beatty. In the centre of the picture facing each other are Jellicoe to the left and Beatty on the right. Behind Beatty, seated at the table on the right, are HSH Prince Louis of Battenberg (later the Marquis of Milford Haven) and Admiral Sturdee. Lord Wemyss, First Sea Lord at the end of the war, is on the extreme right. The picture also includes Admirals Cradock, who died at Coronel in 1914 and Hood and Arbuthnot who were killed in action at Jutland. © National Portrait Gallery, London.

Plate 2 *A Panorama of the Battle of Trafalgar*, by W. L. Wyllie. This view from the stern windows of the French ship *Neptune*, shows *Victory* alongside the *Redoubtable* to port with *Temeraire* to starboard. © National Museum of the Royal Navy.

Plate 3 *The Battle of the Texel* (1673), by W. van de Velde the Younger. Purchased in part for the NMM by the Society for Nautical Research's Macpherson Collection Endowment Fund. © National Maritime Museum, Greenwich, London

Plate 4 *James Richard Stanhope, 7th Earl Stanhope (1880–1967)*, Chairman of NMM Trustees, by Sir James Gunn. Reproduced with kind permission of the artist's estate. © National Maritime Museum, Greenwich, London.

Plate 5 *Dr Roger C. Anderson (1883–1976)*, President of the Society, 1951–60, and three times Hon. Editor of *The Mariner's Mirror*, by Bernard Hailstone. By kind permission of the artist's estate. © National Maritime Museum, Greenwich, London

Plate 6 The *Victory*'s cutter at the Royal Dartmouth Regatta, 2003. Image supplied by Keith Chittenden, © Society for Nautical Research.

Plate 7 HRH Prince Andrew, The Duke of York, President of the Society, at a recent reception at the National Maritime Museum. © National Maritime Museum, Greenwich, London.

Plate 8 The Officers of the Society, 2009. From left to right, the Officers are: Dr Peter V. Nash, Hon. Treasurer; Professor Richard Harding, Chairman, Peter Winterbottom, Hon. Secretary, and Dr Hugh Murphy, Hon. Editor. Image supplied by Lt Cdr Lawrie Phillips. © Society for Nautical Research.

aware of this and acted much earlier. With regard to honoraria, a letter from Brian Dolley to Capt. Lapper is instructive. Dolley, it seems, had always taken the view that his honorarium and that of his wife Cecilia, as Assistant Hon. Editor (which was subsumed within the general costs of producing the journal) was a subvention to him for representing the Society on trips abroad, and running his car largely for the benefit of the Society. This 'subvention' for him and his wife amounted to £1,095 in 1987. In Dolley's words, he could:

> Truthfully maintain that my pseudo honorarium is in fact a partial subvention pure and simple of the tangible and intangible expenses on running my part of the ship.[9]

Dolley saw himself as a roving ambassador for the Society, visiting its friends and members all over Europe and, for a period of five years, assisting with the Marsala Punic ship excavation for two to four weeks each summer. He had translated a number of books and many of the papers published in *The Mariner's Mirror*. Dolley was a larger-than-life character with a strong, if not all-consuming, sense of self-worth who evidently thought that the work he did for the Society was far in excess of the honorarium he took. It probably was; but, in effect, his attitude to honoraria challenged the voluntary principle of persons freely giving their time and expertise to the Society. From 1978, honoraria totalling £475 had grown to £3,505 by 1987.[10] Honoraria should, of course, be distinguished from the payment of out-of-pocket expenses, which Rule 27 of the 1978 Rules of the Society permitted. However, the tendency was for expenses to grow too and the distinction between them and honoraria could easily be blurred. For instance, Dolley's attitude to expenses had always been liberal, whether in asking Council to expend sums on office equipment and sundries or in out-of-pocket expenses.

Subsequently Messrs Bartlett de Reya, solicitors, were instructed to seek counsel's opinion on the validity of the remuneration of officers and the charging of management fees, and a proposal by Capt. Lapper that the Society should form a company to provide management services. On receipt of counsel's opinion, Bartlett de Reya, wrote to the Charity Commissioners on 9 February 1988 admitting that the Society had erred in charging management fees and paying honoraria, but had done so in good faith not realizing that it was outside their powers. In reply, a letter from the Charity Commissioners confirmed that:

> Receipt by the original charity (SNR) for fees in respect of management services provided for the subsidiary charities was *ultra vires*, and seriously so when the payment were used to remunerate officers who were at the same time members of the Council of the Charity.[11]

The protection given under section 28 of the 1960 Charities Act to trustees who act in accordance with the Commissioners' advice could not operate retrospectively. Accordingly, all the Commissioners were able to do in this instance was to note the position and confirm that they did not intend to initiate any action in respect of past breaches of trust which were made in good faith. The Commissioners also doubted whether the circumstances called for the setting up of a trading company for the purposes of administering the charities and producing *The Mariner's Mirror*, and suggested that those persons undertaking these duties should be appointed as Assistants to the Officers of the Charity under clause 9 of the Rules, and that 'no member of the Council of the Charity should in future receive remuneration'.[12] Thus, the Society got off lightly as no order to repay the sums gained in management fees was made. However, the question of its financial stability remained.

Internal changes

In May 1987, Helen Wallis and the Hon. Secretary, Lt Cdr Lawrence Phillips, attended the NMM's 50th Anniversary Reception at Greenwich to mark its official opening in 1937. The consequences of changes at the museum for nautical archaeology and navigation led to some disquiet among the membership of the SNR. Underpinning these concerns was the demise of the NMM's Archaeological Research Centre, which had become a casualty of the declining amount of the government grant to the museum. The SNR's Council was aware that this was of particular concern to nautical archaeologists, notably Valerie Fenwick, and a draft resolution expressing concern was put forward at the 1987 AGM by Antony Preston:

> Considering that the Society for Nautical Research played the key role in the establishment of the National Maritime Museum now exactly fifty years old. The SNR views with grave concern the current Museum re-organization which will reduce the Museum's proper role as a national reference centre for all maritime expertise and scholarship. And seeks the prompt re-confirmation of this role by whatever means are necessary.

Helen Wallis informed the meeting that the President, Admiral Gueritz, had spoken to the Chairman of the NMM Trustees, Lord Lewin, and was assured that the Trustees would seek the advice of the Society among others. Moreover, at the 50th anniversary reception she had also been assured that a closer relationship between the Society and the museum would be welcome. In the light of this she urged 'that it was important that the Society should avoid any counterproductive action'. Rear-Admiral R. O. Morris viewed the terms of the draft resolution with dismay. He felt it was not appropriate for the Society to interfere directly with the museum's

Director and, as 'they were under pressure . . . the Society should give support'.[13] Admiral Morris admitted that the relationships between the Society and the museum had not been close in recent years but were now improving and thought that 'intemperately expressed concern might prejudice this desirable reapproachement [sic] and destroy any possibility of our influencing events'. Helen Wallis concurred, and from the Chair proposed an amended resolution:

> Considering that the Society for Nautical Research played the key role in establishing the National Maritime Museum the Society expresses its deep concern that the Museum should have the means to retain its role as a national reference centre for all maritime expertise and scholarship and promises the Museum all possible support towards this end.

Just what this 'support' could mean, given the state of the Society's finances, was not minuted, but after extended and vigorous debate the amended resolution was carried *nem con*.[14] What this debate highlighted was that there was now a far more critical element in the membership than before, and that it was led, by and large, by nautical archaeologists and academics. Furthermore, the NMM now had successive Directors, Neil Cossons and Richard Ormond, who were museum professionals and not SNR men, unlike their predecessors, Callender and Carr, and to a lesser extent, Greenhill. Neither were the vast majority of NMM Trustees members of the SNR. Another cause of concern from the academic historians' perspective was the fact that the NMM had acquired large paper collections from business and technical sources and that many of these remained uncatalogued and stored off-site. The SNR's hands-off approach and the largely unquestioning support for the NMM, which had characterized the Society's relationships to the museum since 1937, had finally been challenged but, ultimately, to no great effect.

At the 1988 AGM, Admiral Gueritz, admitted that the Society had been living beyond its means. He also referred to the negotiations with the Charity Commissioners, their impact on the Society, and said that the Commissioners' views had been respected. Lt Cdr Peter Whitlock – at his last AGM before handing over the office of Hon. Treasurer to his successor, Antony Preston – put the Society's time-honoured solution to its financial woes before the meeting, the raising of the subscriptions on 1 January 1989 from £10 to £15 for individual members and from £20 to £30 for institutions. This was carried 'with regret' but without dissent. There was no increase in North American rates as these had already been raised at the 1987 AGM. As the first step in a review of the Society's administration, the Chairman, Helen Wallis, explained that the titles of certain posts had been revised to enable payment to be made for services. The Hon. Membership Secretary became the Assistant Membership Secretary, the Hon. Deputy Editor became the Assistant

Editor and the Hon. Assistant Secretary became the Assistant Secretary. During 1988 Lt Cdr Andrew David, who since his appointment as a Trustee had been privately critical of past and present practices, particularly regarding management fees, resigned.[15] Professor Eila M. Campbell was appointed to the vacancy in February 1989. Lt Cdr Phillips, who had felt increasing disquiet at the way the Society's business was being run, also resigned as Hon. Secretary soon after the departure of Lt Cdr David. Cdr Phillips was promptly co-opted on to Council and he, with Capt. Sainsbury, Antony Preston and Eric Grove, formed a group determined on reform.

At the 1988 Trafalgar Day meeting of the Society of Friends of the Royal Naval Museum, Portsmouth, which Helen Wallis chaired, a resolution was passed by a show of hands recommending an amendment to the constitution. The effect of the resolution, from which SNR members abstained, was that they would become a joint Society of Friends of the Royal Naval Museum and of HMS *Victory*. The SNR members saw this as an encroachment on the role of the STVF. It was understood that the resolution was proposed subject to the approval of the C-in-C Home Command, the SNR and the Portsmouth Naval Base Heritage Trust. The resolution had not taken Wallis by surprise, as it had been discussed on 13 October between SNR Officers and the Friends. The SNR, according to Wallis, was concerned that the proposed change should be carefully considered in the light of 'the best interests of *Victory* and of the SNR, which [had] been actively supportive in the ship's preservation for almost 70 years'.[16] It seemed that the SNR had learned nothing from its attempt to launch the Friends of the National Maritime Museum before the Second World War. That proposal had been made subject to its own conditions, which the NMM Trustees had vetoed. The SNR's proprietorialism in respect of the NMM had resulted in the museum's Friends separating from the Society, and now it risked the same outcome in respect to the Royal Naval Museum. The incident also portrayed the continued 'reverence' that certain sections of the Society had for HMS *Victory*, despite the fact that she remained a commissioned ship, and that ultimate responsibility for her rested with the Ministry of Defence, not the Society who had saved her. While the SNR's attitude to the new Friends of the Royal Naval Museum and of HMS *Victory* was initially hostile, after a succession of meetings the Society eventually viewed the process as a *fait accompli* and thereafter sought to avoid a 'dog in the manger' attitude to them.

In a determined effort to involve more Council members in the management of the Society and to inject new dynamism and efficiency into it, three additional committees were set up during 1988, each chaired by a member identified with the reform process. Given contemporary events in the Soviet Union, the reform process became known as '*perestroika*'. These new bodies were the Publications Committee (chaired by Captain A. B. Sainsbury), the Research, Technical and Programmes Committee (chaired by Eric Grove), and the Recruitment and Publicity Committee (chaired by Lt Cdr Lawrence Phillips). Of the recently constituted committees arguably the most important was Publications. To the extent that *The Mariner's Mirror* was the Society to many members, its editor, Brian Dolley, had been given great latitude in producing it during the 1980s, with no effective control over his activities exercised by Council. The new Chairman of the Publications Committee, Tony Sainsbury – a gentleman of great strength of character and political sense – viewed his Committee as a supervisory body with power delegated by Council to overrule the Editor in certain circumstances. In an extreme situation, all members of the Committee might put forward a vote of no confidence in the Hon. Editor. Dolley was unlikely to accept advice impinging on his editorial freedom. Through his years of editing, he knew from past experience that Council was not prepared to interfere although, given the strength of feeling against him in certain quarters, a crisis was almost certain to arise.

Change was symbolized by Helen Wallis stepping down as Chairman of Council at the 1989 AGM after seventeen years in office and being replaced by the former Hydrographer of the Navy, Rear-Admiral R. O. Morris, a committed proponent of reform. In his address, Admiral Morris paid tribute to his predecessor and noted the successes of the Society, HMS *Victory*, the NMM and *The Mariner's Mirror*, and its one unfulfilled ambition, the creation of a nautical dictionary. Despite the potential collaboration with a distinguished lexicographer (Laurence Urdang) the nautical dictionary had made no progress and in reality was now defunct. Although all three successes could be said to have had an international impact, by association and by example, the Society, despite its large international membership of individuals and institutions could still be deemed parochial by its overwhelmingly Anglocentric concerns. As if in confirmation of the latter, Morris, in a statement in *The Mariner's Mirror*, then looked to the future and noted three 'fields' for the future activities of the Society:

1. First, the formal Study of Nautical History in Britain is not as active as any of us would like to see; indeed it can hardly be said to exist in an organized form at all. We must all try to generate interest and enthusiasm for it, and throw the influence of the Society behind any efforts to raise national or regional perceptions of Nautical History. Does anyone know of a rich philanthropist who might be persuaded to endow a chair of Naval History at one of our universities?

2. Secondly, there are moves afoot to revise the legislation on marine archaeology to grant our nautical historical heritage, both that consciously discovered and that stumbled upon accidentally, the same protection as that

afforded to sites and artefacts on land. We already have members active in the field, and in the Heritage at Sea campaign. We must throw the Society's influence behind the campaign.

3. Thirdly, we must seek out and encourage authors and publishers to ensure that the fields of nautical research and naval history are not only tilled, but also harvested in the form of publications.[17]

Morris proposed that the Society should achieve these objects by a combination of Council and Officers 'backed, or in some cases driven, by the Committee structure now in place'. He claimed that a pattern was emerging of greater co-operation between societies and organizations active in 'Marine History and Research'. Morris laudably urged that self-interest should be set aside. The way forward was 'to add influence to influence and interest to interest to maximize our leverage and achieve our joint aims'. Realistically, Morris stated that this could not be achieved on the part of the Society without its membership increasing, thus making its finances sounder and from this its influence would grow.[18]

The increase in subscriptions took effect in 1989. As Admiral Morris noted at the AGM, this 'should not lull the Society into a false sense of security as committees were looking at tighter budgeting and also looking at costs and outgoings generally; the aim being for the Society to live within its income and to be able to spend on new activities in support of its aims'. The Recruitment and Publicity Committee was preparing a drive for new members as recent falls in numbers had now stabilized. A new publicity leaflet and application form was also being produced. At 31 December 1989, membership stood at 1,941 made up of 1467 individual members, 40 life members and 434 institutional members. A new list of members was to be published in 1990, the first for 25 years. To this end, a questionnaire had been circulated to obtain information on members' interests, and to seek comment on the Society's activities. On the death of Lt Cdr Peter Whitlock MBE, Vice-President, former CO of HMS *Victory*, and Hon. Treasurer, Brian Lavery took his place on the VATC. It was also recognized that Miss Annette Gould's activities as Membership Secretary more properly concerned the general affairs of the Society than being an adjunct to the distribution of *The Mariner's Mirror*. The 'assistant' in her title was dropped and her remuneration was then met from the general fund. The publication of the 75th anniversary volume of *The Mariner's Mirror* in 1989 was marked by a full-colour cover, while the February 1989 issue included a congratulatory message from the Society's Patron, HRH The Duke of Edinburgh, together with a brief history of the journal.[19]

By August 1989, the Publications Committee had set up an Editorial Panel with the expertise to assist the Hon. Editor. Members would:

> Both advise the Hon. Editor on the suitability of the articles submitted, and
> help him to identify potential authors to provide cover of periods and subjects
> for which unsolicited articles are not forthcoming.

In addition, the Publications Committee appointed a Reviews Editor, Dr Michael
Duffy, to lighten the load on the Hon. Editor.[20] With the restriction already in place
that the total cost of production, printing and distribution and administration of *The
Mariner's Mirror* should be limited to £30,000 or a figure not exceeding 75 per cent
of the Society's subscription income, whichever was the greater,[21] it is clear from the
combined effects of these decisions that the editorial discretion previously enjoyed
by Brian Dolley had been severely curtailed. In addition, the changes in the office
holders of the Society promised a more pragmatic approach than hitherto. With the
exception of Ann Shirley, the Hon. Secretary, the Chairman, President, Hon.
Treasurer, and the chairmen of the committees were all from naval backgrounds and
were also members of our sister society, the NRS. By the provision of an Editorial
Panel, albeit in the background, but acknowledged on the back cover of the journal,
the previous objections of Brian Dolley were swept aside. His method of checking
prospective articles had been to take soundings on the standing of authors and on
occasions obtain some referees' advice, but he had never commissioned an article.
Dolley tried to achieve a reasonable 'mix' of interest and topicality; while at the same
time he felt that the journal should be 'readable rather than authoritative'.[22] Plainly,
the academic element on Council and in the committees was aghast at this and had
resolved to do something about it.

The Competition

How was *The Mariner's Mirror* affected by competition from other international
English-language academic journals devoted to maritime history in its broadest sense,
that is, mankind's relationship with the sea? The answer was hardly at all until the latter
years of the twentieth century. In 1971, a British journal, *Maritime History*, was
founded. It owed much to Robin Craig, a lecturer at University College, London, and
his efforts were backed mainly by British academics, particularly economic and nascent
business historians. The new journal was devoted to mercantile matters and its foundation was partly predicated on the misapprehension that *The Mariner's Mirror* was too
naval in its outlook, and that it was not academic enough. Unfortunately, *Maritime
History* ultimately sank with little trace; running to four volumes by 1974, and to a fifth
volume in 1977. Ostensibly, the reason given for its demise was that a new publisher
could not be found. The reality was that it did not have enough subscribers and
institutional support: had it done so a publisher would have been willing to carry it on.[23]

The Mariner's Mirror could justifiably claim to have been the pioneering journal for nautical archaeology, and from the earliest days its pages contained significant articles on the subject. It was not until 1972 that *The International Journal of Nautical Archaeology* appeared under the editorship of Joan du Plat Taylor. From 1941, the Peabody Museum of Salem, Massachusetts, had published a quarterly journal, *The American Neptune*,[24] and from 1979, the Australian Association for Maritime History began to issue a semi-annual journal, *The Great Circle*. Not to be outdone, the Canadian Nautical Research Society, founded in 1984, began to publish its quarterly journal, *The Northern Mariner/Le marin du Nord*, and by 1989, there was another new academic journal on the scene, the semi-annual *International Journal of Maritime History* (*IJMH*), based at Memorial University, Newfoundland, and co-edited by Lewis 'Skip' Fischer and Helge Nordvik. The *IJMH* was financed through membership of the contemporaneously created International Maritime Economic History Association. Thus, by the 1980s, *Mariner's Mirror* had international competition in the English language from refereed academic journals covering many aspects of maritime history. This explains, in part, the later decision by the Publications Committee to set up an Editorial Panel for *The Mariner's Mirror*. Nevertheless, although there was no room for complacency, *The Mariner's Mirror* had easily more subscribers, with the exception of the now defunct *American Neptune*, than all other English-language maritime history refereed journals combined – as it does today.

A Decade of Change: into the 1990s

In 1990 the Rules of the Society, previously last revised in May 1978,[25] were altered with the intention of setting them out in a more logical sequence, removing the compounding of subscriptions and clarifying the positions of the Officers and Council of the Society. A new Rule (18) was proposed to regularize the appointment of paid staff.[26] In June 1990, Admiral Gueritz resigned as President at the AGM, after sixteen years, and was succeeded by Admiral of the Fleet The Lord Lewin of Greenwich. He did not attend the meeting and his presidency turned out to be benign and 'hands off', a reflection of the more businesslike way in which the Society's affairs were now being carried on by the Officers and Council.[27] Gueritz noted that Lord Lewin was at first reluctant to take the presidency on the grounds of his age and the need to shed rather than acquire commitments. However he had stated that if members elected him he would be honoured to accept. On election his aim was to strengthen the links between the Society and the NMM, and his belief was that those two 'splendid institutions' could together do much to promote interest in maritime history. Lewin, in a letter of acceptance expressed his sadness that the Society 'had become isolated in the world of Maritime History organizations – a position needing to be changed'.[28] This was not necessarily a bad thing; museums all propound their own agendas with limited horizons, given that they are, on the whole, beholden to their political masters. However, in this respect the Society, as was the case for almost its entire history, lacked perspectives and priorities.

The year 1990 marked a major upheaval in the Society. The Chairman of the Publication Committee, Capt. A. B. Sainsbury, wrote to Brian Dolley offering him a choice. He could resign with suitable honours or measures would be taken to remove him. Dolley duly resigned from the editorship of *The Mariner's Mirror* after nineteen years' connexion with the journal – as assistant editor, joint editor, and editor since 1979. He paid tribute to the compiler of the *Annual Bibliography*, Miss Mary Shepherd (NMM) and to his 'uxorial assistant' and indexer for vols 71–75, Mrs Cecilia Dolley. Dolley intimated that he would 'haul down his quill' on 31 December 1990 and wished his successor well.[29] True to his word, Capt. Sainsbury 'expressed a very warm appreciation of Mr Dolley's work during his long service in his editorial capacities'.[30] Underlying questions about honoraria and management fees during Brian Dolley's editorship had seen the beginning of dissatisfaction within the ranks of Council, initially led by Antony Preston, Lawrence Phillips and Eric Grove. Concerns over the Hon. Editor's role and influence in the Society were also underpinned by academics who wished to see a more rigorous approach to issues of quality in the journal, particularly over haphazard refereeing. In short, the real issue was over the Hon. Editor's use of the Society as his own personal fiefdom, a situation which had been allowed to develop by previous Chairmen and Council members. Dolley had nevertheless made a huge contribution to the Society, and was allowed to resign with dignity to avoid unnecessary unpleasantness. Had he not resigned such was the strength of feeling against him that chairmen of committees and many other members would have resigned thereby jeopardizing the Society's future. This is not to say that Dolley had no measure of support in Council: he had; however, that support had waned. Dolley was replaced from the beginning of 1991 by Dr Michael Duffy, who had been Reviews Editor since 1989. He, in turn, was succeeded as Reviews Editor by Dr David J. Starkey. During 1990, the Hon. Secretary, Ann Shirley, also resigned and was replaced by Derek Law. At its October 1990 meeting the Council voted to give Brian Dolley Honorary Life Membership of the Society and a bronze medal for his contribution to it. However, with his remaining dignity intact, Dolley subsequently declined both awards.[31]

In 1991 the Hon. Editor, Michael Duffy, removed the subtitle 'The International Journal of the Society for Nautical Research' from the frontispiece of *The Mariner's Mirror*, presumably on the basis that this was implied. Its omission gave other journals more of an international cachet than their contents warranted. On the financial side, the 1990 accounts showed an acceptable surplus even though the cost of producing *The Mariner's Mirror* remained the Society's largest single expenditure. During the year a number of possibilities to reduce its cost had been explored and introduced. Whilst Staples of St Albans remained the Society's printer, it was decided that copy-editing and typesetting should be done separately, giving a substantial saving in cost with the penalty of longer lead times before each issue. The content of the cover pages had been revised, as were changes to the typefaces and the layout of the main letterpress. In addition, a decision was made to introduce acid free paper. The decision to launch a *Newsletter* had also been taken, in part to offset the longer lead times, but also to remove ephemera from *The Mariner's Mirror*. The first issue of the new-style, but cramped, *The Mariner's Mirror* came out in February 1991, accompanied by the first issue of the *Newsletter*, which was designed and edited by Lt Cdr Derek Howse.

Some 534 replies to a Members' Questionnaire out of 1,500 dispatched in 1989 had been received. With 1,466 individual members at 25 March 1990, this represented a 36 per cent response rate. Overall, the vast majority expressed satisfaction with the Society's structure and work, and there was clearly no great groundswell for radical change. In respect of *The Mariner's Mirror*, 422 members were entirely satisfied with it as it was, and 48 dissatisfied.[32]

The new production schedule and format for *The Mariner's Mirror* under Dr Michael Duffy, Dr David J. Starkey and typesetter Linda Jones had been underpinned by savings in production costs in the previous year. Even with the addition of the *Newsletter*, costs for it and the journal combined, at that stage, were less than those formerly absorbed by *The Mariner's Mirror* alone. In the wider United Kingdom sphere, the government had issued a White Paper on the Environment, which announced that responsibility for marine heritage was being transferred to the Department of the Environment in line with national heritage on land, and the Royal Commission for Historic Monuments was required to prepare a list of historic sites under the sea. As the Society noted, no resources seem to have been allocated to either the Department or the Royal Commission to enable them to make progress with their tasks. In consequence, the SNR was working with the Joint Nautical Archaeology Policy Committee to maintain pressure for action.[33]

With a new *List of Members* published, membership at 31 December 1990 was down on the comparable figure a year earlier and stood at 1,865, comprising 1,413 individual members, 36 life members and 416 institutional members. However, at the 1991 AGM of the Society, Admiral Morris reported that membership had now stabilized at just over the 2,000 mark. A new fund, created by Mrs Romola Anderson's will, the Anderson Bequest Fund, appeared in the SNR's accounts.

Money from this, together with funds from the other two beneficiaries (the NMM and the NRS), was set aside to produce a new 'scholarly but popular Naval History of Britain'. In addition, the Society continued to sponsor the International Commission for Maritime History Seminar Series in conjunction with the Department of War Studies at King's College, London. These initiatives, combined with plans to sponsor future conferences, marked a new appreciation that the Society had a wider role to play in the academic life of the nation. However, this rather belated appreciation included a new departure of sponsoring a modestly attended one-day conference at the NMM in November 1991. There was also a first 'out-of-town' visit to the ss *Great Britain* at Bristol, which only attracted ten members. The Osborne history project, which had begun well, with Evan Davies undertaking considerable amounts of research in national and private collections, was slowing down. Although the project fund stood at £2,500 after all research and transcription costs had been met,[34] the progress in writing was disappointing and no firm date for publication had been set.[35]

Meanwhile, events surrounding the administration of the PRNMTC had taken a decided turn for the worse. During 1990, it emerged that two of the Company's personnel had appropriated company funds for their own gain and that false accounting for catering functions had regularly taken place. Moreover, many small suppliers were paid in cash without any documentation, and in the case of the 1988, 1989 and 1990 Navy Days at the Dockyard no records or documentation had been created. Subsequently, in October the Business Manager and assistant were summarily dismissed by letter from the Company Secretary, Brian Dolley.[36] That this deplorable situation had been allowed to arise called into question the level of supervision exercised by the Society's Officers and by Council.

On a more positive note, HMS *Victory* began a decade of improvements. Stimulated, perhaps, by the display standards set by HMS *Warrior* on her return from Hartlepool, the VATC was compelled to look hard at the presentation of their charge and created, as its sub-committee, the Interpretation Committee. In September 1991, Peter Goodwin was appointed as *Victory*'s curator and began applying his lifelong interest and research to the improvement of the ship's display. The dressing of the ship was willingly accepted by the SNR as a natural charge upon the STVF.

In the Annual Report for 1992 it was noted the *Newsletter* had proved so popular and had been attracting so much material that it was likely that its growth would have to be limited to control its cost. At the end of 1992, after two years in office, Lt Cdr Derek Howse relinquished the editorship of the *Newsletter* and was replaced by Dr Michael Partridge. By the AGM in June 1993 the first one-day New Researchers in Maritime History Conference, co-sponsored by the Society and the British

Commission for Maritime History, had taken place at the NMM.

At this point, a major change in the status of the Society occurred. Since its inception in 1910, the SNR had remained a body without legal incorporation:

> A congregation of people interested in nautical history and maritime research, raising and disbursing money, holding meetings and generally going about its business as a group of individuals all collectively responsible for our affairs.[37]

In the wider world, however, liability law had mushroomed, as had litigation; and as a consequence individuals could no longer carry the burden of full liability. It was therefore decided to incorporate the Society as a company with limited liability. However, this apparently did not alter the Society's charitable status or the manner in which the Society was run. The Society's Officers and Committees would still be responsible to Council, and Council, in turn, would be still be responsible to the membership, and have to come before it annually at the AGM. As a result of the proposed change in status there would no longer be Trustees who, in any event, had never been established by a Trust Deed. The financial management of the Society would now be vested in Council. Accordingly, a resolution was put to the 1993 AGM to put the new Constitution of the Society into effect and this was passed unanimously, as was a second technical resolution, an 'amendment of the Constitution to dissolve the [old] Society'. All that remained was to finalize the details of incorporation. As some years had elapsed since the subscription had been raised, an increase was proposed, but on a differential basis. Members choosing to pay by either standing order, or by direct debit, would pay £24 per annum but for all other members the sum would be £26. Overseas and institutional membership fees would also be increased by comparable amounts. A change in the Society's printers from Staples of St Albans to the Alden Press of Oxford, now made it affordable to produce *The Mariner's Mirror* on a regular basis at 128 pages per issue.[38]

In his Annual Report for 1993, Admiral Morris indicated his decision to resign and looked back at his five years as Chairman in terms of what the Society had achieved and where it now stood. The three committees set up at the beginning of his tenure, had now been joined by a fourth, the Finance Committee, which supervised the transfer of the Society's investment portfolio to a then private bank, Adam & Co. The Finance Committee assumed the responsibility for those financial matters formerly exercised by the Trustees, and also for a wider supervision of the Society's financial affairs. As a result of the deliberations of this committee, Council decided that the Society should be incorporated as a charitable limited company which the 1993 AGM endorsed. The last meeting of the Council of the old Society and the first meeting of the new SNR (a private limited company by guarantee with no share capital) took place consecutively on 1 September 1993.[39] The Hon.

Treasurer, Chris Swinson, a qualified accountant, played a key role in this major reorganization. Nevertheless, the charitable aspect of the company, *viz* its restricted funds, the STVF and the Macpherson Collection Endowment Fund, still remained to be determined. In addition to the new memorandum and articles of association, the formal documents of the Society's new constitution, a Guide to the Conduct of Business had been drawn up to be given to each new member of Council.

On HMS *Victory*, the Royal Navy guides to the ship were replaced by civilians in a uniform modelled on that of a RN Petty Officer with an embroidered 1805 Royal Arms as an arm badge. The Council was also in consultation with the VATC to have a 25-foot replica cutter built for HMS *Victory* as a memorial to her late CO, Lt Cdr Peter Whitlock. At the instigation of its distinguished small-craft specialist, Austin Farrar, the Research, Technical and Programmes Committee had recommended the Society produce two cutters for HMS *Victory*, one constructed in modern materials by Chippendale of Wroxham and capable of being rowed and sailed. This was presented during the 1993 *Victory* visit. During the summer, the cutter participated in several events crewed by members of the Society under David Page, another small-craft specialist, appointed its Sailing Master. The second cutter, built of traditional materials by apprentices in Chatham Historic Dockyard was handed over on Trafalgar Day 1993 and was displayed alongside *Victory*. This proved to be as great (and expensive) a disappointment as the Wroxham cutter had been a success, Chatham having built the boat using insufficiently skilled and knowledgeable supervision. Too much had been taken on trust by the Research, Technical and Programmes Committee and it was soon clear that, far from being a model replica, it had been shoddily constructed. It was doomed to a short life, some of its materials being 'rebuilt' by *Victory* into a yawl completed in 2009.

In 1994, Admiral Morris, who had done much to turn the Society around, concluded that he had presided over 'an eventful and exhilarating five years' as Chairman.[40] He was succeeded by Rear-Admiral Richard Hill. The Hon. Secretary, Derek Law, the Hon. Treasurer, Christopher Swinson, and the Membership Secretary, Annette Gould, also relinquished their offices and were replaced in 1995 respectively by Lt Cdr W. J. R. 'Jock' Gardner, Peter V. Nash and Peter Garvey. At the 1995 AGM, the new Chairman, Rear-Admiral Hill, described how the Society proposed to complete the process begun in 1993 to constitute it as a charitable company limited by guarantee, by sealing a scheme whereby it was empowered to administer the STVF and Macpherson Funds. All that remained for the scheme's completion was the Charity Commissioners receiving a copy of the newspaper notice to that effect. The Commissioners had already agreed the conclusion of an agreement with the Society's investment advisers, Adam & Company, and this had been signed. By this stage the reorganization of the Society's administration had taken place and a new Finance and General Purposes Committee (FGPC) had overall responsibility to co-ordinate policy and recommend it to Council.

Council

With the earlier setting up of the Finance Committee and now its successor, the FGPC, members may have thought that a form of centralization of the Society's affairs had taken place and that a hierarchical order of importance in terms of Committees had been created. Would the FGPC unduly influence Council – the body with power to oversee all the Society's activity? That, of course, depended upon Council's willingness or disinclination to scrutinize committee recommendations actively. Moreover, with the Society's Chairman in charge of the FGPC, were its recommendations ever likely to be seriously challenged in Council? *De facto* power, in terms of policy decision-making in the Society was heavily weighted in favour of its Chairman and Chairmen of Committees. *De jure* power is vested in the Council but it was generally loath to overturn recommendations from its Chairman. Throughout its history, the Council reflected a wide range of sometimes competing interests. It had never been an elected body in the sense that all members were balloted before the AGM and the results read out accordingly. Nonetheless, the Society's Officers and Councillors were re-elected on an annual basis at the AGM, and any member could recommend a person or persons for office by nominating them beforehand. In practice, the latter course, rarely, if ever, occurred. Chairmen and Council tended to make the big decisions before AGMs and these went through, normally without protest. In fact, AGMs basically served as getting-to-meet-the-members occasions and to reiterate what the Society had achieved during the previous year. Underpinning the entire edifice of accountability, or the lack of it, was the fact that Officers and Councillors expected to serve the Society 'emerged' on the recommendations of those already serving on Council, and not at AGMs.

During 1995 the Society's funds were boosted by a legacy of nearly £40,000 left to it without conditions as to its use, from the estate of Lt Cdr Richard Tomlin. Council decided to create a separate Tomlin Fund, the income from which would finance or supplement expenditure on events it otherwise could not afford. The commissioned history of the Royal Naval College, Osborne, had stalled repeatedly due to Evan Davies' inability to complete the manuscript. Dr Michael Partridge took on the task of writing it, and therefore resigned as Newsletter Editor. He was replaced by Dr Margarette Lincoln of the NMM. A newly formed Small Craft Committee headed by David Page added to the panoply of Society Committees, and also managed the activities of the Wroxham-built *Victory* Cutter. Membership, which had stabilized at just over 2,000 in 1991, had been subject to a year-on-year decline and stood at 1,863 at the end of 1996. To encourage growth in membership a publicity leaflet had been produced under the aegis of Lt Cdr Lawrence Phillips's committee on Marketing and Publicity and was available for distribution. The Society appointed a Publicity Officer, Mr Barry Teate, who served as Secretary of the Small Craft Committee.

On Trafalgar Day 1995, the official Nelson Decade began.[41] *Victory*'s CO, in his annual report, noted that her foretopsail measuring 3,618 sq feet, and a true artefact of Trafalgar, had been returned after drying. The sail had been on display in a glass case on the orlop deck alongside the so-called Nelson shrine, crumpled and un-touched for more than fifty years. It had suffered water ingress during its previous storage, which led to mould developing; that had been treated and it had been cleaned and folded. The curator of HMS *Victory*, Peter Goodwin, had photographed and provided a scholarly analysis of it. Eighty per cent of the funding for this had been provided by Hampshire County Council, with a further £4,000 from the STVF. The availability of a suitable building within the Dockyard was awaited before it could be viewed by the general public.[42]

The Charity Commissioners finally sealed the scheme whereby the Society was authorized to administer and manage the STVF and Macpherson Collection Endowment Funds on 10 July 1996. This completed the process began in 1993 to constitute the Society as a company limited by guarantee. Peter Nash, the Hon. Treasurer, explained at the 1997 AGM that the Society's Annual Accounts had to be presented in the form of restricted and unrestricted funds in accordance with the new rules introduced by the Charity Commissioners. This tended to reduce their previous clarity as activities in the restricted funds were merged with general SNR transactions. Also, investments had been revalued to reflect market rather than book values, resulting in a pronounced increase in Society assets.

Portsmouth Dockyard

At his last AGM as Chairman in 1994, Admiral Morris noted that the run-up to the bicentenary of the Battle of Trafalgar in 2005 had already begun with an interior restoration programme on *Victory*, partly funded from the STVF. This had started in tandem with the ongoing programme of major restoration in Portsmouth Dockyard, about which the Society seemed largely unconcerned, despite changes which might affect its interests, as when the October 1987 hurricane stripped off the entire roof of the Victory Gallery. The Defence Review in 1982 encouraged the MoD (N) to re-evaluate the use of its assets. The MOD (N) considered the south-western area of Portsmouth Dockyard had no functional future for the modern navy but was suitable for development as a heritage site. Portsmouth Naval Base Property Trust

(PNBPT) was set up in 1985 by the MoD and Portsmouth City Council in partnership with English Heritage to take responsibility for the long-term preservation of the historic area of Portsmouth Naval Base released under the 1982 Dockyard Review. It was also intended to safeguard any further historic defence estate which might either be released in the future by the MoD or become available on the open market. The PNBPT is therefore a property development agency holding a ninety-nine-year lease and specializing in the re-use of the historic buildings associated with Britain's naval past. Its assets included the area surrounding HMS *Victory*, the Victory Gallery (as the Victory Museum had become known) and the Royal Naval Museum – but without any recorded consultation involving the SNR. The possibility that the area might be subject to 'aggressively commercial development' receded with the withdrawal of Sea Containers Ltd in 1989.[43] In the case of the Royal Naval Museum, which had by now assumed full control over its Trading Company; the appointment of a commercial manager from outwith its ranks promised a greater income from this source to augment the STVF.

The Royal Naval Museum's status also changed in 1985. Under the provisions of the National Heritage Act of 1983, the museum was devolved from MoD (N) to become an Executive Non-Departmental Public Body, supported by Grant-in-Aid. Its grant income was calculated to reflect the level of support and general financial assistance formerly provided directly by MoD (N). At this juncture its name changed again to become the Royal Naval Museum, Portsmouth (see p. 130–1). It was all too predictable, as other 'heritage' associations have found to their cost, that funding under these circumstances would never be enough to fulfil the ambitions of successive Directors and staff in furthering the interests of the museum. Thus the Director had to look to other bodies to fund projects and to make bids to the National Heritage Lottery Fund. In addition, the Royal Naval Museum later became a registered charity within the provisions of the Charities Act 1993.

By November 1997, the PRNM's fundraising appeal for its modernization schemes had reached £3.8m of the £5m required. According to the museum's Director, H. Campbell McMurray, its fundraising activities had reached a critical point. There was a need to concentrate on funding the fitting out of No. 11 Storehouse in order that the design and construction work on new displays could proceed on schedule. McMurray was deeply grateful for the generous help the museum had already received from the Society. The SNR had advanced £40,000 for the Victory Gallery to enable the museum to carry out the all important preliminary work, which contributed to the museum's successful National Heritage Lottery bid.[44] McMurray then sought the Society's funding in respect of the McCarthy Gallery, which dealt with Nelson's life and career and his enduring popularity as an English hero. He emphasized that an entire corner of the gallery would be devoted to a section called 'The Commander-in-Chief', which would look at Nelson's time as C-in-C Mediterranean, 1803–5, and which would feature furniture and other items he had with him in HMS *Victory*. McMurray wondered if the SNR would contribute a donation of say, £30,000, which would attract matching Lottery funding of about £45,000. Together these sums would cover the cost of the design and fitting out of the entire section. In return for this generosity the museum would be delighted to make prominent mention of the Society in the section, 'with, perhaps, a graphic panel explaining about the Society and its aims'?[45] In the space of a month the Society had agreed to advance £30,000 for the 'Nelson as Commander-in-Chief' component of the McCarthy Gallery.[46] The Society's justification for agreeing to fund or part-fund the Royal Naval Museum projects had already been set out by its Chairman, Admiral Hill, in a letter to McMurray:

> Before any payment is made, the Society will need to be satisfied that the moneys are to be devoted to the specific purposes and no other. While Council has taken the view that in this case the purposes are directly connected with 'the presentation to the public of HMS Victory'. It reiterates that that is the only proper application of the Save the Victory Fund.[47]

Writing at the same time to the CO *Victory*, Lt Cdr Cheshire, who had expressed reservations about the use of the STVF for projects other than *Victory* herself, Admiral Hill enlarged upon Council's reasons for advancing moneys from the STVF to the Royal Naval Museum:

> The presentation of the ship herself is aided, and not degraded, by the supplementary presentations ashore, and the enhancements to them that are now proposed; and that in the 'Nelson Decade', as in no other, resources must be deployed to the full to ensure maximum public impact.[48]

On a more prosaic level, charities were expected to spend the moneys that accrued to them on their stated purposes.

It had often been said within the legal profession that the old Admiralty Court, for historical reasons, dealt with wills, wives and wrecks. To critics of the Society, particularly academic ones, few of whom, if any, would voice their concerns; the SNR was both too naval and too Nelson-obsessed. Similarly, in some academic circles, *The Mariner's Mirror* was seen as all triremes and naval history. There is a grain of truth in the former contention although it has been vastly overplayed, but the *Mirror*, like the Admiralty Court in its general application of many diverse areas of law, existed as a journal focusing on *all* aspects of maritime and naval history broadly defined. Nevertheless, the Society, through its Council and committees, was firmly fixed on a course leading to the celebrations of the bicentenary of Trafalgar in 2005 and the death of Nelson. Council in January 1997 gave unanimous approval to the Chairman regarding finding a suitable home to display *Victory's* foretopsail. In 1997 Dr Eric Grove gave up his long tenure as chair of the Research Programmes and Technical Committee as he was leaving the country to take up a research fellowship in Australia. Brian Lavery, who had already played a major role in the committee, succeeded him.

The 1998 income and expenditure account showed a substantial deficit and, despite the Society's growing cash holdings, the AGM again raised subscriptions from 1 January 1999 to £32 for individuals and £42 for institutions. In November 1998, Dr David J. Starkey indicated his intention to stand down as Reviews Editor of *Mariner's Mirror*.[49] He was subsequently replaced by Dr Richard Gorski, the current Reviews Editor. At Admiral Hill's last Council Meeting as Chairman on 20 April 1999, he announced, consequent upon the death of Lord Lewin, that HRH The Duke of York had accepted nomination for the office of President of the Society. Hill was succeeded by F. A. (Alan) Aberg of the Historical Monuments Commission. Before his retirement, Hill received a letter from H. Campbell McMurray, the Director of the Royal Naval Museum, inquiring whether the Society would be prepared to give further support towards the restoration and re-interpretation of Wyllie's *A Panorama of the Battle of Trafalgar*. It will be recalled that the Society through the STVF had already pledged £30,000 in February 1996. This time Hill felt unable to put the proposal to Council as it would involve the Fund going into overspend, that is, dipping into capital, not income. Moreover, Hill had in mind the possible effects on the STVF of displaying *Victory's* foretopsail, which would incur heavy expenditure from the Fund. However, he did invite the museum to make another application if it wished to cover any shortfall on the project in the autumn.[50]

During 1999, Lt Cdr Lawrence Phillips further revised the membership leaflet, a new membership list was in preparation, and Dr Michael Partridge had nearly completed the history of the Royal Naval College, Osborne. The cost of the publication was subsidized by £3,000 which Lawrence Phillips had raised from industry. A small book launch was held at Portsmouth in 2000 at which the Society's Honorary Vice-President, Countess Mountbatten of Burma, addressed members and guests. In addition, the Chairman of the VATC, Dr Alan McGowan, had written a monograph, *HMS Victory, Her Construction, Career and Restoration*, the royalties of which he donated to the ship's preservation. The Society also entered the internet age, due to the initiative and hard work of Barry Teate and students at Kingston University, Surrey. Members could now consult www.snr.org to find the membership leaflet and the current Newsletter list of events. Discussions on the Bethell Watercraft Index of the British Isles had advanced with the International Sailing Craft Association involved. Progress on this ambitious and needed project had been slow, not in its compilation, but in the funding needed for its application, and John Bethell, David Clement and David Page strove to move the project forward so that the Index was not further delayed. The Society had also taken the lead, prompted by SNR (South) in restoring W. L. Wyllie's grave in Portchester churchyard. Hampshire County Council made a grant of £250, the 1805 Club contributed £100 and the Society made up the balance.[51]

References

1   *Mariner's Mirror*, 75:3 (1989), AGM of the SNR, 1989.

2   *Mariner's Mirror*, 71:3 (1985), AGM of the SNR, 1985.

3   *Mariner's Mirror*, 72:3 (1986), AGM of SNR, 1986. It was announced at the AGM for 1987 that the many benefactions of Mrs Lily McCarthy should be acknowledged by the presentation to her of a hand-carved replica of the launching box of HMS *Dreadnought*, made from the original English and American oak from the timbers of HMS *Victory*.

4   Uncatalogued Treasurer's paper's (Lt Cdr Peter Whitlock) in the authors' possession: letter from Nigel Lloyd, Blease Lloyd Auditors to Captain Lapper, Senior Trustee, 22 June 1987.

5   *Ibid.*: letter from Bartlett de Reya to Charity Commissioners, 15 February 1987

6   Uncatalogued Treasurer's papers (Lt Cdr Peter Whitlock) in authors' possession: Minutes of Council Meeting, 16 September 1987.

7   *Ibid.*

8   *Ibid.*

9   Uncatalogued Treasurer's papers (Lt Cdr Peter Whitlock): letter from Brian Dolley to Captain Lapper, 1 December 1987.

10 Uncatalogued Treasurer's papers: List of Honoraria from 1978 to 1987 compiled by Lt Cdr Peter Whitlock, Hon.Treasurer. In 1978, honoraria were: Hon. Editor (£150), Hon. Treasurer (£225) and Membership Secretary (£150).

11 Uncatalogued Treasurer's papers, (Antony Preston): letter from R. W. Groves, Charity Commission, to M. Rose, Bartlett de Reya, 12 April 1988.

12 *Ibid.*

13 By this stage Richard Ormond had replaced Neil Cossons as Director.

14 *Mariner's Mirror*, 73:3 (1987), AGM of SNR, 1987.

15 David's disquiet is evident in a series of letters in uncatalogued Treasurer's papers (Lt Cdr Peter Whitlock) in the authors' possession.

16 *Mariner's Mirror*, 74:4 (1988), Statement on HMS *Victory* and the SNR by Helen Wallis.

17 *Mariner's Mirror*, 75:3 (1989), From the Chairman.

18 *Ibid.*

19 The costs of the full-colour cover were borne by the Society's printers, Staples of St Albans.

20 NMM SNR 19/1 Minutes of Publications Committee, 30 August 1989. *Mariner's Mirror*, 76:2 (1990), Annual Report for the Year 1989.

21 NMM SNR 3/27 Minutes of Council Meeting, 12 April 1987.

22 Uncatalogued Treasurer's papers (Antony Preston): Meeting of Publications Committee, 19 July 1989.

23 For an analysis of the links between business and maritime history in Britain, see L. Johnman and H. Murphy, 'Maritime and Business History in Britain: Past, Present and Future', *International Journal of Maritime History* XIX No, 1, (2007), 239–270.

24 Founded by Samuel Eliot Morrison: *American Neptune* was published by the Peabody Museum, Salem, Massachusetts, from 1941 to 1992, the Peabody and Essex Museum from 1992–3 and the Peabody Essex Museum from 1993 to its demise in 2002. For *The American Neptune*, see E. S. Dodge, *Thirty Years of the American Neptune* (Cambridge, Mass, 1972), and *The American Neptune: Fifty Year Index* (Salem, 1997).

25 *Mariner's Mirror*, 64:1 (1978).

26 *Mariner's Mirror*, 76:1 (1990), Rule 18 read as follows: Where necessary for the efficient administration of the Society's affairs, suitably qualified persons may be employed and remunerated as the Council may deem appropriate. Such persons may not be members of Council, though they may attend at Council Meetings to report as required.

27 Rear-Admiral Gueritz's first choice for the presidency of the Society had been Admiral Jeremy Black on the 'hopeful' basis that 'if he became First Sea Lord in two or three years time, he would follow the distinguished line of Prince Louis of Battenberg, Admiral Sturdee, Admiral Beatty, Prince George and Admiral Hope'. The last attribution was erroneous in that Admiral Sir George Hope had been Chairman initially (and only President later) and Deputy First Sea Lord. See NMM SNR 3/27 Minutes of Council Meeting, 21 February 1989. Later choices that emerged were Sir Brookes Richards, Admiral Sir David Hallifax, Lord Hood and, on the recommendation of Basil Greenhill, Sir John Morrison, see NNM SNR 3/27 Minutes of a Council Meeting, 27 September 1989. By November 1989 it had been reported that Rear-Admiral Gueritz had approached Admiral Sir David Hallifax as his successor, see NMM SNR 3/27 Minutes of Council Meeting, 23 November 1989.

28 NMM SNR 3/27 Minutes of Council Meeting, 1 February 1990.

29 *Mariner's Mirror*, 76:3 (1990), AGM of SNR, 1990.

30 *Ibid*.

31 NMM SNR 19/1 Letter from B. H. Dolley to Rear-Admiral R. O. Morris, 3 January 1991.

32 Supplement to the Newsletter of May 1991: Annual Report for 1990.

33 *Ibid*, and AGM of SNR, 1991.

34 *Mariner's Mirror*, 75:2 (1989), Annual Report for 1988.

35 *Mariner's Mirror*, 78:3 (1992), Annual Report for the Year 1991.

36 Uncatalogued papers of Antony Preston, SNR Treasurer: Memorandum from B. H. Dolley, Company Secretary PRNMTC to the Chairman and Directors, 18 October 1990.

37 *Mariner's Mirror*, 79:3 (1993), Society Records, Annual Report for 1992, 350.

38 *Ibid.*, Annual Report for the Year 1992 and AGM of SNR,1993.

39 Companies House London Information Centre, Bloomsbury, Company No. 02848095 incorporated 26 August 1993.

40 *Mariner's Mirror*, 80:3 (1994), Annual Report for the Year 1993, and Secretary's Report of the AGM of SNR, 1994.

41 The Royal Navy and the NMM established a Committee to co-ordinate events between 1995 and 2005. It was chaired by Colin White of the PRNM. The Vice-Chairman was Peter Warwick of the 1805 Club. See Chapter 7.

42 *Mariner's Mirror*, 82:3 (1996), Annual Report of the SNR for the Year 1996, and AGM of SNR, 1996.

43 A second disposal of land from the naval base was not given to the PNBPT. In a separate transaction, the MoD sold HMS *Vernon* to the Berkeley Group in 1996. The Gun Wharf Quays development opened in February 2001 and the Spinnaker Tower in 2005. Berkeley Homes retained the Old Infirmary, originally a nineteenth-century Royal Marines' hospital, among its residential properties.

44 PNBPT, *20 Year Review 1986–2006*, 6, takes credit for the re-roofing of the *Victory* Gallery.

45 NMM 17/8 Letter from H. C. McMurray to Rear-Admiral Richard Hill, 5 November 1997.

46 NMM 17/8 Letter from H. C. McMurray to Rear-Admiral Richard Hill, 1 December 1997.

47 NMM 17/9 Letter from Rear-Admiral Richard Hill to H. C. McMurray, 2 February 1996.

48 NMM SNR 17/9 Letter from Rear-Admiral Hill to Lt Cdr M. Cheshire BSc, RN, 2 February 1996.

49 NMM SNR 3/24 Minutes of Council Meeting, 4 November 1998.

50 NMM SNR 17/9 Letter from Rear-Admiral Hill to H. C. McMurray, 23 April 1999.

51 *Mariner's Mirror*, 86:3 (2000), Society Records, Chairman's Annual Report for the Year 1999.

7

Crossing the Bar:
the Society enters a new century

The Society made landfall in the new century intact: that, itself; was worthy of note – for the world had changed substantially since a group of Edwardian gentlemen and two ladies brought it into existence in 1910. In spite of all the changes, the Society's outlook had altered remarkably little. HMS *Victory* still held a central place in its affairs. To this end, the Society's expenditure on the ship was reviewed and a five-year plan devised to take the Society up to the bicentenary of the Battle of Trafalgar on 21 October 2005. This included preparations for displaying the ship's foretopsail.[1] After a decade as Hon. Editor, Dr Michael Duffy was succeeded in January 2001 by another naval historian, Dr Richard Harding. Earlier, in 1999, Dr Margarette Lincoln had succeeded Dr Andrew Lambert as Chair of the Publications Committee and, at the AGM of June 2000, Elizabeth Verity of the NMM succeeded Lt Cdr Jock Gardner as Hon. Secretary. During 2001, Professor Sarah Palmer succeeded Brian Lavery as Chairman of the Research, Technical and Programmes Committee. In conjunction with a relatively new Chairman, Alan Aberg, this represented a substantial change to the officeholders of the Society as the new century began.

The VATC had been meeting formally twice yearly since 1955. It now included the CO of HMS *Victory* and a representative of the Procurement Executive responsible for the provision of timber. From 1985 onwards the representation of the Society and that of the NMM had been modified with the agreement of the Chairman of the SNR and the Director of the NMM. Committee members have not necessarily been replaced when they retire, providing that the range and quality of advice available to the Dockyard authorities is not compromised. However, the Society and the NMM reserved the right to revert to the 1955 agreement at their discretion.[2] Currently, the Society has two representatives on the VATC. On Trafalgar Day 2000, the completely refurbished Victory Gallery at the Royal Naval Museum, to which the Society had generously contributed, and the restored Wyllie *Panorama* were opened under Phase 1 of its re-development programme.[3]

The Society continued to contribute to the purchase of objects and paintings at the NMM through the Macpherson Fund. A second grant of £10,000 from the Macpherson Fund to supplement the £30,000 granted in 2000 enabled the NMM to purchase Isaac Sailmaker's painting of the Eddystone Lighthouse. Also *The Mariner's Mirror* recovered from its previously tarnished reputation. Pre-publication orders for *The Mariner's Mirror on CD-Rom* containing every issue from 1911 to 2000 reached 600. Analysed and edited by John Bethell, with the aid of David Clement, and published in conjunction with Chatham Publishing, the five-CD set contained over 45,000 pages of maritime history, over 11,000 indexed articles and over 2,000 illustrations. This was a remarkable achievement and it had many innovative features ahead of its time. Nevertheless, the Society's role had remained an occluded one and 'raising its profile' beyond maritime history into the wider 'heritage community' was considered to be a priority.

In financial terms, as noted at the 2000 AGM, the Society entered the new century with a small deficit in its non-restricted accounts apparently due to decreased income from subscriptions. This was caused by over-inflating the membership figures by retaining too many non-payers. In fact, the underlying financial position of the Society was remarkably strong. Subscription income had risen during the 1990s and remained stable from 1999 to 2003 while from 1996 to 2001 'other income' including yields from investments exceeded £100,000. However, the three years from 1998 to 2000 did show losses of over £50,000 annually due in large part to unusually heavy expenditure. This caused a decline in the Society's cash balances from 1998 to 2002 but was followed by substantial increases thereafter. Overall, the Society's total revenue hovered around £180,000 per annum from 1997 to 2008. Importantly, one necessary balance in the Society's affairs was no longer a problem in the new century: during the interwar years and again during the period of post-war inflation, the cost of the Society's publications, principally *The Mariner's Mirror*, regularly exceeded subscription income. Over recent years, however, publication costs have been clearly well below subscription income.[4]

At the 2000 AGM, in what had been a familiar refrain of past Chairmen down the years, Alan Aberg urged members to make a special effort to enlist new recruits, and promised to strike off non-payers more rigorously in future after reminder notices had been sent. One further gain from subscription income sources was offered by a new scheme of Gift Aid. This allowed the Society to reclaim 25 per cent of subscriptions from the Inland Revenue in future years, if UK-based members (totalling around 900) supported the scheme. Some 200 members joined the Gift Aid scheme which produced an additional £2,800 for the Society's funds. In addition, the Hon. Treasurer, Peter Nash, instituted a Reserves Policy to conform to new guidelines from the Charity Commission. Barry Teate's resignation as Publicity

Officer meant that the SNR website was currently unavailable, but it was hoped to re-establish it not later than mid-2001.[5] At the end of 2002, overall membership stood at 1,684.[6]

Throughout 2001 the Society's Publications Committee discussed options to mark the bicentenary of Trafalgar. A special edition of *The Mariner's Mirror* for November 2005 was planned and contributions were sought on themes related to 1805. The Society continued to support the Official Nelson Commemorations Committee (ONCC) chaired by Colin White of the PRNM, who was seconded to the NMM, Greenwich, for the planning of the programme for the bicentenary. In August 2001, Portsmouth hosted the International Festival of the Sea and the Chairman, Alan Aberg, helped man an SNR stand alongside *Victory* to advertise the Society. R. E. G. Harris organized the stand, and in recognition of this and other selfless work for the Society, the Council awarded him a medal. *Victory's* curator, Peter Goodwin, explained at the Society's 2001 AGM that new research had revealed that the red paint covering the orlop deck planking 'to disguise bloodstains' was not authentic. Consequently, all red paint had to be removed in the interests of historical accuracy.

The Department of Culture Media and Sport commissioned Dr Alan Borg to produce a review of the Portsmouth Historic Dockyard. Borg had been asked to assess the effectiveness of the management in the Dockyard and consider changes which might be made to improve its long-term efficiency. The most significant of his recommendations was that there should be a single unified management, which would form a National Museum for the Royal Navy on a par with the National Army Museum and the Royal Air Force Museum. The future relationship with other Royal Navy museums at Southsea, Gosport, and Yeovilton was also considered.[7] By 2002, however, it was announced that neither the Department of Culture, Media and Sport which had commissioned the review nor the Ministry of Defence would provide the financial resources needed to put the report's recommendations into effect. The SNR, given its long and enduring association with HMS *Victory* and the Royal Naval Museum, had participated in the review and therefore sought a solution which would address the report's concerns. Discussions on the future of the Dockyard continued with various organizations. These occurred against the background of the Royal Navy having initiated dialogue on widening public access and commercial development in the southwest corner of the dockyard – the location of the most important historic buildings. Meanwhile, the Society, as a member of the ONCC continued to make an input to the shape of the bicentennial Trafalgar celebrations. It was planned for these to be linked to an international Year of the Sea for 2005 initiated by the NMM and the British Tourist Authority.

HMS *Victory* would obviously be the centrepiece for many of the events of 2005, and to this end the Society maintained its financial support for the conservation and eventual display of her shot-torn foretopsail worn at Trafalgar. In conjunction with the Royal Navy and Fleet Support Limited, the Society agreed a contract to clean the sail again and, importantly, to find a permanent cure for its mould problem. It was hoped that the sail would be displayed in Storehouse No. 10, but the provision of stable environmental conditions in the building was essential. The Society contributed £42,120 to the cost of the work from the STVF. This outlay was partly offset by £20,000 to the STVF in 2002, from the Royal Naval Museum Trading Company. It was planned to display *Victory's* foretopsail with explanations of its history in an exhibition commencing in April 2005 which would remain open until November.[8]

Preparations for the bicentenary of the battle of Trafalgar also made progress during 2003. The Society agreed that a grant of £15,000 from the STVF should be used towards the cost of recruiting a part-time Learning Development Officer for HMS *Victory*, Mrs Rachel Rhodes. She was appointed until 2006 to assist in the education of the public during the bicentennial celebrations, technically as a member of staff of the Royal Naval Museum. The SNR agreed to fund a DVD programme to enable disabled visitors of all ages to make a virtual tour of otherwise inaccessible parts of the ship. Also in 2003, a new organization, the Portsmouth Historic Dockyard Trust, was created to direct and co-ordinate the varied agencies involved in the Dockyard.[9]

The Society's President, HRH The Duke of York, attended the SNR Annual Lecture at the Society of Antiquaries given by the Hon. Editor, Professor Richard Harding, and also presented the Anderson Medal for Research in Maritime History to Dr Lewis Johnman and Dr Hugh Murphy.[10]

In his Chairman's Report for 2003, Alan Aberg noted that subscription income had remained stable but overall income had declined, partly due to lower investment returns but principally because of a reduction in donations and legacies. However, the Society's Anderson Fund received a considerable boost at the end of the year from a legacy of £20,000 bequeathed by Mr W. O. B. Meyer. Nevertheless, reflecting improved market conditions, the Society's investment portfolio across all funds increased, enabling it to finance an operating deficit of £3,845 from the overall gain on investments of £236,033 for the year. Rear-Admiral David Pulvertaft succeeded Dr Margarette Lincoln as Chairman of the Publications Committee, and Helen Jones relinquished her post as Editor of the Newsletter. She was replaced by Lizelle de Jager. In turn, Professor Sarah Palmer relinquished her post as Chairman of Research and Programmes to be replaced by Captain Peter Hore RN. The Society also gave a grant to meet some of the translation costs for a monograph *Science and the French and British Navies* published by the NMM and, through the Research, Programmes and Technical Committee, collaborated with the East Kent Trust and the Royal Meteorological Society in a conference at Ramsgate in November 2003 on 'The Great Storm of 1703'.[11]

In January 2004, annual subscriptions were raised to £37 for individual members (with a discount of £3 for direct debit) and £46 for institutions.[12] During the year, the Hon. Secretary, Emma Dunn, who had replaced Elizabeth Verity at the June AGM, resigned for family reasons and was replaced by Peter Winterbottom. Regarding the financial year ending at 31 December 2004, the Hon. Treasurer reported that 2004 had been a busy year for the Society:

> The financial year ended with a realized surplus of £86,744 as at 31 December 2004 compared with £27,296 for the previous year. However, it is important to understand why this was an exceptional figure. As recorded in pages 2 and 7 of the Financial Statements, the Society had received during the year the sum of £175,000 from the National Christina Foundation. This sum was held in custody through the STVF in order that it and the Society's own contribution could be combined towards financing the project to display the foretopsail in Portsmouth. The STVF contributed £60,000 to the project. Between the two a total sum of £100,000 was remitted to Fleet Support Ltd during the year. A further £140,000 was representing the balance of the capital committed to the project is to be released during the 2005 financial year. It was to be regretted that the language in the printed accounts was not as clear on this point as in hindsight it might have been.

Thus, a further £140,000 representing the balance of the capital committed to support the exhibition was released during 2005, and the Society's Patron, HRH Prince Philip KG, duly opened what proved to be a deeply moving and historically important exhibition of the foretopsail in April 2005.[13]

The Bicentenary of the Battle of Trafalgar and the Year of the Sea 2005

The Year of the Sea offered a unique opportunity for the Society to raise its public profile and in so doing increase its membership. That remained to be seen: however, the exhibition to the public of *Victory's* foretopsail at Portsmouth Dockyard was a great success. In addition, as a lasting legacy, the Society also helped to sponsor a Trafalgar Woods Project in conjunction with the Woodland Trust. Moreover, many members, including the Small Craft Committee's cutter crew actively contributed to a host of Nelsonian celebrations and memorials.

The special bicentenary of Trafalgar edition of *The Mariner's Mirror* in May 2005 contained some 20 articles. Attractively presented in its dust cover, the issue was generally well received. In June, Professor Richard Harding succeeded Alan Aberg

Figure 31 HRH The Duke of Edinburgh, Roy Clare and Colin White (1951–2008). (© National Maritime Museum, Greenwich, London)

as Chairman of the Society. In turn, Dr Hugh Murphy succeeded the new chairman as Hon. Editor. Dr Murphy expanded the Editorial Board, revised the journal's Style Sheet and Notes for Contributors and, with the assistance of David Page, placed them on the Society's website. The new Editor's emphasis was firmly on empirical research. He believed double-blind refereeing of articles was essential, and introduced triple-blind refereeing for submissions from members of the Editorial Board. In addition, rigorous refereeing of notes was now seen as a *sine qua non*. The Hon. Editor also reinstated the title 'International Journal of the Society for Nautical Research' on the front cover of *The Mariner's Mirror* and endeavoured to ensure that each issue contained as wide a spectrum of material as possible. This formed the basis of future editorial policy. Above all, the quality of submissions remained the key criterion regardless of the qualifications of the authors submitting. In this respect, the Society can be justly proud of the breadth of articles and notes received for its journal, which marks it out from most academic journals.

169

Contributions from academics and from non-academic authors and the wider public with a special interest in all aspects of maritime history broadly defined make *The Mariner's Mirror* a unique publication. In addition, its lively answers, queries and correspondence sections continue to provide evidence of correspondents pricking pomposity, elucidating long-forgotten controversies, and generally adding to the store of maritime knowledge.

By 2006 it became apparent that despite the Society's heavy financial contribution to the Year of the Sea celebrations, the expected rise in membership had failed to materialize. This prompted a degree of introspection on the Society's wider role in maritime history and in particular how it could raise its profile. At least the Society's impending centenary in 2010 and the centenary of *The Mariner's Mirror* in 2011 offered an opportunity to involve many of the present membership in some way, however small. The Society's Chairman, Richard Harding, viewed 2005 as a year of consolidation which proved that with proper preparation 'the public could be interested in their maritime heritage'.[14] This was hardly a ringing endorsement of the substantial effort and expense expended during 2005. Nevertheless, both Harding and Council were acutely aware that the future of the Society – in line with its purpose of disseminating the best research in maritime history – depended upon engaging more people, including 'a new generation of enthusiastic members'. As this generation were deemed to be very much 'web conscious', Council took the far-reaching decision to develop a new website for the Society, which went online in January 2007. It was preceded in December 2006 by the Council's linked decision to form a new Marketing and Membership Committee. The need for this committee dedicated to a more outward-looking focus was considered 'vital for the future of the Society'. The membership of the Committee under the chairmanship of Dr Helen Doe, reflected the efforts of those members who had brought the new website to fruition, ably assisted by David Page who had for so long single-handedly maintained the Society's web presence. Council had also approved a re-definition of the membership of the Society's FGPC, and a clarification of the role of the Society's Vice-Presidents was put in hand. Council also approved an extension in the page length for the August issue of *The Mariner's Mirror* each year – at the Editor's discretion – and decided to re-institute the publication of the Society's Annual Lecture in its pages.[15]

From 2004 to 2006 subscription income exceeded £60,000, having never been higher. However, SNR activities in 2005 led to an expenditure of £280,020 against total revenue of £169,422, so that the Society posted its biggest financial loss ever of £110,598. The accumulated contingency reserve was called in to meet the costs of the Trafalgar bicentenary issue of *The Mariner's Mirror* and it was planned to set aside similar amounts in reserve in every year thereafter towards defraying the costs of the

Society's centenary celebrations in 2010–11. However, the years 2006 and 2007 witnessed a substantial increase in the Society's total asset value to exceed £2.9m, reflecting substantial gains in the investment portfolios achieved during the course of these years, and a marked increase in cash holdings for 2007 and 2008 to over £400,000.[16]

Richard Harding reported in 2007 that its auditors 'were not just satisfied but impressed with the financial health of the Society', and that its Officers intended that this position should continue. The 2006 review of vice-presidential posts concluded that future Vice-Presidents could only stand on the basis that they continued to serve the Society. This change underlined that in future Vice-Presidents would hold 'working posts' not honorific ones. During 2007, the Hon. Editor and two members of his Editorial Board, Professor D. J. Oddy and Philip Pugh, were charged with identifying common themes in the historical content of its journal for possible inclusion in its centenary issue of February 2011.[17] Towards the end of the year, *The Mariner's Mirror*'s typesetter and administrative editor, Linda Jones (who had acted in that capacity since the early 1990s) indicated her desire to resign – a decision which the Hon. Editor accepted with great regret. She was replaced by Dr Paula Turner.

The theme of modernizing the Society continued into 2008. The Marketing and Membership Committee continued to develop the Society's website and during the year its chairman, Dr Helen Doe handed over the reins to Professor Derek Law, a Vice-President of the Society. Whether the suggestion put to Council regarding the Society gaining a 'Royal' prefix could be termed modernizing is debatable. It had been first raised by Dr C. Northcote Parkinson in 1949 and discussed in a Council Meeting that year. Dr Parkinson wished the Society to apply for leave to add the word, 'Royal' to its official title. The arguments rehearsed then were partially repeated during the course of 2008. In 1949 it was thought that the title would emphasize the Society's national character. Sir Alan Moore thought it an honour that should be offered not sought. Typically, Roger Anderson thought that the motion was unnecessary. Frank Carr, on the other hand, thought it would attract new members though Professor Michael Lewis thought that increased membership might perhaps lower the standard of the Society's work. Basil Greenhill felt that the Society could ill afford the necessary moneys to pursue a royal appellation.[18] During 2008, after the Society's Hon. Secretary, Peter Winterbottom, had exhaustively explored the steps necessary and the attendant costs which would be incurred in seeking 'Royal' status, the Council decided not to pursue the matter.

By November 2008, with the British economy in recession, the effects began to be felt by the Society. Not only was this seen in the relatively poor performance of the SNR's investments in the wake of turmoil in world financial markets, but also through its effects on manufacturers, small businesses and on members of the general public at large. In September, the makers of the cover-board for the *The Mariner's Mirror*, Curtis Fine Papers, of Guardbridge, near St Andrews in Fife, went into administration, and by December the journal's printers since 1993, Alden Press, of Witney, Oxfordshire, also succumbed to the 'credit crunch' with no warning to the Hon. Editor. After an exhaustive tendering process with the aid of Dr Paula Turner, the Hon. Editor was able to ensure that a new printer was in place before the next publication date on 1 February 2009. Bell & Bain of Thornliebank, Glasgow, were chosen to be the Society's printers. For some time, the Hon. Editor had urged the Publications Committee to effect economies of scale by combining the printing of *The Mariner's Mirror* and the Newsletter at one printer rather than two. This was finally achieved from the May 2009 issue. The Newsletter Editor since 2006, Suzanne Davies, resigned, and was replaced by Barry Coombs in time for the November 2009 issue. Earlier, at the 2009 AGM, Rear-Admiral David Pulvertaft relinquished his post after six successful years as Chairman of the Publications Committee, and was succeeded by Cdr David Hobbs.

During 2009, the Society had debated how it could take cognizance of the 'heritage agenda' on which much government policy has been predicated. A suggestion that the Society's Small Craft Committee be reorganized as the Heritage and Historical Small Craft Committee was considered by Council, but this was temporarily abandoned after being met with dogged resistance from the membership of the Small Craft Committee. In part, members of the Small Craft Committee, who had done so much to initiate the Society's electronic media strategy through *The Mariner's Mirror on CD-Rom* and the creation of the website, felt aggrieved that their endeavours were not sufficiently appreciated by the newly formed Marketing and Membership Committee. In fact, members of the Small Craft Committee perform an important ambassadorial role for the Society through the activities of the *Victory* Cutter Crew at Portsmouth Dockyard and at various regattas around the country. Their work is priceless, and in reality has always been recognized. The Small Craft Committee continues to reach out to the leisure sailing and boating community – a body of people that the Society should have more actively recruited to its membership in the past. Nevertheless, in a series of meetings during 2009, the Society's Chairman, Richard Harding met members of Small Craft Committee and listened to their concerns. As a result, moves are in hand to inaugurate a Heritage and Small Craft Committee of the Society, under the chairmanship of David Clement.

Thus far, Marketing and Membership has necessarily concentrated more on marketing rather than on increasing membership. Nonetheless, potential and actual new members have become more aware of the Society through its revamped website www.snr.org.uk (webmaster: Dr Gareth Cole) which now includes a 'members only' area (the Members' Forum Moderator is Justin Reay).[19] There is clear evidence that the website has attracted new members and has in fact stabilized numbers of members to some extent, thus reversing the trend towards a small year-on-year decline. Throughout 2009, the Marketing and Membership Committee debated its web strategy, in particular, the digitization of *The Mariner's Mirror*. How this will be achieved presents the Society with some hard choices. Does it continue on its own or should it involve a journal aggregator such as EBSCO or JSTOR who would digitize past content for free while including *The Mariner's Mirror* in a package of journals it offers to university libraries? That would give academics and students free access to the journal at the expense of ordinary members who pay subscriptions. Moreover, the Society would risk losing its high level of institutional support in university libraries around the world. Or should the Society digitize on its own account, which, if it is to achieve current international archival standards, would be a hugely costly undertaking? If the former and a decision were taken to go with an aggregator, *The Mariner's Mirror* would be available to a far wider population of readers than at present and the Society would benefit from an annual licence payment. If the latter, the Society in digitizing its own content, perhaps in conjunction with like-minded learned societies, would have to develop its website far beyond present capabilities to include a payment platform and link to a much more powerful server. Such decisions, necessarily, are not made overnight and require at the very least a cost–benefit analysis and a great deal of individual and collective soul-searching. However, a decision on which way to go on digitizing the content of *The Mariner's Mirror* will have to be made sooner, rather than later, if the Society is not to run the risk of being permanently left behind in the digital revolution.

Furthermore, in the currently adverse financial climate the Society can only do so much – increases in membership numbers are a *sine qua non* for its future aspirations. This is underpinned by continued turmoil in the financial markets, and reflected by a decline in total asset values for the year ending 31 December 2008 of £614,649 from the previous year in terms of the market values of investments. The Society ended the financial year 2008 with a surplus of just under £60,000 plus over £400,000 in cash.[20] While the year 2008 had been difficult, the Society had taken steps at an early stage to try to mitigate any damage to its investment position by deciding to move to a more conservative composite index measure of 70 per cent FTSE shares to 30 per cent Government stocks.[21] The shift in the underlying asset allocation for the Society's investments had helped to weather the current volatile markets and, with the outlook for 2009 little better, the Society's Officers need to maintain vigilance in pursuit of members' interests. Even when adopting the recent practice favoured by the Charity Commissioners of dividing reserves into unrestricted or general purpose funds, and restricted or funds designated for specific purposes, such as the STVF, the Macpherson Collection Endowment Fund, and the smaller bequests, the Society has a substantial basis of wealth. Taking unrestricted and restricted funds together, the Society's holdings at market values rose from over £2.2m in 1996 to nearly £3m in 2006 and 2007 before the financial crisis reduced the value to £2.3m in 2008. The value of the Society's unrestricted or general-purpose funds rose from £76,000 in 1996 at cost to £143,000 in 2008, while their market value was put at nearly £96,000 in 1996, rising to over £170,000 in 2006. The STVF was by far the largest of the restricted funds, ranging from £1.5m to £2.3m at market value. The Macpherson Collection Endowment Fund began the period at almost £325,000 in 1996 rising to over £400,000 from 2005 to 2007. However, like other investments its value fell back in 2008 by some £80,000. The Anderson Bequest Fund began these years around £100,000 but, benefiting from a legacy of £20,000 bequeathed by W. O. B. Meyer, increased in value to some £385,000 in 2007. The financial crises caused a fall of £40,000 over the years 2007 to 2008.[22] Despite the financial crisis, the stability of the Society's resources meant that Peter Nash, the Hon. Treasurer, was able to maintain subscriptions unchanged.

Two other linked projects occupied the time of the Society's officers in 2008 and 2009: the proposed creation of a National Museum of the Royal Navy (NMRN) and the Society's relationship with HMS *Victory*. On the latter, the Society now operates the STVF to an agreed five-year plan. However, consternation in the press in 2008 arose over a Ministry of Defence review directed by the then Second Sea Lord, Vice-Admiral Sir Adrian Johns on 11 July 2008. This examined options for the future support of HMS *Victory*, which included the possible creation of a fully independent charitable arrangement. It prompted the Society – as a stakeholder through the STVF – to meet MoD officials in November 2008. The Society's position was that *Victory* should remain in commission and continue as the flagship of the Second Sea Lord and that the ship's future lies with the MoD and the Royal Navy and not with any other government department or heritage organization. Underpinning this review is the fact that HMS *Victory* is in need of substantial expenditure to undertake extensive remedial work to her fabric in order to reverse the ship's deteriorating material state, and to resolve safety issues which could threaten continued public access.

In the latter part of 2008, the Chairman, Richard Harding, met the new Second Sea Lord, Admiral Alan Massey, who had been appointed to the post in a ceremony on board *Victory* on 15 July; and the new CO of *Victory*, Lt Cdr Douglas J. 'Oscar' Whild, the 99th holder of this post. By this stage plans for the new NMRN had moved on apace and, in 2009, a new director-general, Dr Dominic Tweddle, formerly Head of the Jorvik Viking Centre in York, was appointed. The new NMRN was officially launched on 18 September 2009 at Portsmouth Dockyard with the Hon. Secretary,

Peter Winterbottom representing the Society. HMS *Victory*, still a commissioned ship and the flagship of the C-in-C Naval Home Command, fired an impressive broadside to launch the NMRN formally. The rolling broadside consisted of 50 pseudo-random shots running from Forward to Aft. A short delay (approximately two seconds) to allow the Middle Gun Deck crews to reload (!) was followed by a further 14 shots using each of these guns in a more measured fashion as an impressive finale. In all of this, the amount of gunpowder used was less than the gunners on board at Trafalgar would have used for a single shot! Now that the NMRN is formally established, negotiations continue on the future of the Society's trustee role in the new entity, and that of its trading company, in which the SNR still holds an interest. In October 1995, Council had renegotiated terms regarding the trading company with the then Royal Naval Museum. It now receives 15 per cent of profits from the trading company and in the event that it is wound up, 7.5 per cent of its assets.[23] At the time of writing, this arrangement seems likely to continue, as it improbable that the new NMRN would start without a trading company. However, the legal agreement for sharing ticket revenues and management of Portsmouth Historic Dockyard ends in February 2010, and renegotiations begin in November 2009.

In formalizing its plans for its centenary year in 2010–11 the Society's committees have all played a role. This centenary history has been commissioned to be issued in conjunction with *The Mariner's Mirror* in February 2010; a centenary meeting of Council is planned to take place at the RUSI in June 2010 where the inaugural meeting constituting the Society was held a century before. Thereafter, a cocktail reception for members and their guests will begin near the site of the Society's 75th anniversary celebrations. The centenary celebrations will end with the publication of a centenary issue of *The Mariner's Mirror* with invited contributions from leading scholars, in February 2011.

References

1 *Mariner's Mirror*, 86:3 (2000), Society Records, Chairman's Annual Report for the year 2000 and AGM.
2 McGowan, HMS Victory: *Her Construction, Career and Restoration*, 124.
3 *Mariner's Mirror*, 86:3 (2000), Society Records, Chairman's Annual Report for the Year 2000 and AGM.
4 SNR Accounts, 1996–2004, see Appendix IV.
5 *Mariner's Mirror*, 86:3 (2000), Society Records, Chairman's Annual Report for the Year 2000 and AGM.
6 *Mariner's Mirror*, 88:3 (2002), Society Records, Chairman's Annual Report for the Year 2002 and AGM.
7 *Mariner's Mirror*, 87:3 (2001), Society Records, Chairman's Annual Report for the Year 2001 and AGM.
8 *Mariner's Mirror*, 89:3 (2003), Society Records; Chairman's Annual Report for 2003.

9 Chaired by Alison Williams, with Alison Alsbury as the first Chief Executive, the Board comprised the Chief Executives of the Royal Naval Museum, the *Mary Rose* Trust, HMS *Warrior*, Portsmouth, PNBPT and a representative from the Royal Navy.

10 For *British Shipbuilding and the State since 1918: a political economy of decline* (Exeter, 2002).

11 *Mariner's Mirror*, 89:3 (2003), Society Records, Chairman's Annual Report for 2003 and AGM.

12 NMM SNR 3/24 Minutes of 43rd Meeting of the Council of the SNR, 22 January 2004.

13 *Mariner's Mirror*, 90:3 (2004), Society Records, Chairman's Annual Report for the Year 2004 and AGM.

14 *Mariner's Mirror,* 92:3 (2006), Society Records, Chairman's Annual Report for the Year 2006 and AGM.

15 *Ibid*.

16 *Ibid.*, Hon. Secretary's Report of the AGM, 2006. The Hon. Treasurer gave a figure of £2.86m in his report. This had risen when the financial statements were published, see, Total Asset Value for 2006, Appendix IV Financial Summary.

17 *Mariner's Mirror*, 93:3 (2007), Society's Records, Hon. Secretary's and Hon. Editor's Reports.

18 NMM SNR 3/4 SNR Council Meeting, 6 April 1949, Dr Parkinson's Proposal.

19 The Members' Forum on the website now has around ten per cent of the Society's membership enrolled.

20 SNR, Financial Statements for the year ended 31 December 2008.

21 Draft Report of the Annual General Meeting, 13 June 2009.

22 See Financial Summary, Appendix IV.

23 SNR Council Minutes, 12 October 2005.

8

Making Fast and Paying Off

What would the founders of the SNR think of the Society's progress if they were able to view it from the standpoint of 2010? They had created the Society at a time of change and unprecedented expansion in Britain's maritime affairs and to some extent regarded themselves as the last generation who knew commercial sail in the United Kingdom. They felt it was their responsibility to pass on their knowledge before it went out of use and was lost. Their wish for the SNR was not that it should record the current state of maritime affairs in 1910: the newspapers of the day were filled with shipping news and reports from naval correspondents, reflecting the pre-eminence of Britain's naval supremacy and mercantile enterprise at sea, and society's anxiety that it should be maintained. The SNR's founders recognized themselves as 'antiquaries' concerned with 'nautical archaeology' who were determined to publish 'nautical history'. In other words, the SNR was, by its own definition, a group of maritime enthusiasts wishing to record the past while there were still among them seafarers who spoke its language and understood how ships had been propelled by oars and sails, by wind, tide and muscle; and how their crews had lived, dressed, navigated and signalled to each other. This wish to record a passing way of life set the 'nautical antiquaries' of 1910 apart from contemporary commentators on the big-gun navy of their day, with its concern for the threat of torpedoes, mines and submarines, or the mechanically-propelled merchant ships varying in size and sophistication from floating hotels to bulk carriers of grain, frozen meat and oil, as well as the cargo tramps and the ubiquitous colliers without which neither navy nor merchant fleet could operate for long without replenishment.

It was evident to the SNR's founders that some aspects of naval history were covered by the NRS and numbers of the initial membership of the SNR were also NRS members. But the desire to learn and to write about the sea and seafarers went beyond the limits of the NRS, and it is significant that not only historically minded writers, but also artists were attracted by the proposal in 1910 to form a 'Nautical

Antiquary Society'. Thus the initial meeting of those responding to the request to express an interest in forming a society was chaired by the marine painter, W. L. Wyllie, RA. The founders who planned the SNR came from literary and artistic backgrounds as painters, authors and journalists with historical interests – especially naval correspondents – and, among the younger ones, university undergraduates with interests aroused by summer yachting. A few had connexions through freemasonry. Naval officers, both serving and retired, were also attracted to the idea. On the face of it, the initial members of the SNR were a group of the professional middle classes of Edwardian Britain but with neither the time available nor the fortunes to support such a venture as 'nautical archaeology', other than as a pastime. For a Society to survive on this basis would be a struggle on subscriptions of half-a-guinea a head.

While there were casualties in both wars, a nucleus of the founders survived until the middle of the twentieth century. Although some were approaching middle age when the SNR was formed in 1910, half-a-dozen or more lived well beyond the end of the Second World War and would certainly have known what the SNR had achieved by then. It was an impressive accomplishment but it by no means matched the original three objects set out in 1910. Of those, two could be recognized as having been attained: to research and publish. *The Mariner's Mirror* would be the most identifiable success by the mid-twentieth century, even though it was then stunted by post-war restrictions and rising costs. However, these founders of the SNR would have looked in vain for the nautical dictionary or encyclopaedia, which was central to their desire to record maritime Britain in transition at the beginning of the twentieth century but which had never enthused their successors, who felt its moment had gone. The great triumphs of the SNR's first thirty years, the preservation of HMS *Victory*, the Victory Museum and the establishment of a national maritime museum were beyond the expectations of the founders. However, the Society's successes reflected the fact that it had been swept along by a few individuals with the financial and political influence that could extract privileges and concessions from governments and Whitehall departments, at a time when economic circumstances left them bereft of public money to spend on such projects as preserving maritime artefacts of a former age.

The old hands, the Marquis of Milford Haven, Douglas Owen, W. L. Wyllie and C. N. Robinson – the oldest founder, known respectfully as 'Skipper' by the 'young bloods' – were all gone by the 1930s as was Milford Haven's successor as President, Admiral Sturdee. Although Sturdee had been a dynamic leader of the Society who relied on his reputation as war hero to maintain his connexions with many influential people, it was James Caird's response that changed the fortunes of the SNR. Sturdee's death in 1925 might have ended the 'navalist' policies he had embraced but it gave Geoffrey Callender an opportunity to extend his influence over the Society to the point of controlling its opinions and policies for the next twenty years.

In 1921, Callender had been able to alarm Council members by his analysis of the financial weakness of the Society and his view that the SNR was over-dependent upon *The Mariner's Mirror* for revenue. Callender had also suggested that a further weakness of the SNR was its lack of focus upon maritime topics other than readers' interest in the journal. In some respects prior to the Save the *Victory* campaign this was true, but Callender was not a man of enough vision to revive the founders' objects nor yet sufficiently secure of his position in the SNR to press hard for change. Nor, when Sturdee was appointed President, was Callender confident of his own status vis-à-vis the victor of the Battle of the Falklands. The few surviving letters to Sturdee from Callender show him providing material – including nautical anecdotes – for Sturdee's speeches. But the interregnum between the death of the Marquis of Milford Haven in 1921 and the appointment of Sturdee as his successor gave Callender an opportunity to set out his vision of the SNR as the popularizer of Britain's naval heritage, by saving HMS *Victory* – eagerly taken up by Sturdee – and by creating a museum which would be a 'People's Palace of the Sea'. That was a strange image and one palpably at odds with Callender's distaste for the flippancy of the guides and the frivolous and disrespectful behaviour of visitors on board HMS *Victory*. But the respect Callender felt was due to the ship as a symbol of British naval history encompassing the victory of Trafalgar and the death of Lord Nelson was not uncommon at the time: Cdr C. N. Robinson even referred to *Victory* as a 'sea cathedral', and it attracted James Caird to fund the undertaking as symbolic of British patriotic achievements. There was undoubtedly some feeling in naval circles that the Great War had not gone well for the Royal Navy. The Grand Fleet had won no decisive victories and the outcome of the war had been decided on land. The Armistice had not been followed by any victory fleet review at Spithead.[1] With its future under threat from the Washington Treaty and the emergence of air power, the Royal Navy was eager to rekindle the pre-war popular patriotism which had championed its pre-eminent role.

It was therefore easy for Callender to divert the SNR away from the broad canvas of its founders which was to see nautical history in its widest sense, back towards the patriotic navalism of pre-war Britain. Whether this was to play to his strengths as a lecturer and teacher of naval history to cadets is unclear since hardly any personal papers of his have been available on which to base this account of the SNR's history. Indeed, the SNR files preserved as Secretary's Papers from Callender's time in office all too frequently contain nothing more than office 'rubbish' – old cheque-book stubs, receipts, and printers' invoices. Notwithstanding this gap, it is clear that soon after his appointment to Greenwich, Callender realized that there was a large collection of naval relics – notably sea paintings and ship models – either owned directly by the Admiralty or deposited elsewhere haphazardly, but principally in the Painted Hall at the Royal Naval College, Greenwich – and set about cataloguing it. The patriotism of the post-war years was supportive of Callender's enthusiasm for popular naval history rather than academic research and writing about Britain's maritime past. Popular patriotism was personified by Sir Doveton Sturdee and his successor, Sir George Hope, suitably acculturated by his term as President and Flag Officer Commanding the Royal Naval College, Greenwich.

Although Callender was not able to influence the senior members of the SNR Council to accept Sir George Hope, his preferred choice for President after Sturdee's death, their selection of Admiral of the Fleet David, Earl Beatty, played into his hands. Beatty, never known as an energetic organizer, and burdened with his appointment as First Sea Lord and later Chief of Staff, was happy to be honoured but not to play any active part in the Society's affairs. This allowed Callender to put forward Admiral Sir George Hope's name a second time, as a candidate for a new post as Chairman of Council. With Hope's appointment as President of the Royal Naval College, Greenwich, coming to an end and his retirement due, his availability, and Callender's previous knowledge of his careful attention to detail and to duty, made him an ideal candidate. Hope would be the perfect patriotic figurehead and mouthpiece for Callender who, it was said, rarely spoke at SNR Council meetings.

With the *Victory* restoration project under way and the death of Sturdee creating a hiatus in the SNR's policies, Callender found it possible to detach James Caird from funding the restoration of *Implacable* and to promote his earlier claim that the SNR's 'duty' to establish a National Naval and Nautical Museum was the all-important item on the Society's agenda. A call to establish central meeting premises for the SNR in 1922 was easily brushed aside, and Callender, building his reputation upon cataloguing the naval ephemera at the Royal Naval College, put forward the view that the Admiralty deposits there should form part of a much larger collection. Apart from the clutter of models and paintings at the Royal Naval College, Callender became aware that the development of a new museum – the Imperial War Museum – threatened any idea of a unified naval collection and also that some material had already been dispersed to the Science Museum.

The impetus strengthening the SNR's interest in creating a maritime museum came from the increasing tendency of American collectors to attend fine art sales in Britain and the opportunity this presented for collectors to sell at high prices. Patriotic feelings in the interwar years expressed the view that Britain's heritage was being sold to the United States and led the Royal Commission on National Museums and Galleries, 1927–9, to propose regulating museums in Britain. SNR interests in this field originated through a desire to acquire Nelson relics and memorabilia. Callender was able to interest James Caird in it and in purchasing the Macpherson Collection 'for the nation'. With the Macpherson Collection deposited at Greenwich, the problem of suitable accommodation became acute. Fortunately, it caused the Seventh Earl Stanhope, while Civil Lord of the Admiralty from 1924 to 1929, to come to the Society's aid. Stanhope's connexions in both the Civil Service and the Cabinet enabled him to establish an Admiralty Board of Trustees to plan for a museum within which its historical collections might be preserved. Without any ostensible interest in the preservation of the naval past Stanhope's family tradition in public life showed an historical awareness.[2] Furthermore, his experience as a Trustee of the National Portrait Gallery – which his grandfather, the Fifth Earl Stanhope, had founded in 1856 – made him familiar with the whole range of museum requirements. Earl Stanhope's connexions with the First Sea Lord, Earl Beatty, as President of the SNR, and Sir George Hope, the former Deputy First Sea Lord, as SNR Chairman from 1925 – both of whom were present or past members of the Lord Commissioners of the Admiralty during Stanhope's term as Civil Lord – created a powerful link to press the Society's case for a Naval and Nautical Museum.

Professor Geoffrey Callender was a conspicuously hard worker able to impose his own agenda upon a passive SNR. As a bachelor, living with his sisters in Blackheath, Callender frequently spent evenings and weekends working in the College. One observer thought he worked eighteen hours a day, six days a week. From the 1920s onwards, Callender appears to have paid Reginald Lowen, then a clerical officer in the College, to do additional work for him in the evenings. Remaining papers from the 1930s show that Callender routinely used Lowen as an unofficial membership secretary for the SNR. There is no evidence to show how Callender paid Lowen for this work or his other temporary assistants, C. Northcote Parkinson and Michael Robinson. Since the Society's income and expenditure accounts include regular headings for postage, typing, and even for the use of an 'amanuensis', the implication is that Callender used the SNR funds available at his discretion to employ them. Once the Society's AGM in 1927 received Sir George Hope's report on the proposal that a 'National Naval and Nautical Museum' should be established, it seems likely that Callender had begun to think of himself as its director, especially if, as rumoured, the Royal Hospital School was to evacuate its buildings at Greenwich. When Earl Stanhope's Board of Trustees was appointed, Callender was included, as custodian of the Greenwich collection, together with Sir George Hope and, almost by a sleight-of-hand, James Caird's attendance at the meetings was ensured. With Caird continuing to acquire art works for the collections, there was an impasse in housing them. This was accentuated by the collapse of the Gold Standard in 1931 and the 'Great Slump' in trade and industry which limited government expenditure.

By the time the Royal Hospital School buildings stood empty in the summer of 1933, the problem was to initiate progress. At Stanhope's suggestion, James Caird wrote to James Ramsay MacDonald, the Prime Minister, offering to pay for the conversion of the buildings provided an Act was passed in the current session of Parliament. This was decisive. It enabled Stanhope to designate Callender as Director, much to his relief, and, with the conversion completed, for the museum to open in 1937. This success was followed by the fulfilment of the Society's wish to have a shore-based Victory Museum at Portsmouth for the display of Nelson souvenirs, which opened in 1938 but, in doing so, breached Sturdee's earlier principle that the SNR should not pay for what was the State's responsibility.[3]

Once the NMM was opened, the full effect of Callender's influence over the Society can be assessed, even though he remained in his post as the museum's Director until his death in 1946. The wartime dispersal of the NMM's contents and the winding down of much SNR activity, together with his own evacuation to Oxford to the house of his architect friend, H. S. Rogers, limited Callender's opportunities to create or implement SNR policy. His main responsibility for that was over by the end of the 1930s, but from 1921 to 1938 the passive but patriotic interwar membership gave Callender a free hand to shape the SNR to his liking and to attain his own goals. Callender was by no means an academic historian. Before assuming the office of Hon. Secretary and treasurer he contributed a number of wide-ranging articles to *The Mariner's Mirror* but his history of the sea had been intended for cadets at Osborne. His other contribution was to write 'The Story of HMS *Victory*' which was used as the script for the Victory Appeal film in 1923.[4] Callender made little effort to bring the 'Maritime Miscellany' to publication to mark the SNR's twenty-first birthday and steadfastly ignored the Society's objective of producing a nautical encyclopaedia or dictionary. After volunteering himself for the post of Hon. Secretary and Treasurer, Callender found it relatively simple to manipulate the SNR to his own ends. Despite an initial lapse, he operated a policy which required him to have automatic membership of all Committees of the Society even including those that were not official formally constituted committees of the Society, but with which the SNR associated itself. Thus, having become Deputy Chairman of the *Implacable* Appeal Committee in the late 1930s, Callender was able to ensure that no financial burden for the restoration fell upon the SNR. Throughout his term as Hon. Secretary and Treasurer, Callender's two principal objectives were to save HMS *Victory* and to create a national maritime museum of which he would be director. To this end he did all he could to deny any SNR support for the campaign to restore *Implacable* and operate her as a youth holiday ship. After Sturdee's death in 1925, Callender exerted his influence to bring about the end of the Sea Fund by which Caird and Sturdee had intended to preserve

Implacable, and which might otherwise have diverted Caird from the restoration of HMS *Victory*. On realizing this, Owen Seaman, editor of the humorous paper, *Punch*, and Sir Vincent Baddeley of the Admiralty approached Callender to request access to the 'Anonymous Donor' knowing that he had provided over £19,000 for the restoration of *Implacable*. Callender discouraged their efforts and maintained his opposition to the *Implacable* project despite the Admiralty-approved appeal by Earl Beatty in 1925 which initially yielded £25,000, a sum which later rose to over £30,000 after further appeals, including one by the Duke of York. However, by the late 1930s, the *Implacable* Committee was adopted by the SNR and its accounts managed and published annually by the Society. This made Capt. Bosanquet's announcement at the 1947 AGM that there was no connexion between the SNR and the *Implacable* all the more incredible!

A good deal has been made of Callender's charm and stimulating companionship. Certainly he was a great influence upon Sir James Caird, lunching regularly with him and accompanying him to London's fine art showrooms to view potential purchases for the museum's collections. In the long run this was to Callender's benefit as the NMM's holdings were augmented. But a case can be made for regarding Callender as short-sighted in respect of the future role of the SNR and, on occasion, as ungenerous. As he wrote, after Sturdee's death, 'out of fairness to the man who is gone we want someone who will not teach the public to forget Sturdee as Sturdee taught them to forget Milford Haven'.[5] Callender also took the opportunity during the restoration of HMS *Victory*'s bow to comment on the difficulties of working with L. G. Carr Laughton though, as correspondence cited in Chapter 1 indicates, he was not alone in that view. Another close observer of Callender, C. Northcote Parkinson, thought him waspish as well as amusing but a man who 'disliked most women, if not all'. His reaction when a 'good lady broke through my defences and was escorted into my office by an admiring police officer' was that 'she had evidently used her eyes to good purpose on him'.[6] To Parkinson: 'After years of inhuman concentration he was no longer entirely sane'.[7]

In the longer perspective, Callender failed to recognize three problems that survived him. The first was that during the restoration work on HMS *Victory*, he did not address the problems of the ship's ownership and negotiate some legal status for the SNR's work. As a commissioned warship, HMS *Victory* remained government property despite the SNR's long-term expenditure of over £1 million on both restoration and maintenance. Indeed, restoration was not simply a one-off expenditure, as became obvious after the Second World War when the lack of an agreement on what was maintenance and what was restoration remained unsolved. Secondly, the SNR's difficulties were compounded by Callender's self-centred recommendation of closing down the VATC in 1938 and switching responsibility for the ship to the NMM under his directorship. The longer term effect of this was for the SNR to find itself effectively excluded from discussions about HMS *Victory*, even though the Society had raised the funds and initially possessed the knowledge and expertise which had brought about the ship's restoration. Callender's third failing was that once in his office in the museum, he did not foresee how the interests of the museum and the SNR would diverge. He neglected to establish any interlocking relationship between the NMM's trustees and the SNR or even the presence of a statutory SNR trustee on the NMM's Board. While Stanhope was Chairman of the Board of Trustees a solution to this problem could and should have been found. It left the post-war relationship between the Society and the museum unclear and the SNR feeling hurt as its progeny's path diverted from its own and fell far short of its parent's expectations.[8] In addition, the interests of those of the museum's employees who were SNR Officers or Councillors were increasingly incompatible with the objectives of the Society.

The post-war years did not provide a good climate for solving the SNR's outstanding problems. Its leadership was older and less enthusiastic for engaging in the major projects which had been the Society's hallmark in the interwar years. The *Implacable*, badly damaged and brought near to destruction by the Royal Navy's mishandling during the war, was abandoned when Sir James Caird refused to consider financing the cost of her restoration. The navy was left to scuttle her ignominiously in 1949, despite the large amounts of money donated by the public for her restoration. Although much was made of the post-war difficulties of the SNR, the Society's income and investments had held up well, though rising costs threatened *The Mariner's Mirror*. In addition, rationing and restrictions imposed on the use of imported materials, particularly timber, delayed war damage repairs to the Victory Museum and maintenance to *Victory* herself. Yet a mood of remarkable optimism prevailed: in 1949 the NMM's VTC thought that 'the ship was being very well looked after' and with additional mechanical ventilation 'could well be preserved for a thousand years or more', a view which later reports suggested was far too sanguine.[9]

The success of the Society's investments should have enabled the SNR to adjust to post-war economic circumstances but the Society's new regime was soon in difficulties. As Reginald Lowen had effectively run the Society single-handed from Greenwich during the war while Callender was in Oxford, the separation of the functions of Secretary and Treasurer occurred after Callender's death for the first time since the Society's foundation in 1910. Poor personal relations between Lowen as Treasurer and George Naish as Secretary (and between Naish and the museum's new Director, Frank Carr) were bad enough for the Society but both Lowen and Naish were more concerned by personal rivalry over their positions and status in the NMM than regenerating the SNR. Both held their SNR offices for a considerable time – Naish for almost thirty years as Secretary and Lowen for fifteen years as Treasurer – in the process of which the initiative for SNR policymaking, tightly controlled by Callender pre-war, passed to the chairmen who succeeded Sir George Hope from 1951 onwards, and to the newly established SNR Trustees after 1954. With Caird's death in 1954 and Earl Stanhope's resignation as Chairman of the NMM's Board of Trustees in 1959, the last of the pre-war connexions and influence were gone.

Taking its cue from Caird's withdrawal of support for *Implacable*, the SNR's activities entered a retrenchment phase during which the Society failed to initiate any of the major post-war 'heritage' rescues – *Cutty Sark*, HMS *Warrior*, ss *Great Britain* or the *Mary Rose,* and although its members were involved with all of them, the SNR was only associated through a series of small grants. There were minor echoes of the former SNR activities in its Small Craft Committee, the formation of its Photographic Collection, its recording of working sail in Falmouth Harbour and its interest in the excavation of the North Ferriby boats. However, HMS *Victory* still required significant outlays for teak, hemp and polypropylene to repair and re-rig her and the war damage to the Victory Museum in Portsmouth was a further drain on investments. In retrospect, while still tied to some extent to its interwar 'navalist' patriotism; the Society seemed to have lost its way compared with its interwar and wartime role. During the war HMS *Victory* had been a great symbol of patriotic feeling: the King and Queen had visited the ship, as had various dignitaries, foreign heads of state and servicemen from the Commonwealth. Despite the bomb damage to her hull, the ship had been re-rigged in time to fly Vice-Admiral Nelson's Trafalgar signal on 21 October 1945.

The origins of the post-war lack of vision may be traced back to Callender's time. While Callender was ruthless in his own self-promotion, his stewardship as Director of the NMM was inauspicious. Not a natural researcher or academic scholar, Callender did not encourage these original objects of the SNR at the museum. His interest was limited to the presentation of the artefacts the museum held, as shown when income from the Macpherson Collection Endowment Fund ceased to be applied to its specific purpose. Callender's over-generous interpretation of the Fund's use extended to applying it to providing and planting shrubs around the museum rather than for acquisitions and maintenance of the museum's art collection. This practice continued despite the disapproval of the Society's Auditor. Later, post-war directors persisted in regarding the NMM's annual income from the Macpherson Fund as for their personal use, to be applied to a variety of purposes of their choice. With hindsight, it was the beginning of a trend that began to emerge post-war whereby the initiators and organizers of various projects turned to the SNR for cash, but not for ideas.

Post-war Britain was less open to the enterprise and individualism that had been the hallmark of the SNR's activities during its first forty years. It was a more bureaucratic and professional society, but less imaginative than the earlier one in which enthusiastic amateurs flourished. The excavation of the North Ferriby boats in the mid-1940s was a case study in point. After the excavation work on the Humber was completed in 1946:

> The timbers were transported to the National Maritime Museum at Greenwich, where in 1948, after a period in the open during which they were subjected to considerable desiccation, they were placed in tanks of glycerol in an effort to preserve them. After some time, disagreeable smells issued from the tanks and the Trustees of the Museum decided to 'dispose' of the remains of F1. The Keeper, Commander G. P. B. Naish RN, did so in an act of Nelsonian insubordination, and squirreled away the better-preserved pieces of timber in a dry basement under the Queen's House, thus preserving irreplaceable evidence for future study.[10]

This allowed modern techniques to establish radiocarbon dating of F1, the oldest of the Ferriby boats. In effect, the institution for nautical antiquities which the SNR had created was not as conducive to research as the Society's original object had desired, and increasingly unresponsive to the SNR's blandishments. Without any new focus for the energies of the Officers and Council, the SNR's horizons contracted. The officeholders in the Society continued to be 'naval men' by and large, for whom its pre-war achievements could not be surpassed or equalled now that the age of the Society's major benefactors and political advocates was over. By the 1970s, despite its crucial support for the creation of the Portsmouth Royal Naval Museum, the Society was basically resting on its laurels. There followed years of drift and indecision, which ultimately meant a lack of protection for the Society's interests. There was no coherent attempt to support or fund the various vessel preservation projects. There was no attempt to maintain overall responsibility for nautical archaeology as its funding and provision was dismantled at the NMM. Nor, without an Editorial Board, did the Society's journal maintain its reputation in an age when professional and academic journals were increasingly technical in their scholarly and production standards. However, there was a 'new' membership from the 1960s onwards which leaned more to the professions and academic life and sought to transform the amateurism of the SNR into the context of formal academic research. It was an opportune moment in the late 1980s and early 1990s when a new and far more critical cohort of influential members emerged who were eager to run the Society.

The post-war benefactors who enabled the Society to create the Tomlin, Anderson and McCarthy funds provided sums which could not match the scale of the interwar donations. This, too, was at a time when the value of the Society's investments was being eroded by inflation, slowly at first in the 1950s and 1960s but accelerating dramatically in the 1970s and 1980s. By then the SNR was reduced to existing as a small society living on the edge of improvidence, its income from subscriptions over the years being insufficient to sustain its main activity, the publishing of its journal. Successive Presidents and Chairmen were driven to bemoan the lack of members and the need to raise subscriptions. The Society was forced into a repetitious Micawber-like debate on how to fund its activities which did not always recognize the Society's responsibilities in terms of its charitable status. Yet the SNR never explored the possibilities of linking with other organizations engaged in nautical archaeology or which had a more general interest in antiquities. The reorganization of the SNR into a company limited by guarantee in the 1990s was a far cry from the attitudes of the founders eighty years earlier but, in part, it reflected change in society in general as well as the changing social composition of the Society's membership. However, during the 1990s the SNR was able to find a new focus for its activities as the bicentennial celebrations of Trafalgar approached and the preserved foretopsail of HMS *Victory* was put on display.

Had they survived, the Edwardian founders of the SNR would have wondered at the changes from the maritime scene with which they had been familiar. On a day-to-day basis they would have been struck by the emptiness of the seas around Britain: where were the coasting vessels, colliers or fishing fleets to be found? Why were the great ports which had buzzed with passenger liner and commercial traffic so empty? Why were the great rivers devoid of the shipbuilding, fitting out and commissioning of ships? How had this collapse of maritime communities come about? While our Edwardian founders would have wondered at the huge container ships berthing in unfamiliar settings, such as Tilbury or Felixstowe, and occasional sightings of gargantuan cruise liners or the concentration of short sea traffic through Dover, it would have dawned on them that maritime activities in Britain in the early twenty-first century were much less significant than they had been before 1914. Mass passenger transportation by air or through an undersea tunnel linking Britain to the continent of Europe was unachievable in the early twentieth century, even if conceivable. Equally so would have been the dismantling of the British Empire and the reduction of the Royal Navy to a size that was barely sufficient for the most limited operations and would struggle to mount another South Atlantic expedition. No wonder, the SNR's founders might muse, that Britain's coinage had lost Britannia. No wonder that Trafalgar's anniversary was celebrated in 2005 in abstract form between 'blue' and 'red' fleets rather than between Britain and the Combined Fleet of France and Spain. This was the ultimate degeneration of historical fact into heritage entertainment. Yet it was the 'heritage' function which in 2008 threatened the Ministry of Defence's future support of HMS *Victory* as a commissioned ship.

There were also aspects of social change which the SNR seemed not to recognize adequately or react to positively. Since the 1950s Britain has experienced a huge growth in waterborne leisure activities which might have interested the founders, but perhaps not the navalists who gained control of the SNR's agenda in the 1920s. Activities on water varied from sailing dinghies to cruising yachts, both sail and power, from basic facilities to extreme luxury of a kind unknown to Edwardian yachtsmen. The range of craft was matched by environment: they were used at sea, in coastal waters and river estuaries, and also inland on rivers, canals, lakes, reservoirs and even gravel pits. Waterborne activities varied from pottering about to ocean racing and Olympic competitions, and fostered a burgeoning specialist press, mainly of monthly journals which lay beyond the purview of *The Mariner's Mirror*. With leisure tourism becoming the world's largest industry, the popularity of ocean voyages in cruise liners offers surrogate exploration coupled with passive entertainment and consumption.

The SNR was set up to co-ordinate the individual interests in maritime antiquities among a group of enthusiasts from a wide cultural base in history, archaeology, literature and art. Over time these interests have narrowed, partly through the personalities of the Society's members but partly as society has become more specialized, more professionalized and more concerned with entertainment than scholarship – with heritage rather than history. Thus the SNR's interdisciplinary approach to their studies has been a casualty of society's institutionalization. Professional museum administrators and heritage managers have not accorded to the SNR its due value; nowhere more so than in Portsmouth Dockyard where the Society has been air-brushed out of the picture by organizations such as the PNBPT.[11] It remains to note that the biggest tribute to the founders of the SNR, and one which they themselves would have recognized, is *The Mariner's Mirror*. Its growth from a small club-style monthly magazine to the leading peer-reviewed high quality international journal of maritime history would have given the Society's founders their greatest pleasure. Begun for an Edwardian gentlemen's study group with common interests in maritime antiquarian matters, the SNR's journal has gone far beyond the founders' expectations in its first hundred years of existence. It has been instrumental in turning the hobby of nautical antiquarianism into the academic discipline of maritime history.

That the Society has reached this milestone is cause for congratulation but not complacency. A remarkable number of people over the years have given their time and experience to the Society to support its plans and achieve its goals. Can this continue when there are moves in other learned societies and charities to professionalize their administration? To the vast majority of members *The Mariner's*

Mirror is the glue that binds the Society and its membership around the world. In its pages lies a treasure trove of a century of scholarship. From the very beginning those who ran the Society did so on the voluntary principle of the giving of one's time and expertise for a greater good – that of scholarship. That aim was somewhat lost at times, but nevertheless remained firmly entrenched in the mind-set of almost all the editors of *The Mariner's Mirror*, despite other distractions, which at times diverted the SNR's leadership.

Having read this account of the Society's first hundred years, members will realize that there are problems to be faced in the future. It is evident that the Society needs to retain or increase its membership if its economic stability is to be ensured. However, in what has increasingly become an electronic age, the problems of digitization must be solved and the challenge of electronic publishing must be met to the members' satisfaction if the Society's publications are to continue in their present form and regularity. Perhaps the development of a commissioned series of SNR monographs in maritime history would be an additional option that would be attractive to members, and increase their satisfaction that the Society is active and committed to its original aims. Given the limited opportunities for personal contact beyond the AGM and various local meetings such as seminars in maritime history – which hitherto the Society has sponsored – some additional meetings may be attractive or some association with like-minded societies may be welcome. However, any expansion of the Society's activities may strain the voluntary principle which underlies the SNR's objectives, and justifies its charitable status. Is it time for the Society's members to muster aft bearing a round robin setting out their wishes for the future of the SNR?

References

1 Rüger, *Great Naval Game*, 257–8.
2 See Newman, *The Stanhopes of Chevening*, 273–4. The fifth Earl was a member of the Historical Manuscripts Commission from 1869 until his death in 1875. He was also Vice-President and later President of the Society of Antiquaries.
3 Sturdee's 'principle' died with him if not before him, since the *Victory* restoration project to which he was so devoted was, in reality, the State's responsibility.
4 Professor Callender's publications included: *Sea Kings of Britain* (London, 1907); *The Life of Nelson* (London, 1912); *The Story of HMS Victory* (London, 1915); *Spindrift. Salt from the Ocean of English Prose* (edited by Geoffrey Callender) (London 1915); *Realms of Melody* (An anthology of English Verse) (London, 1916); *Bibliography of Naval History*, two parts (Historical Association Pamphlets No. 58, 61) (London, 1924); *The Portrait of Peter Pett and the* Sovereign of the Seas (London, 1930); *The Queen's House, Greenwich* (London, 1937); *Sea Passages. A Naval Anthology and Introduction to the Study of English* (London, 1943).
5 Letter inserted into Cdr C. N. Robinson's bound copies of *The Mariner's Mirror*, G. Callender to C. N. Robinson, 22 May 1925.

6 NMM 24/3 (1), Callender to Sir James Caird, 18 January 1933.
7 C. N. Parkinson, *A Law unto Themselves* (London, 1966).
8 Recently, owing to Freedom of Information difficulties, access to Trustees' Minutes has been selectively limited; and the SNR has been charged by the NMM for illustrations used in this book.
9 NMM, Trustees' Minutes, 3 October 1949. For the VATC assessment in 1955 and the shortcomings of the original restoration work, see Chapter Four.
10 E. V. Wright, R. E. M. Hedges, A. Bayliss, R. Van de Noort, 'New AMS radiocarbon dates for the North Ferriby boats – a contribution to dating prehistoric seafaring in northwestern Europe', *Antiquity*, December, 2001.
11 See PNBPT, *20 Year Review 1986–2006*.

Appendix I
Patrons, Presidents and Officers

Patrons

1926–42	Lieut. HRH Prince George RN (HRH The Duke of Kent)
1951–79	Admiral of the Fleet the Earl Mountbatten of Burma
1980–	HRH Prince Philip KG, KT (HRH Duke of Edinburgh)

Presidents

1910–21	Vice-Admiral HSH Prince Louis of Battenberg (Admiral of the Fleet the Marquis of Milford Haven)
1921–5	Admiral of the Fleet Sir F. C. Doveton Sturdee Bt
1925–36	Admiral of the Fleet the Earl Beatty
1936–51	Admiral Sir George P. W. Hope
1951–60	R. C. Anderson
1960–70	Professor Michael Lewis
1970–4	Alan J. Villiers
1974–91	Rear-Admiral E. F. Gueritz
1991–9	Admiral of the Fleet The Lord Lewin
1999–	HRH Prince Andrew The Duke of York

Chairman of the Council

1925–51	Vice-Admiral Sir George P. W. Hope
1951–60	Professor Michael Lewis
1960–70	Alan J. Villiers
1970–2	Professor C. Christopher Lloyd
1972–89	Dr Helen Wallis
1989–94	Rear-Admiral R. O. Morris
1994–9	Rear-Admiral J. R. Hill
1999–2005	F. A. Aberg
2005–	Professor R. Harding

Hon. Secretary and Treasurer
1910–19   (Sir) Douglas Owen
1919–21   Col. W. G. Simpson
1921–46   (Professor Sir) Geoffrey Callender
1946–7   Reginald Lowen (Acting)

Hon. Secretary
1947–77   Lt Cdr G. P. B. Naish RNVR
1977–79   Philip J. W. Annis
1979–84   John Munday
1984–8   Lt Cdr Lawrence Phillips RNR
1988–91   Ann Shirley
1991–5   Derek G. Law
1995–2000   Lt Cdr W. J. R. Gardner RN
2000–4   Liza Verity
2004-   Peter Winterbottom

Hon. Treasurer
1947–63   Reginald Lowen
1963–78   E. C. D. Custance
1978–88   Lt Cdr Peter Whitlock RN
1988–91   Antony Preston
1991–5   Christopher Swinson
1995–   Peter V. Nash

Hon. Editor
1910–13   L. G. Carr Laughton
1913–23   R. C. Anderson
1923–31   W. G. Perrin
1931–2   R. C. Anderson
1932–9   D. Bonner-Smith
1939–46   R. C. Anderson
1946-54   Cdr H. P. Mead
1954–61   G. R. G. Worcester
1961–72   Capt. T. D. Manning RNVR
1972–9   Professor C. Christopher Lloyd
1979–91   Brian H. Dolley
1991–2000   Dr Michael Duffy
2000–5   Professor Richard Harding
2005–   Dr Hugh Murphy

Appendix II
Honorary Vice-Presidents

1928	Sir James Caird Bt (1954)
	H. S. Wellcome LLD (1936)
1929	W. L. Wyllie RA (1931)
1932	Cdr C. N. Robinson RN (1936)
1933	The Rt Hon. The Earl of Stanhope DSO, MC (1967)
1937	Captain Bruce Ingram OBE, MC (1963)
	Sir P. Malcolm Stewart Bt, OBE (1950)
1939	Admiral G. A. Ballard CB (1948)
	The Rev. Hugh H. E. Nelson-Ward (1953)
1950	D. Bonner-Smith FRHistS (1950)
1951	Admiral of the Fleet The Earl of Cork and Orrery GCB, GCVO (1967)
	Admiral Sir George Hope KCB, KCMG (1959)
1953	L. G. Carr Laughton (1955)
1955	R. Morton Nance (1959)
1957	Captain H. T. A. Bosanquet CVO, RN, FSA (1959)
1960	Professor E. G. R. Taylor DSc, FRGS (1966)
1961	R. C. Anderson DLitt, FSA (1976)
1964	G. R. G. Worcester (1969)
1970	Lt Col Harold Wyllie OBE (1973)
1972	Viscount Runciman of Doxford OBE, AFC, DCL, DL. (1989)
1973	Frank G. C. Carr CB, CBE, MA, LLB, FSA (1991)
	Cdr H. O. Hill RN (1973)
1974	Admiral Sir Horace Law, GCB, OBE, DSC (2005)*
1976	Sir Victor G. Shepheard KCB (1989)
1977	Professor C. C. Lloyd (1986)
1978	Alan J. Villiers DSC, FRGS (1982)
1981	The Rt Hon. The Countess of Mountbatten of Burma CP, JP, DL

	Professor C. R. Boxer FBA (2000)
	Professor J. S. Bromley (1985)
	George A. Osbon (1983)
1982	Mrs John G. McCarthy CBE (2006)*
1985	John Munday MA, FSA
	David R. MacGregor MA, FSA (2003)
1988	Admiral of the Fleet Lord Lewin KG, GCB, LVO, DSC, DSc (1989)
1990	Austin Farrar CEng, FRINA (2004)
	Rear-Admiral E. F. Gueritz, CB, OBE, DSC (2008)
	Helen Wallis OBE, FRHistS (1995)
1991	Surgeon Vice-Admiral Sir James Watt KBE, MD, MS, FRCP, FRCS
	M. S. Robinson MBE (1999)

Note. The granting of Honorary Vice-President Status was the Society's highest award. Bracketed dates denote the year of death.

*Admiral Sir Horace Law last appeared in the Society Records as an Honorary Vice-President in May 1990. It cannot be ascertained whether or not he resigned in that year. Mrs John McCarthy (Lily Lambert McCarthy) resigned in 1985.

Appendix III
Lectures and Publications

Annual Lectures: 1930–2009

1930	R. C. Anderson — The 'Santa Maria' of Columbus
1931	L. G. Carr Laughton — The *Henri Grace à Dieu*
1932	H. H. Brindley — Primitive Craft – Evolution or Diffusion?
1933	Edwin Chappell — Samuel Pepys
1934	Frank Carr — Surviving Types of Coastal Craft of the British Isles
1935	Lt Cdr R. T. Gould — Harrison's Time-keepers
1936	Cecil King — Flags in Marine Art
1937	J. P. Bowen — Lighthouses, Lightships and Buoys
1938	Lt Cdr R. T. Gould RN — Sea Monsters
1939	Professor E. Walker — The Cape of Good Hope and its Many Masters
1940–46	*Annual Lectures cancelled*
1947	Eric Marx — Ancient Egyptian Shipping
1948	Lt Col H. Wyllie — The Story of the *Implacable*
1949	G. R. G. Worcester — Chinese Junks
1950	E. W. Bovill — The Shipping Interests of the Hon. East India Company
1951	Alan J. Villiers — Fishing on the Grand Banks under Sail
1952	Cdr W. E. May RN — The History of the Mariner's Compass
1953	R. A. Skelton — Captain James Cook as a Hydrographer
1954	Lt Cdr G. P. B. Naish — Naval Uniforms
1955	Alan J. Villiers — Boats Fishing off the Coast of Portugal
1956	Capt. T. D. Manning — Warship Names
1957	Alan J. Villiers — The New 'Mayflower' Voyage
1958	Basil Greenhill — The Boats of East Pakistan
1959	D. M. Wilson, A. E. Werner and Lt Cdr G. P. B. Naish — The Kentmere Boat
1960	Barone Gianni Rubin — The Shipping of Venice

1961   Lt Cdr G. P. B. Naish — The Tresco Valhalla

           Honor Frost — Ancient Wreck Formations in the Mediterranean

1962   C. R. Boxer — The Dutch East Indiamen, Their Sailors, Their Navigators and Life on Board

1963   E. V. Wright — The North Ferriby Boats: A Reappraisal

1964   D. R. MacGregor — The Sailing Ships of Today in Home Waters

1965   E. W. Paget-Tomlinson — Ideas for a Maritime Museum in Liverpool

1966   John Munday — E. W. Cooke, Marine Artist

1967   Major-Gen M. W. Prynne — King Henry the Fifth's *Grace Dieu*

1968   R. H. C. Gillis — The Pilot Gigs of Cornwall and the Isles of Scilly.

1969   J. C. Beaglehole — Some problems of Cook's biographer

1970   *Not held.*

1971   Jonathan Coad — The Architecture of the Royal Dockyards

1972   Helen Wallis — The use of the Globe on Land and Sea

1973   E. C. B. Corlett — The Iron Age of Shipbuilding

1974   Margaret Rule — The *Mary Rose* Revealed

1975   Cdr Eric McKee — Traditional Boat Building Methods

1976   Colin Martin — The Wreck of HMS *Dartmouth*, Isle of Mull

1978   Honor Frost — The Punic Ship

1979   Surgeon Vice-Adm. J. Watt — Medical Aspects of Cook's Voyages

1980   Richard Harrison — The *Mary Rose* in 1980

1981   C. R. Boxer — From Cape Town to Trondjhem: The Adventures and Misadventures of a Dutch Naval Officer 1791–1795

1982   N. A. M. Rodger — Sea Officers and Seamen of the Mid-eighteenth Century

1983   M. Lucien Basch — The *Kardirga*

1984   Barry M. Gough — The Royal Navy and Canadian Dominion

1985   John Munday — Men Dressed as Seamen: Sailors' Attire through Centuries

1986   Rear-Adm. R. O. Morris — Surveying Ships and Craft of the Royal Navy from Cook to the Computer Age

1987   Antony Preston — Has the Royal Navy Won its Battles in Spite of its Ships? An Assessment of British Warship Design Since 1900

1988   John de Courcey Ireland — Philip of Spain's Enterprise of England: An International Agony of Seamen

1989   John S. Morrison — Lessons of the Trireme Project

1990   John Keegan — Naval and Military History – What is the Difference?

1991   John Munday — The Life and Works of E. W. Cooke, marine artist

1992   David B. Quinn — Who Discovered America, Then? Columbus in

Perspective

1993   Brian Lavery — The Royal Navy in the Great War with France: Why
        Was It Successful?

1994   Andrew Lambert — Preparing for the Long Peace: The Reconstruction
        of the Royal Navy 1815–1830

1995   Rear-Admiral R. O. Morris — Two Hundred Years of Admiralty Charts
        and Surveys, 1795–1995

1996   Daniel Baugh — The Royal Navy and the Naval 'Military Revolution'
        1650–1750

1997   Andrew Gordon — Not Born Yesterday

1998   Adrian Jarvis — The Conflict between the Civil Engineer and the Naval
        Architect in Nineteenth-Century Port Development

1999   Rear-Admiral Richard Hill — Prizes of War

2000   Robert Prescott — Ship Timbers from the *Victory*, Chesapeake Mill,
        Wickham and Chatham Dockyard

2001   Geoffrey Snell — The Defences of Scapa Flow: The Royal Navy's Fleet
        Anchorage 1914–1945

2002   David Clement — Square Rigger Sunset: The Final Days of Deep-water
        Commercial Cargo Carrying under Sail

2003   Richard Harding — The British Way of Warfare: Amphibious
        Operations in the Eighteenth Century

2004   Glyndwr Williams — A Fraud Exposed: Ferrer Maldonado's
        'Discovery' of the North-West Passage

2005   Richard Woodman — The Horseshoe Nail

2006   Eric Grove — Battleship or First-Class Cruiser? HMS *Dreadnought* and
        the Limitations of Jackie Fisher's Radicalism

2007   Roger Knight — Politics and Trust in Victualling the Navy, 1793–1815

2008   Brian Lavery — The Sea and the British National Identity

2009   *Not held*

Occasional Publications, Reprints and Maritime Miscellany Series

1. R. C. Anderson, *The Rigging of a Ship* (1921).
2. G. Callender *The Wooden World Dissected by the Character of a Ship by Edward
   Ward*
3. G. S. Laird Clowes, *The length of Masts and Yards c.1640* (1931).
4. *Deane's Doctrine of Naval Architecture* (not published)
5. *Lists of Men-of-War, 1650–1700*:
   Part I, *English Ships* compiled by R. C. Anderson (1935).
   Part II, *French Ships* compiled by Pierre le Conte (1935).

Part III, *Swedish Ships* compiled by P. Holck (1936).
> *Danish-Norwegian Ships* compiled by H. J. Borjeson
> *German Ships* compiled by W. Vogel and S. Szymowski

Part IV *Ships of the United Netherlands 1650–1700* compiled by
> A. Vreughenhil (1938).

Part V *Indexes* (1939).

6. W. Sainsbury and R. C. Anderson (eds) *A Treatise on Shipbuilding and a Treatise on Rigging written about 1620–1625* (1959).
7. R. C. Anderson, *List of English Men-of-War, 1509–1649* (1959).
8. R. C. Anderson, *List of English Naval Captains, 1642–1660* (1964).

Reprints

Leopold A. Vidler, *The Rye River Barges*
H. O. Hill, *East Cornish Luggers*
James Hornell, *The Fishing Luggers of Hastings*
Boyd Cable, *The World's First Clipper*
James Hornell, *The Curraghs of Ireland*
J. H. Hornell, *British Coracles*
Basil Greenhill, *The Boats of East Pakistan*
C. R. Boxer, *The Dutch East Indiamen*

Maritime Miscellany Series

1. W. Voorbeytel Cannenburg, *The Van de Veldes*
2. P. Gosse, *The Pirates*
3. J.W. van Nouhoys, *The Anchor*
4. A. G. H. Macpherson, *Old Maritime Prints*
5. R. G. Albion, *The Timber Problem of the Royal Navy, 1652–1862*
6. Adm. G. A. Ballard, *The Fighting Ship from 1860 to 1890*
7. Cecil King, *The King's Flags*
8. W. Senior, *The History of Maritime Law*
9. Capt. L. E. Holland, *The Development of Signalling in the Royal Navy*
10. R. Morton Nance, *The Ship of the Renaissance*
11. Sir Alan Moore, *Rig in Northern Europe*
12. Basil Lubbock, *Merchantmen under sail, 1885–1932*

Plans

Model-maker's plans for the *Victory*, 10 plans on 3 sheets from those used in the restoration of 1923–1935

Note: All of the above are now out of print.

Appendix IV
Consolidated Financial Summary, 1911–2008

Part 1: Financial Summary, 1911–1938

Part 2: Financial Summary, 1940–2008

Part 1: Financial Summary, 1911–1938

Date	Subscriptions	Sales, etc.	Investment income/interest	Total revenue	Expenditure	Surplus/Loss	Cash	Securities at cost	STVF assets	Macpherson Fund assets
	(£)	(£)	(£)	(£)	(£)	(£)	(£)	(£)	(£)	(£)
1911	265	153	–	419	260	139				
1912										
1913						214				
1914	159	96	–	484	228	256	256			
1915	104	65	1	425	35	90	300			
1916	85	12	11	197	12	12	185			
1917	78	2	13	579	6	193	192	380		
1918	70	2	19	284	6	138	138	473		
1919	146	165	19	330	290	15	116	473		
1920	303	272	18	593	555	38	3	473		
1921	309	316	18	642	590	52	276	473		
1922	323	297	19	639	666	(28)	248	473	n/a	
1923	362	259	19	640	665	(25)	107	473	n/a	
1924	381	305	19	708	602	106	337	473	n/a	
1925	403	246	20	695	377	267	596	473	n/a	
1926	406	146	40	592	543	49	390	728	27,177	
1927	462	148	40	650	549	101	491	728	8,029	
1928	511	107	43	660	580	80	571	728	2,435	10,709
1929	588	143	51	782	658	125	696	728	435	11,527
1930	627	105	40	773	693	81	776	728	621	11,527
1931	690	8	49	747	837	(91)	476	937	1,651	11,527
1932	711	49	53	813	776	37	513	937	2,159	11,527
1933	743	55	28	826	817	9	522	937	2,662	11,527
1934	771	138	30	939	796	143	665	937	264	11,527
1935										
1936	874	119	30	1,023	1,096	(74)	628	937	649	11,527
1937	890	24	28	942	870	71	699	937	1,289	11,527
1938	892	100	28	1,020	1,024	(4)	695	937	37	11,527
1939									1,138	11,527

Source: NMM, SNR/2 Annual Reports; SNR/3/1 Minute Book 1; SNR/4 Accounts.

Note 1: The 1911 accounts include subscriptions paid in advance for 1912 and 1913 and donations by people declining to join.

Note 2: The accounts for 1915–18 consist of a single handwritten sheet inserted in the Council Minute Book. There are no balance sheets.

Note 3: Interest received. From 1926 the Society opened a deposit account at Coutts in addition to its original current account.

Note 4: Securities. All sums represent the net cost to the Society at time of purchase. The Society held £500 5% War Loan (redeemable 1929–47) from 1919 to 1925. This holding was increased to £750 5% War Loan (1929–47) in 1926 and £950 in 1931. The government conversion in 1932 reduced the interest and extended the term. The holding became 3½ War Loan (1952).

Note 5: No accounts have been traced for the years 1912, 1913, 1935 or 1939.

Note 6: The STVF entry for 1926 is a cumulative figures for the years 1922–26. No further breakdown is available. It seems that this figure was used to conceal the transfer of the Sea Fund to the STVF. n/a = not available.

Note 7: STVF assets exclude the purchase and sale of securities, which cannot be traced fully.

Part 2: Financial Summary, 1940–2008

2A Second World War, 1940–6

Date	Subscriptions	Sales, etc.	Investment income/ interest	Total revenue	Expenditure	Surplus/ Loss	Cash	Securities at cost	STVF assets	Macpherson Fund assets
	(£)	(£)	(£)	(£)	(£)	(£)	(£)	(£)	(£)	(£)
1940	816	356	25	1,197	637	559	1,260	937	974	11,527
1941	779	16	23	819	571	248	1,508	937	986	11,527
1942	764	511	26	1,302	577	725	2,233	937	1,143	11,527
1943	774	82	42	898	640	259	492	2,937	1,541	11,527
1944	785	516	78	1,380	585	794	286	3,937	2,147	11,527
1945	901	1,437	96	2,433	721	1,712	998	4,937	2,905	11,527
1946	911	46	143	1,100	940	160	1,158	4,937	4,035	11,527

Source: NMM, SNR/2 Annual Reports; SNR/4 Accounts.

Note 1: Securities. In 1943 the Society invested £2,000 in 3% Savings Bonds (1960–70) and a further £2,000 in 1944–5 in 3% Savings Bonds (1965–75).

Part 2: Financial Summary, 1940–2008

2B The Post-war Era, 1947–69

Date	Subscrip-tions	Other income, Sales, etc.	Invest-ment income/ interest	Total revenue	Expend-iture	Surplus/ Loss	Cash	Securities	STVF assets	Macpherson Walker Fund assets	Bequest
	(£)	(£)	(£)	(£)	(£)	(£)	(£)	(£)	(£)	(£)	(£)
1947	990	74	157	1,221	997	223	382	5,937	10,035	13,027	
1948	1,061	104	165	1,331	1,201	130	511	5,937	7,797	13,396	
1949	1,048	313	165	1,361	1,270	91	603	5,937	9,798	13,500	
1950	1,075	255	173	1,503	1,565	(62)	80	6,399	11,414	13,765	
1951	1,092	236	191	1,519	1,417	102	182	6,399	14,183	13,890	
1952	1,103	218	193	1,514	1,486	28	210	6,399	16,521	13,883	
1953	1,026	194	215	1,435	1,339	96	306	6,399	16,892	12,646	6,825
1954	1,036	178	206	1,420	1,350	70	376	6,399	20,028	12,687	7,311
1955	1,031	5,568*	218	6,817	6,817#	(79)	411	5,969	20,304	14,075	7,975
1956	1,431	604	258	2,293	1,926	367	321	6,359	13,117	14,061	8,402
1957	1,437	1,101	345	2,883	2,056	238	548	6,010	17,531	14,403	8,521
1958	1,399	708	284	2,391	2,298	93	653	6,010	19,267	14,805	8,893
1959	1,464	813	287	2,564	2,377	187	835	6,263	22,260	15,024	9,345
1960	1,411	1,064	360	2,835	1,902	932	945	7,078	16,724	14,977	9,780
1961	1,427	833	421	2,681	2,087	594	1,468	7,279	21,475	15,314	10,403
1962	1,421	751	484	2,656	1,883	773	1,912	7,525	24,622	16,003	11,033
1963	1,791	1,057	560	3,409	2,619	789	786	9,421	29,077	15,345	11,754
1964	2,007	1,216	655	3,877	2,942	936	1,067	9,921	19,761	15,875	12,501
1965	2,234	1,207	656	4,097	3,846	252	1,463	9,452	26,275	14,006	14,343
1966	2,357	1,586	806	4,749	5,069	(320)	1,306	9,257	22,674	14,946	15,392
1967	2,471	1,431	770	4,672	4,234	438	1,368	9,257	24,111	15,762	16,205
1968	2,541	1,560	846	4,947	4,660	287	1,604	9,255	23,777	16,835	17,039
1969	2,735	1,933	818	5,486	5,402	85	2,214	11,945	38,619	22,115	20,830

Source: NMM, SNR/2 Annual Reports; SNR/4 Accounts.

Notes *Including Savings Bonds valued at £5,461 7s 0d (1954) sold for £5,031 6s 6d. # Stock market investment = £5,031 6s 6d.

2C From Decimalization until Incorporation, 1970–93

Date	Subscriptions	Other income, Sales, etc.	Investment income/interest	Total revenue	Expenditure	Surplus/Loss	Cash	Securities at cost	Securities market value	STVF assets	Macpherson Fund assets	Walker Bequest	Anderson Bequest
	(£)	(£)	(£)	(£)	(£)	(£)	(£)	(£)	(£)	(£)	(£)	(£)	(£)
1970	2,891	2,231	877	5,999	6,746	(747)	1,541	11,945	15,226	50,512	23,293	22,068	
1971	2,915	2,552	876	6,343	6,830	(487)	2,536	11,945	nk	53,842	23,653	23,773	
1972	6,762	953	863	8,578	7,762	816	3,005	12,352	nk	65,122	22,829	25,130	
1973	7,432	1,794	1,197	10,423	9,615	808	3,710	11,784	15,231	78,008	22,470		
1974	7,639	1,944	1,410	10,993	14,606	(3,613)	607	12,662	7,886	55,832	25,877		
1975	7,876	3,011	1,028	11,915	12,911	(996)	81	13,550	14,408	63,655	27,596		
1976	8,565	2,259	1,078	11,902	14,847	(2,945)	72	12,514	12,499	79,249	28,278		
1977	12,684	3,038	1,532	17,254	16,380	874	164	13,445	15,044	127,605	33,104		
1978	15,036	3,612	1,679	20,327	20,327	3,682	2,901	13,445	14,694	150,994	34,090		
1979	14,255	5,536	1,676	20,553	21,467	(914)	5,491	13,454	14,167	184,231	38,624		
1980	23,843	7,609	2,667	34,119	27,128	6,991	10,682	13,454	14,870	211,171	38,749		
1981	27,298	6,125	2,580	36,003	26,250	9,753	22,148	13,285	14,627	264,425	45,768		
1982	27,007	10,423	3,052	40,482	30,452	10,030	24,174	13,285	17,410	298,164	45,955		
1983	25,393	16,352	3,315	45,060	38,475	6,585	52,095	13,285	20,171	336,216	49,510		
1984	27,364	12,349	4,719	44,432	38,582	5,850	46,430	13,285	22,631	403,930	50,038		
1985	29,204	13,730	5,326	48,260	48,808	(548)	36,975	13,285	24,715	434,635	54,834		
1986	31,891	12,070	3,535	47,496	46,832	664	27,258	13,285	38,251	488,844	56,295		
1987	31,356	5,179	4,455	40,990	46,610	(5,620)	46,184	13,285	29,364	630,438	63,202		
1988	34,377	5,832	6,068	46,277	46,582	(305)	57,990	13,285	35,442	735,299	72,869		11,890
1989	40,906	7,497	7,548	55,951	47,503	8,448	67,388	13,823	43,178	867,773	89,181		12,620
1990	41,665	8,173	9,948	59,786	56,031	3,755	116,908	6,620	26,166	1,005,246	132,718		13,434
1991	41,831	20,184	8,557	70,572	55,494	15,078	26,508	62,834	66,105	1,038,803	166,206		80,457
1992	50,158	6,805	3,973	60,936	62,774	(1,838)	24,501	66,007	73,127	1,039,396	179,992		81,161
1993	31,084	3,350	4,173	38,607	37,525	1,082	25,370	70,379	85,395	1,105,775	202,037		81,846

Source: SNR Annual Reports and Acccounts

Note 1: The SNR was incorporated on 26 August 1993. The 1993 accounts cover 9 months until 30 September 1993; the 1994 accounts run from 26 August 1993 to 31 December 1994.

Note 2: No accounts have been traced for 1991. Figures shown have been derived from the 1992 accounts. nk = not known.

Note 3: The 1992 Cash at Bank sum was corrected in 1993 to 20,484, a discrepancy of £4,017.

Part 2: Financial Summary, 1940–2008

2D: From Incorporation to the Present Day, 1994–2008

Date	Subscriptions	Other income, Sales, etc.	Investment income/interest	Total revenue	Expenditure	Surplus/Loss	Cash	Securities at cost	Securities market value	STVF assets	Macpherson Fund assets	Anderson Bequest	Tomlin Bequest	Total asset value
	(£)	(£)	(£)	(£)	(£)	(£)	(£)	(£)	(£)	(£)	(£)	(£)	(£)	(£)
1994	60,927	13,002	13,473	87,402	68,637	18,765	51,280	146,334	173,205	1,248,976	223,694	80,046		2,029,265
1995	48,401	57,696	11,073	117,170	63,803	53,367	78,272	154,345	189,643	1,307,048	225,858	92,563		2,282,565
1995												112,991	39,436	2,516,222
1996	48,320	6,430	104,137	158,887	97,799	61,088	173,235	76,324	95,581	1,870,499	324,940	118,782	41,167	2,790,565
1997	46,983	10,346	124,025	181,354	136,232	45,122	251,807	79,935	114,394	2,132,724	363,441	138,113	46,077	2,974,518
1998	47,903	10,477	107,030	165,410	219,312	(53,902)	190,617	79,935	123,356	2,246,383	403,370	149,876	51,321	2,728,021
1999	56,264	7,382	126,206	189,852	243,621	(53,769)	160,695	96,388	125,552	2,347,774	443,135	157,877	50,701	2,471,834
2000	53,789	4,203	108,066	166,058	221,402	(55,344)	171,643	108,914	132,617	2,163,441	392,249	159,241	48,763	1,953,874
2001	55,449	10,508	105,213	171,170	147,824	23,346	143,386	107,480	129,977	1,927,762	348,956	156,093	45,404	2,130,969
2002	58,365	33,904	90,720	182,989	138,484	44,505	184,256	106,001	108,193	1,527,928	300,321	131,607	36,511	2,285,558
2003	58,958	16,664	86,870	162,492	166,337	(3,845)	211,771	97,049	119,994	1,665,165	342,837	162,654	39,709	2,625,020
2004	61,402	184,098	92,387	337,887	247,337	90,550	367,423	96,787	132,639	1,903,688	347,083	178,585	44,736	2,903,243
2005	60,140	12,567	96,715	169,422	280,020	(110,598)	248,661	107,405	148,927	2,036,386	403,905	203,473	51,844	2,932,865
2006	60,645	18,590	109,437	188,672	154,160	34,512	287,745	112,180	170,749	2,286,430	421,163	224,781	56,712	2,318,216
2007	58,571	178,058	118,716	355,345	159,660	195,685	459,154	134,343	168,765	2,309,146	431,716	385,073	53,814	
2008	57,524	9,231	117,236	183,991	124,563	59,428	401,029	143,399	126,405	1,829,383	351,403	343,495	41,955	

Source: SNR Annual Reports and Acccounts

Note 1: From 1996, subsidiary accounts for restricted funds (STVF, Macpherson Collection Endowment Fund) were incorporated in the SNR's company accounts

Appendix V
Selected Obituaries

Sir Douglas Owen KBE (1850–1920)

Sir Douglas Owen, a founder member of the SNR, died on 15 November 1920 at his London home after a long illness. Educated at King's College School, he later joined the staff of the Alliance Marine, and eventually became the secretary of the company. Douglas Owen acquired an intimate knowledge of the law regarding marine insurance, and was always the leading figure at the annual meetings of the Average Adjusters Association, at which he represented the underwriters. Owen was called to the Bar of England and Wales but never practised. In 1895 he became a member of Lord Herschell's Special Committee on the Marine Insurance Bill, and afterwards served as the Hon. Secretary of the Mansion House Committee on the Port of London in 1902. He was also a representative of the Colonial Office at the Shipping Freights Conference at Johannesburg in 1904.

Douglas Owen was one of the first to respond to the Preliminary Circular inviting support for the proposed Society, and was a member of the General Committee appointed at a meeting on 14 June 1910 and of two of its sub-committees, one to consider Ways and Means, and the other to draw up a set of rules. Finally, at the first Annual General Meeting of the Society on 2 December 1910 he was elected Hon. Secretary and Treasurer. This double post he held until he was compelled by illness to resign in October 1919.

During the war, Owen became the chairman of the Advisory Committee of the State War Risks Insurance Office and of the Coal Exports Committee. His services were recognized by a knighthood in 1915 and a KBE two years later, while France bestowed on him the knighthood of the Legion of Honour and Belgium the Order of the Crown. He was also the author of a number of works on the law of marine insurance and kindred subjects

It would be difficult to exaggerate the debt which the Society owed to him and his efforts in setting it on a working basis and keeping its affairs in working order for the first four years of its active existence, and through its enforced wartime hibernation. The latter period might well have proved fatal to a young Society, but thanks to Sir Douglas Owen it emerged from its retirement, not only in full vigour, but in a stronger state than before.

HSH *Prince Louis of Battenberg 1st Marquis of Milford Haven, GCB, GCVO, KCMG (1854–1921)*

Count (later, Prince) Louis of Battenberg was born at Graz on 25 May 1854, the eldest son of Prince Alexander of Hesse, formerly a Major General in the Russian Army and a divisional commander in the Austrian Army. In 1862 Prince Alexander retired to Hesse (North German Confederation). In that year his cousin Prince Frederick married Queen Victoria's second daughter, Princess Alice, thus the Battenbergs became related through marriage to the British Royal Family. With Queen Victoria's consent, Louis Battenberg joined the Royal Navy as a cadet in October 1868 and became a naturalized British subject. After experience at sea as a midshipman he became an acting sub-lieutenant in April 1874, and was promoted to lieutenant in May 1876. He was appointed to the armoured ship *Sultan* commanded by the Duke of Edinburgh in the Mediterranean Fleet. In 1878, war threatened between Britain and Russia over the Turkish question. HMS *Sultan* was in the fleet sent to Constantinople (Istanbul). Battenberg went ashore to visit his brother Prince Alexander, an officer in the Russian Army and brought him back to be entertained in *Sultan*. Battenberg's personal contacts with the Russians sparked criticism in the English press (in a foretaste of what was to come in the run up to the First World War) which impugned his integrity, even though the Duke of Edinburgh was married to the daughter of the Russian emperor. Battenberg considered resignation, but Queen Victoria eventually placed the blame for the episode on her son, the Duke of Edinburgh. After returning home in April 1878, Battenberg was sent back to serve in the armoured ship, HMS *Agincourt*, flagship of the second-in-command of the Mediterranean Fleet, Rear-Admiral J. E. Commerrell. In February 1880, while attending a banquet in St Petersburg, Battenberg narrowly escaped death when a bomb, intended for his uncle the emperor, exploded shortly before the Imperial Party arrived.

After a spell in the Mediterranean Fleet, and a year or so on half pay, Battenberg married his distant cousin Princess Victoria of Hesse at Darmstadt in April 1884. They had a family of two sons and two daughters, one of whom married Prince Andrew of Greece and later became the mother of Philip, Duke of Edinburgh. Throughout his later career Battenberg's German connexions were vilified in the press (he never lost his accent), and his promotions were (unfairly to many in the service) put down by his critics in the Navy, including Lord Charles Beresford, to his royal connexions. From 1897 to 1899 Battenberg commanded the battleship HMS

Majestic, the flagship of the Channel Squadron before becoming Assistant Director of Naval Intelligence at the Admiralty. In September 1901 he was appointed Commodore, 2nd class, of HMS *Implacable* in the Mediterranean Fleet under the command of Sir John Fisher. He returned to the Admiralty as Director of Naval Intelligence where he renewed his association with Fisher, who had been appointed Second Sea Lord in February 1904 and First Sea Lord in October. Battenberg, who had been awarded the KCMG in 1905 despite the continuing hostility of Beresford, was his own man and did not always see eye-to-eye with Fisher. Prince Louis returned to service in February 1905 as acting rear-admiral in command of the Second Cruiser Squadron in the Atlantic Fleet. In February 1907 he became acting vice-admiral and second-in-command of the Mediterranean Fleet, and was later promoted to vice-admiral and C-in-C of the Atlantic Fleet from June 1908 to December 1910. That month, Prince Louis presided over the first AGM of the SNR as its President. In March 1911 he commanded the Third and Fourth Divisions of the Home Fleet, and in December Winston Churchill, the newly appointed First Lord of the Admiralty, made Battenberg (on Fisher's recommendation) Second Sea Lord. Coming only a few months after the Agadir crisis, Battenberg's German connexions again provoked the fury of the press, but Churchill was resilient in Battenberg's defence – promoting him to First Sea Lord in November 1911. With war declared in August 1914 and anti-German hysteria at its height in the British press, Battenberg's German birth again became an issue. Newspapers demanded his removal and Battenberg, who always knew that his position would be compromised by a war with Germany, resigned at the end of October 1914 to the regret of many in the navy. He was replaced by Lord Fisher. Anti-German feeling grew stronger as the war progressed and in July 1917 King George V disclaimed his German names and titles and ordered his relatives to do likewise. Accordingly, the Battenbergs changed their name to Mountbatten and Prince Louis was briefly known as Sir Louis Mountbatten, after which he accepted a peerage as the Marquis of Milford Haven. He retired voluntarily from the navy on 1 January 1919. From then on he actively devoted himself to the affairs of the SNR. A promotion to Admiral of the Fleet on the retired list was welcomed and he was accordingly promoted on 4 August 1921. He died suddenly at his London home in Piccadilly on 11 September 1921 and was buried at Whippingham on the Isle of Wight. His elder son succeeded to the peerage and his younger son, Lord Louis Mountbatten, later became the Society's patron as Earl Mountbatten of Burma.

John Leyland (1858–1924)

John Leyland, naval historian and travel writer, was born in Halifax, Yorkshire, the son of Francis A. Leyland of the Halifax publishing firm of R. Leyland & Son. In 1881 the census described the family as living at Oak Wood, Skircoat, York, and John as a publisher's assistant. By 1892 he had moved south to Elm Lea, Forest Hill, London; and at the beginning of the twentieth century described his occupation as author. His first book, *The Peak of Derbyshire: Its Scenery and Antiquities* came out in 1891 and was followed by a number of travel guides, among them *The Yorkshire Coast and the Cleveland Hills and Dales* in 1892, *Wensleydale and Swaledale Guide*, 1896, and *Teesdale and District Guide* in 1897. Leyland began writing for George Newnes, the publisher of *Country Life Illustrated*, in 1897. His first volume for them was *The Thames Illustrated: A Picturesque Journeying from Richmond to Oxford*, but in 1900 he published *The Shakespeare Country* over their Country Life imprint. He edited volume two of their *Gardens Old and New: The Country House and Its Garden Environment* series, and revised and extended *The Shakespeare Country* in 1904.

Leyland's change of course which brought him into naval history began in 1895 through an association with Charles Napier Robinson (q.v.) with whom he became joint author of *For the Honour of the Flag: A Story of Our Sea Fights with the Dutch*. This led to him editing *Dispatches and Letters relating to the Blockade of Brest, 1803–1805* for the NRS in 1899. Leyland later collaborated with Robinson to produce *In the Queen's Navee: The Adventures of a Colonial Cadet on His Way to the 'Britannia'* in 1902; and he contributed 'The Place of the Sea Officer and Seaman in Naval History' in C. N. Robinson's *The British Tar in Fact and Fiction* in 1909.

From 1907 onwards, Leyland produced a number of publications on maritime subjects beginning with articles on *The Literature of the Sea: From the Origins to Hakluyt* and *Seafaring and Travel: The Growth of Professional Text-books and Geographical Literature* in the Cambridge History of English Literature. In 1914 he brought out *The Royal Navy: Its influence in English History and in the Growth of Empire* in the Cambridge Manuals of Science and Literature series. During the Great War, Leyland edited a *Souvenir of the Great Naval Battle [of Jutland Bank], and Roll of Honour*, for United Newspapers in 1916 and the following year, *The Achievement of the British Navy in the World-War* for Hodder & Stoughton, which ran to a second revised edition in 1918. John Leyland was sixty years of age by then and his output ceased.

John Leyland was a founding member of the Society, serving on the Council from 1910–11 and contributing to the first volume of *The Mariner's Mirror*; he was also member of the original Editorial Committee and remained active in the Society's affairs until his death in 1924.

Admiral of the Fleet, Sir Frederick Charles Doveton Sturdee Bt GCB, KCMG, CVO (*1859–1925*).

Frederick Sturdee, the eldest son of a captain in the Royal Navy, attended the Royal Naval School at New Cross in south-east London and joined the navy in July 1871 as a cadet in the Training Ship *Britannia*. He passed out first in his class and became a midshipman in July 1873. Promoted to lieutenant in July 1880, Sturdee qualified as a torpedo officer at the torpedo school, *Vernon,* in Portsmouth in 1885. From 1886 to 1889 he was a torpedo lieutenant on HMS *Bellerophon* on the North American and West Indies station but rejoined *Vernon* in 1889, remained on the staff there and was promoted to commander in June 1893. Thereafter he was appointed to the Admiralty as a torpedo specialist in the Directorate of Naval Ordnance until in November 1887 he became commanding officer of the cruiser HMS *Porpoise* on the Australian station. Promoted to captain in June 1889, Sturdee returned to the Admiralty during 1902 as Assistant Director of Naval Intelligence. He left to command the armoured cruiser HMS *Bedford* in the Home Fleet and in May 1905 became Chief-of-Staff to Lord Charles Beresford, C-in-C Mediterranean Fleet, in the battleship, HMS *Bulwark*. He followed Beresford when the former became C-in-C Channel Fleet in 1907. Thereafter Sturdee commanded the battleships HMS *King Edward VII* and HMS *New Zealand* before being promoted to rear-admiral in September 1908. In 1910 Sturdee was appointed to command the First Battle Squadron in the Home Fleet. He was sceptical about the claimed advantages of the long range guns of the new Dreadnought class battleships on the grounds that weather conditions in the North Sea usually restricted visibility to a range when the perceived advantage would count for little. During 1911 Sturdee was president of an Admiralty committee on submarines but returned to the Home Fleet in December 1911 to command the Third Cruiser Squadron. In 1913 he transferred to command the Second Cruiser Squadron where he remained, with the honour of KCB, until promoted to vice-admiral in December 1913.

As Sir Doveton Sturdee, he succeeded Sir Henry Jackson as Chief of War Staff at the Admiralty in July 1914. His immediate superior, the First Sea Lord, Prince Louis of Battenberg resigned at the end of October 1914 and was succeeded by Lord Fisher. The latter regarded Sturdee as a Beresford man and after the disaster of Coronel on 1 November 1914, the First Lord, Winston Churchill, and Fisher despatched Sturdee in command of a task force including two modern battle cruisers HMS *Invincible* and HMS *Inflexible* to the South Atlantic to seek and destroy the commerce raiders of the German East Asiatic Squadron commanded by von Spee. Luckily for Sturdee, while he was coaling at Port Stanley, von Spee's squadron missed the opportunity of shelling the British squadron in port, choosing instead to flee from a superior force. Sturdee set off in pursuit of the German squadron and at the Battle of the Falklands on 8 December 1914 his force destroyed all but one of Spee's ships, including Spee's flagship *Scharnhorst*. Sturdee returned to England victorious and to an extent restored some public faith in the Royal Navy's offensive capabilities. Sir Doveton then became the first admiral since the Napoleonic Wars to receive a baronetcy for his endeavours. In January 1915, Sturdee was given command of the Fourth Battle Squadron of the Grand Fleet, served at the Battle of Jutland and was not impressed by Jellicoe's conduct of the battle. Sturdee was promoted to admiral in May 1917. However, when Jellicoe was appointed First Sea Lord in December 1916, Sturdee expected to take his place as C-in-C of the Grand Fleet. He had the support of the king, but was overlooked and the post was taken by the largely ineffectual David Beatty. Sturdee became C-in-C Nore in March 1918 and remained there in post until being promoted Admiral of the Fleet in July 1921. He retired to his home at Wargrave House, Camberley, Surrey, and succeeded the Marquis of Milford Haven (formerly HSH Prince Louis of Battenberg q.v.) as President of the SNR some four months after the former's death in September 1921. In the eyes of the Society he was the only possible candidate. Apart from his battle honours he had been an original member and later a Vice-President of the Society. Sir Doveton built upon Prince Louis's initial efforts and campaigned relentlessly to save HMS *Victory* for the nation and was the public face of the Society's efforts to do so. He travelled all over Great Britain to raise funds, broadcast appeals on radio and wrote articles in the press. The British public, particularly the business community, were even more apathetic than Sir Doveton anticipated. He was however, greatly heartened by the contributions of the poorer sections of the community, including children who donated their pennies. His relationship with the Scots shipowner, Sir James Caird, was vitally important in saving the ship, as was his vast array of contacts in Whitehall. As President of the Society, Sir Doveton did not suffer fools gladly and was always prepared to stand his ground to protect it. He died on 7 May 1925 and was buried in the nearby parish church St Peter's at Frimley, Surrey.

William Lionel Wyllie RA (1851–1931)
William Lionel Wyllie RA, an Honorary Vice-President of the Society, died on Easter Monday, 6 April 1931: the Society therefore lost one of its firmest friends and most enlightened benefactors. He took the chair, some twenty-one years earlier, at the foundation meeting of the SNR held at the RUSI on 10 June 1910. In 1922 at the invitation of Sir Doveton Sturdee, Wyllie joined the VTC, and thereafter never missed a meeting. No scheme was dearer to his heart than the resolution to create a Victory Museum, and he undertook to paint his *A Panorama of the Battle of Trafalgar*. In recognition the Society conferred upon him its highest honour in its gift and, in 1929, elected him an Honorary Vice-President. As the royal message of sympathy on his death put it 'his name will be handed down to posterity as a great Marine Artist'. His impressive funeral took place on Thursday 9 April 1931. The first part of the service was held at Portsmouth Cathedral and from there the coffin was carried to the waterside between a guard of honour of Sea Scouts and Boy Scouts, for whom W. L.

Wyllie had done so much; and embarked in a ten-oared naval cutter manned by Sea Scouts and lent by HMS *Nelson*, flagship of the Atlantic Fleet. Wyllie's pendant as commodore of the Portsmouth Sailing Club was at half mast at the jackstaff as the cutter proceeded slowly to Portchester. On the way, as the cutter passed each battleship, a bugle call rang out and the ship's company saluted and the colours were lowered to half-mast. At Portchester the coffin was taken ashore and borne through the Watergate of the castle to the quiet churchyard. The Society was represented at the funeral and at a later memorial service at St James's Church Piccadilly.

W. G. Perrin OBE (1874–1931)

W. G. Perrin, Admiralty Librarian and Hon. Editor of *The Mariner's Mirror* from 1922, became ill at the beginning of January 1931, with a breakdown occasioned by overwork, from which he appeared to be making a good recovery. However, on 9 February the illness took a more serious turn, and he died on 12 February 1931.

W. G. Perrin lost his father at an early age and his education was accordingly curtailed. He owed his success in later life to sheer hard work. He entered the Civil Service by examination and was eventually posted to the Admiralty in August 1893. He served in the Record Office and later in the Legal Branch and in December 1900 he became private secretary to Sir Evan MacGregor, Secretary to the Admiralty, and subsequently to his successor, Sir Inigo Thomas. He was appointed librarian to the Admiralty on 10 April 1908, where he was the moving spirit behind the re-organization of the Admiralty Library. His knowledge of flags pointed him to the naval signal book of 1804, from which he established that the flags which had been accepted as denoting Admiral Nelson's historic signal at Trafalgar were incorrect, having been taken from an earlier code.

On the outbreak of war in 1914, the Anti-Aircraft Section of the Air Department, Admiralty, took over part of the Library for its headquarters. Perrin was commissioned as lieutenant RNVR. He served as Lord Fisher's assistant secretary (for anti-aircraft and bomb-dropping questions) on the Board of Invention and Research. In January 1917 he became Secretary to the Fifth Sea Lord, Sir Godfrey Paine, and a year later was awarded the Order of the British Empire. Perrin accompanied Sir Godfrey to the Air Council in January 1918 and, on the formation of the Royal Air Force three months later, became temporary lieutenant colonel and was placed in charge of the Pay and Records Branch of the Air Ministry before returning to the Admiralty Library in 1920.

One of his tasks after the war was to revive the NRS, of which he had been Hon. Secretary since 1912. In 1921 he was elected as a Fellow of the Royal Historical Society, and in 1924 to the council of that body. In 1922, Cambridge University Press published his work, *British Flags: Their Early History and Their Development at Sea*.

He also edited several volumes for the NRS and contributed several articles to *The Mariner's Mirror*. In 1927 he was appointed by the Admiralty to be Secretary to the Trustees of the NMM and the Macpherson Collection at Greenwich.

Perrin became proficient in foreign languages and became an expert palaeographer. A prominent Freemason, he had passed the chair of the Royal Naval College and United Service Lodge, No. 1593, and had held London rank in the Craft for some years. He left a widow but no family.

Sir Henry Wellcome (1853–1936)

Born in a frontier log cabin in Almond, Wisconsin, Henry Wellcome's father was an itinerant missionary who preached from a covered wagon. In 1880 Wellcome established a pharmaceutical company, Burroughs Wellcome with his colleague Silas Burroughs, who died in 1885. In 1910 Wellcome became a British subject and in 1924 he consolidated his commercial and non-commercial activities into one holding company, The Wellcome Foundation Limited. For the last twenty-five years of his life he became an avid collector of curios and amassed a collection of some 2,000,000 items including Nelson's razor and Darwin's walking stick. Knighted in 1932, Wellcome and Sir James Caird became the first Honorary Vice-Presidents of the SNR. He personally outfitted the Dispensary on *Victory*, and after he died in 1936 the Wellcome Trust was established through his will.

Admiral of the Fleet the Earl Beatty GCB, OM, GCVO, DSO (1871–1936)

David Beatty was born in Stapely, Cheshire on 17 January 1871: in January 1884 he joined the Training Ship *Britannia* tenth out of 99 candidates and passed out 18th of the 33 remaining cadets. Beatty served as second-in-command of Lord Kitchener's river flotilla in the Khartoum Expedition. He commanded the gunboat *Fatah* at the Battle of Omdurman (2 September 1898) and was promoted to commander. Beatty later served as a member of the Naval Brigade during the Boxer Rebellion (1900), which he joined from the battleship *Barfleur* on the China Station where he was second-in-command. During the capture of Tientsin in June, he was twice wounded in an arm, and rewarded for his bravery by promotion to captain at the age of 29 – at a stroke, the youngest captain in the Royal Navy.

In 1900 he also found time to marry a wealthy heiress, Ethel Field Tree – the divorced daughter of the department store founder, Marshall Field. She bought him a steam yacht, and houses in London and Leicestershire and a grouse moor in Scotland. Beatty moved in flamboyant style in high society circles, and was promoted to rear-admiral in 1910 – the youngest in the navy. Offered a posting to the Atlantic Fleet, Beatty declined and asked for one in the Home Fleet. This did not endear him to sections within the Admiralty; however, his career was effectively saved by Winston Churchill (who knew him from Omdurman) then First Lord of the Admiralty who appointed him as his Private Naval Secretary. On 1 March 1916, Beatty was appointed to command the First Battlecruiser Squadron with the rank of vice-admiral. The Battle of Jutland and Beatty's part in it remain controversial to this day. He succeeded Jellicoe as C-in-C of the Grand Fleet and was promoted to admiral and later received the surrender of the German High Seas Fleet (after humiliating its officers) in November 1918. In 1919 he was promoted Admiral of the Fleet and thereafter served as First Sea Lord until 1927, when he became the first Chairman of the Chiefs of Staff. On retirement he was created Earl Beatty. He died after catching a chill when acting as a pallbearer at Jellicoe's funeral, which he had attended when clearly unwell. He was buried at St Paul's Cathedral. Beatty also served as the SNR's third President from 1925, after the death of Sir Doveton Sturdee. Beatty accepted the office on the proviso that someone else would do the work, which is why the Society appointed as its first Chairman Admiral Sir George Hope on the recommendation of Sir Geoffrey Callender.

Sir Owen Seaman Bt (1861–1936)

Educated at Shrewsbury School and Clare College Cambridge, where he was placed in the first class of the Classical Tripos in 1883, Owen Seaman then became a schoolmaster at Rossall School before going on to become a professor of literature at Durham College of Science, Newcastle upon Tyne. In 1897 he was called to the Bar at the Inner Temple, and in the same year joined the staff of the satirical magazine, *Punch*, becoming assistant editor in 1904 and editor from 1906 to 1934. He was knighted in 1914 and created a baronet in 1933. Seaman was an indefatigable supporter of the campaign to save the *Implacable* and a Vice-President of the SNR. A confirmed bachelor, he died in 1936 and was buried in Putney Vale Cemetery.

Cdr Charles Napier Robinson RN (1849–1936)

C. N. Robinson was one of the founder members of the Society, and a member of the original Council of 1910–11. In 1921 he became a Vice-President of the Society and in 1931 was appointed an Honorary Vice-President. To the end he remained a member of the Publications Committee. For forty-three years he was naval correspondent of *The Times*, and witnessed as a spectator or correspondent all naval reviews over a period of eighty years.

Robinson came of an old naval family. The son of a paymaster of the Royal Navy, he joined *Britannia* in 1861, and two years later was appointed to the 40-gun frigate *Liverpool*. With Admiral Dacres he made a cruise round the United Kingdom in the first squadron to which ironclads were attached. He was later involved in the suppression of slavery on the East Coast of Africa, and piracy in the Malacca Straits.

He retired in 1882 with the rank of commander. In 1884 he was appointed assistant editor of the *Army and Navy Gazette*, which position he held until 1927, and from 1885 to 1920 he was also the naval correspondent in London of the *New York Herald*. Robinson was appointed to the staff of *The Times* in 1893. He was also a founder and original Councillor of the NRS and for many years belonged to the Royal Navy Lodge of Freemasons. His only son, Rear-Admiral Cloudesley Varyl Robinson, retired in 1934 after a varied service career.

In 1932 Robinson was awarded the Chesney Gold Medal of the Royal United Services Institute for his services to naval literature. He was profoundly interested in the social life of the navy and the personalities of seamen received greater attention in his many books than they had done previously.

Sir Oswyn Murray CB, KCB, GCB (1873–1936)

Oswyn Alexander Ruthven Murray was the fourth son of Sir James Murray, the great lexicographer who was the first editor of the *Oxford English Dictionary*. He was elected a scholar of Exeter College, Oxford, in 1891, took a triple first and won the Vinerian law scholarship in 1897, the year in which he entered the Secretary's Department of the Admiralty. In 1904 he left the Secretariat to become Assistant Director of Victualling, and in December 1905 he succeeded Henry Yorke as Director of Victualling. In seven years, Murray transformed the Department. In 1911 he was appointed Assistant Secretary at the Admiralty, and in August 1917 became Permanent Secretary. Sir Oswyn served on the Council of the SNR from 1927 to 1931, in which year he became a Vice-President and was re-elected annually until his death.

George Ernest Manwaring FRHistS (1882–1939)

George Manwaring enjoyed few of the advantages which education could supply, but entered the London Library as a junior assistant at the age of 17 and, under the guidance and tuition of Sir Hagbert Wright, gradually won for himself recognition as a scholar whom other scholars were proud to consult. Manwaring elected to specialize in naval history and naval antiquities. He served on the Council of the Society from 1922 to 1925, was an assistant editor of *The Mariner's Mirror* under W. G. Perrin, and was for a long period, until the time of his death, on the council of the NRS.

Manwaring edited *The Life and Works of Sir Henry Mainwaring*, whom he liked to think of perhaps as a distant ancestor, in 1920–1 for the NRS. This presaged a long series of edited collections and single-authored works, including *Woodes Rogers's Cruising Voyage around the World* and a biography of Rear-Admiral James Burney. He rose to be assistant librarian of the London Library and unfailingly aided all who asked his advice. Throughout, his health was never robust and he died peacefully in a nursing home at Sutton, Surrey, on 13 November 1939.

HRH *Prince George, Duke of Kent* KG, KT, GCMG, GCVO *(1902–1942)*

Born at Sandringham, Norfolk on 20 December 1902, HRH Prince George was at that time fifth in the line of succession to the throne. After preparatory school at Broadstairs, he joined the naval college at Osborne, and later enrolled at Dartmouth. He left the Royal Navy in 1929 and joined the Civil Service becoming he first royal to do so. In 1926 he became the SNR's first Patron – an honour he held until his death. The title of Duke of Kent was conferred on him in 1934. As a Freemason, in 1939, he was elected Grand Master of the United Grand Lodge of England, an office he held until his death

Prince George had a racy lifestyle, but did eventually marry Princess Marina of Greece and Denmark in 1934. At the beginning of the Second World War he returned to active service with the rank of rear-admiral, briefly serving in the Intelligence Division at the Admiralty before transferring to the Royal Air Force. Prince George was killed – in highly controversial circumstances – in northern Scotland on 25 August 1942 while a passenger in a Sunderland flying-boat aircraft, which crashed apparently *en route* to Iceland and Newfoundland.

Harold Hulme Brindley FSA *(1885–1944)*

Harold Hulme Brindley was a founder member of the Society and a frequent and valued contributor to *The Mariner's Mirror*. Born in June 1885, son of Jon Beavis Brindley, barrister-at-law, he entered St John's College Cambridge in 1884 and graduated BA with Third Class Honours in the Natural Sciences Tripos. He was Demonstrator in Elementary Biology, 1915–26, and thereafter University Demonstrator in Zoology until 1934. He contributed to the study of the Mollusca and the Orthoptera group of insects, and acted as an examiner in zoology at Glasgow University, 1915–18 and 1925–6. Brindley was also a Fellow of St John's, and, from 1914–23, Steward of the College; he also rose to distinction as a nautical archaeologist.

Sir Geoffrey Arthur Romaine Callender Bt (1875–1946)

Sir Geoffrey Callender died of heart failure, aged 71, in his office at the NMM, on Wednesday, 6 November 1946. For twenty-six years he had served the Society as its Hon. Secretary and Hon. Treasurer. Callender had an innate power to interest others, which first made him an outstanding teacher of youth. The generations of naval officers who came under his influence, whether children at Osborne, boys at Dartmouth, or young or middle-aged men at Greenwich learned much. He was not a great scholar in the academic sense but, on his chosen ground, his knowledge was prodigious, and in getting across a message he had few equals. Callender was always a man on a mission to transmit to the British people the debt which they owed to the sea and to impel them to realize it. He always marched head-on to his goals, knowing exactly what he was doing and striving to achieve. Above all he had a single-minded clarity of purpose in playing the leading part in steering the Society towards his goals particularly toward the establishment of the NMM, of which he became its first Director.

The son of a mill owner, whose grandfather was the first Conservative MP in Manchester, Geoffrey Callender was educated at St Edward's School, Oxford and went on to read Modern History at Merton College, Oxford, graduating in 1897. He joined the staff of the Royal Naval College, Osborne, in 1905, and was promoted to be head of English and history in January 1913. He moved to the Royal Naval College, Dartmouth, in 1921 as Head of History, and in 1922 became the first professor of history at the Royal Naval College, Greenwich, which moved him to the heart of the Society's affairs. He retained the chair until 1934, when he was succeeded by Michael Lewis. A bachelor to the end, he lived with his two sisters in Blackheath. He was knighted in 1938.

David Bonner Smith, FRHistS (1890–1950)

David Bonner Smith was a frequent contributor to *The Mariner's Mirror* and its Hon. Editor from 1932 to 1939. As Admiralty Librarian, he was of even more influence in matters of nautical research. He joined the staff of the Admiralty Library in March 1911, was made deputy librarian on the death of W. G. Perrin in 1931. He was appointed librarian in March 1932. He retired in May 1950 at the age of 60, and in recognition of his long and useful services to the Society, was elected an Honorary Vice-President at the 1950 AGM. It has been said of Bonner Smith that he not only knew every one of the 100,000 books in the Admiralty Library, but was also familiar with all their contents. It is a fact that he could direct students and enquirers to whatever references were needed, and have the necessary books at once placed before them. Scores of our members owed a debt of gratitude to his ever ready and encyclopaedic acquaintance with books and documents dealing with the sea and sea services. David Bonner Smith also served as Hon. Secretary of the NRS from 1944 to 1948.

Sir James Caird of Glenfarquhar Bt (1864–1954)

James Caird was born in Glasgow on 2 January 1864, the elder son in a family of six. He was educated at Glasgow Academy and then joined the firm of William Graham and Co., East India Merchants, in 1878. In 1889 he moved to London, and a year later joined Turnbull, Martin and Co., managers of the Scottish Shire Line of steamships. In 1891 he became manager and by 1903 he was sole partner and owner of the Shire Line. In co-operation with the Houlder and Federal Lines, he opened up trade between the west coast of England and Australia and New Zealand.

Caird started a new shipyard at Chepstow from scratch to build standard ships in 1916, and in 1917 the government bought him and his associates out in what became known as the National Shipyard. In the same year, probably foreseeing the likelihood of a shipping slump after a short-lived post-war boom, Caird sold his shipping interests to the Glen Line (later owned by Cayzer Irving & Co.). He remained a director of some 25 companies connected with maritime industries and was also the chairman of the Smithfield and Argentine Meat Company.

He was created a baronet in 1928, but later refused a peerage offered by Neville Chamberlain. Stocky of build and generous by nature, he retained his Scots accent to the end. Sir James went daily to his London Office until 1949 when illness took hold. He died at his home in Wimbledon, South East London on 17 September 1954. Sir James also had a home in Glenfarquhar, Kincardine, which he marked in his title. His wife, Henrietta, predeceased him in 1953: they had a daughter but no son; thus the baronetcy died with him.

But for Caird's munificence, *Victory* would not have been saved for the nation and the NMM would not have been created and filled with his magnificent donations. In monetary terms, he gave the huge sum of £1,250,000 to the NMM alone, and as a result his cultural legacy has endured.

Leonard G. Carr Laughton (1898–1955)

On 30 April 1955 the SNR suffered a severe loss by the death of L. G. Carr Laughton, who might be said to have been its founder, as far as that title should be given to any one man. A son of Sir John Knox Laughton, he naturally grew up with naval history in his blood, and Carr Laughton added both archaeology and etymology to his vast store of knowledge on almost any subject connected with the work of the SNR, a store which he was always ready to share with others. For one whose knowledge was at the same time so extensive and so detailed, Carr Laughton wrote surprisingly little on a large scale, but on one subject at least he produced something not likely to be superseded for many years, if ever. This was his study of the decoration of ships in the sailing-ship epoch, published in 1925 under the somewhat inadequate title of *Old Ship Figure-heads and Sterns*. He was responsible for three long and important chapters in Laird Clowes's *The Royal Navy*, these being connected with history rather than archaeology, and he wrote certain naval or nautical sections of the *Victoria County Histories*. Another piece of work which deserves special attention was his Report to the VTC of his search among the

Admiralty Records for information which would help in the restoration of the ship to her Trafalgar state. This was printed in *The Mariner's Mirror* in 1924.

Even before the foundation of the SNR, Carr Laughton had begun to accumulate material for the 'complete and scholarly Nautical Encyclopaedia or Dictionary', which was then included among the Society's original objectives. Unfortunately, his very thoroughness made him something of a perfectionist; he was never satisfied that he had found enough to justify publication.

Admiral Sir Aubrey Clare Hugh Smith KCVO, KBE, CB (1872–1957)

Sir Aubrey Clare Hugh Smith was a scion of a well-known merchant banking family in the City of London. His father was Governor of the Bank of England in 1897–8. Hugh Smith went to sea at the age of 13. Promoted to commander in 1905, he commanded successively two small ships – the boys' training ship *Iris*, and a third-class cruiser, *Foresight*. After two years at the Admiralty he received the first of his long series of diplomatic appointments as naval attaché at St Petersburg, and later Stockholm and Oslo. In the course of the first three-year appointment he was promoted to captain. When the fleet was mobilized in 1914, he became flag captain of HMS *Drake*, flagship of the 3rd Cruiser Squadron. In March 1915, he was posted as Assistant Director of Naval Intelligence under Captain Reginald Hall. After eighteen months in that post, he was appointed C-in-C in the Eastern Pacific, with his broad pendant in the famous HMS *Glasgow*. He remained in command there until after the end of the war. In 1921, he was promoted rear-admiral and became head of the British Naval Mission to Greece. He then became Naval Representative on the Advisory Committee of the League of Nations until 1927. In 1928 he was promoted vice-admiral and, not having flown his flag at sea, was placed on the retired list, from which he was promoted admiral in 1930.

In retirement, Hugh Smith became a director of Hay's Wharf, an important and long-established London business, which was largely controlled by his family. As a member of the Fishmongers Company – he was in turn elected Prime Warden, and he was active in its charitable work. Until his death he was an active member, Councillor and Vice-President of the NRS and the SNR.

Sir Alan Moore Bt (1882–1959)

Before the death of Sir Alan Moore, the Society had hoped to recognize his work for nautical archaeology and the SNR by adding his name to the list of its Honorary Vice-Presidents. Alan Moore was a founder member of the SNR and played an important role as an intermediary in bringing together Leonard Carr Laughton and Robert Morton Nance which ensured its success. Moore contributed to the very first issue of *The Mariner's Mirror*, and during the Great War served as a Temporary

Surgeon RN. In 1925, he published *Last Days of Masts and Sail* (illustrated by Robert Morton Nance) and, in the following year, *Sailing Ships of War, 1800–60*. In 1953 Moore published his recollections on the foundation of the SNR in *The Mariner's Mirror*.

Admiral Sir George Price Webley Hope KCMG, KCB *(1869–1959)*

George Hope was born on 11 October 1869 at St Andrews, the son and grandson of admirals. He was educated at Mannamead School, Plymouth, where his father was the dockyard superintendent in Devonport. He entered *Britannia* as a cadet in 1882 and was appointed lieutenant at the age of 20 having obtained firsts in every subject. Hope went to the Mediterranean in the *Colossus* but returned in 1891 to qualify in gunnery at HMS *Excellent*, then under the command of Sir Percy Scott. Promoted to captain on 30 June 1905, he was appointed flag-captain in HMS *Good Hope*, flagship of the First Cruiser Squadron. After two years, Hope joined the staff of the Inspector of Target Practice, attending gunnery practices, reporting on them and offering suggestions for improvement at a time when gunnery practice was becoming a standard organized procedure for the whole Navy. In March 1911, Hope was appointed Assistant Director of the Mobilization Department at the Admiralty and, when Churchill inaugurated the War Staff scheme in 1912, he was appointed Assistant Director of the Operations Division of the Staff at the Admiralty. A short-term command of the battleship *Superb* was followed after mobilization by a working-up command of the reserve cruiser *King Alfred*. However in October 1914 he was given command of the newest battleship, *Queen Elizabeth*, which he took into the Mediterranean and from February 1915, bombarded the Dardanelles forts. Hope was Admiral de Robeck's flag-captain and was awarded the CB for his organization of the landings. He was honoured by being made *aide-de-camp* to the King and brought the *Queen Elizabeth* home in May 1915 to join the Grand Fleet. In 1916 Hope was appointed director of the Operations Division of the Naval Staff. He was promoted rear-admiral on 3 April 1917 and was appointed Deputy First Sea Lord on 18 January 1918, in succession to Sir Roslyn Wemyss, when Wemyss became First Sea Lord. Hope accompanied Wemyss to France in November 1918 for the Armistice negotiations and when Wemyss was the British signatory to the Armistice agreement. Hope was appointed to the Board of Admiralty 24 January 1919, and was the Admiralty representative at the Peace Conference. After the Peace was signed Hope commanded the Third Cruiser Squadron in the Mediterranean for eighteen months in HMS *Cardiff*. He was promoted Vice-Admiral on 26 November 1920 and spent two years on half pay before being appointed President and Flag Officer Commanding the Royal Naval College, Greenwich in February 1923. He served for three years, being promoted admiral on 24 November 1925.

Vice-Admiral Sir George Webley Hope was invested as KCMG in 1919 and as KCB in 1923

Sir George Hope was the Society's President from 1936–51, and to all intents 'Acting President' for eleven years before that. When the Society invited Earl Beatty to be its President in 1925, he asked it to appoint a Chairman who would – to put it bluntly – do the work for him. Sir George was then Admiral President of the Royal Naval College, Greenwich, so that Professor Geoffrey Callender had a good deal to do with the Society's choice of Chairman. For twenty-six years Sir George presided at SNR meetings with unfailing regularity and guided the Society wisely in many important decisions. He was also one of the original Trustees of the NMM, who helped to form a close relationship between the museum and the Society.

Sir George Hope died on 11 July 1959. A memorial service was held in the chapel of the Royal Naval College, Greenwich, at which R. C. Anderson, President of the SNR, gave the address, before his family and the Director of the NMM and senior staff and officers of the SNR.

Robert Morton Nance (1873–1959)

Born in Cardiff to Cornish parents, Robert Morton Nance moved to Cornwall in 1906 to the small village of Nancledra near St Ives. He was a leading authority on the Cornish language and the author of many books, and pamphlets, including a Cornish–English dictionary. He was also a nautical archaeologist of distinction, a founder member of the SNR and a frequent contributor to *The Mariner's Mirror*. As a young man he had made a very extensive collection of drawings from all sorts of contemporary representations of ships and could redraw these in pen-and-ink for reproduction. His book, *Sailing Ship Models*, was published in 1924 and reissued in 1949 and remains a standard work

Captain Henry Theodore Augustus Bosanquet CVO (1871–1959)

Henry Bosanquet joined *Britannia* in 1883 and his name first appears on the Navy List on his appointment to HMS *Raleigh*, a fully rigged steam frigate and the flagship of the Cape of Good Hope and West African Station in 1885. He retired from the Navy on grounds of ill health at the age of 27, and joined the Marine Society which he served with distinction as its secretary. He was promoted to captain on the retired list as a reward for his work mainly at the Admiralty during the First World War, where for a time he was head of the navigation section of the Royal Naval Air Service.

A founder member of the SNR and a contributor to its journal; he was its Hon. Auditor until 1946, Treasurer in 1947, Councillor in 1948 and Vice-President in 1951. He published a catalogue of the NMM's collection of naval officers' swords in

1955, and in 1957 the Society honoured Henry Bosanquet's very great contribution to it by the award of Honorary Vice-President.

Cdr Hilary Poland Mead RN (1889?–1962)

Hilary Mead went to sea as a midshipman in 1904. By the outbreak of the Great War he had been promoted to lieutenant and had become a signals specialist. In that capacity he served in the *King George V* and the *Dreadnought*. After the war his last appointment was at the Hong Kong Wireless Station. Hilary Mead joined the Society in 1932. He wrote four books, and contributed many articles connected with flags and signalling to *The Mariner's Mirror* between then and 1961. From 1946 he succeeded Roger Anderson as Hon. Editor and remained in post until the end of 1953 when he was succeeded by G. R. G. Worcester. Mead's editorship spanned a difficult period of paper restrictions, controls and rising prices all of which he bore with consummate professionalism.

William McQuie Mather (1898–1963)

William Mather died in Ramsey, Isle of Wight on 14 July 1963; he was born in Liverpool in 1898 and had hoped to serve in the Royal Navy. Unhappily he was prevented by ill-health from following this career, although during the Great War he became a wireless operator in the Merchant Service, being engaged on the North Atlantic convoys.

After the war he entered the family business, but his real interest lay in maritime history, and he was able to make an outstanding contribution within this field, particularly by his studies of early nineteenth-century naval and merchant shipping. His maritime library was wide in scope and of particular value to the researcher. As such, before his death it was his wish that his collection and that of a highly detailed, 1:96 scale-model of HMS *Victory*, which had taken him ten years to produce, should go to the projected maritime museum of Liverpool. This it did.

Rear-Admiral Henry George Thursfield (1882–1963)

Henry Thursfield was the only son of Sir James R. Thursfield, naval historian and naval correspondent of *The Times*, and friend and supporter of Admiral Sir John Fisher. Henry joined the navy by way of *Britannia* and became lieutenant in 1902 and captain in 1920, when he was appointed Deputy Director of the Royal Naval Staff College at Greenwich. Between 1922 and 1924 he commanded ships in the Mediterranean Fleet. In 1928 he became Director of the Tactical Division at the Admiralty. He was appointed *aide-de-camp* to King George V in 1932 and the same year retired with the rank of rear-admiral.

Admiral Thursfield was naval correspondent of *The Times* from 1936 to 1952 and was editor of *Brassey's Naval Annual* from 1936. He joined the SNR in 1937 and was soon elected a Councillor. In 1954 he was elected as one of the Society's original trustees. He also served on the Council of the NRS and edited a volume of *Naval Journals, 1789–1817*, published in 1951. He also served as a trustee of the NMM from 1948 to 1955.

Admiral of the Fleet The Earl of Cork and Orrery GCB, GCVO (1873–1967)

Earl Cork and Orrery (known in the Royal Navy as Ginger Boyle) joined *Britannia* in 1886 aged 11. He was promoted to lieutenant in 1895 and served in the China Squadron at the time of the Boxer Rebellion. Promoted to commander in 1906 and captain in 1913, when he served as the Naval Attaché, Rome. He joined the Society in 1929 when he was serving as Admiral President of the Royal Naval College, Greenwich, during which time his former Professor of History and English, Geoffrey Callender, was planning the formation of the NMM. In 1938, as C-in-C Portsmouth, he opened the Victory Museum and from 1940 to 1947 he was a Trustee of the NMM.

Gregory Robinson DSC (1876–1967)

Gregory Robinson was one of the more immediate founder members of the SNR and was also prominent in its foundation. At the time of his death he was a Vice-President of the Society. The son of Captain Charles R. H. Robinson, RN, believed to have been the last Master in the Navy before they became navigating officers, Gregory Robinson was born in the parish of St Anthony, Willcove, Cornwall, overlooking Plymouth Sound on 22 February 1876. Educated in the Mathematical School of Christ's Hospital, at the age of 13 he was presented by Queen Victoria with a gold pencil case as a reward for the drawing of a ship which took her fancy. After a three-year course at the Royal Academy School he made a voyage on his father's ship HMS *Wye*, a steam-powered store ship of 1,370 tons. He then made a voyage round the world in a four-masted barque, *Carradale*. He settled as a marine artist on the Quay House at Hamble, and afterwards in Satchel Lane, where he brought up a family of four boys. In 1912 he sailed with friends through the Kiel Canal in the yacht *Silver Crescent* and was locked-up for a time by the German authorities, being mistaken for a spy. In the Great War he held a commission as lieutenant RNVR for four years and was awarded a DSC for his services. From his studio at Hamble he painted many water colours of sailing ships, which were particularly popular with Americans. However, no modern artist has captured so well the grace and detail of a seventeenth-century English warship.

James Richard Stanhope, 7th Earl Stanhope (1880–1967)

James Richard Stanhope, 7th Earl Stanhope and 13th Earl of Chesterfield, KG, PC, was born on 11 November 1880. He was an army officer in the Grenadier Guards between 1900 and 1908 and again from 1914 to 1918 rising to the rank of colonel at the end of the Great War. Later he served as a Territorial Army inspecting officer. The Earl Stanhope married Lady Eileen Browne (1889–1940), the eldest daughter of George Ulick Browne, 6th Marquis of Sligo, and Agatha Stewart Hodgson. He succeeded to the 7th Baron Stanhope and later to 13th Earl of Chesterfield but never used the more senior title, and continued to be known as Earl Stanhope. As he had no close heirs, both Earldoms and the Barony of Stanhope became extinct upon his death.

Earl Stanhope was a Conservative politician holding the post of Civil Lord of the Admiralty from 1924 to 1929. In the National Government, he was Under-Secretary of State for Foreign Affairs 1934–1936 and First Commissioner of Works 1936–1937. In Neville Chamberlain's ministry Stanhope was President of the Board of Education 1937–8; Leader of the House of Lords 1938–1940; First Lord of the Admiralty 1938–1939; Lord President of the Council 1939–1940.

Earl Stanhope's connexions with the Civil Service and among the Cabinet enabled him to press the Admiralty in 1927 to establish a Board of Trustees which could agree on the future deposit and display of their historical collections. Stanhope had no obvious interest in the preservation of the naval past, but his family's interests showed a distinct historical turn. Also, his experience as a Trustee of the National Portrait Gallery – which his grandfather, the Fifth Earl Stanhope, had founded in 1856 – made him familiar with the whole range of museum requirements. Following the passing of the NMM Act, 1934, Earl Stanhope became Chairman of the Board of Trustees, a post he held until 1959. He was elected a Vice-President of the SNR in 1932 and raised to be an Honorary Vice-President in 1933.

The 7th Earl Stanhope died on 15 August 1967. He left Chevening, his country seat, to the Nation.

G. R. G. Worcester (1890–1969)

G. R. G. Worcester, Hon. Editor of *The Mariner's Mirror* from 1954 to 1961 died on 5 January 1969. He entered the navy at an early age and as a midshipman rounded the Horn under sail. During the Great War he served in submarines until 1919, when he left the Navy to join the Marine Department of the Chinese Maritime Customs Service.

As River Inspector, Worcester assisted in surveying, marking and opening the Yangste to steam navigation to a point 155 miles west of Chungking and 1,450 miles from the sea. But 'Paul' Worcester's permanent claim to fame arose from Sir Frederick Maze getting the permission of the Chinese Nationalist Government to allow Worcester to spend all his time visiting every port in China in order to make a study of Chinese shipping from earliest times. A large number of books and articles on junks ensued, accurately and amusingly illustrated from his pen. His auto-biography *The Junkman Smiles*, became a best-seller overnight. He was mainly responsible for building up the unique Maze Collection of Chinese junks (some made by his own hands) now housed in the Science Museum, Kensington, and writing the authoritative guide to that collection of models. During the Second World War, Worcester spent three years as a prisoner of war of the Japanese.

Professor Michael Arthur Lewis CBE (1890–1970)

Educated at Uppingham and Trinity College, Cambridge, Michael Lewis joined the staff of the Royal Naval College, Osborne, in 1913. During the Great War he was commissioned into the Royal Marine Artillery and rejoined Osborne to serve as a Term Lieutenant. In 1922 he transferred to the History and English Department of the Royal Naval College, Dartmouth. In 1934 he succeeded Geoffrey Callender as Professor of History and English at the Royal Naval College, Greenwich, and retired in 1955 to live locally.

With his friend Callender whom he had first served under at Osborne, he shared a lasting interest in nautical research and naval history. A councillor of both the NRS and the SNR, he became the Chairman of the latter from 1951 until 1961, and President until his death in 1970. On the death of Callender in 1946, Earl Stanhope the Chairman of the Trustees of the NMM suggested to Lewis that he might become Director, but he was too happy in his job at Greenwich to leave it.

Captain T. Davys Manning CBE, VRD, RNVR retd (1898–1971)

Captain T. Davys Manning was Hon. Editor of *The Mariner's Mirror* from the November issue of 1961 until his death on 28 November 1971. Educated at the junior and senior departments of Weymouth College, Manning joined the Royal Navy in 1916, serving in the RNAS with experience of airships. After demobiliz-ation he joined the Sussex Division of the RNVR as a sub-lieutenant.

He was an assistant master at Newlands School, teaching principally mathematics and history. Recalled during the Abyssinian crisis in 1936 he served for six months. He was a lieutenant commander at the outbreak of the Second World War. His duties during the war included command of the coastal forces working-up base at Ardrishaig and serving in the Second Sea Lord's office. After the war he rejoined Newlands School and became assistant headmaster until he died. He also com-manded the Sussex Division of the RNVR from 1946 until 1951, and in 1949–51 was *aide-de-camp* to HM King George VI. His war services were acknowledged by the award of the CBE, as well as the Volunteer Reserve Decoration.

Lt Col Harold Wyllie OBE *(1880–1973)*

Harold Wyllie, who died in London on 22 December 1973, at the age of 93, was one of the last surviving founder members of the Society and for many years a Vice-President in both active and honorary capacities.

The elder son of the marine painter W. L. Wyllie, RA, Harold inherited a life-long love of the sea from his father, which led him in later life to specialize in painting men-of-war through all the ages of sail. In 1898 he was sent to New York as special artist to the *Graphic*, but this career was interrupted in 1900 when he received a commission in the Royal West Kent Regiment and served in the Boer War, gaining the Queen's Medal with three clasps. After the war he returned to painting and exhibited at the Royal Academy and at many other galleries across the land. During the Great War, he was granted a permanent commission in the Regular Army in the field in 1916, and was posted to the Wiltshire Regiment. He was one of the first to volunteer for transfer to the newly formed Royal Flying Corps and he later commanded various squadrons both in France and in the defence of Britain. He was awarded the OBE in 1919 and retired from the army in the following year with the rank of lieutenant colonel. After the war he qualified as a pilot and was later granted the honorary rank of wing commander.

An original and valued member of the VTC from 1922, Harold Wyllie brought his vast knowledge and experience to bear on the committee whose work culminated in the opening of the ship to the public in 1928. He was also a great supporter of the Victory Museum. He also became Captain Superintendent of HMS *Implacable* and the *Foudroyant* and encouraged their youth work.

At the outbreak of the Second World War he was granted a temporary commission in the RAFVR, but in 1943 he transferred to the RNVR as a Lieutenant for Special Duty and commanded HMS *Implacable* at Portsmouth. Promoted to lieutenant commander, he was demobilized in November 1945. By this stage he had had a distinguished career in all three armed services in three separate wars.

After the war, Col. Wyllie returned to being Captain Superintendent, and in 1948 the Implacable Committee was re-formed as the Foudroyant Committee. In 1949, despite all efforts to save her, HMS *Implacable* was towed out to sea and met her watery grave. In the same year it was possible to re-open *Foudroyant* as a training ship, and in that year Harold Wyllie resigned his post as Captain Superintendent but continued as a member and later Vice-President of the Foudroyant Committee.

A few years before his wife Hilary's death in 1960, the Wyllie's moved to her birthplace at Hillhead of Dunkeld, Perthshire. There, until a short time before his death, Harold Wyllie continued to produce works of art.

Roger Charles Anderson DLitt, FSA (1883–1976)

Roger Charles Anderson died at the impressive age of 95 on 3 October 1976. With his friends, L. G. Carr Laughton, Alan Moore, H. H. Brindley and Gregory Robinson he was a founder member of the SNR. He became Hon. Editor of *The Mariner's Mirror* for the first time in 1913, and many of the informative articles in the early issues of the journal were written by him. He also used the *nom de plume* 'South Goodwin' to contribute through the years. Roger Anderson was Hon. Editor from 1913–23, 1931–2 and 1939–46, and President of the Society from 1931–61. An original member of the Board of Trustees of the NMM as first constituted, he went on to succeed Earl Stanhope as Chairman of Trustees from 1959 to 1962 and donated many of the items and books that grace the museum today.

Anderson had a special interest in the building and rigging of early sailing ships and this led to a number of books which still stand the test of time including *Naval Wars in the Baltic* (1910); *The Rigging of Ships in the Days of the Spritsail Topmast, 1600-1720* (1927); *Naval Wars in the Levant* (1952); *Seventeenth Century Rigging* (1955); and *Oared Fighting Ships* (1962).

Although his writing style was rather dull, Roger Anderson's conclusions were always trustworthy. He thrived on facts and figures, and always named the ships, the guns they carried and noted the captains' Christian names. He was scrupulously fair to foreign interpretations. His nautical library contained many important overseas works, and these, in conjunction with his equally important collection of ship models, were donated to the NMM.

Bernard Pool CB, CBE (1898?–1977)

A former Councillor of the SNR and a contributor to *The Mariner's Mirror*, Bernard Pool joined the Admiralty division of the Civil Service in 1914 and was called to the Bar of England and Wales in 1921, later becoming a senior Bencher of the Middle Temple. He served at the Admiralty throughout his career, becoming Director of Naval Contracts from 1948 to 1960. On his retirement he became Hon. Treasurer of the NRS from 1960 to 1971 and later Vice-President. His most valuable contribution to naval history was his book *Navy Board Contracts, 1660–1832* (London, 1966).

G. B. P. Naish FSA, RNR (1909–1977)

George Prideaux Brabant Naish, the Society's Hon. Secretary from 1947 to 1977, was educated at St Edward's School, Oxford, and Southampton University. George Naish was an original member of staff at the NMM, and rose to become keeper in 1969. He became Historical Consultant to the Director in 1971. Naish had an unrivalled acquaintance with the museum's collections, and was prodigal in the generosity in which he imparted his knowledge to others. His enthusiasm for nautical archaeology and for maritime and naval history was boundless.

During the Second World War he volunteered for the RNVR, transferring after de-mobilization to the RNR, in which he became lieutenant commander. He was also a keen yachtsman and an active member of the Royal Cruising Club to the end of his life.

Naish's individualism was marked and he had a remarkable memory. His most important contributions were his NRS edition of Spanish documents relating to the Armada, together with Ubaldino's second narrative, in the *Naval Miscellany* (London, 1952), and his volume of *Nelson's Letters to his Wife* (London, 1958). Perhaps his most original work where his chapters on the history of sailing ships and shipbuilding from the sixteenth to the twentieth centuries in volumes 3 and 4 of Sir Charles Singer's *History of Technology* (London, 1954).

At the Society's AGM of 1977 Naish was elected an Honorary Vice-President of the SNR by acclamation. He served on the VATC, the Council of the NRS and was also President of the Council for Nautical Archaeology.

Captain T. E. Jackson, FMA, RN (1896–1977)

After an outstanding career in the Instructor Branch of the Royal Navy, which he joined in May 1919 and left in February 1952, Captain Jackson was appointed by the Society as the first curator of the Victory Museum on 1 May 1952. With no previous museum experience, he applied himself with dedication, vigour and thoroughness and in a short space of time turned around the fortunes of the museum whose visitor numbers rose rapidly year-on-year. He found time to study for the Museum's Association diploma, which he was awarded in 1957, becoming an Associate and, subsequently, a Fellow of the Association. He was an extremely kind and gentle man who never lost the self-discipline which, as a pedagogue in his earlier life, he had to develop in others.

Major-General Michael W. Prynne CB, CBE (1912–1977)

On 27 September 1977 Michael Prynne and his wife were killed in a motoring accident at Wells-next-the Sea, Norfolk only a few days after attending the memorial service for George Naish. Educated at Bedford School, the Royal Military Academy, Woolwich, and St John's College, Cambridge, he was commissioned with the Royal Engineers in 1932 and served in the Second World War in Persia, Iraq, the Eighth Army in North Africa and Italy (at Monte Cassino) being mentioned in despatches. He attended the Joint Services Staff College in 1948 and from 1951–3 was Military Attaché in Moscow. His last military appointment was as Chief of Staff, Headquarters Southern Command from 1966–7.

Michael Prynne had twice served on the Society's Council and as a young subaltern he had worked with the Naish family on the remains of the *Grace Dieu*. A man of very wide tastes and interests, on his retirement in 1967 from a distinguished military career, he became secretary of the Association of Consulting Engineers. But for his untimely death, the November 1977 issue of *The Mariner's Mirror* would have carried the announcement of his appointment as chairman of a committee to organize the collection of material towards the publication of 'a complete and scholarly Nautical Encyclopaedia or Dictionary', under the terms of Rule II, 3 of the Society – to which task he had just begun to devote his customary energy and enthusiasm.

Professor Ralph Davis FBA (1915–1978)

Born in Hull in 1915, Ralph Davis was a long-term member of the SNR and contributor to *The Mariner's Mirror*. From 1968 to 1975 he was a Trustee of the NMM. At the time of his death he was Professor of Economic History at the University of Leicester. He was generally acknowledged as the leading authority on the early modern history of merchant shipping, his *The Rise of the English Shipping Industry in the Seventeenth and Eighteenth Centuries* (1962), being the standard work on the subject. This book was followed by others, such as *English Overseas Trade, 1500–1700* (1973), and The *Rise of the Atlantic Economies* (1973), which gained him an international reputation as a scholar of distinction.

Admiral of the Fleet The Earl Mountbatten of Burma KG, GCB, OM, GCSI, GCIE, GCVO, DSO (1900–79)

Louis Battenberg was born at Frogmore House, Windsor on 25 June 1900. He became a cadet at the Royal Naval College, Osborne, in May 1913 and was there when his father, Prince Louis of Battenberg resigned as First Sea Lord after the outbreak of the First World War. After attending the Royal Naval College, Dartmouth, he was appointed as a midshipman in the battle-cruiser HMS *Lion* in July 1916, and later transferred to the battleship, HMS *Queen Elizabeth* in February 1917. In June 1917 his father renounced his German titles and took the surname Mountbatten.

In August 1941 Mountbatten flew to the USA to take command of the aircraft carrier HMS *Illustrious* then under repair at Norfolk, Virginia but was recalled by Churchill in October to succeed Sir Roger Keyes as adviser to Chiefs of Staff on Combined Operations, with promotion to commodore. His rapid advancement occasioned a deal of resentment among senior officers, but Churchill nevertheless appointed him Chief of Combined Operations in March 1942 with full membership of the Chiefs of Staff Committee and acting promotion to vice-admiral, lieutenant general and air marshal. The failure of the raid on Dieppe brought in its wake a great deal of criticism of Mountbatten and his Combined Operations organization.

However, Mountbatten survived the criticism and in August 1943 accompanied Churchill to the Quebec Conference, where he was appointed Supreme Allied Commander, South East Asia, with acting promotion to admiral. He established a large headquarters in Delhi, but after April 1944 moved to Kandy, in Ceylon. His relationships with his operational admirals and commanders in the field at times left much to be desired, with Mountbatten no stranger to courting publicity. Post-war he declined the offer of a baronetcy, instead settling for a viscountcy in the New Year Honours List of 1946. He declined to use his new title of Viscount Mountbatten of Burma and continued to be known as Lord Louis Mountbatten. At the end of May 1946 he left his headquarters in Singapore and returned to England with the substantive rank of rear-admiral.

Mountbatten's progressive views on the end of Empire found favour with the 1945 Labour Government, and he was offered and accepted the post of Viceroy and Governor General of India. He assumed office in March 1947 committed to ending British rule there. He and his wife became friends with the Hindu leader of the Congress Party, Jawaharlal Nehru but he was unable to influence the Muslim leader Muhammad Ali Jinnah. Faced with an impending collapse of imperial authority owing to the fracturing along religious lines of the supporters of the Hindu and Muslim parties, Mountbatten brought forward the date of independence to 15 August 1947. Partition of the sub-continent between a secular, predominantly Hindu India, and a Muslim Pakistan ensued amid intercommunal violence, rape, murder and destruction of property, leaving over a quarter of a million people dead and many more displaced as refugees. Mountbatten stayed on as Governor General of the new Dominion of India and as Chairman of a Joint Defence Council set up to divide the assets of the British Indian Army. Pakistanis came to regard him as over-sympathetic to India especially over Nehru's home state of Kashmir, to this day a continuing source of tension between India and Pakistan. By October 1947 Indian politicians came to suspect that the Supreme Commander of both Dominions' armies, Field Marshal Sir Claude Auchinleck (no friend of Mountbatten) favoured Pakistan. Mountbatten arranged for Auchinleck's retirement and the disbandment of his headquarters. At the end of his period in office as Governor General, Mountbatten became Earl Mountbatten of Burma in August 1947.

After leaving India at the end of 1948 Earl Mountbatten was given command of the First Cruiser Squadron in the Mediterranean Fleet. He was promoted to vice-admiral in June 1949, and from June 1950 to April 1952 he was Fourth Sea Lord at the Admiralty. In June 1952 he was given command of the Mediterranean Fleet, promoted to admiral in February 1953 and, in April 1955, appointed First Sea Lord, with promotion to Admiral of the Fleet in October 1956. In July 1959, Mountbatten became Chief of the Defence Staff and embarked on a policy of unifying the defence establishment. Consequently, in 1964 the Admiralty, the War Office and the Air Ministry were renamed the Army, Navy and Air Force Departments and combined in a new Ministry of Defence. Mountbatten left office in July 1965, by which stage a Labour government had been elected after thirteen years of Conservative Party rule.

On 27 August 1979, Earl Mountbatten of Burma, together with his grandson, Nicholas Knatchbull, and an Irish boy, Paul Maxwell, were murdered by elements within Irish republicanism who planted a bomb that blew up his fishing boat off his country house in Mullaghmore Co. Sligo. His daughter Patricia, her husband, Lord Brabourne, and their other son were injured, and Lord Brabourne's mother died of her injuries. Mountbatten received a state funeral in Westminster Abbey and was buried in Romsey Abbey near Broadlands. His elder daughter, Patricia, Lady Brabourne, succeeded him as the second Countess Mountbatten.

After the Earl's death the following tribute by the Society's President Rear-Admiral Edward F. Gueritz was published in *Mariner's Mirror*:

On Monday 27 August 1979, a letter was lying on my desk ready for despatch and addressed to Admiral of the Fleet the Earl Mountbatten of Burma. The letter, written in my capacity as President of this Society, informed Lord Mountbatten that next year the Council wished to offer a tribute to him as the Society's Patron, on the occasion of his 80th birthday and in the 30th year of his Patronage. The first part of the tribute was to take the form of an article in *The Mariner's Mirror*, and for this we sought permission to print the text of the Admiral of the Fleet's speech at the Annual Jutland Dinner in HMS *Warrior* in 1978, in which he gave an appreciation of the Battle of Jutland. It is hoped that publication of this address will be possible in due course.

For the second part of the Society's tribute it was hoped that there would be an opportunity for Members to greet the Patron in person and for him to address them at some suitable gathering. Although the Diamond Jubilee of the STVF falls in 1981 it seemed appropriate that our tribute should be directly related to HMS *Victory*, whose survival was the result of the launching of the STVF on the initiative of Lord Mountbatten's distinguished father Admiral of the Fleet Prince Louis of Battenberg, First Marquis of Milford Haven and President of this Society from its inception in 1910 to his death in 1921.

The shock news of his violent death was exacerbated, therefore, by the personal distress shared by thousands who encountered this great man at various stages in his brilliant career. Members of the Society at home and abroad will mourn the loss of their most distinguished Patron and all will share in the feelings of revulsion at the manner of his passing.

Professor John Horace Parry CMG *(1914–1982)*

Professor Parry was Gardiner Professor of Oceanic History at Harvard University from 1965 to 1981. Educated at Clare College, Cambridge, he took his PhD in history there in 1938, and served in the Royal Navy during the Second World War rising to the rank of lieutenant commander. One of the most distinguished maritime historians of the twentieth century; Parry was especially concerned with Latin American history and with maritime exploration in the Renaissance. His books, *The Age of Renaissance* (1963), *The Spanish Seaborne Empire* (1966), *The Discovery of the Sea* (1974), and *The Discovery of South America* (1979) are regarded as standard works, followed by his *Romance of the Sea* (1981), a splendidly illustrated general history.

At the time of his death he had already concluded a five-volume collection of early Spanish and Portuguese discovery and settlement in the Americas.

Captain Alan J. Villiers DSC, FRGS *(1903–82)*

Alan Villiers served as Chairman of the SNR from 1960, becoming President from 1970 to 1974 and thereafter as Honorary Vice-President. For many years he was Chairman of the Society's Photographic Records Sub-Committee, a member of the VATC, a Trustee of the NMM, from 1948, and a Governor of the *Cutty Sark* Trust. His death marked the passing of one of the last of the great men of sail. Alan Villiers, an Australian by birth, went to sea at the age of 15. Having served five years in square-rigged ships, he turned to journalism for his livelihood, which stood him in good stead and he later became a professional and prolific author. It was his habit to write up a series of disparate experiences – sailing around the Horn, serving in the Portuguese cod fishery, exploring the Indian Ocean in Arab dhows – in books with an authentic flavour, which earned him a wide public. After the success of his first book on the grain ships, *Falmouth for Orders* (1928), he drew on his wide experience of windjammers and four-masted barques in many books of reminiscences, such as The *Way of the Ship* (1953) or his latest lively memoirs, *Give Me a Ship to Sail* (1958).

Alan's life at sea began when he went to sea in a small square-rigger in the Tasman trade and later joined the Norwegian Antarctic Ross Sea whaling expedition. In 1931 he became part-owner of the four-masted barque *Parma*, then the largest sailing ship in the world, which twice won the grain race from Australia to England. In 1936 he purchased the Danish full-rigged training ship *Georg Staag* (which he re-named *Joseph Conrad*) and sailed her around the world with a crew half full of cadets. For two years before the Second World War he had his first experience of sailing in Arab dhows on the Persian Gulf–Zanzibar run. During the war he joined the RNVR and rose to the rank of commander, having won the DSC when in command of landing craft during the Normandy landings. After the war he found time to command the *Warspite*, the training ship of the Outward Bound Sea School based at Aberdovey, the *Mayflower* replica ship, which he took across the Atlantic without auxiliary power, and several square-rigged ships for such notable cinematic films such as *Moby Dick* and *Billy Budd*. Villiers was a born lecturer and broadcaster. Endowed with a quarter-deck voice and a keen sense of the dramatic, he could keep an audience on its toes like no other man.

Arthur Bugler OBE (?–1982)

Arthur R. Bugler was for over twenty years the constructor at Portsmouth Dockyard in charge of the restoration of HMS *Victory* for which he was awarded the rare distinction of Honorary Membership of the SNR. Apart from the ship herself there can be no finer memorial than his monumental two-volume, HMS *Victory: Building, Restoration and Repair* (London, 1966), now long out of print. Austere in both appearance and in his insistence on correctness, Bugler's immense contribution to Nelson's flagship was appropriately marked by the attendance of past and present COs of HMS *Victory* at his funeral.

Captain Stephen Roskill CBE, DSC, MA, DLitt (Oxford), DLitt (Leeds), FBA FRHistS RN (1903–82)

Born into a legal family, deafness was an affliction which precluded Captain Roskill from achieving the full distinction he deserved in the Royal Navy. However, when he was appointed official historian of the Royal Navy in 1949, naval history gained immensely from his subsequent work, notably his *The War at Sea 1939–1945*, 3 vols, (London, 1954, 1957, 1960–1). His mastery of evidence, clarity and brevity of presentation, and frankness of judgement won him many admirers, not only in naval circles but also in the historical profession. He received many honours in recognition of his literary and historical achievements including an Honorary Life Presidency of the NRS and the Chesney Gold Medal of the RUSI.

Michael Dolley DLitt (London),, Hon. DLitt (National University of Ireland), MRIA, FSA (1925–83)

Michael Dolley joined the Society in 1948 and was a member of Council from 1960 to 1964. The twin brother of the Hon. Editor of *The Mariner's Mirror*, Brian Dolley, he read history at King's College London and then went to the NMM as assistant keeper of oil paintings, working closely with Michael Robinson. In 1951, he moved to the British Museum as an assistant keeper in the Department of Coins and Medals until 1963. He returned to academic life to teach at Queen's University, Belfast, and was granted a personal chair in historical numismatics from 1975 to 1978. By then his health had began to deteriorate and after three years at the University of New England in Australia, he had to retire early.

Notwithstanding his specialization in Anglo-Saxon and Norman numismatics, he retained an active interest in maritime affairs and contributed to *The Mariner's Mirror*. Over the years he abandoned his baptismal names in favour of his confirmation name of Michael; hence many of his earlier works were under the name of R. H. or R. H. M. Dolley.

Professor Robert G. Albion (1896–1983)

Robert Albion was a true salt-water historian, whose discipline properly included economic history, as his work on shipping lanes, tramp steamers and sea ports abundantly demonstrated. He found Princeton 'a very pleasant place' but it was miles from the sea, though Harvard, where he concluded his teaching years, had the Atlantic Ocean at its doors. He was a life member of the SNR for over fifty years.

Albion took his doctorate at Harvard in 1924. His thesis grew into a book, *Forests and Seapower* (1926), followed by *Square Riggers on Schedule* (1938), *The Rise of New York Port* (1939), *Sea Lanes in Wartime* (1942) and many other works. Perhaps his favourite publication was a reference work: *Maritime and Naval History and Bibliography*, which included among major works, lists of MA and PhD theses on naval or maritime subjects from recognized universities. He retired from Harvard as Gardiner Chair of Oceanic History.

Professor J. S. Bromley (1917–85)

John Bromley was Professor of Modern History at the University of Southampton from 1959 until his retirement in 1977. A graduate of New College, Oxford, he was appointed in 1937 to a lectureship at the University of Liverpool, to which he briefly returned after war service with HM Treasury. In 1947 he returned to Oxford where he was lecturer and Fellow of Keble College until his appointment to the chair of modern history at Southampton. It was at Keble that he joined the SNR to which he contributed much, being elected an Honorary Vice-President in 1981.

Among English historians Professor Bromley's reputation rests principally on his masterly edition of volume VI in the *New Cambridge Modern History* series. In maritime history, his great interest was privateering on which he produced many learned and elegant essays. He was the principal founder of SNR South, and its first chairman in 1963.

Professor Christopher Lloyd (1906–86)

Christopher Lloyd joined the Society in 1946 and was elected to Council in 1950, 1956 and 1962. He became Vice-President in 1964, and succeeded Alan Villiers as

Chairman in 1970. He was Hon. Editor of *The Mariner's Mirror* from 1972 to 1979 when he was elected as Honorary Vice-President.

Educated at Marlborough and Lincoln College, Oxford, Christopher Lloyd lectured at Bishop's University, Quebec, from 1930 to 1934. In the latter year he began his career of teaching generations of naval officers, first at the Britannia Royal Naval College, Dartmouth, and from 1945, at the Royal Naval College, Greenwich, where he became professor of history from 1962 until his retirement in 1966.

Lloyd was one of the very few naval historians who appreciated the influence of health and disease upon the course of naval history. He was a champion of the sailor and provided revealing insights into his character, his life on board and ashore. This was exemplified, perhaps most of all, by his book on *The Navy and the Slave Trade* (1949) which drew heavily upon the personal experiences of the officers and men of the West Africa Squadron. It paid a long overdue tribute to a forgotten generation who had given their lives for the suppression of this evil.

To a younger generation Christopher Lloyd was ever helpful. He gave a great deal of his time to the NRS, particularly when he was Publications Secretary between 1949 and 1962.

W. O. B. Majer (1900–87)

Bill Majer died on the very day (23 July) that the TS *Foudroyant*, to which he had devoted much of his energies, was due to leave Portsmouth Harbour for restoration at Hartlepool.

Bill was born on one of his father's ships off Hong Kong on 12 March 1900. Not only had he sailed around the Horn more than once with his father under sail; at the age of 8 he had even spent several weeks drifting in the China Sea on a sailing vessel which had been dismasted in a typhoon.

He was sent home to attend school in England and flew in the Royal Flying Corps in France towards the end of the Great War. After reading engineering in London, he joined Lloyd's Bank and took early retirement so that he could devote himself to his wide-ranging maritime interests. He joined the SNR in 1948, and was elected to Council in 1959 and 1966. Bill also served as a Trustee from 1967 until 1978 when he became Vice-President until his death. He was a founder member of SNR South and was their President for four years.

Bill's energy belied his years. Married for fifty years, his first wife, Violet, died in 1983. He married again in 1986, to Marlisa North, who, like Bill, worked hard on the *Mary Rose* project.

Cdr W. E. May RN (1889–89)

In 1951 Edward May was appointed as Deputy Director of the NMM, Greenwich –

a post he held until 1968 when he retired. An expert on the history of marine compasses and navigation he also had curatorial responsibility for costume, uniform, weapons (swords, small arms) and also medals and decorations. He co-authored, with Philip Annis, a two-volume work, *Swords for Sea Service*. His anecdotes about the Great War were memorable and during his tenure at the museum he accomplished a great deal, but was not fully supported by the Trustees in matters of disciplinary action. As John Munday recalled, one would see him running up to the drinking-water tap to add to his gin and lime with the words, 'This water tastes of mice'!

Sir Victor G. Shepheard KCB, RCNC (1893–1989)

Sir Victor Shepheard was the last of the traditional Directors of Naval Construction (1952–8) whose instructions from the Board of Admiralty read, 'He is the final authority on the design of warships and other vessels for H.M. Navy.'

He entered HM Dockyard, Devonport, in 1907, as an apprentice from which he won one of the very few cadetships to the Royal Naval College, Greenwich. He graduated as assistant constructor, Royal Corps of Naval Constructors, in 1915 and joined the Grand Fleet as constructor lieutenant. He fought at Jutland in *Agincourt* as damage control officer. Later, he was the junior member of a Board of Inquiry into damage to HMS *Courageous*. He was brave enough to forward a minority report, in opposition to the admiral, and the Admiralty finally accepted Shepheard's views.

On return to Whitehall he worked on cruiser and production problems. After a round of appointments in Dockyards and design he became professor at Greenwich in 1934. He worked hard to bring the expertise of the RCNC into the design of naval aircraft, introducing aerodynamics into taught courses. During the war he rejoined the Director of Naval Construction's department as Chief Constructor, rising to Assistant Director in 1942, and Deputy Director, in charge of the department at Bath in 1947.

In 1952 he became Director of Naval Construction, aged 59, at a time of change when his balanced judgement was invaluable. The *Porpoise*-class conventional submarine programme, the guided missile ships of the County class, the first gas-turbine ships, and eventually the *Dreadnought* nuclear submarine programme all benefited from his wise counsel.

However, the ship of which he was most proud was the Royal Yacht *Britannia*, designed in 1952, when the health of HM King George VI began to fail. Sir Victor was a frequent visitor to the palace as the king and other members of the royal family took a keen interest in the design.

Viscount Runciman of Doxford Bt OBE, AFC, AE, DCL, DL *(1900–89)*

The death of Walter Leslie Runciman was announced on 1 September 1989. Lord Runciman succeeded to the title on the death of his father in 1949. His family business was in shipping in the north-east of England. In addition he was a member of the board of directors of the Moor Line, the Anchor Line and of Doxford of Sunderland. He was also a director of Lloyd's Bank and of the Consett Iron Co., Ltd.

Before the Second World War, he had been chairman of the North-East Coast Shipowners Association and, during the war; he was Director-General of the British Overseas Airways Corporation (1940–3) and Air Attaché in Tehran (1943–6). In 1952 he was president of the Chamber of Shipping and also became chairman of the General Council of British Shipping. In 1955 he was appointed a Trustee of the NMM. He served as Chairman from 1962 until he retired in 1972. In that year he was made a Hon. Vice-President of the SNR and a year later he was persuaded to become the first chairman of the Advisory Committee on Historic Wreck Sites, and remained as such until 1986. During his tenure it had become known as the Runciman Committee. He was justifiably proud of his grandfather, an apprentice at sea in the 1860s who had founded the family business.

Lt Cdr Peter Whitlock RN, MBE *(1926?–89)*

Lieutenant Cdr Peter Whitlock, formerly CO of HMS *Victory*, and the Society's Hon. Treasurer for a decade, died at the Royal Naval Hospital, Haslar, on the morning of Trafalgar Day, 21 October 1989. His affection for *Victory* was infectious and his knowledge of her encyclopaedic. He was the archetype of the English seaman, rugged of feature, utterly professional, wholly devoid of any 'side', and a 'veritable Heart of Oak'. He saw action during the war in HMS *Kent*, among other ships, and was the last incumbent of at least two ancient offices: Master Rigger and Boatswain of the Dockyard – a post he held twice at Portsmouth. Peter Whitlock became a Vice-President of the SNR in 1988, and was for several years a Trustee of the PRNM, and a director of its Trading Company. For almost a decade he acted as a Consultant for the *Mary Rose*. His funeral took place at St Anne's Church in HM Naval Base, Portsmouth, on 26 October. 1989. The bearer party was provided by HMS *Victory* and the address was read by the Society's President, Rear-Admiral E. F. Gueritz.

Mrs Romola Anderson (1890–1990)

The death of Mrs Romola Anderson, widow of Roger Charles Anderson, whom she married in 1916, occurred a month short of her hundredth birthday. Among her wedding presents was life membership of the SNR, a gift from her husband.

That present was a forecast of the close collaboration which was the hallmark of their marriage. Not only did they go sailing in the Eastern Baltic along the coasts of the emerging Baltic republics in the early 1920s, she worked in the mud of the Hamble on the timbers of the *Grace Dieu*, and was joint author with her husband of *The Sailing Ship*, a classic work that first appeared in 1927.

A lively talker and correspondent, she showed great interest in the SNR and, even as late as 1985, attended the 75th Anniversary Commemoration in the Banqueting House, Whitehall. She contributed much useful material for the account of the excavation of Henry V's great ship.

With her death, the Society lost its last direct link with its foundation members, and was saddened by the loss of such a charming and active Life Member.

Reginald Lowen MBE (1900–90)
Reginald Lowen did much for the Society and for the NMM. After naval service as a signalman, he joined the Royal Naval College, Greenwich, as a clerical officer in the 1920s, where he impressed Professor Geoffrey Callender. Lowen became Callender's right-hand man in the new NMM. During the war much of the burden in running the museum fell on Lowen as Callender spent most of the time in Oxford. On Callender's death in 1946, Lowen became acting director until Frank Carr arrived in May 1947, and also replaced Callender as Acting Secretary of the Society until George Naish took over. Lowen then held office as Hon. Treasurer of the Society until shortly after his retirement in 1960. He was awarded the MBE for his service to museums in 1953.

His retirement began in tragedy. He had built a bungalow on the Isle of Wight, but within six months his wife died and he went to Australia for a time, but he found the climate trying and he returned to live with his daughter at Meopham. Among other activities he prepared material for a history of the museum, which was never published.

Frank George Griffith Carr CB, CBE (1903–91)
Frank Carr read Law at Trinity Hall, Cambridge. In 1928, before his finals, he made a voyage to Antwerp on a spritsail barge at a wage of £1 per week, all found. He also took his Board of Trade Yachtmaster's (Deep Sea) Certificate at this time. In 1929 he was appointed assistant librarian to the House of Lords. On the death of Sir Geoffrey Callender in 1946, Frank Carr became the NMM's second Director in May 1947. Unlike Callender, Carr had a great deal of practical experience of seamanship and had written many books on various types of vessels. His *Sailing Barges* (London, 1931), reached a fourth edition in 1989, and his *Yacht Master's Guide and Coaster's Companion* (London, 1940) was highly regarded.

Carr became a member of the Society and Secretary of its Coastal Craft Sub-committee formed in 1934. He was a member of Council in 1932 and again in 1948, and was made Honorary Vice-President. From 1948 to 1976 he served on the Society's VATC, and was the prime mover in the restoration and preservation of the *Cutty Sark*. He left the NMM in rather acrimonious circumstances at the end of 1966. However, his tenure there was a success as he expanded the museum's activities, its collections and its premises. He was a founder member of the World Ship Trust in 1978 and its Chairman. He fought tirelessly, often against the odds, to achieve what he wanted both for his beloved *Cutty Sark* and for the museum.

Desmond Wettern (1934–91)

The son of a building contractor, Desmond Wettern was educated at Winchester and completed his National Service in the Royal Navy. Thereafter, he wrote widely on naval affairs as a freelance journalist and in 1961 became the first naval correspondent of the *Sunday Telegraph*. He moved to the *Daily Telegraph* as Naval Correspondent in 1965. Desmond covered almost every major event in which the Royal Navy was involved for a quarter of a century and was never happier than when embarked with the Fleet. He was as much at home in the mess decks as he was in the Admiral's quarters or the wardroom. His books included *The Decline of British Seapower* (London, 1982), a detailed history of the Royal Navy from 1945 to 1970.

Ronald Lothar De Bunsen (1910–92)

A Vice-President of the Society since 1984 and first elected to Council in 1955, De Bunsen also served as a Trustee from 1964 to 1984. He was formerly head of the Shipping Department of Barclay's Bank, Treasurer of the Books Department of the Society for Promoting Christian Knowledge and saw war service in the Royal Air Force. He also served on the Committee of TS *Foudroyant*.

Lt Cdr Richard John Tomlin RD, CEEng, MIMechE, RNR (1925–93)

Richard Tomlin, who died in December 1993, bequeathed to the Society a sum not far short of £40,000. His main interest for more than thirty years was nineteenth-century marine engineering and his enthusiasm for research in this area led him to take a keen interest in the restoration of HMS *Warrior*. The present state of her engines and boilers is, to a great extent, due to his researches. In recent years poor health confined him to his home in Cardiff.

A bachelor, Tomlin had a successful career in the power generation and petrochemical industries in South Wales, where he was maintenance superintendent at Carmarthen Bay Power Station from 1965 to 1970, and Power and Utilities

Group Engineer and Superintendent of the Engineering Branch Drawing Office, British Petroleum Chemicals at Port Talbot from 1970 to 1982, when he retired.

His bequest formed the nucleus of the Society's Tomlin Fund administered through the Society's Research Technical and Programmes Committee, which is still disbursed today.

Professor Eila Campbell MA, FSA (1915–94)

Eila Campbell was a staunch supporter of the SNR and served as a Councillor from 1986, Trustee from 1989 to 1993 and a Vice-President from 1993. She will be best remembered by her students in cartography and in geography for founding the E. G. R. Taylor Lecture which the Society still sponsors, for saving the journal *Imago Mundi* from eclipse in the 1970s, and for promoting the history of cartography internationally through her management of the History of Cartography Conferences.

She took her degree in Geography at Birkbeck College, London in 1941, and then assisted Professor H. C. Darby on the *Domesday Geography of England*. She was a serving officer on many societies, including the Society of Women Geographers and the British Federation of University Women. As head of the Geography Department at Birbeck she also taught evening classes and was an inveterate traveller. After her retirement in 1981 she continued to work just as hard, and will be fondly remembered by her students, friends and colleagues.

Helen Wallis OBE, DPhil, FSA, FRHistS (1924–95)

Dr Helen Wallis, a historian of international renown in cartography, exploration and discovery, was Chairman of the SNR from 1972 to 1989, and subsequently, an Honorary Vice-President. During 1971, when the Chairman, Professor Christopher Lloyd, took over as Hon. Editor of *The Mariner's Mirror* on the sudden death of Captain T. Davys Manning, the then President, Alan Villiers, asked Helen Wallis – a Councillor of the Society – to assume the vacant chair as a temporary measure. In the event that temporary measure was to last seventeen years.

Born in Barnet, Hertfordshire, on 19 August 1924, the daughter of a north London headmaster, she attended St Paul's Girls School, and then read geography at St Hugh's College, Oxford. She joined the Map Room at the British Museum in 1951 as an assistant keeper under R. A. Skelton, whom she succeeded as superintendent in 1967, becoming map librarian in the newly-founded British Library in 1973. She retired from that post in 1986.

As Chairman of the SNR, she played an active role in the formation of the PRNM, and the Heritage Area. She was held in great affection by the Society's members but had much to contend with during her tenure.

Lt Cdr Derek Howse MBE, DSC, FRIN, FRAS, RN (1919–98)

Born in to a naval family in Weymouth, Derek Howse entered Dartmouth in 1933 and began his career at sea in HMS *Rodney* in 1937. He was appointed First Lieutenant on the destroyer HMS *Sardonyx* before his 22nd birthday. Thereafter, Derek Howse qualified as a specialist navigating officer and while at sea was twice mentioned in despatches. After the war Howse completed the Fighter Direction Course and during the Korean War (1950–3) he served as Lt Cdr (N) aboard the cruiser *Newcastle*. He was appointed MBE in 1954 and retired from the navy in 1958, not yet forty years old.

In 1963, he was appointed assistant keeper in the Department of Navigation and Astronomy at the NMM, joining other Society stalwarts such as D. W. Waters and W. E. May, and later becoming head of department. Howse published widely and retired from the museum in 1982, to become a Caird Research Fellow. In 1983-84 he was the Clark Library Visiting Professor at UCLA. He was also a Fellow of the Royal Astronomical Society and of the Royal Institute of Navigation, which awarded him its Gold Medal in 1998. Derek Howse was a widely respected member, Councillor, and Vice-President of the SNR over a period of thirty years, and also a member of its Publications Committee from its inception in 1990, and was also the first Editor of the Society's *Newsletter* from 1991 to 1996.

M. S. Robinson MBE (1910–99)

Michael Strang Robinson's death on Christmas Eve 1999 removed a distinguished and delightful character and severed a tie with the SNR's beginnings. His father, Gregory Robinson DSC, marine watercolourist, was one of our founders, and a prolific contributor to *The Mariner's Mirror*. On the foundation of the NMM in 1937, Michael was appointed a junior assistant. During the war, as Sergeant Robinson, he served in the Middle East from 1941, and was attached to the SAS Regiment in 1942. In the following year, he joined the Special Boat Squadron. Wounded and captured on Leros, in 1944, he was first imprisoned in Athens and later at Stalag IVB at Mulhberg-on-Elbe near Leipzig. There Robinson studied the Dutch language and sea terms, his teacher being a fellow Dutch prisoner of war. He was demobilized in December 1945 and returned to the museum. He formally became head of the Department of Pictures in 1951, was appointed MBE in 1959, and retired from the museum at 60 (rather than at 65) to forward his continuing work on the van de Veldes, on whom he was an unrivalled authority. In 1985 the NMM awarded Michael Robinson its Caird Medal. It was a fitting reward for a man of principle and innate modesty; his monument however, can be seen in his influence on the museum's collections and their understanding.

Admiral of the Fleet The Lord Lewin of Greenwich KG, GCB, LVO, DSC, DSc *(1921–99)*
Terence Thornton Lewin was educated at the Judd School, Tonbridge, and joined
the Royal Navy as a special entry cadet in 1939. During the war he served in the
Tribal class destroyer, HMS *Ashanti,* acquiring a DSC and three mentions in
despatches. Post-war, Lewin specialized in gunnery. He was promoted to
commander in 1953 and, after an Admiralty appointment, he commanded a
destroyer, HMS *Corunna,* and thereafter served as second-in-command of the Royal
Yacht *Britannia.* Promotion to captain followed in 1958. Thereafter, Lewin
alternated between Ministry of Defence and sea command appointments, including
the aircraft carrier HMS *Hermes.*

Promoted to rear-admiral, Lewin was appointed Assistant Chief of Naval Staff
(Policy). There followed two years as flag officer, Second-in-Command of the Far
East Fleet (in effect its seagoing commander). Following this Lewin was appointed
as Vice-Chief of Naval Staff, which he held from 1972 to 1974, a highly demanding
post in a period of great uncertainty in the Royal Navy as to its future role and
composition. Lewin sought to preserve the Navy's worldwide capability. There
followed stints as C-in-C of the Fleet and then Naval Home Command. Experience
in these positions, including the NATO post of C-in-C Eastern Atlantic, equipped
him to be First Sea Lord, which he took up in 1977, and then Chief of the Defence
Staff in 1979. His first year included the decision to replace the ageing Polaris
submarine force with one equipped with the Trident missile. During the Defence
Review by the then Conservative Party Defence Secretary, John Nott, Lewin was
powerless to prevent large cuts in the surface fleet and in manpower. Somewhat
fortuitously, the Falklands crisis and subsequent conflict intervened, proving the
short-sightedness of the Conservative government's approach. Lewin's contribution
during that conflict was recognized by a life peerage and the award of the Order of
the Garter – the first awarded to a naval officer since Earl Howe in 1797. As
Chairman of the Trustees of the NMM, he became a benign President of the SNR in
1991 until his death.

Brian H. Dolley LLB *(1925–2000)*
Brian Dolley graduated from King's College, London with an LLB, and was a
member of Gray's Inn, specializing in company law. He became a director of the
United Dominions Trust. He spent much of the war on east-coast convoys in HMS
Vivian, most of whose officers seem to have been from the legal profession. When
Professor Christopher Lloyd became Hon. Editor of *The Mariner's Mirror* in 1972,
Dolley was appointed Assistant Editor. In 1978–9 he was Joint Editor and then Hon.
Editor from 1980.

A large, vigorously opinionated man, Dolley was a controversial figure during his tenure, but to his credit he firmly believed in the international character of the Society's journal. Fluent in Italian and French with a strong working knowledge of Spanish, in his frequent business trips to Europe he spent much time making contact with Society members, and encouraging them to publish in *The Mariner's Mirror*, often translating their contributions himself. Dolley also encouraged and promoted the publication of much classical and medieval maritime history and nautical archaeology in the journal. He had a particular interest in ships of classical times and spent five summers helping with work on the Marsala Punic ship.

Dolley's Editorship was marked by his independence and the great deal of latitude afforded to him by Council. Unfortunately, near the end of his tenure, he did not see eye-to-eye with newer members of Council and the newly formed Publications Committee. Dolley did, however, retire with dignity intact. He later contracted diabetes which eventually led to blindness. His staunch Roman Catholicism aided his later travails. His wife Cecilia, who served as Assistant Editor during his tenure, herself lost a leg due to infection, and some time after his death she was admitted to a nursing home before she, too, passed away.

David Lyon (1942–2000)

Maritime history suffered a grievous loss when on 13 March 2000 David Lyon succumbed to a brain haemorrhage on the last day of his holiday on Tortola in the British Virgin Islands. The son of an officer in the Fleet Air Arm, he was born of Scottish descent in Crosby, Lancashire, on 20 October 1942. He later attended the King's School, Rochester, and went on to read history at King's College, Cambridge. David Lyon joined the NMM in 1964 as a research assistant to the Director, but he is best known for his work in charge of the museum's collection of Ships' Plans and technical records, including ships' covers. As a committed enthusiast Lyon sensed commitment in others and went out of his way to help and assist researchers in their studies, especially those from the non-university sector whom he selflessly encouraged to publish their work. With a cavalier attitude to publisher's deadlines, David's most famous works were the four-volume *Denny List* (1975) and the *Sailing Navy List 1688–1862* (1993).

A keen seaman, he met his future wife Eleanor Sharpston – a barrister, Queen's Counsel and a Fellow of St John's College, Cambridge, on a cruise on a Baltic trader in 1989. Lyon also helped in the foundation of the Ordnance and Nautical Archaeological Societies and made a huge contribution to the SNR as a founder member of the Research, Technical and Programmes Committee and as a member of Council. His innate honesty and integrity did not allow him to suffer fools gladly. He had no time for career-enhancing political correctness or modish managerialism, and those who knew him well cherished him for it.

Professor Charles Ralph Boxer (1904–2000) FBA

An Honorary Vice-President of the SNR for many years and a prolific contributor to *The Mariner's Mirror*, Charles Boxer had a stellar reputation on a truly international stage as an author and historian. Without any formal academic training he began his scholarly career while still a regular soldier. His interests embraced numismatics, maritime archaeology, Golden Age Iberian literature, Japanese art, the history of the early Catholic missions in Asia, navies, ships and seafaring, and the social, political and economic structure of the Portuguese and Dutch colonial empires in the first era of Europe's overseas expansion. He was probably the last representative of that breed of scholarly serving officers that empire produced, and his career was a splendid realization of that classical ideal, of a life devoted to 'arms and letters'.

Born on 8 March 1904 in Sandown, Isle of Wight, and educated at Wellington and Sandhurst, Boxer's scholarly output was phenomenal, amounting to nearly 400 books, articles and reviews. This astonishing flow reflected the keenest and most lucid of minds, immense erudition, legendary industry, sheer intellectual zest, a formidable memory and a willingness to accept new fields for, and methods of investigation. His private wealth allowed the upkeep of a magnificent library; he was fluent in Japanese and could get by in most of the major European languages.

Boxer was born of an old and distinguished service family. At 23 he was commissioned into the Lincolnshire Regiment. Throughout his life he remained in many ways the old-style officer; he had an unfailing eye for a pretty girl and a legendary capacity for alcohol. There was a strong element of the iconoclasm of his class about him, and his forthright expression of his views and uncompromisingly independent behaviour helped to ensure that he was denied the knighthood or other honour usually accorded to scholars of his eminence.

Boxer was wounded and taken prisoner by the Japanese at the fall of Hong Kong in 1941 and served in the Army until 1947. On leaving the army he held the Camões Chair in Portuguese in London until 1967, interspersed with a brief spell (1951–3) as Professor of the History of the Far East. From 1969 to 1972 he was professor of the History of the Expansion of Europe at Yale, having held various other appointments in the USA previously. Early in his academic career at King's College, London, he ruefully remarked that as he was the only professor there without a degree, when he had to appear at degree ceremonies unrobed, people might have thought he was the man they had called about the gas! His first honorary doctorate was awarded by the University of Utrecht in 1950, which gave him something in common with his hero, Beachcomber's Dr Strabismus. His contributions to scholarship and his reputation were recognized by his election to the British Academy in 1957. In all probability we shall not see his like again.

Professor Bryan Maclean Ranft (1917–2001)

Educated at Manchester Grammar School and Balliol College, Oxford, Bryan Ranft rose to the rank of major in the Royal Artillery during the Second World War. Post-war he joined the academic staff of the Royal Naval College, Greenwich, which he led as Professor of History and International Affairs between 1967 and his retirement in 1977. In 1970 Bryan Ranft was invited to teach at Sir Michael Howard's innovative Department of War Studies at King's College, London. Over the next dozen years his remarkable educational skills were much in evidence inspiring a new generation of naval historians.

Over a period of fifty years, Ranft's contribution to the NRS was immense as editor, Councillor, Vice-President and adviser. His major published works include *The Vernon Papers* (1958), and a two-volume edition of *The Beatty Papers* (1989 and 1993). Ranft also served as a Councillor of the SNR from 1966 to 1970.

Former NATO Secretary-General Joseph Luns (1911–2002)

Joseph Marie Antoine Hubert Luns, Dutch diplomat, Minister of Foreign Affairs, and Secretary-General of NATO, was one of the very few honorary members of the SNR. He was born in Rotterdam and attended schools in Amsterdam and Brussels. At the age of 20 he spent a year as an ordinary seaman in the Royal Netherlands Navy.

Joseph Luns took a degree in Law from the Universities of Leiden and Amsterdam in 1937 and then studied at the London School of Economics and Berlin University before entering the Foreign Service of the Netherlands. Luns spent the Second World War in Berne, Lisbon and then with the Dutch government in exile in London, where he later served in the embassy. In 1949 he became permanent delegate to the United Nations, until his appointment as Minister for Foreign Affairs in 1952, a position he held for 19 years, a record in Dutch parliamentary history. During this time he fiercely opposed De Gaulle's anti-American and British policies.

He was a convinced Altanticist, and in 1971 was appointed Secretary-General of NATO, a post he held until resigning in 1984.

A. G. E. Jones (1914–2002)

Godfrey Jones was born in Cardiff, moved to Surrey, and was educated at school in Croydon, later gaining a Batchelor of Commerce (Economics) degree through London University. During the Second World War he served in the Royal Army Pay Corps. Godfrey Jones took a teacher-training course and from 1949 until retirement in 1974 was employed in Colleges of Further Education at Ipswich, Bristol and Braintree. He ended his career as Head of the West Kent College of Further Education at Tunbridge Wells and later moved to Eastbourne. He was a Life Fellow of the Royal Geographical Society.

Jones was especially interested in the whaling industry of the late eighteenth and early nineteenth centuries, both in the Greenland and Davis Strait and in the South Seas trade. Polar exploration, both North and South, was also of interest to him as his many publications testified. In his later life he donated his library of maritime books to the Scott Polar Research Institute, Cambridge, and after his death his remaining papers were also donated there.

Basil Greenhill CMG, CB (1920–2003)

Basil Greenhill joined the SNR while still at Bristol Grammar School, having his first article 'The story of the Severn Trow', published in *The Mariner's Mirror* in the summer of that same year, 1936. The following year he absented himself from school to sail from Bristol to Finland in the four-masted barque, *Viking*. His war service in the Royal Navy saw him train as a radar mechanic and after being commissioned he spent his time at the radar research establishment at Malvern.

After the war, Greenhill returned to his interrupted studies at the University of Bristol to complete his degree in Politics, Philosophy and Economics. He then joined the Dominions Office (later the Commonwealth Relations Office) where he remained until December 1966. Greenhill rose steadily in that branch of the diplomatic service. A tour in East Pakistan (now Bangladesh) was followed by a term in Japan as Head of Chancery and in 1958 he was the British delegate at the Law of the Sea Conference. Later that year he returned to East Pakistan as Deputy High Commissioner, but the posting was cut short when his wife contracted amoebic dysentery. They returned to England but she died in 1959. Greenhill then served in Nigeria before what was to be his final posting as Deputy High Commissioner in Ottawa.

The first volume of his best known work, *Merchant Schooners* appeared in 1951, and the second in 1957. His long membership of the Society and his writing meant that he was well known at the NMM and to its Director, Frank Carr. With his interests and proven administrative experience, Greenhill was seen as a likely candidate to succeed Carr as Director. Carr had passed the normal age of retirement but wished to serve two or three more years, and with this in mind, he supported Greenhill's candidature. The latter, aged 46, was sounded out concerning his interest in applying for the post, and apparently stated that he would come from Ottawa at the end of 1966 but not later.

As they had the right to do, given Carr's age, the museum Trustees terminated his appointment, invited applications for the post in open competition and subsequently appointed Greenhill who took up his post on 1 January 1967. When the appointment was announced an enraged Carr launched a vitriolic attack on his successor in a letter to *The Times*. Given Greenhill's irascibility – never far from the surface – it was inevitable that he would reply in kind and there followed a public correspondence that was unfortunate for the museum.

It is no exaggeration to say that during the next twelve to fourteen years Greenhill transformed the museum. The staff was enlarged; new departments and galleries created, huge exhibitions were mounted and an association with foreign museums established. As the museum's stock rose, so did that of its Director: he was elected Chairman of the National Museums Conference in 1980, continuing until his retirement from the museum in 1983, when he was succeeded by Neil Cossons.

A Vice-President of the SNR, Greenhill rarely attended meetings and in retirement he kept busy chairing the ss *Great Britain* project from 1982 to 1992. He was awarded honorary doctorates from the universities of Plymouth and Hull. To the latter he donated his extensive collection of authored and other maritime books.

David MacGregor (1925–2003)

David MacGregor was educated at Eton and Trinity College, Cambridge, where he read Architecture. His father was an officer in a Scottish regiment who, for the most part, was based in India. A Cambridge friend introduced him to Basil Greenhill, who became a great influence on his life. After leaving Cambridge in 1948, David MacGregor took a job in the architectural office of Fulham Borough Council and remained there for eleven years, during which he avidly researched materials for his first book in the evenings and at weekends. That book, *The Tea Clippers* was published in 1952.

In 1961, MacGregor quit his job and went to the Clyde to study and copy the plans of old clippers in the offices of such shipyards as Alexander Stephen and Barclay Curle. He traced, copied, worked-up, re-drew and re-created innumerable plans, and he repeatedly published sail plans where none had previously existed, thus adding to historical knowledge.

MacGregor's approach to research was serious, detailed and accurate and the product of a genuine love of his subjects. He was a talented painter who, at the age of 13, had two paintings hung in the Royal Institute of Oil Painters. As an avid collector of all things maritime, he never ceased to be fascinated by the long-gone commercial years of sail.

Austin 'Clarence' Packard Farrar CEng FRINA (1913–2004)

Austin Farrar, known as Clarence to his friends and colleagues, died on Tuesday 6 July 2004, aged 91. His father was lost at sea in 1917 and Austin Farrar was raised by his mother and grandfather, Edward Packard, who ran a company that eventually became Fisons. At preparatory school in Folkestone, Farrar was taught to write by a trainee teacher, Enid Blyton. He served a marine engineering apprenticeship at

Phillips and Son Ltd., Dartmouth. On leaving, Farrar, a keen sailor, became a yacht designer. During the Second World War, he worked at the Admiralty on torpedo nets.

After the war Farrar established the Wolverstone Shipyard where he designed and built the most successful International 14-foot dinghies of the post-war period, such as the *Windsprite* and *Bolero*, as well as many other craft. He developed the cold moulding technique setting the standard for others to follow and designed the curved sliding seat now used on International Canoes.

In 1948, Austin Farrar competed in the Olympic Trials in the Swallow class finishing second, and for many years thereafter he worked with the International Yacht Racing Union and the Royal Yachting Association on technical matters. In 1954, Farrar sold the yard and moved on to establish the renowned Seahorse Sails with Leslie Widdecombe. Thereafter, Farrar was at the forefront of developments in Terylene sail cloth. He designed and made many fittings which are still evident today in racing yachts and catamarans. Although officially retiring in the late 1980s, Austin Farrar never really stopped working and designing. He was an Honorary Vice-President of the SNR and worked on the design of *Victory*'s cutters and on many other nautical archaeology projects.

Anthony N. Ryan (1924–2005)

Born and educated in Liverpool, Tony Ryan was a longstanding member of the SNR and a valued member of the Editorial Board of *The Mariner's Mirror*. After completing his service as a navigator in Bomber Command in the Second World War – which left him with a dread of flying – Tony Ryan became a lecturer at the University of Liverpool in 1950, completing his MA thesis 'The Copenhagen Expedition, 1807' in the following year. He remained at Liverpool until his retirement in 1991. In 1992, he was made an Honorary Research Fellow and Senior Fellow at Liverpool. He published many articles on maritime and naval history in respected peer-reviewed journals and for many years was an Honorary General Editor of the NRS. His own edited volume of *The Saumarez Papers* was published for that Society in 1968.

John de Courcey Ireland (1911–2006)

John de Courcey Ireland was Ireland's foremost maritime historian and a valued Overseas Corresponding Member of the SNR. He was born in Lucknow on 19 October 1911, the son of an Irish-born officer in the Indian Army who, on his deathbed in China as part of the Expeditionary Force in 1914, advised John's mother never to let her son join the army. John de Courcey Ireland was later educated at Marlborough College, where his gift for languages was apparent. Before taking up a scholarship at New College, Oxford, to read Spanish, he embarked on a voyage to South America as a crew member on a tramp ship and was deeply affected by the vast gulf between rich and poor witnessed at first hand in Brazil. Thereafter, de Courcey Ireland became a lifelong pacifist and socialist who abhorred the sectarian nature of Irish politics, and was also a founding member of the Campaign for Nuclear Disarmament in Ireland. Working as a schoolmaster in Ireland, latterly at Blackrock, and as a research officer at the Maritime Institute of Ireland from 1943, de Courcey Ireland regretted that the Irish had turned their backs on their maritime history but resolved to change this. An eloquent speaker, linguist and prolific author on Irish maritime history and affairs, his many publications included *The Sea and the Easter Rising* (Dublin, 1966), *Ireland's Sea Fisheries: A History* (Dublin, 1981), and *Ireland and the Irish in Maritime History* (Dublin, 1986). In 1951 John de Courcey Ireland was awarded a doctorate by Trinity College, Dublin, and thereafter was highly influential in setting up a maritime museum at Dun Laoghaire (Kingstown), later to become the National Maritime Museum of Ireland.

Alan Pearsall (1925–2006)

Born in Leeds, Alan Pearsall had a scholarly background. His father was an eminent botanist and his mother taught botany at Leeds University before she raised a family. The family's temporary move to Morecambe, Lancashire, in the 1930s turned into an association of nearly seventy years for Alan Pearsall, as he maintained a flat there until his death. The north-west of England and the Lake District, in particular, remained the centre of his world all of his life. In 1943 Pearsall volunteered for service in the Navy, although only seventeen, and served in India. He returned to England in 1946 and went to Cambridge to read history, and then research at London University on the nineteenth-century navy in the Far East, under Gerald Graham. Although he did not finish his doctoral study, he gained a reputation for his wide knowledge, and on the strength of that joined the NMM, Greenwich, in 1955.

Pearsall remained at the museum for thirty years, first serving in the Navigation Department and then from 1960 as Custodian of Manuscripts. In the early 1970s he was made historian of the museum, before retiring in 1985. He had a lifetime interest in transport, particularly railways. Alan Pearsall will be particularly remembered for his unselfish sharing of knowledge with three generations of naval and maritime historians. He had an enormous international network of friends. He never married and the scholarly world was his life.

Geoffrey Vaughan Scammell (1926–2006)

G. V. Scammell was a University Lecturer in History and Fellow of Pembroke College, Cambridge, from 1966 to 1992. Thereafter he held an Emeritus Fellowship at Pembroke until his death on 4 February 2006, aged 80.

Geoffrey Scammell's contribution to maritime history was impressive. His publications included *The World Encompassed: The first European maritime empires c. 800–1650* (1981), *The English Chartered Trading Companies and the Sea* (1982), *The First Imperial Age: European overseas expansion, 1400–1715* (1989), and *Ships, Oceans and Empire: Studies in European maritime and colonial history, 1400–1750* (1995). Scammell was a respected reviewer and referee for *The Mariner's Mirror* and for many others. His opinions were always fair minded and helpful and he will be greatly missed.

Richard Ollard FSA (1923–2007)

Richard Ollard was a long-term member of the SNR and until recently a member of the Editorial Board of *The Mariner's Mirror*. He was also a vice-president of the NRS and a recipient of the NMM's prestigious Caird Medal in 1992.

Born and raised in Yorkshire, the son of an Oxford don who was subsequently ordained, Richard Ollard attended Eton College. He joined the Royal Navy in 1942 as a rating, gained a commission in 1943, and served as an intelligence officer in Ceylon, where his primary task was to translate intercepted Japanese signals.

Post-war, Ollard was awarded a scholarship to New College, Oxford, and then went on to a lectureship at the Royal Naval College, Greenwich, until he lost his post due to defence cuts in 1959. In 1960 he joined the publishers, Collins, as an editor. He was extremely loyal to his authors and later found time to pen his first book, *The Escape of King Charles II* (1968). A year later he wrote *Man of War: Sir Robert Holmes and the Restoration Navy* (1969), and in 1974, an acclaimed biography of Samuel Pepys. In 1976, his *This War without an Enemy: A History of the English Civil Wars* was published, and is perhaps the best general history of the conflict.

In 1998 Richard Ollard was the recipient of the Hayward Hill Literary Prize. He was also a Fellow of the Royal Society of Literature and the Society of Antiquaries.

Thomas Allcott Guy Pocock (1925–2007)

Tom Pocock was one of the most distinguished, and certainly the most widely read, of all the post-war generation of naval historians, and played a key role in the recent expansion and development of the profession.

The son of a former history teacher at Dartmouth, Guy Pocock, Tom Pocock joined the Royal Navy at 17 in 1942 and was later present at the Normandy landings. Post-war, Tom had a successful career in journalism. He was variously, defence correspondent for the *Daily Mail*, naval correspondent at *The Times*, and a roving correspondent for the *Daily Express*, before finally settling at the *London Evening Standard* in 1958, where he remained until 1988.

It is, however, as a naval historian that Pocock will be remembered. In 1968 he published his first work of naval history, *Nelson and his World*, followed by a further 23 books over the next 38 years, some of which dealt with his wider interests including biographies of Alan Moorehead (1989) and Rider Haggard (1993). At his peak, Tom produced a book almost every two years. There was bound to be some unevenness, but he was best known for his substantial and influential canon of work on Horatio Nelson.

Basil Wroughton Bathe ISO (1912–2007)
In 1949 Basil Bathe joined the Department of Aeronautics and Sailing Ships at the Science Museum, London, and from 1962 he was in charge of the Sailing Ships and Small Craft collections there. Five years later he was appointed assistant keeper and, later in his career, head of Water Transport Collections until he retired from the Science Museum, aged 65, in 1978.

Basil Bathe served as a Councillor of the SNR and thereafter as long-standing Vice-President. He also served on many other committees, including the Council for Nautical Archaeology, the Waterborne Transport Advisory Committee and on the ss *Great Britain* project. His range of scholarship was impressive; witness his many publications on ship models, sailing ships, small craft, warships and merchant ships. He co-wrote, with Donald McIntyre, *Man-of-War: A history of the combat vessel* (1969), and *Seven Centuries of Sea Travel: from the Crusades to the Cruises* (1972).

Bathe spent most of his retirement at Ickenham, Middlesex, and retained a keen interest in maritime affairs, particularly in sailing ships. He died aged 94 on 24 March 2007.

Robin Craig (1924–2007)
Robin Craig was a long-time member of the SNR and a former Councillor, who passed away in hospital in June 2007 at the age of 83.

Robin Craig was an influential figure in the development of maritime economic history in Britain. He acquired an early love of ships and the sea while growing up in Cumbria, worked in shipping in the City of London and eventually took his first degree at the London School of Economics. Craig went on to a lectureship at University College, London, and remained there until he retired.

While at UCL, Craig inspired a generation of potential maritime historians with his knowledge of shipping and of shipping records, and in the 1970s he founded a journal, *Maritime History*, that eventually folded, due to the withdrawal of the publisher. His particular area of expertise lay in tramp shipping and trade thereof. His enthusiasm for the subject inspired many, and his hospitality at St Margaret's Bay was legendary.

A large part of Robin's published output was brought together in 2003 in a volume published by the International Maritime Economic History Association (IMEHA) in its Research in Maritime History series: *British Tramp Shipping, 1750–1917* (2003). In 2004 Robin Craig gave the keynote address at the Fourth International Congress of Maritime History in Corfu, where his contribution to maritime history was recognized by his unanimous election as Honorary President of the IMEHA.

Up to the end Robin Craig remained generous with his time, knowledge and hospitality and maritime history is the poorer for his passing.

David Keith Brown MEng, CEng FRINA, RCNC (1928–2008)

David Brown was a rare example of a professional engineer who used his knowledge of history to inform and enhance his work as a naval architect for the Admiralty and later the Ministry of Defence. He had actually lived through some of the relevant history, using his knowledge of the war at sea in World War II, especially in areas such as operational effectiveness, damage survival and seakeeping.

Although born in London in 1928, David Brown's family moved to Leeds where a schoolboy interest in warships developed. A high achiever academically, he took a first-class honours degree in naval architecture from Liverpool University, one of the last to do so before the university closed its course. That opened the door to join the then well-paid Royal Corps of Naval Constructors, whose normal intake was bright dockyard apprentices. From 1949 David Brown undertook the RCNC course at the Royal Naval College, Greenwich, finishing with a First-Class Certificate. Students' performance was carefully recorded and referred to in later years, as a guide as to who might reach the highest ranks. The training period included time at sea in a variety of warships, from which every naval architect benefits.

Appointed assistant constructor in 1953 at Bath (to which city the constructors had moved from London in 1940), Brown's first job was concerned with design calculations on small vessels and the occasional ship trial. As with other RCNC staff, there followed a variety of posts and promotions, all building up experience by working on the Tribal class frigates in 1955 and propeller design in 1958 before becoming involved in highly confidential work on the UK's first nuclear-propelled submarine, culminating in the 1963 trials (and troubles) of *Dreadnought*.

In 1970 David Brown was appointed Chief Constructor (equivalent naval rank of RN captain) at the Admiralty Experiment Works at Haslar near Portsmouth – not Experimental, as Brown frequently had to point out. This posting coincided with the centenary of the Admiralty-financed ship model towing tank developed by William Froude at Torquay. Brown set up an exhibition at Haslar, which still retained some of its Victorian equipment, as well as all the model test reports which he perused thoroughly. That prepared the ground for David Brown's centenary history of the

RCNC published in 1983 as *A Century of Naval Construction*. With his access to the records and serving and retired RCNC members, he produced a comprehensive history, although he did admit to pulling a few punches and not naming some individuals of whose actions he disapproved.

On his retirement at 60, Brown had reached the post of Deputy Chief Naval Architect. He was also a Vice-President of the Royal Institute of Naval Architects, a Vice-President of the World Ship Society and a Council member of the SNR from 2001 to 2004. To those outside the MoD, he will be best remembered for his series of five books on British warship design, from 1815 to 1985. These drew together his breadth of experience and depth of knowledge, explaining in layman's terms how and why warship design features evolved in the Royal Navy, each supplemented with many informative appendices. His last book was *Atlantic Escorts* published in 2007. He realized that this was likely to be his last full-length book, partly because he felt he had exhausted most of the subjects where he had detailed knowledge, but also because of failing health, perhaps exacerbated after being knocked down by a car in Bath. Separated, then divorced, from Avis, he lived alone in a flat in Bath from 1993, always pleased to welcome visitors. He died there on 15 April 2008. In Professor Ian Buxton's words, mirroring the thoughts of many, thus passed a man of great intellect, of deep knowledge of his chosen field, whose reputation will endure; but a modest man withal.

Ann Giffard (1924–2008)

Ann Giffard died in Cornwall on 23 August 2008. She was a member of a very old West Country family and from 1961 was the second wife of Dr Basil Greenhill, former Director of the NMM, Greenwich (1967–83). His first wife, Gillian, died tragically in 1959 from amoebic dysentery contracted in East Pakistan, now Bangladesh. Between 1967 and 1984, Ann co-authored a number of Basil's books: *Women under Sail* (1972); *Travelling by sea in the nineteenth century* (1974); *West Countrymen in Prince Edward's Isle* (1967; this became a successful television programme); *The British Assault on Finland, 1854–1855: A forgotten naval war* (1988) and *Steam, politics and patronage: the transformation of the Royal Navy, 1815–1854* (1994). In Andrew Lambert's words:

> Her contribution added a vital human dimension to these projects, and the two last built on the shared experience of living in Finland, and the naval career of her ancestor, the senior British naval officer to be killed in the Crimean War . . . Over time, Basil's long-standing aversion to the Royal Navy was significantly ameliorated. Their books were well reviewed, as befits significant contributions to historical scholarship.

Slim, tall, dark-haired and dark-eyed, she was a pleasant and approachable person at museum functions, though perhaps a little shy. The staff became very much aware of the Director's particular interests, merchant schooners, boat archaeology, the Baltic, and shipbuilding on Prince Edward Island, Canada, which entailed a certain amount of travelling for them both. Ann once related how an injury to her leg in climbing over a stone wall on Prince Edward Island led to the discovery of a vital link in their research, provided by the doctor who attended to her!

In retirement the Greenhills moved to their holiday home, a substantial stone cottage at Boetheric, Cornwall, owned by the National Trust, where they continued a very active life of research, writing and local interests together for nearly twenty years. At the front of the house opened a prospect of the great Brunel bridge at Saltash and the Tamar estuary. They took a particular interest in the preservation and enhancement of the old river port of Cotehele Quay – she with her roots in Cornwall and he with his drive and enthusiasm for the study of merchant shipping. Only a mile from their home, the Quay and the restored Tamar sailing barge, *Shamrock*, were for many years (until 2006) an out-station of the NMM, and a familiar attraction on the river.

With the help of friends, neighbours and latterly, professional carers, Ann was able to stay on at home after Basil's death in 2003, despite increasing infirmity. Her garden was one of her great delights, and a splendid setting for discussions on matters maritime. She broke her arm 2006 and both son and stepson travelled from America and Australia respectively to see her, but had to return to their work and families. They were able to be with her at the end.

Rear-Admiral E. F. Gueritz CB, OBE, DSC (1919–2008)

Teddy Gueritz was President of the SNR from 1974 to 1991. Before his death due to heart failure on 21 December 2008 at Salisbury General Hospital, he was one of four remaining Honorary Vice-Presidents.

Edward Findlay Gueritz was born on 8 September 1919 and was educated at Cheltenham College. He joined the Royal Navy as a special entry cadet in 1937 and was a midshipman in the heavy cruiser HMS *Cumberland* which reinforced Harwood's squadron blockading the German pocket battleship *Graf Spee* off Montevideo in December 1939. He served in the destroyer HMS *Jersey* in the Channel, South Western Approaches, and in the Mediterranean theatre. On 2 May 1941 *Jersey* was mined and sunk in the entrance to the Grand Harbour, Malta, with the loss of 35 men. Gueritz survived the sinking and thereafter joined Combined Operations Command serving in Scotland; the Indian Ocean and India.

Gueritz's first experience of amphibious warfare was as beachmaster of 121 Force during Operation Ironclad, the capture of Madagascar in May 1942: an operation undertaken to prevent the Vichy French forces from offering bases to the enemy. During this operation he was awarded the Distinguished Service Cross. In the winter of 1943–4 Gueritz took an active part in combined training of army and naval personnel at Invergordon. At the Normandy landings on D-day, 6 June 1944, Gueritz went ashore on Sword Beach, an 8 km stretch from Ouistreham to Saint-Aubin-sur-Mer at 08.00 hours as the third most senior member of the beachmaster party. He took over as beachmaster when his commanding officer was badly wounded and his army counterpart was killed. Gueritz had the arduous task of marshalling the troops coming ashore, organizing landing craft and keeping in contact with the naval forces offshore, resplendent in a blue-painted helmet and red scarf armed only with a walking stick. By the evening, despite myriad problems including soft sand, barbed wire and minefields some 30,000 troops and several hundred vehicles and tons of ammunition had been landed.

Teddy Gueritz survived nineteen days under fire on Sword Beach before a piece of shrapnel crushed the back of his skull. He was evacuated to Southampton General Hospital and owed his life to the skill of a surgeon there, John Richardson, who later became president of the General Medical Council and was created a life peer. Gueritz's skill and courage during the landings was recognized by a Bar to his earlier DSC.

Gueritz married Pamela Britton in 1947. In 1948 he attended the Army Staff College, Camberley; and in 1953 the Joint Services Staff College. During the imperial misadventure of the Suez campaign in 1956, he was naval force logistics officer on the staff of General Hugh Stockwell, for which he was awarded an OBE. Promoted to captain in 1959, Gueritz became successively Deputy Director of the Royal Naval Staff College, Deputy Director of the Tactical and Weapons Policy Division, Captain of the Fleet, Far East; Director of Defence Plans (Navy), and Director of the Joint Warfare Staff. He was then Admiral President of the Royal Naval College, Greenwich, and Commandant of the Joint Warfare Establishment, Old Sarum, before leaving the Royal Navy in 1973.

In retirement, Gueritz was a specialist adviser to the House of Commons Select Committee on Defence, and Director of the RUSI. He edited *Brassey's Defence Year Book* from 1977 to 1981 and was joint editor of *The Third World War* (London, 1978), *Ten Years of Terrorism* (London, 1979), and *Civil Defence in the Nuclear Age* (London, 1982). During his long presidency of the SNR, Gueritz unfailingly supported its officers.

Colin Saunders White BA, MA, DLitt, FSA, FRHistS, RNR (1951–2008)
Colin White, who died of cancer aged 59 on Christmas Day 2008, was one of our foremost naval historians. Educated at Culford School, Suffolk, Southampton University, and King's College, London, Colin received an honorary doctorate of

letters from the University of Portsmouth, in 2004, for his contribution to naval history in conjunction with the award of visiting professor.

He was however, best known for his vast contribution towards Nelsonic scholarship. Colin White joined the PRNM, in September 1975 as a research assistant. By 1995 he was appointed to the post of Deputy Director and Head of Museum Services with special responsibility for the Royal Naval Museum's ambitious Development Plan. In 1999, he led the Nelson Letters Project, which discovered over 1,400 unpublished letters from around the world. In 2000, White was appointed chairman of the Official Nelson Celebrations Committee with responsibility for co-ordinating the bicentenary of Trafalgar celebrations in 2005. By 2001, he was seconded to the NMM, Greenwich as Director, Trafalgar 200, to assist the museum with planning its 2005 initiatives. In 2006 Colin White was appointed Director of the Royal Naval Museum in succession to Dr Campbell McMurray.

A talented public speaker, Colin White delivered lectures with élan, wit and considerable warmth. He published, *inter alia*, *The Nelson Companion* (1995), *1797: Nelson's Year of Destiny* (1998), *The Nelson Encyclopaedia* (2002), *Nelson: The New Letters* (2005) and *Nelson the Admiral* (2005). In 2006, White was awarded the Desmond Wettern Media Award 'for being the most visible spokesman for Britain's maritime interests in 2005'. In addition to being a member of the SNR, he was also a Vice President of the NRS and the 1805 Club.

Philip Pugh BSc, CEng, MRAeS (1940–2009)

Maritime and naval history as well as engineering and aviation lost a great scholar with the death of Philip Pugh on 5 January 2009. His erudite contributions to debate and incisive comments at the long-running International Commission for Maritime History Seminar Series at King's College, London, will long be remembered by all those who had the privilege to know him. To the unwary academic Philip's approach to questions as a member of the audience would often put speakers off their guard. He would ask them a relatively innocuous question in a self-effacing manner usually professing no great knowledge of the subject at hand, wait for a response, and then ask a supplementary question which was always incisive. Although he often professed to be no more than 'a simple engineer', Philip's knowledge and under-standing of scientific principles was outstanding. He could give professional statisticians more than a run for their money in cost estimating and mathematical modelling, and was particularly adept at using correlation coefficients in regression analysis to check that the parameters used were not themselves correlated.

Philip Pugh's first book, *The Cost of Seapower: The Influence of Money on Naval Affairs from 1815 to the Present Day* (London, 1986) caused a great stir on its publication not least among the admirals at the Ministry of Defence, but also among politicians who had consistently under-funded the Royal Navy. It was typical of Pugh to write without fear or favour. The book was the product of his long and profoundly sceptical experience of procurement issues and related costs. Future projects, according to Pugh, could only be objectively measured by comparison with similar projects which had entered service in the past, and whose actual cost was a known quantity. From the 1980s Philip Pugh accumulated a vast database of the costs of past national projects, both civil and military, and used it support his development of a series of models as predictive tools for costs and timescales for procurement projects at the concept stage and for which no design drawings yet existed. He knew from experience that early estimates for projects are usually wrong and that the earlier they are made the greater the error is likely to be. Pugh understood that fundamentally the true cost of a project only becomes apparent when it enters service and during its design and manufacture stage it is the estimates that change. Among his many insights, through his work on past data, was the recognition that cost escalation, that is the propensity for each successive generation of systems of a particular type to cost more than the last, even when general inflation is allowed for, is not in any way new. Pugh also showed that different types of systems (ship, tanks, aircraft, etc.) tended to escalate at different rates.

Philip Pugh was born in Pontypridd, Glamorgan on 3 June 1940; however, the family actually resided near Leeds, where his father was a lecturer. His mother felt it safer to move to Pontypridd for the birth, but Pugh spent only six days there. Later, he spent most of his youth in Hull before, at the age of 17, reading mechanical engineering at the University of Leeds. The Oxbridge Colleges would not accept Pugh, as his Latin was not up to scratch. That was their loss as he graduated at the age of 19 with first-class honours and won the Senate Prize at Leeds.

Philip Pugh then joined the National Physical Laboratory at Teddington in 1960 and worked there until 1971. He got married in 1962 to Valerie, whom he met in Hull, and they lived in Kingston, Surrey. Thereafter he spent a decade at the Royal Aeronautical Establishment, Bedford, and chose to live in Clapham, Bedford. In both establishments he was engaged in development of aerodynamic test facilities and in high-speed aerodynamic research with particular reference to the carriage, release and flight of weapons.

In 1981, he joined the Procurement Executive of the MoD in the Directorate of Project Time and Cost Analysis [DPTCAn] where he was responsible for the collation of costs forecasts for MoD central committees. After a short time engaged in the funding of engine technology demonstrator work, he returned to DPTCAn as Assistant Director (Weapons and Electronics). Subsequently, between 1991 and 1994, Pugh had a spell on secondment in academia; first in the Centre for Defence Studies at King's College, London, and then in the Defence Engineering Group at

University College, London. He left government service in 1994 but continued to specialize in cost analysis and forecasting as an independent cost consultant. In association with HVR Consulting Services Limited, he was the originator of their Family of Advanced Cost Estimating Tools (FACET), now in use within government and industry in the UK, France, Germany and Australia.

A chartered engineer and member of the Royal Aeronautical Society, Philip Pugh was much in demand to give talks to various bodies and was always happy to give his time to do so. He was a Visiting Fellow at the Centre for Defence Economics at the University of York, and he also lectured regularly at Cranfield University. Philip Pugh was extremely proud to be a member of he Editorial Board of *Mariner's Mirror* and brought to it a sense of the practical and also his long experience and encyclopaedic knowledge of engineering. He was exceedingly clever and could strip down arguments to their fundamentals with ease. As a referee he was always helpful, particularly in pointing out ways in which an article or note could be improved. Above all else his innate sense of fairness and loyalty to his friends was admirable. He will long be remembered by all he came into contact with. He leaves his widow, Valerie, two sons and a daughter. We will not see his like again.

Michael Stephen Partridge PhD, FRHistS *(1956–2009)*

Michael Partridge who died suddenly on 10 March 2009 contributed a great deal to our Society. He was a compiler of the Society's Annual Bibliography from its beginnings and prepared and edited (with Karen Partridge) the last issue for 2007, published in February 2009. As the Society's second Hon. Newsletter Editor, Michael succeeded Lt Cdr Derek Howse and edited that publication from issue no. 9 of February 1993 to issue no. 22 of May 1996, resigning to complete a history of the Royal Naval College, Osborne. Up to that point the history of what became known in Society circles as the Osborne project had been in abeyance, despite extensive Society support and cajoling, as the original author had failed to make progress. By stepping into the breech Michael effectively saved the Society from considerable embarrassment. The resulting publication, *The Royal Naval College Osborne A History 1903–1921* (Stroud, 1999), was critically acclaimed. The book was based on interviews with Osborne survivors, which he had conducted much earlier (in 1987–8). Accordingly, Michael was a deserving recipient of the Society's Anderson Medal for Research in Maritime History in 2000.

Michael Stephen Partridge was born on 27 January 1956 in Grays, Essex. He read for his first degree (BA (Hons) Medieval & Modern History) at the University of Birmingham, graduating in 1977. Michael then undertook his PhD at the London School of Economics. He was a part-time student, supporting himself by working as a receptionist in the Accident & Emergency department at University College

Hospital, London. He completed his doctoral thesis in 1984 and his first book, *Military Planning for the Defence of the United Kingdom, 1815–70* (Westport, Conn., 1989), was based on it.

Michael had an abiding interest in nineteenth-century political, diplomatic and military history, and this included naval history but was never confined to that. His non-naval publications included two bibliographies in the Greenwood Bibliographies of British Statesmen series, *Wellington*, published in 1990, and *Palmerston*, in 1994. He wrote a biography of *Gladstone* for Routledge in 2003. Recently he had been a co-general editor of the Pickering & Chatto series *Victorian Political Figures* and had edited two and a half volumes in the first series of these, on Gladstone and Palmerston. He was also involved from 1982 in the very large publishing project *British Documents on Foreign Affairs*, firstly as a research assistant but from 1992 as a general editor. This is a very large series of volumes, reproducing the Foreign Office Confidential Print from its beginnings in the 1840s until 1956. Michael was a general editor of the later nineteenth-century volumes and also of the three more recent series relating to documents from the Second World War, and 1946–50 and 1951–6.

Michael taught at various places in the 1980s, including the London School of Economics and the City of London Polytechnic. From 1985 onwards he was at first part-time but then a full-time member of staff at St Mary's College, Strawberry Hill (Twickenham). He was very popular with the students and regarded as an inspirational teacher by many of them. Their loss and the Society's loss is a great one.

Jan Glete (1947–2009)

With the death of Jan Glete the world of maritime history has lost one of its great original thinkers. He will probably be best remembered for his seminal *Navies and Nations: Warships, Navies and State Building in Europe and America, 1500–1860* (Stockholm, 1993), but his contribution to history spans some ten books and countless papers, covering not just maritime history but also Swedish business history and wider issues of military history and state-building.

He was born in Västerås in 1947 and after gaining his PhD at the Department of History at Stockholm University in 1975 he spent his entire academic career there. His first published work on maritime history came in 1985 with a study of the Swedish coastal defence service. Typically, this was not simply a conventional military history, but a more complex investigation of the interaction of technology, doctrine and organization. This was to be a recurring theme throughout his work and in 1993 he published *Navies and Nations*, one of the most significant books on naval history ever to have been published. Naval history had been characterized by national studies of individual nation states, largely concerned with military hardware and naval strategy. Glete, by contrast, undertook a detailed comparative analysis of some seventeen navies ranging from the obvious contenders of England, France and the United States, through to the virtually unknown navies (at least in Western eyes) of Egypt and Oman. In total he considered 59 navies from around the world as diverse as Siam, Haiti and Colombia. He looked at them not just in strictly naval terms, but also in their political, technical and bureaucratic contexts. Never had such a task been contemplated before. Where he was unable to read texts in different languages he famously just learnt those languages. This was no great showman historian's trick, he simply wanted to be sure he had considered an issue in the light of all published research on the subject.

His theory was that there was a great interconnectedness between naval organization, naval technology and state building and he was able to demonstrate that in many cases the development of navies and nation states went hand in hand.

In 2000 he published *Warfare at Sea, 1500–1650: Maritime Conflicts and the Transformation of Europe* (London, 2000), which took up some of the themes developed in *Navies and Nations*. His introduction is telling: 'I have attempted to carry out the historian's basic responsibility of setting the record straight by reading studies from several countries and looking at the same problem from more than one perspective'. What he produced is one of the most challenging and stimulating surveys of early modern naval history, looking not just at the military conflicts, but at the political, economic and social changes that lay behind them, and all from a global perspective. Reading this short book you are forced to acknowledge that naval history cannot, or at least should not, ever be the same again. Many naval historians over the years have paid lip-service to the international nature of their subject. Jan Glete on the other hand has laid the foundations for a truly inter-nationalized study of naval history.

Glete's work also made a significant contribution to advancing the 'military revolution' debate in wider historical circles through his exploration of the 'fiscal-military state'. His *War and the State in Early Modern Europe* (London, 2002) examined the three main players of Spain, the Dutch Republic and Sweden in a by now familiar lucid and challenging fashion.

His great strength was his ability to handle both minute details of, for example, an individual ship's tonnage or ordnance as well as large over-arching concepts. He was very much an empirical historian, examining the data carefully before developing any theoretical arguments, but he was also a great theorist and able to come up with new and clearly argued ideas. Not only was Jan Glete a great historian, he was also a very humble and generous person. He kindly agreed to contribute to the centenary issue of *The Mariner's Mirror* but illness prevented this. Jan Glete died of cancer in July 2009. He will be sadly missed.

Index

Page numbers in *italic* show a Figure. The suffix 'n' indicates further material in a reference note. Subheadings are arranged in ascending page order.

Aberg, F. A. (Alan): quotes Sir Geoffrey Seymour on *Victory* 29, 47n18; becomes Chairman of Council 160, 164, 168; urges recruitment 165; at International Festival of the Sea 166

Adam & Co. (private bank) 154, 155

Addis, Lt Cdr Charles P., CO HMS *Victory* 135

Admiralty: subscribes for *The Mariner's Mirror* 9, 23, 68; arranges survey of *Victory* 30; terms for restoration of *Victory* 30; agrees to undertake maintenance 38; proposes combined Dockyard and Victory Museum 43; entrusts Dockyard Museum to VATC 44; approves discharge of VATC 46; commissions SNR to catalogue Royal Naval Museum 51; accepts proposal for NMM at Greenwich 53; appoints Trustees for NMM at Greenwich 53; donates contents of Royal Naval Museum, Greenwich 55; appoints Sir James Caird as Trustee 58; approves name 'National Maritime Museum' 58; withdraws support for *The Mariner's Mirror* 83; agrees Victory Museum and McCarthy Collection combined 117

Albert, Prince, HRH The Duke of York (later HM King George VI): lays Royal Hospital School foundation stone 57; *Implacable* Appeal 67, 183

Albion, Professor Robert G., obituary 233

Alden Press of Oxford 154, 172

American Neptune, The (quarterly journal) 150, 162n24

Amery, L. S., First Lord of the Admiralty 32; explains the Navy Estimates 33; receives donation from Caird 34

Anderson Medal for Research in Maritime History 167, 257

Anderson, Mrs Romola: Bequest 152; obituary 236–7

Anderson, Roger Charles 6; Hon. Editor *The Mariner's Mirror* 15 *bis;* organizes Amsterdam display 17; contributes articles 22, 226; editorial policy 22; wartime service 22; never refused articles 27; relinquishes post as Editor *The Mariner's Mirror* 27; further service as Editor 28; opposes quarterly issue 28; Royal Naval Museum Committee 51; appointed Trustee of NMM 53; investigates Hamble wreck 63; keeps photographs as evidence 68; third period as Editor 68, 71; three-anchor flag 76; counsels delay in choosing Patron 79; argues for change after Callender 80; becomes President of SNR 82; has to apologize on behalf of Society 82; *Sailing Ships* 82; resigns as Editor *The Mariner's Mirror* 84; calls for STVF to be controlled by NMM Trustees 88; compiles index to

Anderson, R. C. contd: *The Mariner's Mirror* volumes 1–35 97; pledges to produce Nautical Dictionary 97; dashes hopes for Nautical Dictionary 98; retirement portrait 98; VATC 104n92; death 124; 'Royal' prefix unnecessary 171; Hon. Vice President 193; *nom de plume* 'South Goodwin' 226; obituary 226

Anderson, Sir Colin, VATC 105n92

Andrew, Prince, HRH Duke of York, SNR President 160; attends Annual Lecture 167

Anglo-Japanese Naval Treaty 1902 2, 18n8

Anglocentricity 106, 140, 147

Annis, Philip: Hon. Secretary 125; resigns to be Deputy Director NMM 126

Annual Bibliography 131; first year appears 133; grant from British Library 139; compiled by Miss Mary Shepherd 151; compiled by Michael Partridge 257

Archbishop of Canterbury 69

Army and Navy Gazette 6, 7

Ashley, Anthony 11

Baddeley, Sir Vincent 60, 66, 183

Baker, Mr, Forest Research Laboratory 122

Ballard, Vice-Admiral 28; *The Black Battlefleet* 130; Hon. Vice President 193

Barclay, Lady 61

Bartlett de Reya, solicitors 143

Basch, Monsieur Lucien 130

Bathe, Mr Basil: joins Executive Committee of PRNM 125; obituary 250

Battenberg, Vice-Admiral HSH Prince Louis of (later Marquis of Milford Haven): First President xiii, 11, 16, 17, 133, 178, 230; supports formation of Society 7; death 25, 29; obituary 206–7

Beamish, Admiral T. P. H. 37

Beatty, Admiral of the Fleet David, The Earl: elected President 39, 180; needs Chairman to do the work 39, 180, 213, 220; death 40; *Implacable* restoration appeal 66, 67, 183; NMM Trustee 73n40;

obituary 212–13

Beechey, Sir William, Nelson portrait 107

Bell & Bain, of Thornliebank 172

Beresford, Admiral Lord Charles: criticizes Navy League 3; confronts Fisher's policy 4, 19n15, 26; hostility to Battenberg 206, 207

Bermuda Maritime Museum Trust 132

Berry, Sir William, NMM Trustee 73n40

Bethell, John 161, 165

Bethell Watercraft Index of the British Isles 160–1

Blease Lloyd, SNR auditors 140

Board of Trade, abandons sail qualification 5, 19n18

Bonner Smith, David: Admiralty Librarian 28; Hon. Editor *The Mariner's Mirror* 68; Hon. Vice President 193; obituary 216

Borg, Dr Alan, recommends unified museum management 166

Bosanquet, Captain Henry T. A. 77, 80 *bis*, 183; audit objections ignored 113; Hon. Vice President 193; obituary 220–1

Boulton, E. H. B., VATC 104n92

Boxer, Professor Charles Ralph: Hon. Vice President 194; obituary 243

Bracher, Lt Cdr V. H., CO HMS *Victory* 100

Brindley, Harold Hume 6, 9; on Editorial Board 27; expense of restoring *Victory* 32; obituary 215

British Library 131, 139

British Maritime History (journal) 149

British mercantile marine 4

British Museum 60, 104n82

Britton, C. J., indexer 84

Bromley, Professor John S. 100; Hon. Vice President 194; obituary 233

Brown, Captain R. S. Clement 125

Brown, David Keith, obituary 251–2

Brunel, Marc 111

Buck, Sir Anthony, MP 117

Bugler, Arthur, obituary 232

Caird Medal 240, 249

Caird, Sir James 34, *34*; underwrites *Victory* project 34–5, *40*; letter to Sturdee 35, *36*; Hon. Vice President 41, 49n59; pays for Macpherson Collection purchase 56–7, 113, 181; appointed to Macpherson Collection Trust 58; becomes NMM Trustee 58; further purchases for museum 59; forms close friendship with Callender 60; agrees to finance West Wing conversion 61, 182; offers full cost under conditions 62; bust for the Caird Rotunda 63; 'The Sea Fund' account 65 *bis*, 182; covers cost of training four boys 66; pays for towing *Foudroyant* to Portsmouth 67; advises Trustees to boycott *Implacable* 77, 184; offers to pay for *Implacable* survey 77; his support had kept Callender in post 80; pays for Callender's funeral 80; Society's greatest benefactor dies 83, 178; personal philanthropy 95, 179; obituary 216–17

Callender, Professor Sir Geoffrey A. R. *24*; Hon. Secretary and Treasurer 24, 39, *40*, 47n7; revises Society's aims 24–5, 179; controls Society from Greenwich 25, 47n11, 181; omitted from Board 27; shocked by unseemly crowds 30, 179; *The Story of HMS Victory* 35, 182, 189n4; appoints architect for Victory Museum 45; advises discharge of VATC 46, 183; catalogues Royal Naval Museum collections 51; revives Royal Naval Museum at Greenwich 51, 179–80; sees Queen's House as home for maritime museum 52, 180; appointed Trustee of NMM 53, 181; adviser to NMM Trust 57, 59; advises Caird on purchases 59, 60, 181, 183; near mental breakdown 61, 183; first Director of the NMM 62, 75, 182; reports on Friends of the NMM 64; blocks restoration of *Implacable* 65, 182; Cobb's request for Anonymous Donor 66; deputy chairman *Implacable* Committee 66, 182; service to Society 79–80; sudden death 79; domiciled in Oxford during the war 80; dislike of Carr Laughton 82–3, 183; writes to Admiralty about *The Mariner's Mirror* 83; uses Macpherson Trust to plant shrubs 113, 185; failure to recognize future problems 183–4, 185; ungenerous remark after Sturdee's death 183; obituary 215–16

Cambridge University Press: prints *The Mariners' Mirror* 28, 97, 98; improved marketing 99 *bis*, 101, 110, 118; last issue 119

Campbell, Professor Eila 146; obituary 239

Canadian Nautical Research Society 150

Carlyle, A. E.: Appeal Secretary 32; persuades First Lord to write to Sturdee 32–3; celebrates success 33–4

Carr, Frank George Griffith 77 *bis*; appointed Director of the NMM 80, *81*; conflict over *Victory* curator 89; calls for round table conference on *Victory* 93; sees *Cutty Sark* as Merchant Navy icon 95; inaugural lecture SNR South 100; committee of experts for death-watch beetle 104n82; VATC 104n92; forced to retire 106, 136n3, 245; uses Macpherson Fund 113; supports 'Royal' prefix 171; Hon. Vice President 193; obituary 237–8

Carr Laughton, Leonard George: creates SNR 5; canvases support for Society 6; letter shows differing opinions 6; Acting Secretary 7, 9; article in the *Morning Post* 7; drafts Prospectus 7, 8; initial steps 7; requests publicity 7; Hon. Editor *The Mariner's Mirror* 11 *bis*; retired as Editor 15; researches *Victory* plans 32, *40*, 217–18; researches Hamble wreck 63; disputes restoration of *Victory*'s bows 82–3; Hon. Vice President 82; entries to Nautical Dictionary 97, 218; obituary 217–18

Charity Commissioners 106, 141, 142 *bis*, 143–4, 145, 155, 157, 173

Chatham Historic Dockyard 155; bicentenary of launch of *Victory* 100, 105n112; Chatham Publishing 165

Cheshire, Lt Cdr M, CO HMS *Victory* 159

Chippendale of Wroxham, build *Victory*'s cutter 155

Clare, Roy *169*

Clement, David 161, 165; chairs Heritage and Small Craft Committee 172

Cobb, Geoffrey Wheatley 32, 64–5, 66, 73n47, 73n48

Cobb, Mrs Wheatley 66, 71

Connaught, HRH The Duke of 31

Coombs, Barry, Editor of *Newsletter* 172

Corbett, Sir Julian S. 6, 7; on Editorial Board 27; urges *Victory* restoration begins 35

Cork and Orrery, Admiral of the Fleet, Earl of 46, 80, 89; Hon. Vice President 193; obituary 222

Corlett, Dr E. C. B. 110

Cossons, Dr Neil, Director of NMM 132, 145

Coutts and Co. 23

Craig, Robin: founder *Maritime History* journal 149; obituary 250–1

Crawford, W. S. (publicity agent) 32

Creasy, Admiral Sir George 93

Crimmin, Ms Patricia 132

Culture, Media and Sport, Department of 166 *bis*

Currie, Sir William 94

Custance, Admiral Sir Reginald 9

Custance, Mr Eric C. D.: Hon. Treasurer 80, 100, 105n111; PRNM Trustee 117, 118 *bis*; financial concern for SNR 120, 124; resists transfer of STVF assets 120; resigns over SS *Great Britain* Project 125, 126, 137N54

Cutty Sark (composite clipper 1869) 94–5, 105n94; moored at buoys for 1951 Festival of Britain 95, *96*

Cutty Sark Preservation Society 95, 185, 238

David, Captain H. F., NMM Trustee 73n40

David, Lt Cdr Andrew 132, 146

Davies, Dr Evan, history of RNC, Osborne project 139, 153, 156

Davies, Suzanne, Editor of *Newsletter* 172

Davis, Professor Ralph, obituary 228

De Bunsen, Ronald Lothar, obituary 238

De Jager, Lizelle, Editor of *Newsletter* 167

death-watch beetle 70, 92, 104n82, 122

Department of the Environment 152

Devastation, HMS (turret ship 1871) 55

Devitt & Moore 19n18

Doe, Dr Helen , chairs Marketing Committee 170, 171

Dolley, Brian: Assistant Editor 119; becomes Hon. Editor *The Mariners' Mirror* 126; requests editorial assistants 128; objects to censorship 129; canvasses Overseas Corresponding Members 130; Journal at reduced rates for students 132; purchases computer and word processor 132, 133, 138n79; membership records on computer 133; suggests management fees 140; unsupervised control leads to academic weakness 140; reduces number of pages 142; attitude to expenses 143; honorarium is subvention of expenses 143; editorial methods 149; agrees to resign with dignity 151; obituary 241–2

Dolley, Michael, obituary 232–3

Dolley, Mrs Celia: Hon. Assistant Editor 130, 242; indexer Volumes 71 to 75 151

Domvile, Sir Barry, Admiral President, RNC Greenwich 58

Dorrien Smith, Lt Cdr Thomas 97, 105n105

Dowman, Captain Wilfred 94

Dreadnought, HMS (battleship 1906) 3, 4, 32, 55

Duff, Sir Patrick 60, 61, 62

Duffy, Dr Michael: Reviews Editor 149; Hon. Editor *The Mariners' Mirror* 151, 152, 164

Dumanoir de Pelly, Rear-Admiral Pierre 64

Dunn, Emma, Hon. Secretary 168

Earle, Sir Lionel 53, 60
Edward VII, HM The King 9, 65
Elizabeth, HM The Queen *85*, 95
Engholm, Frederick (film-maker) 35
Engineers and Shipbuilders, North East Coast, Institute of 5, 19n20
Engineers and Shipbuilders in Scotland, Institute of 5, 19n20
English Heritage 158
English, Lieutenant, CO HMS *Victory* 46
Environment, Department of the 113, 152
Eyres-Monsell, Sir Bolton, First Lord of the Admiralty 58

Falklands, 1914 Battle of the 26, 209
Falmouth Harbour, working sail 185
Farrar, Austin 'Clarence' Packard: recommends two *Victory* cutters 155; Hon. Vice President 194; obituary 246–7
Fenwick, Valerie 144
figureheads collection, Valhalla, Tresco Abbey 97
Fischer, Lewis 'Skip' 150
Fisher, Dr R. C. 104n82, 104n92
Fisher of Kilverstone, Admiral of the Fleet John Arbuthnot: First Sea Lord 1904–10 3; strengthens Nore Division 3; reforms officer training 4; speeds up shipbuilding 4; torpedo-boat destroyer programme 1893 4; distrusts Sturdee 26
Fisher, Sir Warren 61
Forest Research Laboratory 104n82, 122
Foudroyant, TS 1897 (ex-*Trincomalee*): training ship 65, 66, *67*, 67 *bis*, 78, 234; Admiralty uses as storeship 70; bomb damage 70; Training Establishment 71; history 73n48; post-war state 76–7; Foudroyant Trust 125; Foudroyant Committee 225, 238
Fraser of North Cape, Admiral Bruce, Lord 89, 90
Friends of the National Maritime Museum 64, 75, 146

Friends of the Royal Naval Museum and HMS *Victory* 146
Friends of the Royal Naval Museum, Portsmouth 146
Frost, Ms Honor 114 *bis*, 115, 129
Fry, C. B. and Beatrice 60
Fuller, Admiral Sir Cyril 71

Gales of Detroit, Michigan 132
Gardner, Lt Cdr W. J. R. 'Jock', Hon. Secretary 155, 164
Garvey, Peter, Membership Secretary 155
George, Prince, HRH The Duke of Kent: first Patron 40, 56, 71, 78; obituary 215
George V, HM The King 35, 40; visits *Victory* 30, 38, *40*, 44, 46
George VI, HM The King (previously Prince Albert, Duke of York) 69, 185, 235
German Navy Law: 1898 and 1900 2; 1906 3
Giffard, Ann, obituary 252–3
Glasgow, HMS (Type 42 destroyer 1976) 131
Glete, Jan, obituary 258–9
Goodwin, Peter, *Victory*'s curator 153, 157, 166
Goodwin, S. 15
Goold-Adams, Richard 110, 111, 125
Gorski, Dr Richard, Reviews Editor 160
Gould, Miss Annette, Membership Secretary 148, 155
Grace Dieu (Henry V's ship 1418) 63, 237
Grant, Captain, CO HMS *Victory* 69, 70 *bis*
ss *Great Britain* Project 111, 125, 136n9, 246, 250
Great Britain, ss (screw steamship 1843) 110, 136n8, 153
Great Circle, The (semi-annual journal) 150
Green, R. & H, of Blackwall 19n18
Greenhill, Basil 76; becomes Director of NMM 107, *109*, 136n3; uses Macpherson Fund to pay travel expenses 113; refuses SNR office in museum 124; retires 132; opposes 'Royal' prefix 171; obituary 245–6
Greenwich: Queen's House 52 *bis*, 53, 57,

Greenwich: Queen's House contd: *59*, 62, 80;
  Royal Hospital School, relocation to
  Holbrook 52, 53, 57, 60, 181; proposal to
  dry-dock *Implacable* 77 *bis*; *Cutty Sark*
  moored at buoys for 1951 Festival of Britain
  95, *96*; dry-dock for *Cutty Sark* 95 *bis*
Greenwich Hospital 51, 61, 62, 71n3
Grove, Eric 146, 147, 151, 160
Gueritz, Mrs Pamela 100
Gueritz, Rear-Admiral E. F.: President SNR
  111, 124, 125–6; seeks attention to youth
  facilities 126–7; notes requests for reform
  127; attends Mountbatten's funeral 128;
  prefers Council over editorial board 128–
  9; sees threat to publication of *The
  Mariner's Mirror* 141; concern at NMM
  re-organization 144; admits Society living
  beyond its means 145; resigns 150; choice
  for next President 162n27; Hon. Vice
  President 194; tribute to Lord Louis
  Mountbatten 230; funeral address for Lt
  Cdr Whitlock 236; obituary 253–4

Hakluyt Society 5, 20n21
Halifax, Lord 87
Hall, Admiral 84
Hall, Viscount, First Lord of the Admiralty
  91–2
Hamble wreck 63
Hampshire County Council 157, 161
Harding, Dr Richard: Hon. Editor *The
  Mariners' Mirror* 164, 167, 168; Chairman
  of Council 170, 174
Hardy, Thomas 56
Harris, Reg 166
Hartelie, Olaf (C. N. Robinson) 15
Hay, Dr H. 104n82
Hayward, Jack 111
Henry Grace à Dieu (galleon 80 1514) 63
Higham, Cdr 89
Hill, Engineer-Cdr H Oliver 76; Hon. Vice
  President 193
Hill, Rear-Admiral Richard: Chairman of

Council 155; justifies RNM funding 159;
  retires as Chairman 160; unable to support
  Wyllie's *Panorama* 160
*HMS Victory, Her Construction, Career and
  Restoration* 160
Hobbs, Cdr David, chairs Publications
  Committee 172
Holbrook, Suffolk 52, 53, 57, 60, 182
Holland Rose, Professor J. 71
Hope, Admiral Sir George Price Webley:
  chairs Victory Finance Committee 37;
  chairs Victory Advisory Technical
  Committee 38; elected Chairman of
  Council 39, 180; past career 39, *41*, 180;
  becomes President 40; resurrects Victory
  Museum proposal 43; proposes VATC be
  discharged 46; appointed Trustee of NMM
  53; endorses proposal for NMM 53;
  'People's Palace of British Sea-Power' 55,
  63; urges retention of Macpherson
  Collection 55–6; suggests Friends of the
  National Maritime Museum 63–4; sees no
  prospect of Greenwich site 67; three-
  anchor flag 75–6; partnership with
  Callender 79–80; resigns after long service
  82; transfers STVF to NMM Trustees 88;
  memorandum to Admiralty concerning
  Victory 91; Hon. Vice President 193;
  obituary 219–20
Hore, Captain Peter, chairs Research,
  Technical and Programmes Committee 167
Houston, Richard 13
Howe, Earl 37
Howse, Lt Cdr Derek: edits *Newsletter* 152,
  153; obituary 240
Hugh Smith, Admiral Humphrey 67, *67–8*,
  70; obituary 218
Hughes, Lt Col A. J. L., indexer 110

Ilchester, Earl of, NMM Trustee 73n40
Imperial Maritime League, created 1908 3,
  19n11
Imperial War Museum 51, 55, 60, 180

Implacable Committee 66, 67 *bis*, 70–1, 77, 225; Admirals' Appeal 68, 74n59; radio appeal by Christopher Stone 68, 74n58; reformed as Foudroyant Committee 225

Implacable, HMS (Third rate 74 1805) 42, 66, 67; formerly *Duguay-Trouin* 64; sale cancelled 65; Admiralty uses as storeship 70; work stopped 70; Training Establishment 71; post-war state 76–7; stripped and scuttled 78, 184, 225

indexing: lack of 84; volumes 1 to 35 97 *bis*; indexers change 110; Cumulative Index funded 114; Cumulative Index 119, 132; at five year intervals 130; volumes 36 to 55 published 130; Mrs Celia Dolley, volumes 71 to 75 151

Ingram, Captain Bruce, Hon. Vice President 193

International Journal of Maritime History (semi-annual journal) 150

International Journal of Nautical Archaeology, The 150

International Maritime Economic History Association 150

International Sailing Craft Association 160

International Year of the Sea for 2005 166

Ireland, Dr John de Courcey: Overseas Corresponding Member 130; obituary 247–8

Jackson, Instructor-Capt. T. E.: Victory Museum Curator 82, 97, 100; obituary 227

Jal, Auguste, *Glossaire nautique* 5

Jal Society, proposed 5, 6

James, Admiral Sir William 69

Jane, Fred Thomas 22

Jay, Cdr Lawrence, CO HMS *Victory* 135

Jellicoe, Admiral of the Fleet Sir John 26

Johnman, Dr Lewis 167

Johns, Vice-Admiral Sir Adrian, Second Sea Lord 174

Jones, A. G. E., obituary 244–5

Jones, Helen, Editor of *Newsletter* 167

Jones, Mrs Linda, typesetter 152, 171

Kenyon, Sir Frederick, NMM Trustee 73n40

King, Cecil 42, 71

Kneller, Godfrey 13

Knight, Roger 129

Kraus, Messrs, of Liechtenstein 118

Laird Clowes, G. S. 63, 64

Lambert, Dr Andrew: chairs Publications Committee 164; eulogy for Ann Giffard 252–3; Lang, Sir John, Secretary of the Admiralty 93 *ter*, 105n93

Langley, Lt Cdr, CO HMS *Victory* 97

Lapper, Capt. William 142, 143

Laughton, Sir John Knox: edits *Naval Miscellany* 5; founds NRS 5; secretary of NRS 6; publicizes Prospectus 7; supports new Society 7; at inaugural meeting 9

Lavery, Brian, Hon. Treasurer 148, 160, 164

Law, Admiral Sir Horace 115–16; Hon. Vice President 193, 194

Law, Professor Derek: Hon. Secretary 151, 155; chairs Marketing Committee 171

Layton, Admiral Sir Geoffrey 90

Lecky, Cdr H. S. 27

Lewin, Admiral of the Fleet Sir Terence 131, 144; becomes 'hands off' President 150–1; death 160; Hon. Vice President 194; obituary 241

Lewis, Admiral Andrew 117

Lewis, Professor Michael: turns down NMM Directorship 80; elected Chairman of the Council 82; concern over *Victory* alterations 92–3; becomes President 98; seeks economy in *The Mariner's Mirror* costs 98–9; VATC 105n92; lack of northern members 106; announces retirement 110; doubts 'Royal' prefix 171; obituary 224

Leyland, John 6, 9, 28; obituary 207–8

Lincoln, Dr Margarette: *Newsletter* Editor 156; chairs Publications Committee 164, 167

Little, Admiral Sir Charles 90, 92
Lloyd, Professor Christopher: Hon. Editor *The Mariner's Mirror* 119; retires as Editor 126, 129; Hon. Vice President 193; obituary 233–4; Chairman of Council 234
Lloyd's Register of Shipping 95
London County Council 77, 95 *bis*
Londonderry, Lady 11
Lowen, Reginald: Acting Hon. Secretary 78–9, 181; administers NMM during the war 80; becomes Acting Director and Hon. Secretary 80, *85*, 102n28; becomes Hon. Treasurer 80–1, 85, 97, 106; poor relations with Secretary, George Naish 81–2, 107, 184; resigns 100; uses Macpherson Fund 113; obituary 237
Luns, Joseph, former NATO Secretary-General, obituary 244
Lutyens, Sir Edwin 63
Lyon, David, obituary 242

McArdle, Rear-Admiral S. L., PRNM Chairman 117
McCarthy Gallery 158–9
McCarthy, Mrs Lily: donates Nelson Collection 115; Royal Naval Museum Trustee 116; Lily Lambert McCarthy Foundation 130, 135, 138n79; retires as Hon. Vice President 135, 161n3, 194 *bis*; Hon. Vice President 194
McCutcheon Craig, Sir John H. 61
MacDonald, James Ramsay, Prime Minister 58, 62 *bis*, 73n40, 182
McGowan, Dr Alan 46; Chairman VATC 160
MacGregor, David R.: Hon. Vice President 194; obituary 246
McKenna, Reginald, Treasurer STVF 31
Mackinnon, Sir Percy, NMM Trustee 73n40
McMurray, H. Campbell, RNM Director 158; relies on SNR funding 158–9; seeks funds for restoring Wyllie's *Panorama* 160
Macpherson, A. G. H. 55–6, 71, 113

Macpherson Collection: Endowment Fund 42, 70, 87 *bis*, 127, 140–1; Backhuysen Ludolf 56; Brueghel, Pieter the Elder 56; Monamy, Peter 56; Storck, Abraham 56; van de Velde, Willem, father and son 56; *Battle of the Texel*, Willem van de Velde the Younger 87; *Eddystone Lighthouse*, Isaac Sailmaker 165
Macpherson Collection Appeal 56–7, 113
Madden, Admiral Sir Charles, chairs NMM Trustees 124
Mainwaring George Ernest 27; obituary 214–15
Majer, Mr W. O. B.: keeps index cards 110; obituary 234
Manning, Capt. T. Davys, RNVR : Hon. Editor *The Mariner's Mirror* 98, 119; obituary 224
Mariner's Mirror, The: printers *see* Bell & Bain; Cambridge University Press; Staples and Co., St Albans; Alden Press of Oxford; Kraus, Messrs, of Liechtenstein; future contributors 6; proposal for journal 7, *8*, 9, 177; Admiralty subscribes for 250 copies 9; Editorial Committee 11, 15, 20n43, 20–1n51, 23; name and cover 11, *12*, 13, 127; contents of first issue 13, *14*; teething troubles 13; resumes post-war 22; 1914–18 war-time subscriptions 23; Admiralty increases to 300 copies 23; costs inflation 23; increased subscriptions 23–4; production re-examined 25 *bis*; Editorial Board appointed 27; Admiralty increases to 900 copies 68, 83; paper rationing 68; reduced size due to paper rationing 68; Admiralty cancels support 83, 86, 102n42; Covenant subscription 84, 97, 99, 110, 124; increased production costs 84; indexers 84, 97, 110; lacks general index 84; 'Maritime Miscellany' 84, 102n45, 182; index to volumes 1–35 97; inexorable rise in production costs 98–9; Publications Committee abolished 98; Macpherson Fund

finances Cumulative Index from volume 35 114; volumes 1 to 35 reprinted 118; costs of production 1968-75 119; Cumulative Index 119; stock of back numbers 119; costs force subscription rise 126; grants for articles 132; lacks editorial board 140, 186; undistinguished reputation 140, 186; 75th anniversary volume 148, 161n19; brief history of the journal 148; Publications Committee sets up Editorial Panel 148–9, 150, 169; Reviews Editor appointed 149; refereeing of articles 151, 169; subtitle removed from frontispiece 151; new production schedule and format 152; all triremes and naval history 159; CD-Rom of all issues 1911 to 2000 165, 172; special edition for Trafalgar bicentenary 166, 168, 170; subtitle replaced 169; centenary issue 171, 175; leading international journal of maritime history 188

Maritime History journal 149, 161n23

Maritime History Seminars, International Commission for 139, 153, 255

Maritime Institute of Ireland 130

Markham, Sir Clements, FRS 9

Marsala Punic ship, Sicily 113, 114–15, 130, 143, 242

Mary, HM The Queen, purchases Nelson's death mask 44

Mary Rose (60-gun ship 1509) 113, 114 *bis*, 135, 185, 234

Massey, Admiral Alan, Second Sea Lord 174

Massie Blomfield, Admiral Sir R. 9

Mather, William McQuie, obituary 221

Matthews, Rev. E. W. 9

Mattinson, Mr D. A. 104n82

Maudsley, Henry 111

May, Cdr William Edward: Deputy Director of NMM 81, 107 *bis*, 234, 240; obituary 234–5

Mead, Cdr Hilary P.: Hon. Editor *The Mariner's Mirror* 84, 221; obituary 221

Mercury, TS (ex-*Gannet*, composite screw sloop 1878) 60

Meyer, Mr W. O. B., legacy 167, 174

Midland Bank 37

Milford Haven 66, 67

Moore, Sir Alan: recalls formation of SNR 5, 6, 20n22; drafts Prospectus 7, 8; has doubts of 'Jal Society' 7; name *The Mariner's Mirror* already current 9; view of H. H. Brindley 11; disquiet about editor 13, 15; contributes articles 15; on re-rigging *Victory* 32, *40*; *Last Days of Sail* 82; on 'Royal' prefix 171; obituary 218–19

Morris, Rear-Admiral R. O. 139, 144–5; Chairman of Council 147; lays out future activities for SNR 147–8; membership exceeds 2000 152; farewell address 154, 155, 157

Morriss, Dr Roger 132 *bis*

Mountbatten, Admiral Lord Louis xiii, 78, 101–2n20; becomes Patron 79, *79*, 133–4; murder 128; obituary 228–30

Mountbatten of Burma, Countess 160; Hon. Vice President 193

Mountbatten, Lieutenant Philip (later Prince Philip) 79

Munday, John: Society tie 100; Hon. Secretary 126, 128, *134*; resigns 133; Hon. Vice President 194; recalls Cdr Edward May 235

Murphy, Dr Hugh 167; Hon. Editor *The Mariners' Mirror* 169, 171, 172; revises editorial policy 168–70

Murray, Sir Oswyn 61; obituary 214

Naish, F. C. P., and sons 63

Naish, George, Hon. Secretary 80–1, 106, *108*; Assistant Director till post abolished 81; centre of dissension 81–2, 107, 184; attends *Victory* bicentenary functions 100; VATC 104n92; horror at Nelson Exhibition in Japan 108; attends exhibition 110; free use of Macpherson Fund 113;

Naish, George contd: PRNM Trustee 117; retires from NMM 124, 137n49; death 125; defies Trustees and preserves timbers 186; obituary 227

Nance, Robert Morton 6, 7, 15; articles 22; Hon. Vice President 193; obituary 220

Nash, Peter V., Hon. Treasurer 155, 157, 165, 174

National Art Collections Fund 61

National Christina Foundation 168

National Heritage Act 1983 158

National Heritage Lottery Fund 158 bis

National Marine Photograph Collection 76

National Maritime Museum see NMM

National Maritime Museum Bill 62 bis

National Museum of the Royal Navy (NMRN): proposal 166, 174; launch 174–5

national naval museum proposed 25, 27

National Naval and Nautical Museum see NMM (National Maritime Museum)

National Portrait Gallery 54, 60

National Provincial Bank, Southsea 65, 73n51

Nautical Antiquary Society 6, 7, 8, 177–8

Nautical Archaeology Policy, Joint Committee on 152

Nautical Encyclopaedia or Dictionary 9, 15, 25, 75, 84, 97, 124, 178; Sub-Committee 127–8; Gale/Urdang Project 132–3, 147

Naval Architects, Institute of 5, 19n20

Naval Defence Act 1889 1

Naval Miscellany, The vol. II 5

Navy League: formed 1893 2; leads Battle of Trafalgar centenary 2; grows to 100,000 members 3; political campaigns 5

Navy League Journal 6

Navy Records Society 5, 15–16, 19n19, 149, 177

Nelson Exhibition in Japan 107–10

Nelson, Vice-Admiral Horatio, Lord: will 16; chelengk 42, 60–1, 72n33; memorabilia 42–3; Funeral Barge 43, 49–50n64; death mask 44; West Collection of relics 55; portrait by Sir William Beechey 107, 123

Nelson-Ward, Reverend 64; Hon. Vice President 193

Neptune, HMS (battleship 1874) 29, 47n19

New Researchers in Maritime History Conference 153

NMM (National Maritime Museum) Greenwich: SNR pursues the project 44; Trustees take over VATC functions 46; Callender proposes creation 52, 71n1, 179; Trustees appointed 53, 57; ad hoc Committee formed 61; Committee agrees Callender as Director 61; Prime Minister chooses Board of Trustees 62, 73n40; finally opened 63, 73n41; dissension among Trustees 107; demise of Archaeological Research Centre 144, 186; Directors divert income from Macpherson Fund 185

Noble, Admiral Sir Percy 77

Nordvik, Helga 150

North Ferriby boats, excavation 185, 186, 190n10

Northern Mariner, The/Le Marin du Nord (quarterly journal) 150

Notes and Queries (magazine) 7

NRS (Navy Records Society) 5, 15–16, 19n19, 149, 177

Oddy, Professor D. J. 171

Office of Works 53, 59, 60, 61, 63, 104n82

Official Nelson Commemorations Committee 162n41, 166 bis, 255

Ollard, Richard, obituary 249

Ormond, Richard, Director of NMM 145

Osbon, G. A.: edits The Black Battlefleet 130; Hon. Vice President 194

Our Navy (film) 2

Owen, Douglas 9, 11; Hon. Secretary and Treasurer 13; contacts pre-war membership 23; resignation and death 23, 178; obituary 205–6

Pack, Capt. A. J.: Curator Victory Museum 100; to be in charge of new museum 116;

Director PRNM 117, 118

Page, David: Sailing Master *Victory*'s cutter 155; heads Small Craft Committee 156, 161; revives website 169, 170

Palmer, Professor Sarah, chairs Research, Technical and Programmes Committee 164, 167

Parker, Captain Harry 56, 72n17

Parker, T. H., Dealer in Prints, Drawings and Paintings 13

Parkinson, Dr C. Northcote 171, 181, 183

Parry, Professor John Horace, obituary 231

Partridge, Dr Michael Stephen: joint compiler, Annual Bibliography 133; edits *Newsletter* 153; takes on Osborne history 156, 160; obituary 257–8

Patrick, Mrs Mary 133

Peabody Museum of Salem, Massachusetts 150

Pearce, Lt Cdr 117, 118, 119, 125

Pearsall, Alan, obituary 248

'People's Budget' 1909 3, 19n14

'People's Palace of British Sea-Power' 55, 63, 179

Perrin, William Gordon (Admiralty Librarian) 9; becomes Editor 27; champions quarterly publication 27–8; confirmed as Hon. Editor 28; definitive work on British flags 28, 211; Secretary to Trustees of NMM 53; obituary 211–12

Philip, Prince, HRH Duke of Edinburgh: as Patron *Frontispiece* xiii, *129*, *131*, *169*; supports Carr on *Implacable* 77; supports *Cutty Sark* project 95 *ter*; becomes Patron 133, 134; congratulates *The Mariner's Mirror* 148; opens foretopsail display 168

Phillips, Lt Cdr Lawrence, RNR: Hon. Secretary 133, *134*, 144; resigns over management fees 140, 141, 146; Recruitment and Publicity Committee 147, 151; produces publicity leaflet 157; raises money from industry 160; revises membership leaflet 160

Phillips, Mrs Jennifer, Hon. Deputy Secretary 133

Pilgrim Trust 68

Plenderleith, Dr H. J. 104n82

Pocock, Thomas Allcott Guy, obituary 249–50

Pool, Bernard, obituary 226

Poole, John 28

Porchester churchyard 161, 211

Portsmouth: offers berth for *Victory* 30; Dockyard collection boxes 37; Dockyard war years closure 42, 68; Admiral Superintendent houses memorabilia 43; Dockyard Museum 43, 44 *bis*; *Implacable* and *Foudroyant* moored in Harbour 67, *67*; Admiralty House unusable 90; Block Mills 111–13; 1982 Dockyard Review 158

Portsmouth City Council 158

Portsmouth Historic Dockyard 158, 166, 175

Portsmouth Historic Dockyard Trust, created 167, 176n9

Portsmouth Naval Base Property Trust 135, 157–8, 162n43, 188

Portsmouth Naval Heritage Trust 135, 146

Portsmouth Royal Naval Museum: Admiral Law's proposal 115; MoD (N) responsibility 115–16; Board of Trustees 116, 186; Trust Deed 117; changes name to Royal Naval Museum, Portsmouth 131, 158; Nelson as 'Commander-in-Chief' display 159

Portsmouth Royal Naval Museum Trading Company 120; incorporated 122; record profits 125; fraud by employees 153, 157

Powell, Miss Isabel G. 74n75

Power, Admiral Sir John Arthur 92

Power, Rear-Admiral A. M. 111

Preston, Antony 142, 144; Hon. Treasurer 145, 146, 151

Prynne, Major-General Michael: works on the *Grace Dieu* 63; opposes transfer of STVF assets 120–1, 122; chairs

Prynne, Major-General Michael contd: encyclopaedia sub-committee 124, 128; obituary 227–8

Pryor, Mrs Ethel 11

Public Works and Buildings, Ministry of 112, 113

Pugh, Philip: on Editorial Board 171; obituary 255–7

Pulvertaft, Rear-Admiral David, chairs Publications Committee 167, 172

Ranft, Professor Bryan Maclean, obituary 244

Reay, Justin, Members' Forum Moderator 173

Redoutable (French Third rate 74) 44

Reid Dick, Sir William 63

Restronguet Creek, near Falmouth, last fishing fleet under sail 76

Rhodes, Mrs Rachel, Learning Development Officer 167

Richardson, Professor A. E., chairs VATC 94, 104n92

Richmond, Admiral Sir Herbert William 73n40

Riddle of the Sands, The, Erskine Childers 3, 19n13

Risdon Beazley Ltd, Messrs 111

Robertson, J. N., VATC 104n92

Robinson, Cdr Charles Napier: advises small society 6; doubts on funding 6, 7; The Times naval correspondent 6, 213; article in The Times 7; publicizes Prospectus 7; at inaugural meeting 9, 178; receives criticism of Carr Laughton 13, 15; on Editorial Board 27; sees Victory as 'sea cathedral' 30, 40, 179; seeks advice on raising money 32; joint author with John Leyland 208; Hon. Vice President 213

Robinson, Gregory 6, 11, 28, 83, 240; obituary 222

Robinson, Michael S. 181, 232; Hon. Vice President 194

Rodger, Dr N. A. M. 128, 129; edits The Black Battlefleet 130; doubts dictionary contract viable 132

Rogers, H. S., architect 38, 45, 182

Rolfe, Mrs Elizabeth, indexes volumes 36 to 55 130

Romance of HMS Victory (film) 35, 182

Rose, Dr Susan 132, 139

Roskill, Captain Stephen, obituary 232

Rosyth: designated as naval base 3

Royal Commission for Historic Monuments 152

Royal Commission on National Museums and Galleries 56, 180

Royal Commission on Supply of Food and Raw Materials in Time of War 1905 3, 18–19n10

Royal Hospital School, relocation to Holbrook 52, 53, 57, 60, 72n31, 182

Royal Marines Museum, Southsea 166

Royal Naval College, Dartmouth 24

Royal Naval College, Greenwich 24, 25, 37 Royal Naval Museum collections 51

Royal Naval College, Osborne 24, 139, 153, 156, 160, 257

Royal Naval Museum, Greenwich: collections 51, 180; reorganized by Callender 51; Royal Naval Museum Committee 51; Admiralty collection of ship models 52, 55; Captain James Cook's compass and dipping needle 55; Drake's astrolabe 55; half-models collection 55; National Gallery of Naval Art 55, 72n12, 180; oldest Chatham Chest 55; sheer draughts, plans and profiles 55; West Collection of Nelson relics 55; Caird's purchases housed 59

Royal Naval Museum, Portsmouth: previously Portsmouth Royal Naval Museum 131; registered charity 158; devolved from MoD (N) 158

Royal Naval Museum Trading Company: profits to STVF 167; renegotiated terms 175

Royal Navy Fleet Air Arm Museum, Yeovilton 166
Royal Navy Submarine Museum, HMS *Dolphin*, Gosport 115, 166
Rubin de Cervin, Barone G. B. 130
Runciman of Doxford, Lord: Chairman of NMM Trustees 73n40, 104–5n92, 107, 131; Hon. Vice President 193; obituary 236
RUSI (Royal United Services Institute): organizes 1891 Naval Exhibition 2; first general meeting of SNR 9–10; inaugural meeting of SNR 9; presented with replica of *Victory*'s belfry 134
Ryan, Anthony N., obituary 247

Sainsbury, Captain A. B. 146, 147, 151
Sainsbury, Mrs A. B. 100
Scammell, Geoffrey Vaughan, obituary 248–9
Science and the French and British Navies, NMM monograph 167
Science Museum 51, 55, 60, 112, 180
Sea Containers Ltd 158
Sea Fund 65, 73n51
Seaman, Sir Owen, editor of *Punch* 64, 66 *bis*, 67, 183; obituary 213
Seppings, Sir Robert 35
Seymour, Sir Geoffrey, condition of *Victory* 29
Shepheard, Sir Victor: Director of Naval Construction 93; Hon. Vice President 193; obituary 235
Shepherd, Miss Mary, compiles *Annual Bibliography* 151
Shirley, Ann, Hon. Secretary 149, 151
Simpson, Colonel W. G., Hon. Secretary and Treasurer 23
Skelton, Mr R. A. 87
Smallwood, Arthur, Director of Hospital School 52
Smith, Admiral Sir Aubrey 78, 83
Smith, J. 13
Smith, Mr Lints 32

SNR (Society for Nautical Research): bankers *see* Coutts & Co.; Midland Bank; Adam & Co. (private bank); briefly Nautical Antiquary Society 7, 8; aims and objects 9, 20n40; final name adopted 9; *List of Members* published 1990 12; Code of Laws 16; financed by *The Mariner's Mirror* 16; lacks London headquarters 16, 25; display at 1913 Amsterdam Shipping Exhibition 17; launches public appeal for the *Victory* 30; appoints Victory Finance Committee 37; discharges Victory Finance Committee 38; enlarged with public image 40; Battle of Trafalgar Panorama annexe 44; catalogues Royal Naval Museum collections 51; Coastal and River Craft Sub-Committee 64, 76, 238; distances itself from *Implacable* 77, 101n8; drive for new members 99; endows annual E. G. R. Taylor Lecture 105n106, 239; annual meetings with MoD (N) on *Victory* maintenance 130; management fees for administering STVF, etc. 140–1, 142; creation of contingency reserve 141, 142; honoraria 141, 142–3, 151; concern over relations with NMM 144–5, 184, 190n8; Editorial Panel set up 148–9; Constitution of the Society adopted 154; Finance Committee 154, 156; incorporated as a Charitable Limited Company 154, 157; Council's lack of accountability 156; Finance and General Purposes Committee formed 156; advances money for Victory Gallery 158, 186; advances money for 'Nelson as Commander-in Chief' 159; five-year plan for HMS *Victory* 164, 174; financial situation to 2008 165; Gift Aid scheme 165; Anderson Medal for Research in Maritime History 167, 257; conference on 'The Great Storm of 1703' 167–8; biggest ever financial loss 170; application for 'Royal' prefix dropped 171; Heritage and Small Craft Committee 172; adverse

SNR contd: financial climate 173–4; investments 173–4; geographical spread of members 106, 136n2; Marketing and Membership Committee: formed 170; debates digitization of *The Mariner's Mirror* 173, 189; proposed Jal Society 6, 7; membership increased 10, 11, 13, 105n113; relations with NRS 15–16; 'navalist' policy agenda 27; notes condition of *Victory* 29; members granted free access to *Victory* 37, 49n50; pursues NMM at Greenwich 44; public appeal for Victory Museum 45; re-organization and new catalogue 51–2; proposes National Maritime Museum 52, 72n7; public appeal for Macpherson Collection purchase 56–7; prints exhibition loses money 60; ship model exhibition 60; recognizes *Implacable* Committee 67, 101n10; Second World War income 68; post-war membership 71, 78; Photographic Records Sub-Committee 76, 101n2, 185; post-war accounts 85–6; recognized as a Charitable Body 97, 106, 136n1; Overseas Corresponding Members 130; Publications Committee 146–50 *passim*, 240, 242; Research, Technical and Programmes Committee 146–7, 239, 242; Recruitment and Publicity Committee 147; members list and recruitment drive 148; Rules of the Society altered 150, 162n26; *Newsletter* launched 152; Small Craft Committee 156, 168, 172, 185; post-war lack of vision 185; resting on its laurels 186; specific accounts: Chelengk Fund 42, 61; Coastal Craft Fund 42, 64, 87; *Implacable* Fund 42, 70, 183; Macpherson Collection Endowment Fund 42, 56–7, 70, 87 *bis*, 113–14, 127, 165, 174, 200–4; Nelson Relics Fund 42; van de Velde Memorial Fund 42; Victory Museum Fund 42; Victory Panorama Annexe Fund 42, 44; Victory Museum Walker Bequest 87, 112, 116 *bis*, 118 *bis*; Tresco Valhalla Appeal 97, 98, 105n105; Symposium Account 110; Anderson Research Fund launched 139; Anderson Bequest Fund 152–3, 174, 186; Tomlin Fund 156, 186, 238, 239; subscription rates 10, 40; technical advisers to the Admiralty 32; Victory Finance Committee 37, 48–9n47; wartime surplus invested 69; three-anchor flag rejected 75–6; Trustees appointed 87, 185; subscription increase 110–11, 124, 148, 168; too naval and Nelson-obsessed 159; website www.snr.org 160, 169, 170, 172; members only area 172–3, 176n19

SNR South: started 100, 233; restoring W. L. Wyllie's grave 161

Spens, A. T., Appeal Secretary 32

Stanhope, James Richard, 7th Earl, Civil Lord of the Admiralty 53; relevant experience 53–5, *54*, 181, 189n2; chairs NMM Trust 57; creates Macpherson Collection Trust 58; resists attempt at Admiralty control 58–9; lobbies for Office of Works control 59–60; arranges with National Portrait Gallery 60; hopes for Callender as first Director of NMM 60; asks Caird to finance buildings renovation 61; chairs permanent NMM Board of Trustees 62, *85*; proposes second reading of Museum Bill 62–3, 63; support for Callender 80, 182; memorandum to Admiralty concerning *Victory* 91; Hon. Vice President 193; obituary 223

Staples and Co. of St Albans 119, 136n33, 152, 154

Starkey, Dr David J., Reviews Editor 151, 152, 160

Staveley, Captain and Mrs M. C. *33*

Stewart, Sir P. Malcolm, Bt, Hon. Vice President 193

Stone, Christopher 68

Story of HMS Victory, The, Professor Sir Geoffrey A. R. Callender 35

Strachan, Captain Sir Richard 64

Sturdee, Admiral Sir F. C. Doveton: becomes President 26, *26*; views on naval strategy and history 26–7, 47n13; oversees report on *The Mariner's Mirror* 27; confirms quarterly issue 28; chairs Save The Victory Fund 30; *Victory* an imperial asset 31, 179; letter to *The Times* 33; agrees STVF might be permanent endowment 35; promotes film 35; death 37, 178; objects to using private funds for state-owned buildings 43, 182, 189n3; opposes Admiralty policy for combined Museum 43; intends SNR restores *Implacable* 65; opens 'The Sea Fund' account 65, 73n51; obituary 208–10

STVF (Save The Victory Fund) 30, *31*; Victory Appeal Committee 30–1, 32, 48n35; receipt to Captain and Mrs M. C. Staveley *33*; amount raised 34

Romance of HMS Victory (film) 35, 182; appeal plus donations 37; receipts and expenditure 37; sales of commemorative medal 37; fund exhausted 38; income from sale of souvenirs 45; receives the Sea Fund 65, 73n54; donations continue 70; receipts pay off Victory Museum and Panorama debts 86, 102–3n51; post-war buoyant revenue 87; control transferred to NMM Trustees 88; entry fees to Victory Museum suspended 91, 104n77; entry fees to Victory Museum restored 92; funds to purchase teak 94, 98, 104n93, 122, 185; revenue profits increase 100; purchases Nelson portrait by Sir William Beechey 107, 123; funds *Victory* repairs 117; profit to be diverted to PRNM 117; Trafalgar Day Orphans' Fund 117; conflict over transfer of assets 120–2; grant to restore *Victory*'s Great Cabin 123; purchases bus for *Victory*'s crew 123, 136n46; funds polypropylene re-rigging 126, 185; funds foretopsail preservation 157, 164, 167; finance for display of foretopsail 168

Swinson, Christopher, Hon. Treasurer 155 *bis*

Taylor, Joan du Plat 150
Taylor, Professor Eva G. R. 98; Hon. Vice President 193
Teate, Mr Barry, Publicity Officer 157, 160, 165
Temeraire, HMS (Second rate 98 1798) 44
Thames Nautical College, Greenhithe 94
Thursfield, Rear-Admiral Henry George, obituary 221–2
Times, The: employs Naval Correspondent 2, 6, 7, 213; Admiral Sturdee's letter 33
Tomlin, Lt Cdr Richard: Bequest 156; obituary 238–9
Trafalgar, bicentenary of the Battle 157, 164, 187 *bis*; special edition of *The Mariner's Mirror* 166, 168; Learning Development Officer 167; virtual tour DVD 167; *Victory*'s cutters crew in celebrations 168, 172
Trafalgar, Panorama of the Battle annexe 44, 45, 46; repairs and restoration 88; returned from restoration 107; Campbell McMurray seeks funds 160; restored and opened 164
Trafalgar Woods Project 168
Trefgarne, Lord 134
Tresco Abbey, Valhalla, Isles of Scilly 97
Trincomalee, HMS (Fifth rate 46 1817) 65, 73n50
Turnbull Martin & Co. 34
Turner, Dr Paula, administrative editor 171, 172
Tweddle, Dr Dominic, Director-General NMRN 174

United Services Magazine 5
United States Naval Institute, Proceedings 7
Urdang, Mr Laurence 132, 147
van de Velde, Willem, the Younger 13
van de Veldes Memorial 42, 71, 240

van Swinderen, HE Jonkheer R. de Marees 42

VATC (Victory Advisory Technical Committee) 38, 44; functions passed to NMM Trustees 46, 92; formally reconstituted 93, 104–5n92; old VATC criticized 94; approves black polypropylene for rigging 123; creates Interpretation Committee 153; includes CO HMS *Victory* 164; modified representation 164

Verity, Elizabeth, Hon. Secretary 164, 168

Victory, HMS (First rate 100 1765): exhibition of foretopsail xiii, 157, 160 *bis*, 164, 168, 187; rescue needed 25; symbol of naval history 27, *29*; deteriorates for lack of maintenance 28, 47n17; continued deterioration 29; SNR notes condition of *Victory* 29; dry-docked 1922 30, 48n22; pre-restoration survey 32, 48n30; suggestions for restoration 32; estimate of fabric to be replaced 35; rigging to be replaced with hemp 37; three-stage lift 37, *39*; King George V visits 38, 49n53, 49n54; masts and spars installed 38; Dispensary outfitted by Henry Wellcome 41, 212; onboard museum demolished 43, 49n62; Trafalgar Panorama 44; air-raid damage 69; post-war re-rigging (sisal) 70, 86, 99, 103n52; cost of restoration and maintenance 85; cost of upkeep and rigging 88; attempts to appoint curator 89 *bis*; commissioned warship or heritage site? 89–90, 103n69, 103n70, 103–4n71; requisitioned as accommodation ship 89–90; Nelson's furniture displayed in Victory Museum 90, 91, 92, 104n73; official entertainment in Nelson's cabin 90, 104n72; committee of experts on death-watch beetle visit 92, 104n82; test borings find all below orlop deck rotten 93; re-rigging with hemp 99–100, 185; 1973 fire on board 123; re-rigging with black polypropylene 123, 126; restoration of the Great Cabin 123; annual meetings with MoD (N) on *Victory* maintenance 130; Chatham cutter rebuilt as yawl 155; Royal Navy guides replaced by civilians 155; two replica cutters built 155, 156, 172; five-year plan for HMS *Victory* 164, 174; unauthentic red paint on orlop deck removed 166; cutter's crew in Nelson celebrations 168, 172; options for future support 174, 188

Victory Museum: Admiral Sturdee opposes combined museum 43, 49n63; directed and managed by VATC 44; Old Rigging House site 44; completed *45*, 46, 182; dedicated to Nelson and *Victory* 46; Expense Account Department moves in 69; Instructor-Capt. T. E. Jackson full-time curator 82, 92; cost 85; demands on the STVF 87 *bis*; Victory Museum Walker Bequest 87, 112, 116; bomb damage 88, 103n62; war damage repairs and restoration 88, 185; insured value 97; second extension begun 99; Admiral Law's proposal 115–16; extension for McCarthy collection 115, 186; combines with McCarthy Collection 117, 136n25; forms nucleus of Portsmouth Royal Navy Museum 117; 1987 hurricane rips roof off Victory Gallery 157; refurbished Victory Gallery opened 164

Ville, Dr Simon 133

Villiers, Captain Alan J.: chairs Photographic Records Sub-committee 76; VATC 104n92; SNR President 111 *bis*; splits Macpherson Fund income 114; Victory Museum extension 115; regrets no SNR office in the museum 124, 137n49; retires as President 124; death 131; Hon. Vice President 193; Chairman of Council 231, 233; obituary 231–2

VTC (Victory Technical Committee) 32, 48n33; answerable to Council 37; replaced with Victory Advisory Technical Committee 38; too sanguine view post-war 184

Waghenaer, Lucas Janszon, *Speculum Nauticum* 11, 100

Walker, Mrs Dorothy M. 87

Wallis, Helen: Chairman of the Council 117, 119, 128, *131*, 136n26; denies neglect of Victory Museum 118; clarifies role of Executive Committee 130; objects to PRNM name changes 130; reports on meetings with MoD (N) 130; seeks closer relations with NMM 144; reviews Society's administration 145; chairs Friends of the Royal Naval Museum, Portsmouth 146; steps down 147; Hon. Vice President 194; obituary 239

War Studies Department, King's College, London 153

Warrior, HMS (iron armoured ship 1860) 135, 153, 185, 238

Waters, D. W. 240

Watt, Surgeon Vice-Admiral Sir James, Hon. Vice President 194

Watts, Sir Philip 29, 32, 38, 47n20

Wellcome Foundation 122, 212

Wellcome, Sir Henry S.: Hon. Vice President 41, 49n59; obituary 212

Wellington, HMS (Third rate 74 1816) 28

Wemyss, Admiral Sir Rosslyn 82, 219

Wettern, Desmond, obituary 238

'What is the Truth about the Navy' (newspaper article) 1, 17n1

Whild, Lt Cdr Douglas J. 'Oscar', CO HMS *Victory* 174

White, Colin Saunders: plans programme for Trafalgar bicentenary 166, *169*; obituary 254

Whitlock, Lt Cdr Peter 141; CO HMS *Victory* 123; Hon. Treasurer 126, 139, 145; death 148, 155; obituary 236

Whittingham, Lt Cdr, CO HMS *Victory* 100

Williams, Lieut E., RN 9

Willis, Admiral Sir Algernon Usborne 89, 90, 91, 92

Winterbottom, Peter, Hon. Secretary 168, 171, 175

Woolwich Ship report 17

Worcester, Mr G. R. G.: ex-Japanese PoW 82; Hon. Editor *Mariner's Mirror* 84, 98; Hon. Vice President 193; obituary 223–4

Wyllie, Lt-Col H. 32, 66, 67, 70, 77; as Wing Cmdr *40*, 70; as Lt-Cdr, RNVR 70, 71; Hon. Vice President 193; obituary 225

Wyllie, Mrs H. 71

Wyllie, W. L., RA 9, *10*, 32, *40*, 178 *bis*; paints Trafalgar Panorama 44; grave restored 161; Hon. Vice President 193; obituary 210–11

York, Duke of (later HM King George VI) *see* Albert, Prince

York, Duke of *see* Andrew, Prince